The Teacher's Guide to Success

Teaching Effectively in Today's Classrooms

Ellen L. Kronowitz

California State University, San Bernardino

PEARSON

Boston   New York   San Francisco
Mexico City   Montreal   Toronto   London
Madrid   Munich   Paris   Hong Kong
Singapore   Tokyo   Cape Town   Sydney

This book is dedicated to the hard-working teachers who make a difference every day.

———————————

Executive Editor and Publisher: Stephen D. Dragin
Senior Development Editor: Mary Kriener
Editorial Assistant: Katie Heimsoth
Marketing Managers: Weslie Sellinger, Danae April
Production Manager: Elaine Ober
Editorial-Production Service: Kathy Smith
Pre-press Buyer: Linda Cox

Manufacturing Buyer: Megan Cochran
Interior Design: Deborah Schneck
Text Illustration: John DePippo, Schneck-DePippo Graphics
Photo Researchers: Katherine Apone, Naomi Rudov, Annie Pickert
Cover Administrator: Linda Knowles
Composition: Schneck-DePippo Graphics

For related titles and support materials, visit our online catalog at www.ablongman.com.

Between the time website information is gathered and then published, it is not unusual for some sites to have closed. Also, the transcription of URLs can result in typographical errors. The publisher would appreciate notification where these errors occur so that they may be corrected in subsequent editions.

Cataloguing-in-Publication Data not available at press time.

ISBN-10: 0-205-45619-7
ISBN-13: 978-0-2-5-45619-2

Printed in the United States of America

10   9   8   7   6   5   4   3   2   1   RRD-W   10   09   08   07

About the Author

Dr. Ellen Kronowitz epitomizes what it means to be a teacher of young people. As a long-time educator as both a teacher and as a teacher educator, Dr. Kronowitz brings a passion and dedication rarely seen today. At California State University, San Bernardino, Dr. Kronowitz has served as a member of the multiple subjects credential program, instructor of social studies methods, and supervisor of student teachers and interns. In addition, she has served as the CSUSB liaison to the Hillside-University Demonstration School, an award winning partnership that has been recognized nationally and internationally.

A graduate of the Columbia University Teachers College, Dr. Kronowitz began her career as an elementary school teacher and later became program development specialist for a New York University Teacher Corps Project. She has also served as a full time lecturer at Brooklyn College, City University of New York.

In addition to the publication of *A Teacher's Guide to Success: Teaching Effectively in Today's Classrooms,* Dr. Kronowitz has written *Your First Year of Teaching and Beyond,* 4th edition, for new teachers; co-authored three resource books for teachers, *Pathways to Poetry,* and, with her graduate students, published a teacher resource book about Native American cultures, *Circle of Tribes.* She also has written books for early readers in the Dominie Factivity Series, published by Pearson.

Dr. Kronowitz continues to reach out to educators by conducting workshops for new teachers and mentors and presenting various topics, including teacher induction and social studies education and strategies.

Brief Contents

Contents

Unit 3

Classroom Organization and Management 87

Unit 6

Engaging All Learners   259

Unit 7

Assessing and Communicating Student Progress   313

Unit 8

A Professional Life in Balance 357

Epilogue

Final Tips 387

Preface

This handbook was written expressly for the new teacher, kindergarten through high school, in all regions and settings. It is a quick and easy reference to support novices before and during their first years in the classroom.

Supervisors, administrators, curriculum coordinators, mentor teachers, in-service support providers, university methods courses professors, and student teaching seminar leaders will find that this handbook facilitates their work with pre- and/or in-service teachers.

Research on the challenges teachers face in their first years of teaching often concludes that a balance of research and practical advice makes for a successful induction into the teaching profession. The content of this handbook presents that balanced approach, using essential knowledge derived from those engaged in research and those engaged with students in the classroom. Therefore, the advice and guidelines provided in this handbook reflect not only a review of the available literature on the new teacher experience, but the collective wisdom of resourceful and experienced teachers as well.

This handbook is as comprehensive as the format allows, and readers, seeking more information, may read the books or visit the websites recommended at the end of each unit or refer to the comprehensive reference listing at the end of the handbook.

Content and Organization

The 40 chapters divided into 8 units and an Epilogue address the most practical and research-based aspects of the first year of teaching. These chapters will simplify the complex challenges ahead, including having a successful first day, organizing and managing your classrooms, respectfully disciplining students, mapping out a differentiated curriculum, teaching with proven, research-based strategies, assessing student learning, preparing students for standardized tests, and addressing your own personal and professional development needs.

The content has been keyed to the INTASC standards that guide the professional education of teachers. You will find the chart showing the correspondence of the Handbook chapters to these standards in Chapter 2. The tabs and index guide you to material on your immediate concerns, although some readers may prefer the cover-to-cover approach.

Unique Features

The Teachers Guide to Success: Teaching Effectively in Today's Classrooms contains a variety of unique features that will help you make the most of your reading.

- **Effectiveness Essentials** at the beginning of each chapter outline the key concepts within the chapter.

- **Apply It!** activities provide ideas for the reader to work through with or without instructors or supervisors.

- **Avoid It!** features provide tips about mistakes teachers should try to avoid.

- **Classroom Artifacts** features include practices or materials that have been used in the classroom shared by practicing teachers.

- **Watch It!** icons call out video clips that can be accessed in the Live Classrooms section of the DVD that accompanies this book. Many of the video clips are followed by suggested post-viewing activities.

- A series of features that include quotes and shared stories from veterans in the field and students. These include **Myth Busters!** with advice from veterans that dispel common misconceptions and myths; **Teacher Talks . . .** filled with anecdotes from experienced teachers; and **Student Says . . .** reflections from students of all ages on school and schooling.

- Each unit ends with a **Unit Checklist** to help in-service or pre-service teachers prepare and an **annotated list of recommended readings and websites** for use in professional development or in the classroom.

- A **Technology Advantage** is realized with the inclusion of the robust DVD included free with every copy of *The Teacher's Guide to Success*. Divided into three main sections, this valuable resource is designed to help you prepare for day-to-day instruction and plan for the days ahead, as well as inspire you. After a general introduction by Dr. Kronowitz, you have access to:

  – Video clips of various researchers in the field of education speaking on critical issues in education today;
  – Over 30 video clips of concepts-in-action in live classroom settings; and
  – Downloadable blackline masters of resources ready for instant use in the classroom.

Adapt the guidance in *The Teacher's Guide to Success* to your teaching circumstances and subject area. Use the resources provided to help you identify, clarify, solidify and/or modify your currently held beliefs about instruction, discipline, management, assessment, working with parents, and working with colleagues. Use this Handbook as your roadmap to successful first years of teaching beyond which are the rewards that first motivated your choice of this exciting, challenging profession.

Acknowledgments

It takes a committed team of professionals to tend this project from start to finish and I was fortunate to have the best. I would like to express my gratitude to Steve Dragin, Executive Editor and Publisher at Allyn & Bacon, for his belief that I was the person for this project. I relied throughout on his expertise and sound advice. Mary Kriener, Senior Development Editor, provided invaluable feedback and suggested changes for the better. She is a talented and skillful editor, and I am indebted to her for her support, encouragement, and friendship. I am grateful to Elaine Ober, Production Director, who coordinated the artistic team that brought the manuscript to life. The marketing team, Danae April and Weslie Sellinger devised a cutting-edge and inventive approach to bring the book to its audience. Finally, I'd like to extend a thank you to Tyler Cyr, who oversaw the production of the DVD, and Sonja Regelman and Erin Leidel, development editors who provided early guidance on the project. To all of you at Allyn & Bacon who helped along the way I offer my deep appreciation and heartfelt thanks.

I want to thank the following reviewers whose attention to the big picture as well as the details made this a much better book. I am grateful to all of you: Kimberly Bridgers, Dodson Elementary School; Dorotha Ekx, St. Vrain Valley School District; Vicky

Gilliland, Southwestern Oklahoma State University; Jerrie Smith Jackson, Our Lady of the Lake University; Megan Mahoney, James A. Garfield Elementary School; Stephen H. Pulliam, The Stony Brook School; Peggy Redman, University of La Verne; Louise Sayuk, The Kinkaid School; Susan Scott, University of Central Oklahoma; Jolanda Westerhof-Shultz, Grand Valley State University.

My final thank you is to all of the teachers, students, and others who added the spice and flavor to this Handbook with your anecdotes. The following teachers and students from many parts of the country have given freely of their advice.

Students . . . Adam, Lexington, NC; Annie, Cremorne, Australia; David, Satellite Beach, FL; Debbie, Silverbell, AZ; Drew, Glenview, IL; Erik, Brookline, MA; Erin, Glenview, IL; Holland, Redlands, CA; Jeremy, Klamath Falls, OR; Kathleen, Glenview, IL; Kira, Arcata, CA; Kurt, Plano, TX; Mark, Orlando, FL; Megan, Glenview, IL; Natalie, Yucaipa, CA; Niki, Satellite Beach, FL; Riley, South Charleston, OH; Walker, Redlands, CA

Teachers . . . Gabe Aguilar, San Bernardino, CA; Diane Amendt, Colton, CA; C. Francine Apacible, Bilingual Aide, Hillside School, San Bernardino, CA; Barbara Arient, San Bernardino, CA; Cheryl Ayala, San Bernardino, CA; Dottie Bailey, Colton, CA; Sarah Barten, Desert Sands, CA; McKayla Beach, Palm Springs, CA; Kathleen Beard, Morongo Unified, CA; LeTiqua Bellard, Charlotte, NC; Cindy Brewer, Mebane, NC; Kim Bridgers, Hermitage, TN; Shirley Byassee, Colorado Springs, CO; Shirley Casper, North Sydney Boys' High School, Sydney, Australia; Kathleen Cave, Sparks Elementary School, Sparks, MD; Jan Christian, San Bernardino, CA; Kim Ciabettini, Highland, CA; Dion Clark, San Bernardino, CA; Maria Cleppe, San Bernardino, CA; Nina Conine, Principal, Olivehurst, CA; Nancy Derksen, San Bernardino, CA, Sarah Dominick, Preschool aide, Stockholm, ME; Brenda Downs, Pinon Hills Elementary School, Minden, NV; Art Eustace, Fontana, CA; Art Gallardo, San Bernardino, CA; Laurel Garner, Chattahoochee Elementary School, Duluth, GA; Loretta

Gomez, San Bernardino, CA; Laura Graham, Ontario, CA; Elizabeth Hodgson, Durham, NC; Shelley D. Howell, Morongo Unified School District, CA; Mark Horowitz, Bridgeport Middle School; Kevin Jarrett, Northfield Community School, Northfield, NJ; Susan Johnson, Richwood, WV; Thomas Kaszer, Lodi, CA; Deborah Lichfield, St Johns, AZ; Huifen Lin, Doctoral student, Penn State University, State College, PA; C. L. Lopez, San Bernardino *Sun*; Perry Lopez, Bronx, NY; Gordon MacDonald, Montvale, New Jersey; Ivania Martin, Benicia, CA; Mary K., Wellman, IA; Rachel Vogelpohl Meyen, Durham, NC; Linda Meyer, San Bernardino, CA; Eileen Mino, Colton, CA; Becky Monroe, San Bernardino, CA; Gaynor Morgan, Oostende, Belgium; Marsha Moyer, San Bernardino, CA; Ingrid Munsterman, Ruth Grimes Elementary School, Bloomington, CA; Camille Napier, Natick High School, Natick, MA; Dr. Gary Negin, Volunteer Teacher in Costa Rica; Dr. Virginia S. Newlin, Rock Hall Middle School, Rock Hall, MD; Jason Paytas, Arcata, CA; Katia Martins Pereira, Sao Paulo, Brazil; Steven Podd, Nesaquake Middle School, St James, New York Jennifer A. Ponsart, Four Corners Charter School, Davenport, FL; Joan Prehoda, Fontana, CA; Ms. Leticia Price, Rockville School; Stephen Pulliam, Stony Brook, NY; Kelly Rubio, Manhattan Beach, CA; Charles Skinner, South Carolina State Department of Education, Cottageville, SC; Andy Slavin, Bend, OR; Lynn Sleeth, Fontana, CA; Joan Marie Smith, Colton, CA; Robin Smith, Hollidaysburg School District, Hollidaysburg, PA; Brandi Stephens, Mebane, NC; Sandra Stiles, Sarasota, FL; Heidi Thompson, Yucaipa, CA; Hester Turpin, Colton, CA; Abby Ungefug, Student teacher, Montana State University, Lewistown, MT; Kris Ungerer, San Bernardino, CA; Devon Van Dam, McKinleyville, CA; Shannon Vanderford, West Memphis, AR; Matt Villasana, Columbia, MO; Abby Volmer, Odessa Middle School, MO; Laurie Wasserman, Andrews Middle School, Medford, MA Beth Ann Willstrop, Health Careers High School, San Antonio, TX; Kevin White, Charlottesville, VA; Beth Williams, Mobile, AL

From the Author

Hello, my name is Ellen Kronowitz, the author

of *The Teacher's Guide to Success: Teaching Effectively in Today's Classrooms.* As a longtime teacher, I can honestly say that working with young children and helping to shape their futures was some of the most satisfying and fulfilling work I could have asked for. All told, I have devoted forty years to education, and, you know, I have never regretted that initial decision to teach. It started me on a sustained and exhilarating journey around the world of education.

Whether experienced or new to teaching, as that first day of the school year approaches, you may feel some apprehension, regardless of your preparation to this point. Having been through this experience myself, I know that anxiety and apprehension. Teaching, after all, is the only profession I know of that has a first day every year! That's why I wrote *The Teacher's Guide to Success* and created the accompanying DVD. If I'm able to help you feel just a little bit more ready for that first day of school, well, then we both will have succeeded.

The good news is that there is only one very first day in the first year of teaching. The better news is that although each subsequent year evokes the same anticipation and feelings of excitement, each year also produces fewer jitters. Many first-year, novice, and even experienced teachers spend restless nights before that first day of school. But I assure you that with each year, it gets easier and easier. Trust your training, and remember that you know more and are better prepared than you feel. Also remember that there is always a lot of help around you. Mentors and colleagues ensure that no teacher is alone.

There are challenges, and there will be obstacles that will get in the way of your efforts to teach effectively. But along with those challenges come many individual joys and opportunities to develop your skills as a teacher. Each year brings new students, new opportunities for personal growth, and new colleagues. Daily you will delight in the small successes of your students, knowing you have made a difference. Your students bring something new to the classroom, and they are why no school year is ever the same. The key is spending time getting to know and appreciate the various personalities and racial, ethnic, and cultural influences students have on your classes. You have the most sacred trust imparted with your credential—influencing the lives of young people—and the benefits of your efforts may not be known for years. For every feeling of apprehension, it is equally important to remind yourself why you chose this profession in the first place.

Concerns about the first years of teaching bring back memories of sleepless weeks prior to my first teaching assignment. I was anxious and sick to my stomach that first morning until I walked through the door and saw my class. My mother always told me to put my right foot forward before any new endeavor, and that's what I did as I stepped into the classroom. I never regretted my decision to teach.

As years go by, you may not remember each and every student you encounter, but rest assured that they will remember you. Some of your students will keep in touch. Some won't. But students never ever forget a teacher who has touched their lives. To paraphrase Christa McAuliffe, "you touch the future, you teach."

As you look around the faculty meeting or the staff room, know that at one time all teachers experienced the same apprehension. Beyond all the anxiety of the first days and months of school lie all the rewards that motivated your choice of this exciting, challenging profession in the first place.

While I cannot be there in the classroom with you, I believe you will find *The Teacher's Guide to Success* the next best thing.

Now, as my mother used to say, put your right foot forward and do it!

Ellen Kronowitz

Unit 1

Your Induction Into Teaching

I touch the future.

I teach.

Christa McAuliffe,
teacher and first civilian in space

Chapter 1

How Does Teaching Differ from Student Teaching?

Effectiveness Essentials

- Teacher education courses and credentialing are only the beginning steps of a long journey.

- The first year of teaching is different from student teaching.

- Part of the challenge of the first year is fear of the unknown.

- Teachers are a diverse group, although not as diverse as their students.

- Teachers have to assume multiple roles.

Why Don't I Feel Prepared to Start Teaching?

This question, often posed by students in the last phase of the teacher credential program, gives me pause each time I hear it. Having been through this experience myself, I know exactly what they mean. They're anxious and scared. The valuable information they have learned and are still learning doesn't make them feel competent and confident in light of their upcoming first solo day in a classroom.

Listening to my students' concerns about the first years of teaching brings back memories of sleepless weeks prior to my own first teaching assignment. I had many methods courses under my belt, but had not the vaguest idea of how to combine instructional ingredients to meet my students' needs. I was anxious and sick to my stomach that first morning until I walked through the door and saw my class. My mother always told me to put my right foot forward before any new endeavor and that's what I did as I stepped into the room. I never regretted my decision to teach, and I remember each one of the students in my first class. I guarantee that you will too!

As years go by, you may not remember each and every student you encounter, but rest assured that they will remember you. I recently contacted a former student, an environmentalist and a mother of three, and asked her to collect her own children's comments about their favorite teachers.

My unforgettable second class.

Student Says . . .

I have modeled myself after you as a teacher of my own children. You were a patient teacher that gave each person a chance to reach their potential even if it was not evident initially. . . . Any public school teacher that does this gives each student a fighting chance. You gave me confidence that continues to this day. You weren't afraid to love the students in your charge. To a little child with as many challenges in life as I had, this can mean everything.

Much love,
Debbie Bradshaw
Silverbell, Arizona

Student Says . . .

I came across your name within a listing of teacher resources and stopped dead in my tracks. I attended public school in New York City in the 1960s, and had a third grade teacher named Ellen Kronowitz. My Miss Kronowitz was a young and spirited teacher who stood out among the rest of the faculty, and made a very lasting impression on me.

I went to P.S. 15, Queens, and had the same teacher for both first and second grade. My report cards were filled with comments remarking on my inability to focus, my talking out of turn, my tendency to daydream, and other habits now often associated with ADD. I fear she almost had my mother convinced that I just wasn't very bright, until I finally entered the third grade.

Miss Kronowitz, on the other hand, told my mother that she

(continued on facing page)

Debbie was a fifth grader in my third year of teaching thirty-five years ago. We have kept in touch over all these years. She was the student who needed the extra attention and the extra push to excel. I pushed, and she resisted. Finally, she gave in and accepted my challenges to excellence. And, despite a very difficult childhood, she authored some of the most creative stories and poems I have encountered as a teacher.

I have kept Debbie's letters over the years. Each one reminds me of the intangible rewards of teaching. Sometimes your students will keep in touch. Sometimes they won't. But students never ever forget a teacher who has touched their lives.

Mark then

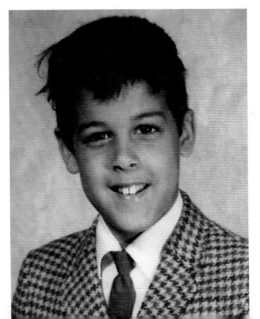

Another former student, Mark Young, pictured below as a third grader and today (and in the class photo on page 3), surprised me by writing to me a few months ago (see the Student Says feature in the outside column).

Teacher education is only the beginning.

The proliferation of induction and mentoring programs and the new standards for the teaching profession all suggest that success in the first year is dependent on having certain knowledge, skills, and dispositions, as well as a great deal of support. Luckily, today there is a greater emphasis on helping new teachers through the challenges of the first year.

Mark now

After all of the educational psychology and methods courses, and the student teaching experience, you still may feel as if you have no idea what to do once you secure a teaching position. But you actually know more and are better prepared than you feel. Ask any veteran teachers you know, and they will tell you that it takes at least five years to build your confidence. We have all experienced the pre-service jitters. The treatment for this affliction is experience in the classroom.

The first year of teaching is different from student teaching.

When you're a student teacher, the supervising teacher can catch you when you fall and cheer you on during rough times. The curriculum has been set, and you are responsible only for portions of students' education. During your practicum, the ultimate accountability lies with the master or supervising teacher. In contrast, once you have your teaching credential in hand, the responsibility is all yours.

If you are an intern teacher, earning a credential while teaching and without benefit of a supervised student teaching experience, you may find that guidance and supervision is less intense than you need during your first year. It is understandable that many first-year teachers spend restless nights before that first day of school. The good news is that after the first year, it gets easier and easier, and there is a lot of help available to you.

thought that I was quite bright indeed, and that difficulties in second grade were likely the result of boredom and a need to be challenged academically. And challenge me she did. Looking back, I realize that Miss Kronowitz taught with a fresh enthusiasm, and not only fostered in me a lifelong love of learning, but also the freedom and courage to march to the beat of my own drummer.

Mark Young
Orlando, Florida

Apply It!

Take a few minutes and divide a paper into two columns. Label one column *Student Teaching* and the other *Teaching* (see Figure 1.1). In the first column, write down your responsibilities as a student teacher. Under *Teaching,* list additional responsibilities you will need to assume when you are in charge. Comparing the columns will help you prepare for the new tasks.

statistics

Why do teachers enter the profession? According to a survey of veteran teachers by the National Education Association (2003) the following responses were given:

- Desire to work with young people   73%
- Concern about social values   44%
- Interest in subject matter   36%
- Influence of a teacher   32%

I always remind myself of the "why" in my teaching. I love my "babies," who happen to be 16–17 years old; and I must remember that they are experiencing my themes, writing requests, and choices in literature for the first time rather than for the hundredth plus time as I am doing. If my "why" is for money, then I am in the wrong position. If my "why" is job security, then I say thanks to my profession. If my "why" is because I love to watch my "babies" struggle with thinking and adjusting earlier thoughts with new information and synthesizing those thoughts into their own new forms that transfer to other disciplines and their own lives and that from them I also learn, then I'm in Nirvana.

Beth Ann Willstrop
Grades 9–12, Reading and Literature
Health Careers High School
San Antonio, Texas

Figure 1.1
Student Teaching/Teaching Comparison Chart

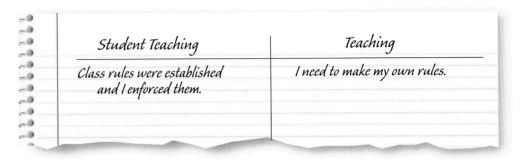

Student Teaching	Teaching
Class rules were established and I enforced them.	I need to make my own rules.

Fear of the Unknown

Part of the challenge of the first year is fear of the unknown. What will it be like when you have to assume total responsibility for a class? Here's what lies ahead (the scary stuff):

- You are accountable for the planning, organization, instruction, and assessment of students.
- You are responsible for your classroom environment and the routines that keep it operating efficiently.
- You will be asked to assume non-teaching duties such as lunch, yard, and bus duty.
- You need to meet new colleagues and possibly explore an unfamiliar community.
- You need to establish and maintain communication with parents and perhaps supervise aides.
- You are responsible for record keeping and ongoing diagnoses.
- You will be assigned a challenging variety of students.
- You may have to teach unfamiliar material.
- You may experience some potential impediments such as lack of parental support; overcrowded classrooms; outdated equipment; lack of adequate texts and materials; poorly maintained campuses; and some students who may be disrespectful, angry, disengaged, or even violent.

Here's what also lies ahead (the fun stuff):

- The joy of watching your students "get it"
- The thank-you notes and letters from students and grateful parents
- The eagerness and excitement you see on kids' faces
- The letters of acceptance to college your high school students share with you
- The painting or drawing a student offers as a gift
- The affectionate comments you receive as the students exit your classroom
- The growth and development you see every day
- A letter from students like Debbie or Mark many years later

- The small successes and the large leaps
- The knowledge that you will make a difference and "touch the future"
- The joy of sharing a joke with your students
- Being able to celebrate your students' achievements with them
- The ability to attend student performances, proms, festivals, homecoming, sports events, carnivals, and other significant school-wide events
- The gratification of attending awards assemblies, promotions, and graduations honoring your students
- The lasting friendships and colleagueship with the school's staff
- Pride in your own professional accomplishments

statistics

- In 2003–2004 there were 3,044,012 teachers in the United States, grades K–12 (NEA, 2005).
- Males comprise 24.9% of teachers (NEA, 2005).
- The average teacher salary for 2003–2004 was $46,752, with the highest salaries in Connecticut, Washington DC, and California, and the lowest in South Dakota, Oklahoma, and North Dakota (NEA, 2005).
- Nationally, about 17% of public school students are African American and 6% of teachers are African American. Likewise, about 17% of public school students are Hispanic and 5% of teachers are Hispanic (NEA, 2004a).
- In more than one-third (38%) of U.S. public schools, there is not a single teacher of color on staff (NEA, 2004a).

Who Are We?

We are a diverse group.

However, we are not as diverse as the students we teach. A key to being a great teacher is spending time getting to know and appreciate the various racial, ethnic, and cultural groups represented in our classes. It is also important to understand that students born into poverty, and across racial and ethnic lines, have developed hidden rules for survival. These hidden rules affect how students born into generational poverty respond to instruction and discipline (Payne, 2001). You will find more information about meeting the needs of the generational poor in subsequent chapters.

Becoming a Teacher
A first year teacher talks about why she became a teacher, and the challenges and joys she has experienced. After viewing the video, write about your motivation for becoming a teacher.

We have to assume multiple roles.

All teachers have to be cheerleaders, interior decorators, artists, systems analysts, efficiency experts, performers, nurturers, assessors, judges, mediators, diagnosticians, psychologists, communicators, bookkeepers, managers, and friends—to name just a few. Many of these roles come naturally to teachers. Good communication skills, for example, are associated with the teaching profession. Other roles such as assessor or diagnostician are practiced during teacher preparation. Some roles, such as mediator and efficiency expert, are often learned on the job.

Every teacher you know was once a novice. As you look around the faculty meeting or the staff room, you need to realize that at one time all teachers experienced the same apprehension that you do now. Beyond all the anxiety of the first days and months of school lie all the rewards that motivated your choice of this exciting, challenging profession in the first place.

Chapter 2

What Does Research Show About the Induction Year?

The beginning is the most important part of the work.

Plato

Effectiveness Essentials

- The beginning teacher dropout rate is alarmingly high.
- Districts recruit quality teachers and want to hold on to them.
- The first year of teaching has its ups and downs.
- Be sure to identify your support system at the school and district level.
- Adequate preparation can diminish your apprehension.

statistics

- In the United States, 46% of all new teachers leave their schools within five years (NCTAF, 2005).
- In high-poverty schools, annual teacher turnover rates approach 20% (NCTAF, 2005).
- The NEA (2004b) reports that the average cost to recruit, hire, prepare, and then lose a teacher is $50,000.

The Teaching Profession as a Leaky Bucket

The beginning teacher attrition rate is alarmingly high. As more teachers are hired, too many spill out of the profession. School district administrators increasingly realize that the effort to recruit new teachers needs to be combined with an effort to retain and support these teachers during the first years, when the going gets a little rough.

Research is needed to stem the attrition and retain effective teachers.

In some areas, there is a severe teacher shortage resulting from growing pupil populations, teacher retirements, class size reduction, and competition from other fields for the pool of candidates who traditionally have entered teaching. Because of the increasing need for new teachers, districts are working very hard to retain the teachers they recruit. That means finding new and improved ways of making the induction year a successful one. Current research focuses on why teachers leave, the cost of teacher attrition to the districts, and the elements that constitute effective induction, including timing and sequencing of inservice instruction and the role of administrators and mentors during the induction process.

The prevailing emphasis is on recruiting *quality teachers.*

In January 2002, George W. Bush signed into law the *No Child Left*

Myth Buster!

Teaching is a lonely profession.

It certainly can be lonely if you isolate yourself from your colleagues and the community. Reach out, form alliances and bonds with people you believe to be like-minded. Become involved in a project with other teachers, other grade levels, other subject specialists and community members. Projects that invite participation may include a global fair, a technology showcase, a writer's festival, or a play. School-wide events, though hard work, can help pull teachers together. Teaching is as lonely as you want it to be.

Andy Slavin
Sixth Grade Teacher
Bend, Oregon

Behind Act that mandates that a "highly qualified" teacher staff every classroom by the 2005–2006 school year. According to the official *No Child Left Behind* website (2002), the act provides grants to recruit and train quality teachers, especially in specific areas of need; creates tax deductions for out-of-pocket teaching related expenses; and establishes loan forgiveness programs for teachers. These initiatives address the quality issue while school districts work on recruitment and retention challenges.

Why do teachers who have studied so hard, endured student teaching, and even survived the first year leave the field?

Other explanations cited in the literature on attrition include:

- Lack of physical and mental conditioning
- Isolation
- Value conflicts
- Assignment to teach the most disruptive and least academically able students
- Lack of long-term commitment
- The differential between beginning teacher salaries and the first-year salaries of other college graduates
- Idealistic and unrealistic expectations
- Inadequate resources

statistics

- According to the NEA (2004b) the top three reasons for leaving are poor school leadership, low pay, and personal reasons.

The First-Year Roller Coaster

The first year of teaching has its ups and downs. Ellen Moir and her colleagues at the University of California at Santa Cruz (1990) identified a five-phase cycle of that first-year roller coaster (see Figure 2.1).

School-wide events bring teachers and students together.

statistics

According to the MetLife Survey of the American Teacher: Expectations and Experiences (2006), 85% of teachers feel their school or district provides adequate opportunities for training.

The first phase is ANTICIPATION.

When your job offer arrives, you are higher than a kite. No more part-time jobs at the supermarket, no more moonlighting as a security guard, no more living from hand to mouth to pay for courses. You have a job! This phase carries you through the first few weeks of school.

Next comes the SURVIVAL phase.

During the first weeks of school, you scramble to keep one step ahead of the kids, staying up too late to write lesson plans, worrying about what your principal thinks about you, and so on. In other words, you are trying to keep your head above water!

The DISILLUSIONMENT phase arrives next.

This phase kicks in when your responsibilities outstrip your energy. This phase can set in six to eight weeks into the school year, and it varies in length and intensity. To your current anxieties, you have to add preparing your room for open house, principal evaluations, and parent conferences. You are exhausted! The job as a supermarket checker or night security guard begins to look appealing. You start to question your commitment, and your morale sinks.

The next part of the cycle, REJUVENATION, coincides with your first sustained rest.

It might occur during Winter Break or even Thanksgiving. You can reintro-

Figure 2.1

Anticipation   Survival   Disillusionment   Rejuvenation   Reflection

duce yourself to your family, read a book for enjoyment, and generally relax and enjoy a few minutes to yourself. You begin to see the big picture and, after a well-deserved rest, you are ready to seek out new solutions.

In the spring comes the REFLECTION phase.

Reinvigorated, you can reflect on some of your practices. By now, you may have gotten good advice, attended inservices, and gotten a handle on some of your paperwork. You begin to think about how you would do things differently next time, and you begin to look forward to next year!

Apply It!

Prepare for the induction year by making a list of behaviors, thoughts, and feelings that might go along with each phase of the first-year teaching cycle shown in Figure 2.1. For example, in the Survival phase:

"I am a nervous wreck, I have to get some help, I'm drowning in paper, I can't sleep, I'll never get these plans written, etc."

Avoid It!

Do not suffer in silence. Ask for help when you feel overwhelmed.

Do not give into disillusionment. This too shall pass.

Recognize and Identify Your Own Concerns

The most important thing you can do is to recognize and address your fears before you begin teaching. Help is available at the school and district levels. You may have mentors, buddy teachers, and/or formal induction programs. Your grade-level colleagues in elementary school, your team in middle school, and your department at the high school are your "first responders" when you want to put out fires or lay your concerns to rest. Most important, you can, on a personal level, be prepared. Your concerns can be substantially reduced by appropriate preparation. This handbook is intended to help you with that preparation.

Teacher Talks . . .

After my first year of teaching was over, I wanted to write an apology letter to all my students for making so many mistakes that first year. I didn't, but maybe I should have.

Dottie Bailey
English Teacher/Speech
Middle School
Colton, California

What teachers know and can do makes the most difference in what children learn.

Linda Darling-Hammond,
teacher educator and researcher

Chapter 3

What Are Some Challenges for the Reflective Teacher?

Effectiveness Essentials

- Standards help you reflect on your teaching practice.
- It is never to early to begin to reflect on your teaching.
- All teachers face common challenges.
- Initially, new teachers request help with the most practical teaching tasks.
- In the middle of the first year, instructional needs move to the top of the list.
- Some beginning teachers are subject-centered, and some are student-centered.
- New teachers face daunting challenges, but help is available.
- Balance research with practical advice.

The Reflective Teacher

John Dewey's definition of *reflective thinking* has been the basis of a teaching construct that we refer to as *reflective practice*: "Active, persistent, and careful consideration of any belief or supposed form of knowledge in the light of the grounds that support it and the further conclusion to which it tends" (Dewey, 1933). Reflective teachers, therefore, think about and analyze their own teaching for the purpose of improving practice and becoming the best teachers they can be.

The biggest challenge is becoming the best reflective teacher you can be.

The National Board for Professional Teaching Standards (NBPTS, 1989) has identified five core propositions that can help you meet this challenge. Each proposition pinpoints an essential aspect of teaching that will enhance student learning. They are listed in Figure 3.1, along with references to which chapters of this handbook are relevant to learning more about them.

Figure 3.1

NBPTS Standard and Corresponding Handbook Chapters

NBPTS Five Core Principles	Correlations in this Book
Teachers are committed to students and their learning.	Chapters 15–34
Teachers know subjects they teach and how to teach those subjects to students.	Chapters 15, 21–34
Teachers are responsible for managing and monitoring student learning.	Chapters 5–20, 30–34
Teachers think systematically about their practice and learn from experience.	Chapters 1-4, 35–40
Teachers are members of learning communities.	Chapters 8, 14, 34, 36, 38

Apply It!

Before you begin reading this chapter, take a piece of paper and jot down what you believe teachers should be able to do to make a difference in kids' lives and learning. Then check your responses against the professional standards mentioned in this chapter. Comparing and contrasting your own perceptions with national standards will enable you to reflect on what you know vis-à-vis the expectations for a first-year teacher.

Apply It!

Write down your biggest fears about being a first-year teacher. Then compare your responses with the following sections, selected from recent reports, that highlight concerns. This activity will convince you that your anxieties are shared among many first-year teachers.

Developing a Philosophy of Education
Teachers reflect on their philosophies and tie them into the standards for the profession. Take some time to write down your own educational philosophy before viewing the video. Afterward, compare your response with those of the teachers in the clip.

Standards help you reflect on your teaching practice.

Standards help you set new goals to improve and assist you in monitoring your practice to meet your professional goals throughout your career. The NBPTS listing of standards can be downloaded in their entirety from the Internet at http://www.nbpts.org/standards. The Interstate New Teacher Assessment and Support Consortium (INTASC) proposes ten standards that are very similar. Additionally, many states have their own set of professional teaching standards that you will need to know.

It is never too early to begin to reflect on your teaching.

A simple six-step process for reflection is shown in Table 3.1.

Table 3.1 Reflecting on Your Teaching

The Steps	Sample Responses to Each Step
1. Clarify Your Beliefs	All kids can learn. Parents must partner with teachers.
2. Own Up to Your Strengths	I know my subject matter. I am funny and explain things well. I am able to sense who needs a kind word.
3. Give Up Perfectionism	I will never be able to carry a tune. My desk will never be as neat as I would like.
4. Question Your Beliefs and Actions	Maybe I shouldn't use time out as a strategy. How can I find more time to work with individuals?
5. Devise a 5-Year Professional Development Plan	I will use more research-based teaching strategies. I will differentiate learning more effectively. I will get a Master's Degree in counseling. I will take more courses in special education. I will learn American Sign Language.
6. Toot Your Own Horn	I will invite administrators and parents to performances/debates/culminating events, etc. I will have business cards made up to hand out. I will send student work to the district office for display. I will call and invite the newspaper education reporter to special events or demonstrations.

Main Concerns and Challenges

If you are not too worried about the challenges you are facing, you are a phenomenon, a rare individual who has it all together. You are definitely atypical. When I look back on my first year of teaching, the first word that comes to mind is *trepidation*. Also, *delight, success,* and *fun.*

All teachers face common challenges.

A decade ago, Brock and Grady (1996) reported that principals and beginning teachers rank classroom management and discipline as the number one problem, and most current research suggests that this holds true today. In addition to discipline, other perceived challenges during the first year and beyond are:

- Dealing with individual differences
- Meeting *No Child Left Behind* requirements
- Implementing standards
- Assessing students
- Preparing students to do well on standardized tests
- Motivating students
- Establishing good relationships with parents
- Organizing class work
- Grading papers
- Having insufficient materials and supplies
- Dealing with individual student problems
- Juggling heavy teaching loads
- Having insufficient preparation time
- Establishing relationships with colleagues
- Planning lessons and preparing for the day
- Being aware of school policies and rules

How did your list compare? These are the types of concerns addressed throughout this Handbook. Research-based ideas and practical solutions from veterans will be presented throughout the book to allay the anxiety you may be experiencing as your induction into the teaching profession draws closer.

When the going gets rough, just imagine you are a new teacher in 1872. Figure 3.2 illustrates the expectations of teachers from that time period.

Teacher Talks . . .

How many people can honestly say that they love their job? I can. When I am enjoying what I do the kids get so much more out of it. They can tell when I am enthusiastic about something and in turn they get excited about it. When a child turns to me at the end of the school day and says "Today was fun," it makes my day.

Kelly Rubio
Fourth Grade
Manhattan Beach, California

statistics

Despite all of these challenges, according to the NEA (2003):

- 32% of teachers would make the same choice of profession
- 29% probably would choose the same profession
- 18% said it was an even chance they would choose the profession
- 16% said they probably would not make the same career choice

Figure 3.2
Rules for Teachers, 1872

Rules for Teachers
1872

1. Teachers each day will fill lamps, clean chimneys.
2. Each teacher will bring a bucket of water and a scuttle of coal for the day's session.
3. Make your pens carefully. You may whittle nibs to the individual taste of the pupils.
4. Men teachers may take one evening each week for courting purposes, or two evenings a week if they go to church regularly.
5. After ten hours in school, the teachers may spend the remaining time reading the Bible or other good books.
6. Women teachers who marry or engage in unseemly conduct will be dismissed.
7. Every teacher should lay aside from each pay a goodly sum of his earnings for his benefit during his declining years so that he will not become a burden on society.
8. Any teacher who smokes, uses liquor in any form, frequents pool or public halls, or gets shaved ina barber shop will give good reason to suspect his worth, intention, integrity and honesty.
9. The teacher who performs his labor faithfully and without fault for five years will be given an increase of twenty-five cents per week in his pay, providing the Board of Education approves.

Myth Buster!

Teaching is easy. Anybody can do it.

First and foremost, teaching is not for everyone. Good teachers make teaching look easy, but it's not. Teachers are responsible for molding and shaping students through academics as well as character building. Sometimes the best lessons are not planned. However, a good teacher knows how to use these teachable moments and tie them into the state standards. Having good classroom management skills is an essential part of teaching. Without classroom management in place, the class will not run smoothly, nor will any learning take place. The students also have to know and feel that the teacher respects and cares for them. This is not as easy as it sounds. Teachers can develop this by being fair, firm, and consistent with all students. It takes a lot of work, but the time and effort you put into doing this will pay off in the end. Believe it or not, students know when teachers genuinely care about and respect them.

LeTiqua Bellard
Math and Science, Grades 7–9
Charlotte, North Carolina

Initially, new teachers request help with the most practical teaching tasks.

These include locating and using teaching resources and materials, securing emotional and instructional support, getting advice about classroom organization and discipline/management, gathering information about the school system, and establishing a classroom environment.

In the middle of the first year, instructional needs move to the top of the list.

These may include conferring with your team or department head about best practices, best strategies, and teaching resources. Effectively teaching essential curriculum standards and benchmarks and test preparation take center stage. Securing adequate resources and materials, emotional

19

Teaching Fifth Grade
A fifth grade teacher discusses why she chose fifth grade. Look at the video clip and try to decide whether Ms. Dorn might be more subject-centered or student-centered.

statistics

- 33 states reported mandated new teacher mentoring programs.
- 22 states reported state funding for those programs.
- 23 states required mentor training.
- These statistics represent an almost 25% increase in mandated new teacher mentoring programs, since 1998 (Hall, 2005).

support, and classroom management assistance continue as mid-year needs. This suggests that only after teachers have control of areas such as resources and materials are they ready for assistance with instruction.

Achieving a balance between subject matter and student needs is another challenge.

Some beginning teachers are subject-centered and some are student-centered. Lidstone and Hollingsworth (1992) were the first to identify this duality. The first group needs help in establishing routines and management, advice on attending to student learning, and encouragement to reflect on their practice and rely on themselves for answers. The latter group, already focused on the students, needs support in management and curriculum, encouragement to balance idealism and pragmatism, and support to avoid excessive self-criticism.

To find out which type you are, ask yourself whether you spend more time organizing the content or figuring out the learning styles of individuals. Do you talk to colleagues about individual kids or your subject area? Are you more concerned with the "what" of teaching than the "how to" of teaching? Not surprisingly, secondary teachers tend to be subject-centered and elementary teachers, especially primary teachers, tend to be student-centered. Which type are you?

As you plan your lessons, make sure that you are balancing both the content and your students' needs. Your lesson plan should include a section for "differentiating instruction" or the means by which you will adapt the content for specific student groups or individuals. You will read more about differentiating instruction in Chapter 28 of this Handbook.

New teachers face daunting challenges, but help is available.

Schools and districts offer a variety of assistance. Mentor and buddy teacher programs help ease the way in more and more districts, and orientation sessions are scheduled for new teachers. Your principal and other administrative and instructional personnel are there to help.

Formal school district induction programs are very common.

These programs assume that the credential is but one stepping stone on the long journey to becoming an accomplished teacher. You may be required to attend presentations, demonstrations, and informal meetings with other new teachers. You may be assigned a mentor, who will do everything from providing a sympathetic shoulder to actually demonstrating effective strategies and classroom management techniques. In some states, your mentor may follow a sequence of state-mandated, beginning-teacher standards and track your progress toward meeting them. If your district has not yet formalized an induction program, seek out a buddy on your grade level, team, or in your department. An experienced teacher on the staff will be a great source of succor, support, and information.

Research is valuable, but practical advice will assuage immediate concerns.

Research on the challenges teachers face in their first years of teaching

Avoid It!

Comparing yourself to more experienced teachers and becoming self-critical is self-defeating, so accept your novice status and do the best you can each day.

Complaining is considered unprofessional. Seek solutions from mentors instead.

often concludes that a balance of research and practical advice makes for a successful induction into the teaching profession. You will find recent research with practical applications throughout the Handbook from such prominent figures as Ruby Payne, Robert Marzano, Carol Ann Tomlinson, Fred Jones, William Glasser, Jacob Kounin, and others. Advice from veteran teachers combined with research results will provide a well-balanced set of guidelines for the new teacher to follow. Balancing research and practical advice is essential for your success.

Myth Buster!

If you ask for help, you will be perceived as incompetent.

I would say that if you don't ask for help in your first year of teaching, the principal will think you are incompetent, unaware of the challenges that you are facing, and possibly arrogant!

Teaching is always a challenge . . . because the challenges are not just the kids we teach, they are the intellectual challenges of understanding how individuals learn, how we can provide the best environment and stimuli for them to learn, how we as individuals can enrich the lives of our students, how we can encourage our colleagues to do the best they can, how we can learn from our colleagues . . . and the list goes on.

Shirley Casper
Science Teacher, Grades 7–12
North Sydney Boys' High School
Sydney, Australia

All the resources
we need are in
the mind.

Theodore Roosevelt

Chapter 4

How Can I Plan Ahead for My First Day?

Effectiveness Essentials

- Mental planning and detailed plans in black and white are key to success.
- Gather teacher's editions, planning documents, and supplies.
- Reach out to your students and parents.
- Familiarize yourself with your district, school, and its community.

Plan Ahead for Success

The two keys to success in teaching are mental planning and detailed written plans. The minute you secure your teaching position is not too soon to begin preplanning for your first year and first day of teaching. Before school starts, you have an opportunity to plan the year ahead by visualizing yourself at work in your classroom and then writing down on paper those ideas and tasks that need to be accomplished before the first day. You will probably revise your drafts, so keep them in a loose-leaf binder.

Apply It!

Ask at least three veteran teachers how they prepare for the first day of school. Every teacher, new and experienced, can always use some fresh ideas. Make a list of relevant, useful, and constructive advice and keep adding to the list as you pick up more tips along the way. The ongoing list will serve as a reminder of tasks still to be done.

Ways to Prepare for the First Day

Somehow, "firsts" seem magical: first date, first prom, first baby, first house. These moments are etched into memory. But the reality is that the first day of school is like any other, and if you are well prepared, the day will pass very quickly, and you will be on to the second!

Gather resources.

These are some resources to help with preparations:

■ **Success-of-the-Day Journal.** Buy yourself a blank journal, and then write the date and three successes of each school day (see Figure 4.1). It might be that your class responded favorably to your poetry lesson. Perhaps your principal gave you a much valued compliment or a colleague told you how well behaved your students were. Or, a parent may have commented on how much his child looks forward to coming to school each day.

Figure 4.1
Success-of-the-Day
Journal Entry

Date	Success
9/5	First day over!
	Plans were appropriate
	I remembered most students' names

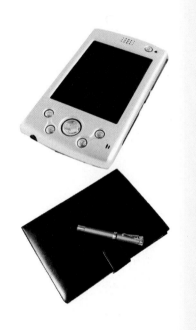

This will become your reflective journal, and initially you are only allowed to write down your successes. Later, you can add suggestions for improvement as you reflect on your day. As you reread the journal at the end of each week, you will see written proof that you know what you are doing.

■ **A Day Planner/Calendar or Electronic Organizer.** You probably used some sort of calendar, date book, or electronic organizer to keep track of appointments, exams, and work during your college years. Now you need to think about a planner in which you can list open house dates, parent conferences, inservice seminars, faculty meetings, and other school events.

■ **Just-in-Case Kit.** Keep a personal "just-in-case kit" in your desk with items such as a change of socks or hose, a toothbrush and toothpaste, sewing kit, band-aids, pain relievers, deodorant, cologne, breath mints, etc.

If you teach a "messy" subject like art or chemistry or teach early grades, you may want a change of shirt or blouse in case of accidental spills. Or, keep an oversized shirt around that you can wear in those "messy" situations. You may want to keep an extra sweater and an umbrella in your classroom and a few snack bars in case your lunch is interrupted. Pretend you are delayed at school for an evening meeting or during an emergency. What would you need to get through that day? Think of this as your school emergency/teacher survival kit.

■ **Autobiographical Bulletin Board.** Gather materials for an autobiographical bulletin board. You might include a report card from your own school days; photos of family, pets, and travels; a list of favorite books; special quotes; certificates you have earned; a statement of your teaching philosophy, and anything else you want to share with your students. This board will serve as

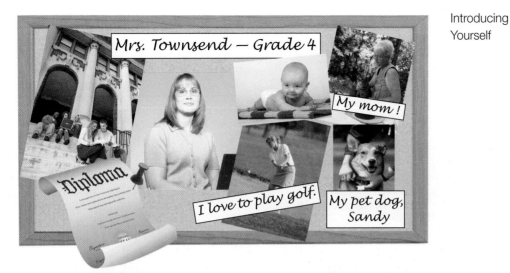

Introducing Yourself

Call parents the first week of school. Let them know something great you have observed about their child. This will start the year off on a positive note, and if you have to call about some problem later, you will have already established a good relationship.

Linda Meyer,
Resource Teacher
San Bernardino, California

a visual when you introduce yourself to your class on the first day of school.

Reach out to your students and their parents before school starts.

Here are some ideas:

- **Parent and Student Letters.** Compose a parent letter that will go home on the first day of school. You can make templates for the rules, policies, newsletters, and open house schedule way before school starts. You can send a postcard, or a letter, to parents or to your students expressing your anticipation of the new school year (see Figure 4.2).

- **One-on-One Visits.** One teacher I know makes home visits or tele-phones parents at the start of the school year. Although this is unusual in this day and age, you can imagine how impressed a parent would be at your level of commitment.

Take the time to get to know your school and the surrounding community if you are unfamiliar with it.

- **Attend a School Board meeting.** You can even introduce yourself infor-mally to the board members. They will be impressed that you took the time to attend.

- **Visit your school.** Take some time to visit or revisit your school site. This will enable you to find the school and see how long the commute takes. Try

Figure 4.2
Back-to-School Postcard

Teacher Talks . . .

During your work days before school begins, seek out other teachers and take the initiative to introduce yourself. You will need the support that they have to offer, and they will appreciate your support as well.

Becky Monroe
*Language Arts and Reading, Grades 7–9
San Bernardino, California*

out your route to school during the times you will be traveling back and forth to see what traffic is like or how to time your arrival by rapid transit. In addition, visiting the site early will help you feel more comfortable in your new surroundings. Find out how to get your own school e-mail address.

■ **Get to know your community.** Many teachers will relocate to a new state, city, or region. Settle down as soon as possible so you can get a feel for the community and learn where best to make friends. Check out key locations in town like the public library, and meet key people, including the movers and shakers. Making friends in and out of school will give you a sense of belonging. Investigate community organizations and other activities that might interest you and enable you to connect with others.

■ **Surf the School and District Websites.** You will find a great deal of information here that you will need to know, such as test scores, school policies and procedures, etc. Ask about any procedures that are unclear. Learn the reasons for any policies that don't seem to make sense. Every school has its own history and challenges. You'll be better equipped to follow policies and procedures correctly if you understand the reasoning behind them.

■ **Read the Community Phone Directory and Local Newspaper.** You will glean a great deal of information about an unfamiliar community by reading these sources of

Apply It!

Become an architect. Take a piece of graph paper and decide what furniture arrangement best reflects your instructional and management goals. Is your designated space a science or technology lab? In your history classes, do you want your students facing one another across a divided room? Will you be using PowerPoint as a primary instructional tool, and do you want all students facing the screen? Will you be using cooperative learning strategies? Do you need areas for small-group instruction and differentiated learning? Does your plan encourage or discourage interaction? Planning your room out on paper will save you time when you actually get into your classroom to move furniture. Create alternative plans just in case one doesn't work out.

good information. Learn the history of the town and read the local newspaper to find out what the local issues are. What are the unique features of the community? What are the after-school opportunities you can refer parents to? What special services are offered to families?

Make your classroom a space you look forward to coming to.

You will spend more hours at school in your classroom than you will at home from Monday to Friday. If you are sharing a room, you need to meet with your "roommates," negotiate some private desk and bulletin board space, and discuss sharing computers, file cabinets, storage cabinets, and technology such as the LCD or overhead projector. Buy a rolling cart to take with you as you move from room to room with materials that cannot be stored in the shared classroom.

Gather materials and supplies for your students.

Teacher supplies you may need include: a plan book, journal, pens and markers, a stapler and staples, paper clips, tape, rubber bands, a seating chart, subject-specific materials, substitute teacher folder, and substitute goodie bag. This last item should be packed with new and different materials that pertain to your subject or subjects and supplement the plans you have prepared in advance. It might

Teacher Talks . . .

I went out and spent $1700.00 on supplies and posters for my room. What I did not take into consideration was that the students did not want to see posters. They wanted to see their own work up. I did not need to spend all that money. . . . Another thing that I did not realize was that other teachers would be more than happy to share what they already had with me. The thing that I should have been working on was where to put all the things that I wanted up. Space is very limited in a classroom. . . . After the first quarter, I'm a little more choosy about what and where I put things up.

Cheryl Ayala
Fifth Grade First-Year Teacher
San Bernardino, California

I teach English to second, fourth and sixth graders at Escuela Concepcion in Costa Rica. Only the sixth graders have four thin, photocopied textbooks. There are no textbooks for students in the other elementary grades. Teachers get one piece of chalk per day. This is back to basics teaching—the students, a blackboard, and me.

Dr. Gary Negin
Volunteer Teacher in Costa Rica

include a History Channel video for your American History class, play scripts for an English class, an edible experiment for a middle school science class, or special arts or crafts projects and one-minute mysteries for elementary students.

Stock up on student supplies at discount or warehouse-type stores. A recent *Los Angeles Times* article (Hayasaki, 2004) reported that teachers commonly dip into their own pockets for supplies, and one profiled teacher spends as much as $2,000 of her $48,000 salary. A science teacher was quoted as spending $3,000 on special equipment and supplies. First, check out what the school provides and then, depending on the grade level of your students, you may need to supplement these supplies with some that

Avoid It!

Being in denial about what lies ahead

Waiting until school starts to prepare yourself

Winging it

Visit your school supply room early.

you provide. YOU DO NOT NEED TO BUY WHEN FREE IS BETTER. There are suggestions for securing free and inexpensive materials in Chapter 23.

Get a copy of the teacher's editions of your textbooks early.

This is the best way you can adequately prepare your curriculum. Many teacher materials can be complex. So you will need time before school begins to get the big picture of all you are expected to teach that first year. This will also give you time to think of additional strategies or activities you can use in your lessons.

Unit 1 Checklist

Preplanning for First Day Checklist	**For more information go to:**
☐ Have I read all the state and district standards?	Chapters 3, 21
☐ Have I read school and district procedures and policies?	Chapter 4, 9
☐ Do I have an overview of the year's curriculum, including texts?	Chapters 21, 23
☐ Have I designed my classroom environment?	Chapter 10
☐ Do I have a discipline plan consistent with the district/school?	Chapter 9
☐ Have I familiarized myself with the school and community?	Chapter 4
☐ Do I have a plan for reaching out to students and families?	Chapters 4, 9
☐ Have I gathered teaching resources, including planning materials?	Chapters 4, 23

Further Reading: Books About the First-Year Teaching Experience

Baldacci, L. (2003). *Inside Mrs. B's classroom: Courage, hope and learning on Chicago's South Side.* New York: McGraw Hill. A journalist gives up her job to teach middle school in an urban school that is overwhelmed by problems. This is a realistic view of teaching in the inner city by a teacher who faced all of the challenges head-on and eventually triumphed.

Goodnough, A. (2004). *Mrs. Moffett's first year: Becoming a teacher in America.* New York: PublicAffairs. This is an account of a legal secretary turned teaching fellow in a pilot program in New York City. She signs on as first grade teacher in an underperforming school in Brooklyn.

Kane, P., Ed. (1996). *My first year as a teacher.* New York: Signet. This is a collection of 25 first-year teacher accounts spanning all grade levels and all kinds of classrooms.

Ladson-Billings, G. (2001). *Crossing over to Canaan: The journey of new teachers in diverse classrooms.* San Francisco: Jossey-Bass. This is an account of the challenges and rewards of teaching diverse learners in real-life situations.

Reed, K. (1999). *Rookie year: Journey of a first-year teacher.* Boston, MA: Peralta Publishing. A first-year teacher recounts the personal and professional challenges in his first year of teaching a fifth grade class, known as "The Wild Bunch," in a Boston school.

First-Year Teacher Websites

Advice for First-Year Teachers
http://www.educationworld.com/a_curr/curr152.shtml
This website is geared to the needs of first-year teachers and includes survival guides, tips, resources, and links to other first-year teacher sites.

Middle Web: The First Days of Middle School
http://www.middleweb.com/1stDResources.html
This website is geared to the middle school teacher, but has ideas relevant for high school as well. There is multitude of short articles about discipline, icebreakers, connecting with parents, successful first-year and first-day advice, etc.

National Education Association
http://www.nea.org
This comprehensive website for educators features ideas, archives of research articles, education statistics, and links to classroom ideas.

New Teacher Resources
http://www.teachersfirst.com/new-tch.shtml
This website will be especially helpful to secondary teachers and includes topics such as the first day of middle school and do's and don'ts for success in middle school along with many other useful resources with links to the U.S. Department of Education publications for new teachers.

What to Expect Your First Year of Teaching
http://www.ed.gov/pubs/FirstYear/
This website offers advice and strategies from first-year teachers and veterans and includes a checklist of tips.

Unit 2

First Day

Unit 2
First Day

You don't have to see the whole staircase, just take the first step.

Dr. Martin Luther King, Jr.

Chapter **5**

What Can Help Me Through My First Day?

Effectiveness Essentials

■ All new teachers are nervous as the first day approaches.

■ Ten basic principles can guide you to a successful first-day experience.

■ Teachers set the tone for the year on the very first day.

■ You will have many opportunities to address first-day slip-ups.

All New Teachers Are Nervous as the First Day Approaches

You are not alone. The night before your first day will be a sleepless one as you worry about what to wear, what to say, whether the kids will stay in their seats and whether your plans will run out before recess or the period ends. Remind yourself that you are as prepared as you can be without actually meeting your students, and then engage in your favorite bedtime stress buster like taking a warm bubble bath or listening to music.

Most teachers do not have a first-day experience before their very own first day. Many university classes begin after the first day of school, whether in late June or September. Teacher education courses combined with student teaching prepare you as well as they can, but only after you have succeeded in your very own first-day experience will you finally relax. You have all the ingredients, but you still worry about whether the recipe will turn out. The first day is an untried recipe. And you can always change, adapt, and revise your plans on days 2–188. Your students are checking you out and trying to figure out what your expectations will be, and they may be as nervous as you are.

Ten Basic Principles Can Guide You to a Successful First-Day Experience

Incorporating and following these principles will give you a sense of control over that first day, and each principle conveys an important message to students that will help set the tone for the coming year. Although sample first-day schedules can be helpful, it is often more useful to provide you with a list of ten principal ingredients for the first day. Then you can create your own gourmet dish (see following page).

Be overprepared.

Arrive very early. You will feel more confident if you can spend time checking out the room and feeling comfortable in it. Make sure your name is on the board along with the daily schedule, a welcome sign is on the door, all your name tags are carefully prepared, the desks are arranged to your satisfaction, all your instructional materials are ready, your bulletin boards are fresh, and your plans are summarized for easy reference.

The one certainty for the first day is that you will forget to do something! On my first day of class, I always

NOTES

Teacher Talks . . .

I learned the importance of "The Rules of the Room" my first semester teaching high school, when I didn't establish any right at the start. I soon learned that it's much easier to ease off on rules than it is to establish them after the fact. Fortunately for me, I taught just semester-long courses, no full-year courses. So, before the start of the second semester, I clearly wrote out the guidelines or rules for my classroom, and that was the first thing we went over after first introductions. It was perhaps the most important on-the-job lesson I learned throughout all my time teaching. There's just no anticipating what that first day is going to be like, and the most important thing you can do is make sure there's order in your room. It carries over for the rest of the semester . . . or year.

*Mary
High School Social Science
Wellman, Iowa*

Guiding Principle	Message Sent to Students
1. Be overprepared	Teacher has it all together.
2. MOTIVATE	School will be exciting.
3. Establish routines and a schedule	School is organized.
4. Establish rules	I will be safe and responsible.
5. Orient students to room	I belong and am comfortable.
6. Preview the curriculum	I will gain mastery of new subjects.
7. Let students choose/decide	I am part of a community of learners.
8. Include a literacy experience	Reading and writing are keys to learning.
9. Acknowledge every student	I am unique and special.
10. Assign easy/review work	I can succeed. It's a snap!

forget something. My students never know because I adapt. Write a summary of your first day or first period plan on an index card and keep it close at hand. Write the outline of activities or schedule on the board as another cueing device for you and a reminder to your students that you are well organized and have given a great deal of thought to this first day. Because you have!

Message Sent to Students: This teacher has put effort into this first day or period and really is businesslike. She knows what she is about and has thought this through. This teacher doesn't "wing it." So I better not either.

Motivate.

Capitalize on students' anticipation and excitement the very first day. Provide a variety of highly motivating experiences. Keep the pace moving and overplan so you never drag anything out to fill time. One kindergarten teacher brings in a chicken and eggs it has laid that week. The students talk about chickens using descriptive words, follow directions to cook the eggs, read *Green Eggs and Ham* by Dr. Seuss, make mosaics with the eggshells, and write about their experiences. That's a first day to remember! Although you need not bring in an elephant to teach the color gray, you may want to think about an exciting activity to start the day.

A middle school social studies teacher I know dresses up like a Roman Senator, complete with toga and laurel wreath and tells students all about the social studies curriculum. An earth science teacher brings in frozen models of the earth made out of melons that have been halved, hollowed out, and filled with different flavored ice creams to represent the layers. Of course, the students eat the earth after this motivating presentation. Even at the high school level, you need to motivate in some way. If you are not comfortable with a flashy activity, at least tie an ice breaker to the subject matter and make an impression. Remember that every one of their teachers is trying hard to get their attention that first day.

Message Sent to Students: This class will be exciting and the teacher has made an effort to convey that he will do his utmost to keep things moving along so we won't be bored.

Establish routines/schedule.

Begin to establish a set of daily routines that first day. Unit 3 will discuss routines at length. Routines are your tools for saving time and ensuring smooth functioning, structure, and security. Introduce some routines on that first day as they are needed; others can be introduced as the week progresses.

Message Sent to Students: School is organized and predictable. This teacher will help me keep all my assignments straight and stay structured.

Establish classroom rules.

No matter what grade level or subject matter you teach, you will need to establish the rules of the classroom that first day. You will have an opportunity to learn about rule making in Chapter 9, and Unit 4 is devoted to discipline and classroom management. Begin to implement your strategies and create a positive discipline system based on mutual respect, responsibility, and dignity. Don't let

Fun While Learning

Figure 5.1
Silhouettes

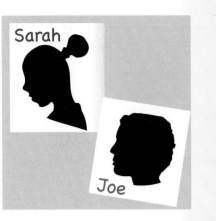

On that first day, design a class motto, class flag, or class mascot to establish a sense of community. Cut up a huge rectangle of butcher paper into puzzle pieces and have every student write his or her name on the piece and decorate it. Call students up to add their piece to the puzzle of friendship. Have each student make a silhouette using a light source projecting the image on black construction paper (see Figure 5.1). Hang these around the room. Younger students can draw their images on paper plates. Or, design your own motivating and inspiring beginning that is subject matter and/or age appropriate.

Class Puzzle

infractions slide that first day. Thirty pairs of eyes (or more!) will be watching!

Message Sent to Students: *I will be safe and I will be responsible for my actions.*

Orient students to school/classroom.

The easiest way to orient elementary students—whether new, second language learners, or returning students—to their school is to take a walking tour that first morning, pointing out such places of interest as the rest rooms, water fountains, principal's office, and nurse's office. You also may need to show students school bus stops, places to line up after lunch, the cafeteria, assigned fire drill locations, and appropriate exits. Let the students know what the bells or other signaling devices mean. Take an "eyes only" tour of the classroom as well. Make sure that your

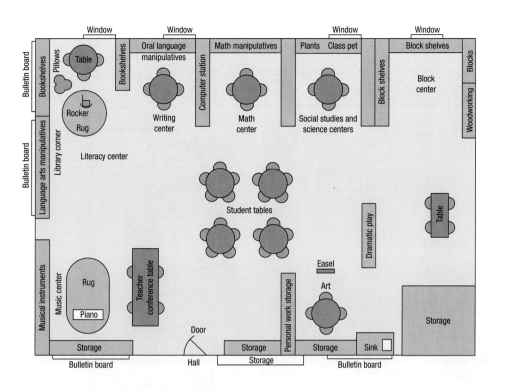

Figure 5.2
Floor Plan for a
Kindergarten Classroom

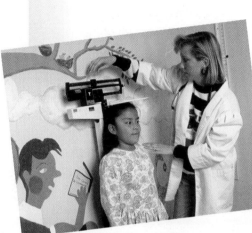

Locations Around Campus

English language learners understand what you are saying. Use gestures, visuals, and peer translators. As you look at Figure 5.2, consider which locations should be pointed out to students.

Middle and high school students also can be oriented to the school, but not in the same way. In large schools, you may discuss key landmarks near your classroom or pathways to the bathrooms, cafeteria, or main office.

Make sure your students have a campus map and go over it. This is particularly helpful to students who are new to the school, such as recent elementary or middle school graduates. Orient your secondary students to the classroom and discuss how it is set up for learning.

Message Sent to Students: *I belong and I am comfortable. I know my way around the school and the classroom.*

Young students can make a simple map of the classroom or the school grounds (see Figure 5.3). Or, have them pinpoint their houses with stickers on a local map of the community. Older students can use MapQuest to locate their houses in relation to the school on a community map. School maps should be distributed to middle and high school students and key locations should be highlighted.

Figure 5.3
Classroom Map

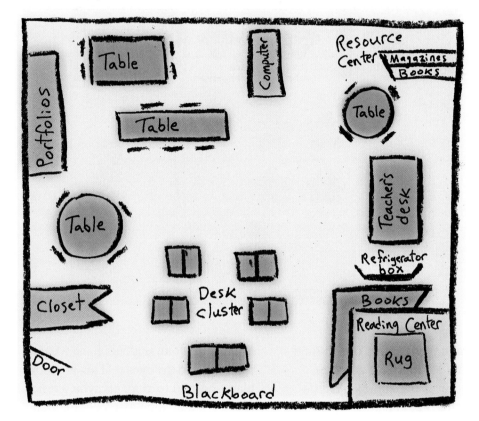

Preview the curriculum.

Preview some of the topics students will cover and introduce them to at least one of their textbooks or readers that first day. Hand out the textbook(s) and take a brief survey of the table of contents. You also can construct a bulletin board that previews the curriculum and highlights the year's or semester's topics, field trips, and upcoming special events. This is the time to present the big picture and connect the content with the students' experience. Think of the first day as a splashy advertisement of the content and what it can do for them later in life.

> *Message Sent to Students: I will gain mastery of this new material, and it looks like the subject(s) will be interesting.*

Let students choose and decide.

Share responsibility for decision making from the outset. Let students know they will be encouraged to make choices and participate in classroom processes. Participatory experiences that first day might include choosing seats, writing classroom rules, and so forth. In secondary school, ask the students what most interests them about the first topic or unit. Seek their input on the subject matter within the parameters of the standards. Let them know that they will have a choice on projects both in terms of content and presentation modes.

> *Message Sent to Students: I am part of a community of learners and I will have input and will be invited to participate in my own education.*

Include a literacy experience.

Demonstrate the value you place on literacy by incorporating some reading-related or writing activity into your plans no matter what grade level or subject you teach. You can turn the tide toward literacy by showing great wonder and enthusiasm for the world of books yourself. For example, read "First Day of School" in Aileen Fisher's book of poetry, *Always Wondering* (1991) to primary students after asking them to describe or write about what they are wondering on this first day of school. The following box lists some books that are appropriate to read on the first day of school, with approximate grade levels.

> *Message Sent to Students: Reading and writing are keys to learning and to success.*

Books About School

Primary (K, 1, 2)

Minerva Louise at School
Janet Stocke

Starting School
Janet Ahlberg

Will I Have a Friend?
Miriam Cohen

Ella Sarah Gets Dressed
Margaret Chodos-Irvine

This Is the Way We Go to School
Edith Baer

Lily's Purple Plastic Purse
Kevin Henkes

The Principal's New Clothes
Stephanie Calmenson

Officer Buckle and Gloria
Peggy Rathmann

Never Spit on Your Shoes
Denys Cazet

The Teacher from the Black Lagoon
Mike Thaler

Grades 3–4–5

I'm New Here
Bud Howlett

My Teacher Glows in the Dark
Bruce Coleville

Math Curse
Jon Scieszka

Sixth Grade Can Really Kill You
Barthe De Clements

Amber Brown Series
Paula Danziger

Junie B. Jones Series
Barbara Park

Class Clown
Johanna Hurwitz

Middle School

Merlyn's Pen: Fiction Essays, and Poems by America's Teens
R. James Stahl

Olive's Ocean (chapter book)
Kevin Henkes

Chicken Soup for the Teenage Soul
Jack Canfield

Soft Hay Will Catch You: Poems by Young People
Sanford Lyne and Julie Monk

Ten Second Rainshowers: Poems by Young People
Sanford Lyne

Poems from Homeroom: A Writer's Place to Start
Kathi Appelt

Swimming Upstream: Middle School Poems
Kristine O' Connell George

High School

In high school, depending on your subject matter, select a short biography of a scientist, historical figure, mathematician, athlete, writer, health worker, political leader, etc., and have your students read and respond orally or in writing with a prompt from you. You can search for biographies at http://www.biography.com

Apply It!

Have your older students write a thank you letter or card to a previous year's teacher. This will provide you with a purposeful writing sample.

Acknowledge every student.

Let each student know with a verbal or nonverbal response from you that she or he is welcome, valued, and special. It can start with an individual greeting to each individual on the way into the room. A greeting in the primary language of second language learners will make them feel welcome.

A high school government teacher I know gives his students note cards and has them write "I _____ (name) am, beyond a shadow of a doubt, cool." Then he signs the cards and laminates them. He tells them to keep it with them at all times, and randomly throughout the year, he gives them extra credit if they have it with them. Some of his students keep those cards for years.

Message Sent to Students: *I am unique and special and this teacher cares about getting to know me as a person, not just as a student.*

Review and assign easy work.

Prepare work for the first day that is slightly below the anticipated level of the class. Why? Everyone should go home that very first day feeling successful, believing that they have accomplished something. Step in when you see that a given task is too difficult or frustrating. You have the whole year to challenge students and expand their capacities and talents.

Message Sent to Students: *I can succeed. It's a snap!*

Teachers Set the Tone for the Year on the Very First Day

The first day should be framed within the regular class schedule you have worked out. The students should experience a routine sequence of activities from the outset. Your new colleagues can help here. Many schools and/or districts will have orientations and teacher-only work days before students arrive. At that time, you can speak with teachers at your grade level or in your department and survey them about what they actually do step by step on the first day. Take very careful notes. Typical first-day schedules for elementary and secondary teachers follow.

Teacher Talks . . .

Every fall I look forward to a teacher's "New Year": a fresh beginning; an opportunity to greet my new middle school kids as their sixth grade teacher, and get to know their wonderful, unique personalities as we go through their first year together. I love watching them grow and change. There's a feeling of excitement and anticipation as I go in to school a few weeks before the year starts: setting up my room, thinking of ways to get the kids energized about learning, and watching their transformation from being elementary kids from our district's four different schools, into a group of middle schoolers who care about one another, help one another, and become friends for many years.

Laurie Wasserman
Learning Disabilities
National Board Certified Teacher
Medford, Massachusetts

Teacher Talks . . .

On my first day teaching first grade, a little boy went missing after lunch. I didn't notice until the end of afternoon recess around 2:00 p.m. He was simply doing what he did in kindergarten the year before at lunchtime. He went home! In a panic I called the principal. She went to his house and found him sleeping on the porch because his parents hadn't expected him home until 3:30.

P.S. I wasn't fired and am still teaching 20 years later.

Linda Meyer
Resource Teacher
San Bernardino, California

A Generic Elementary First-Day Schedule

This schedule is a template of common first-day activities. Your grade-level colleagues will be able to help you adapt this generic agenda since they know about the bell, recess, and lunch schedules and other special first-day events you should anticipate.

Welcome. Post a welcome sign on the door. Welcome your students at the door and direct them to take a seat. Have your name on the board and pronounce it for your students. Let them choose seats or have the seats already assigned. See Chapter 6 for ideas on assigning or choosing seats.

Routines/Morning Exercises/Flag. Have a list of what must be accomplished during the morning routines and establish a sequence that will become habitual after the first few days.

Orientation to Classroom/School. Take a walk around the school site and orient the students to the classroom, stressing what is yours, what is theirs, and what materials are available to use with and without teacher permission.

Rule Making. Either present the rules or engage in rule making with your students. You will read more about this in Chapter 9.

Recess/Snacks. Find out ahead of time what (if any) snacks are allowed and how the snacks are provided. Will parents take turns bringing in snacks? Will you have rules about what kind of snacks are acceptable? Avoid snacks such as peanut butter that may trigger potential allergic reactions. Will milk money be collected? Where is recess equipment stored? Will you have ball monitors?

Language Arts/Reading. Distribute literature books, read aloud, or have the students write for diagnostic purposes.

Centers for Kindergarten or Math. Decide which centers you will have and shorten the time for their first experience. Most of your center time will be taken up with an explanation of the rotation. A math diagnostic test may be administered on the first day, but also excite students' imaginations with some special math activity.

Lunch. Students go to lunch or go home after morning kindergarten.

Science/Social Studies/Art. On the first day, introduce your first science or social studies unit and combine it with artistic expression.

Wrap-up/Clean up. Summarize the day so students will remember what they did when parents ask the question, "So what did you do in school today?"

Preview the Next Day. Tell your students what exciting lessons they will be learning tomorrow so they return to school eager to see what you have planned.

A Generic Secondary First Day Schedule

Consult with your team or department colleagues after you have a tentative agenda. They will help you adjust the agenda since they know about the bell and lunch schedules as well as other special first-day happenings you should anticipate.

Welcome. Welcome your students at the door and direct them to take a seat. Have your name on the board and perhaps a welcome sign on the door. Have them fold index cards and make nameplates or provide nametags. You might take digital photos of the students to help you remember who's who. Small versions can be pasted on the seating chart you develop. Have a mini-agenda of the class session on the board.

Administrative Tasks. Take attendance. Check the pronunciation of the names and ask if there is a nickname or shortened form the student prefers. Make a tentative seating chart.

Introductions. Use any of the introductory devices described in Chapter 8. Tell the students something about yourself and about how you got interested in teaching this particular subject area. Include your schooling background and your approach to teaching.

Expectations. Discuss your expectations and class rules. These should conform to the school and district rules and be posted on the bulletin board. Make sure to let the students know that mistakes are permitted in class but

Student Says . . .

On the first day of school the teacher welcomed us. I was calm. She was easy on us. I felt happy. She explained the rules to us. She told us who our three teachers were. I was really bored. She told us what they taught. I felt interested. She reviewed a lot of things. I felt as if I knew everything. Love, Riley.

Riley,
Third Grade, Age 8
South Charleston, Ohio

Apply It!

This is a short, generic inquiry activity that can be applied to any subject area on that first day. Hide an item related to your subject matter in a mystery box. The students are only allowed to ask yes/no questions about the item. (Is it alive? Is it made out of metal? Is it found in a house?) Before the item can be revealed:

1. Everyone must get a turn
2. Only yes/no questions are allowed
3. Teacher will not answer the same question twice
4. Each student gets to write down his or her answer on a post-it
5. Prizes can be awarded

there is only one pass for each rule that is broken. Discuss the consequences for failure to follow the rules. Discuss your policy for late work, make up work, absences, etc.

Routines. Let the students know what they will need to bring to class each day, how you will take attendance, how to set up their notebooks, homework policies, general expectations, procedures for sharpening pencils, bathroom pass policy, throwing items in the wastebasket, raising hands, and generally what will happen routinely each class period.

Preview Curriculum. Tell students what they will be able to do and give an overview of the content they will master during the semester. Let them know what big projects are coming up, and how your grading system works. Display sample projects from last year to set the standard high. Most teachers distribute a mini-syllabus similar to the ones you have been given in university classes. Syllabi make assignments clear; discuss assessment and grading policies; set due dates; detail penalties for late work, tardies, and absences; spell out rules; list needed supplies; and explain procedures for make-ups, etc., all in one place. See the *Classroom Artifacts* feature for an actual high school syllabus.

Short Activity. Try to fit in one very short activity related to your subject. Enforce all the rules you have just set down regarding hand raising, calling out, listening, etc. Possibilities include:

- A jazzy science experiment
- A math puzzler or shortcut they don't know about
- A two-minute mystery to solve

See Apply It! for an example.

Wrap-Up. Set a timer to let you know the period is coming to an end. Have students gather materials, clean up, and wait for your signal to leave. Remind them of what to bring to class the next day and give a very short homework assignment. Review all rules and procedures every day that week to reinforce them and orient any new students.

Classroom Artifacts

A Real Syllabus
U.S. History: Class Rules and Policies

Place this sheet in the front of your notebook.

Notebook: The skill of taking notes is essential and can only be acquired by experience. Every student must take notes and keep a notebook. A notebook is helpful in developing habits of good organization; good organization means time saved and no searching for papers. Students should take notes from class lectures and discussions. At least 60% of the objective test questions will come from matters discussed in class—topics which may not be covered by the assigned readings. A carefully kept notebook will make studying for tests much easier. Notes may be used on the test for the last 20 minutes. If you are absent, it is YOUR responsibility to copy the notes you have missed from another class member.

Tests: The tests will generally be objective, with at least 40% of the multiple-choice questions coming from the assigned reading. Some of the questions will not be discussed in class, but if you have done the assigned reading, you should do well on them. The remaining 60% of the questions will come from the notes. Some unit tests may have both objective and essay portions. I will usually tell you ahead of time what the essay question will be so that you may prepare for it. I expect that all rules of English will be followed on all essays, along with good organization (i.e., Introduction, Body, Conclusion).

Make-Up Tests: Anyone who misses a regularly scheduled test for any reason must make up the test. The make-up test may or may not be the original test. No notes may be used on the make-up test. Make-up tests may be taken during the class period in another room, or after school (my choice).

Quizzes: Quizzes may come at any time and may cover lectures, discussions, readings, videos, and assignments.

Homework: All homework assignments will be done in ink (blue, black, or purple). Assignments done in pencil or other colors will NOT be accepted. All assignments must be turned in on time—no late papers will be accepted!! There is no penalty for excused absences—papers will be due upon your return to school. If you are absent either on the day an assignment is given, or on the day that assignment is due, the assignment will only be accepted if your absence is excused Note: If you attend school for any portion of the day, but miss my class, you must turn in that assignment or receive a zero.

Copying: While you may desire to work with a friend on an assignment, I expect you to do your own work. Any form of copying will result in zeros for all parties involved. This, of course, does not include any group assignments that might be made.

Attendance: In a class such as history, being in class is very important. Absences do tend to reduce a student's learning and subsequently lower his/her grade. This is especially true because much of the test material is covered in class.

Suspensions and Cuts: No credit will be given for work missed if you are suspended or cut class.

Field Trips, Sports, and Activities: All absences must be pre-arranged before you may be excused from class. Failure to pre-arrange any absence will result in a cut being issued. Any assigned work due on the day of your pre-arranged absence must be turned in before you leave on your trip or you will receive no credit.

Tardies: It is essential that students arrive on time, are prepared, and are ready to work. If you arrive late, you cause the instructor (that's me, hint, hint) extra work (which I detest) and waste valuable class time. If you are not in your seat when the bell rings, you are tardy!! If you are detained by another teacher or school personnel, be sure you have a pass. Find your seat with the least possible disruption. If you arrive tardy (unexcused) for the THIRD time during a grading period, you will be given a choice to either stand up in the back of the room for the entire period and lose your Off Campus Card, or spend one hour of detention after school with me. Standing for the period or one hour of detention will erase the tardy for that day only. You may stand one more time or spend one hour in detention to erase the next (4th) tardy; after that you will lose your Off Campus card and the opportunity to do extra credit. The next tardy (really your fifth tardy of the quarter), you will spend one hour after school on either a Tuesday or Thursday in detention with me!! Failure to spend the assigned detention will result in a one day suspension for defiance. Each quarter begins with no tardies.

Class Rules:

1. Come prepared with notebook, pencil or pen, and paper.
2. Bring your textbook to class every day. If you do not bring your textbook, you will be sent back to your locker to get it and receive a tardy.
3. Be in your seat when the bell rings.
4. Be courteous and raise your hand if you wish to speak.
5. Follow school rules.
6. You will be treated as an adult and will be expected to act accordingly. The rules of common sense and courtesy will be followed by all.

Grade Sheet and Scale: Each student must keep his/her own point totals and grade average. You should therefore be aware at all times of how well you are doing. A cinch notice (my vernacular for "progress report" which

are sent out half-way through each quarter) or poor grade should not come as a surprise. This course is not graded on a curve: each student earns a grade based on his or her individual performance.

$$90-100 = A \quad 80-89 = B \quad 70-79 = C \quad 60-69 = D \quad 59\% \text{ and below} = F$$

Pluses and minuses are added as follows:

0, 1, 2 =	(−)	80% 81% 82% =	B-
3, 4, 5, 6, =	straight grade	83% 84% 85% 86% =	B
7, 8, 9 =	(+)	87% 88% 89% =	B+
.5+	round up to next number		

Research Paper: It is the policy of the Social Science Department that a research paper be done during one of the semesters. We will do the research paper during the SECOND semester. Topics and format will be discussed during that time.

Extra Credit: Extra credit is available only to those students who do the assigned class work and homework. Only students who have successfully completed 80% of their assignments AND have perfectly cleared attendance will be eligible to do extra credit. Incomplete assignments will diminish your opportunity to do extra credit. Extra credit may only be used to raise your grade from "F" to "D," "D" to "C," or "C" to "B." You may not raise your grade from "B" to "A" with extra credit. Extra credit is limited to a maximum of 10% of the points per quarter and must pertain to what has been studied during that quarter. All projects, research reports, drawings, etc., must be approved by the instructor and are due 1 week before the end of any grading period.

Teacher Assistance: Students who find the work difficult should see the instructor early in the quarter. Help will be made available before or after school. It is essential for any student experiencing difficulty to do all the assigned work. It is possible for a student who has difficulty on tests to pass the class by doing all the assignments and extra credit.

My class teaching schedule is:

Periods 1, 2, 3   U.S. History CP   Room SS-6
Period 3–6   Work Experience   Work Exp. Office
Period 7   Work Experience   Classroom SS-2 (Tues. & Thurs. 2:20–3:15)

Work Experience Office phone # _____ Call any time after 10:45 A.M.

Parent and Student Signatures: The purpose of these rules is to inform all concerned as to what I expect and how I intend to run the class. I believe it is important for everyone to know ahead of time what the class policies are so that confusion and future problems can be eliminated. If you have read and understand your responsibilities for being a member of this class, please sign. A parent or guardian must also read and sign this paper.

Thank You.

Mr. Thomas Kaszer
Tokay High School
Lodi, California

Student's Name _____ Date _____

Parent/Guardian Signature _____

Comments or Suggestions:

On the first day of Middle School, I ask the students to brainstorm all of their concerns about middle school. Some of those most frequently mentioned are getting lost, mean teachers, gangs, getting on the wrong bus, too much homework, being offered drugs. They record their lists and on the second day the students take out their lists and we have a reality check to see which of these things actually occurred. Then the students are asked to turn the two lists into an essay. This process serves two purposes: it alleviates anxieties and puts them at ease and secondarily, I have an initial writing sample from each student.

Kathleen Beard
Seventh Grade
Middle School History/English
Morongo Unified, California

Oops, I Forgot Something

Remember, Rome wasn't built in a day, and you don't have to accomplish everything in one day either. Unlike other firsts: first date; prom; graduations from high school and college; job interview; car purchase; and birth of a child, you can redo the first day of school over and over again for the rest of the semester or school year. First days have a funny way of erasing themselves and you can start anew each and every day.

Apply It!

Now it is your turn to design a first-day or first-period schedule. Use the guidelines as a model for your own first day or period.

Avoid It!

By all means, when your students' parent(s) ask them what they did in school or in a certain subject, you **do not** want them to utter the dreaded words, "Nothing much." When you look over your plans for the day, put yourself in your students' shoes and ask yourself, "Would I go home and talk about an exciting day, or would I yawn and say the dreaded words?"

Chapter **6**

How Do I Arrange and Assign Seats?

*At a round table,
every seat is the
head place.*

German proverb

Effectiveness Essentials

■ Your seating arrangement should be consistent with your instructional philosophy.

■ Rows or modified rows reduce distraction and social interaction.

■ Clustering facilitates differentiated and cooperative learning.

■ The horseshoe maximizes space and reduces interaction.

■ Choosing seats can be a first exercise in responsible decision making.

■ Teachers should move students who make bad choices.

■ Seat students with special needs and second language learners to optimize learning.

■ When sharing a room, establish ground rules openly and honestly.

Classroom Arrangement
Teachers discuss how classroom arrangement is dependent on the age of students and type of instruction taking place. After watching the video, make at least two tentative and different floor plans for your room.

When I attended public school in the 1950s, there was one seating design—bolted down desks, and two schemes for assigning seats—alphabetical or size order. Your saving grace was poor eyesight, hearing impairment, or behavioral problems. Those students were placed up front, close and personal next to the teacher's desk. My bottle-thick glasses gave me a front row seat. Some might say it was because I talked too much, but I will never admit to that.

It is time to put on your designer's hat and think about your room arrangement and how you can fit all the 20–40 students in the space that is your home away from home for the year. In this chapter you will encounter some considerations that should guide your "blueprints."

Your Seating Arrangement Should Be Consistent with Your Instructional Philosophy

Another way of saying this is that your seating arrangement should be determined by how you want to conduct business in your classroom. Your classroom reflects your personality and instructional style and takes into account the needs (intellectual, emotional, and social) of your students. If you plan on lecturing using PowerPoint, you may want your students in rows, all facing forward for optimal viewing. If you are a cooperative learning advocate, you can minimize disruption by having students already seated in clusters. Clusters also facilitate the learning center approach favored by many elementary teachers and accommodate differentiated learning at any grade level.

Seating Arrangements Vary from Classroom to Classroom

A first step is to look at various arrangements in classrooms around the school to see the alternatives available. Ask your colleagues which arrangements seem to work best for them and why they arranged the desks or tables as they did. Collect as many ideas as you can. Find out how many students are on your class list and see which configurations accommodate that number best. There are three basic configurations to consider:

Rows or modified rows will reduce distraction and social interaction.

You will find desks arranged in rows or tables oriented toward the front of the room in many classrooms (Figure 6.1a). This arrangement tells the students that you are in charge and literally at the head of the class. This is a way to curb discipline problems at the outset, and many novices rely on this seating arrangement to diminish talking and distractions.

Figure 6.1a

Rows

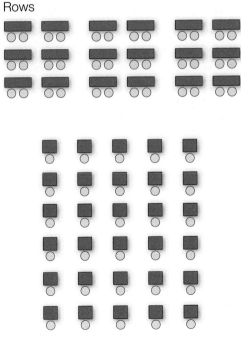

Figure 6.1b

Clustering

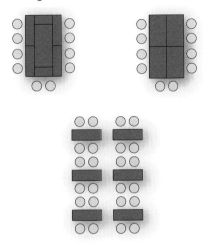

Row upon row of seats may convey the message that cooperative work is not the priority and that students work independently. However, effective teachers model moving desks quietly and quickly to form clusters or groupings when collaborative activities are planned.

Clustering facilitates differentiated learning for students with special needs and second language learners.

Clustered tables or desks (Figure 6.1b) provide a social environment conducive to projects, cooperative learning, and

Teacher Talks . . .

My students are always clustered in groups. I always have at least one high and one low per group. That way the students have someone to scaffold with when they begin independent work.

Kris Ungerer
Kindergarten
Riverside, California

differentiated learning. This configuration allows for sharing of materials and more interaction. The downside is that clustering may create management and even discipline problems. Make sure students at clustered tables can see the board and all technology and instructional locations without twisting into pretzels. No student should have his or her back to the instructional sites.

The horseshoe configuration allows for more space and reduces interaction.

More students are oriented toward the front of the room, and the teacher has greater access to all students (Figure 6.1c). The horseshoe configuration can be used on a larger scale or students can sit in a circle to encourage debate

Figure 6.1c
Horseshoes

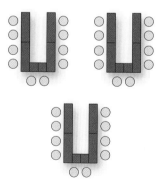

Figure 6.1d
Circular

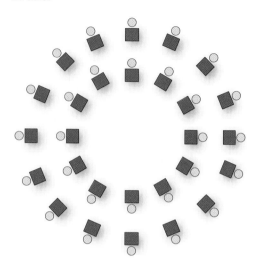

and discussions—especially in middle and high school classes (Figure 6.1d). On the negative side, one high school teacher cautions to stay alert as students in this configuration now have an easy opportunity to communicate non-verbally with each other.

These three basic building blocks— the individual desk, the cluster, and the mini-horseshoe—can be arranged in any number of ways. Or, the three elements can be combined in the same classroom.

If you are working in a team in block schedules, you will want to confer with your teammates about their methods of arranging and assigning

Room Arrangements

Teacher Talks . . .

As an upper elementary teacher, the days of nametags and all the books stacked neatly on each desk is no doubt passé, and certainly not my style. I am concerned about arranging my room so every seat is relatively good and so that my independent work areas are accessible. As far as seating I let students find their own with the warning to find something that fits because it might be a long time before I make changes. Then I adjust seating to compensate for social irresponsibility, language help, or physical difficulties (hearing, "lost" eyeglasses, etc.). I also radically change around the seating at least once a month to promote more diverse social interaction. Also at my present school the difference between initial class lists and who actually shows makes a lot of preplanning in this area a waste of time. I do listen to the moms who tell me on the first day not to let their child sit by . . . That is almost always good advice.

Art Eustace, Fifth Grade
Fontana, California

Apply It!

Your seating chart can be a valuable assessment tool as well. Use your seating chart to assess YOUR teaching behaviors, patterns, and practices as well as monitor your students' in-class behavior and response patterns.

Make several copies of your finalized seating chart. Use the copies to put some symbol next to the students you call on. This will help you identify who is responding the most and who needs to be encouraged to respond more. You want to ensure equity in your questioning. You can also use copies of the seating chart to identify your pattern of movement around the room. Attach a copy of the seating chart to a clipboard every so often and draw lines to see how well you are circulating around the room. Use seating chart copies for other notations as well, such as inattention, rule breaking, unique responses, etc.

seats. Check to see how seats are arranged in the classroom(s) you are assigned to. Since you are sharing space, your choices may be limited. Secondary school teachers generally use a seating chart and/or use nameplates for the desks or tables that facilitate attendance taking. Students take their index cards or nameplates from a table or pocket chart and you will know who is absent at a glance. Use different colors for each period and your nametags or nameplates can be easily sorted if they get mixed up.

Choosing Seats Can Be a First Exercise in Responsible Decision Making

Choosing your own seat is increasingly common in elementary, middle, and even high school classrooms. The teacher should emphasize good decision making and remind students that bad or irresponsible choices are subject to swift teacher modification before the first week of school has ended. From the following options, choose the one that is age appropriate.

The first two are suggestions for elementary school teachers:

1. Drawing numbers from a hat and the #1 gets to choose first, #2 second, and so forth.

2. Determining criteria for choosing first such as white tennis shoes, red clothing, sayings on shirts, etc.

3. Let the students just come in and choose a seat, temporarily or permanently.

4. Have nametags on the predetermined seats.

5. Allow free choice, but during the first week reseat any students with special needs or those with obvious incompatibilities with seatmates, before finalizing your seating arrangement.

Move students who make bad choices. In other words, free seating choices are not final until the teacher says they are final. And even then, students are reminded that seating charts are written in pencil and may be changed at any time. New seat selections can be made every few months or at mid-semester in the interest of fairness. Students can make new friends and have a new classroom vantage point.

Students with Special Needs and Second Language Learners Should Be Your Main Concern

Seat non-native speakers next to native speaker buddies and make sure your students with special needs

Teacher Talks . . .

At the beginning of the year, I assign seats to my students. Midway through the semester, I rearrange the assignments, but I turn it into a logistical challenge. My room has three large tables (islands really); two of them have six seats and the third has four seats. I allow the students to sit anywhere they want with the following restrictions: They cannot sit at the same table. They cannot sit across from or beside anyone whom they were previously across from or beside. It is not that hard for them to figure out, and they have fun figuring it out.

*Stephen Pulliam
High School Science
Stony Brook, New York*

Apply It!

If you have students sit in clusters or grouped at tables, you might ask them to come up with names for their table groups or clusters related to the curricular content. They can be names of constellations, continents, mythological figures, desert animals, etc. Then they can make nametags reflecting their table, row, or cluster identity or hang a cluster identity sign from the ceiling.

have their individual circumstances accommodated. The cumulative record card, parents, teachers, administrators, and your own observations may help you identify those who need special accommodation. If you are using self-selection as your seating method, you need to use utmost sensitivity when reseating students with special needs so as not to draw undue attention to them. Since you have already stated that seat selections are not final until you say they are, making changes of this sort can appear routine.

When Sharing a Room, Have an Open and Honest Discussion to Establish Ground Rules

You may want to address topics such as leaving the room clean and ready for the next occupant, returning moved furniture to an agreed upon arrangement, turning off all computers, removing personal materials to a storage container, use of common supplies, allocation of board and bulletin board space, etc. Another topic to address is how the teacher(s) with whom you share a room feel about your remaining in the room to prep. Some teachers don't want to be "watched" and you need to be upfront with colleagues about your feelings and theirs.

Avoid It!

Do not isolate any student based on hearsay, rumor, or gossip. Give every student a chance to start anew.

Do not hesitate to modify a dysfunctional seating arrangement.

Do not be afraid to modify student seating if you see obvious cliques developing based on race, culture, school social status, etc.

Chapter 7

What Should I Wear and What Should I Say?

Effectiveness Essentials

- Strive for a strong first impression.
- Let students, parents, and administrators know you are a professional through dress, words, and deeds.
- Balance professional dress with comfort.
- Some middle and high school teachers wear subject-related clothing.
- It is most appropriate to be addressed formally.
- Develop rapport with your class.
- Find unique ways to break the ice.

Clothes make the man.

Anonymous Latin Proverb

Clothes make the man. Naked people have little or no influence on society.

Mark Twain

Your First Impression Will Be a Lasting One

Veterans recommend dressing as professionally as possible. Professional dress will help with classroom discipline. When you dress casually, the students perceive you as casual and may not take you as seriously as they should. Model the dress of your principal or administrators to be on the safe side. You need not run out to a color consultant or buy a dress-for-success manual. A few low-cost upgrades to your wardrobe will give you confidence. Try for the "business casual" look.

Even if "all the other teachers are wearing them," save your sweats and shorts for the gym and your flip-flops and backless shoes for the weekend. Think about how midriff-baring tops and very short skirts will play in your classroom, especially when you lean over. Although jeans are worn at some schools, your students will be wearing them and you want to distinguish yourself from them. Students will make judgments about you on that first day, and you can gain an advantage in the respect department by dressing like you deserve it.

Figure 7.1

Professional but Casual

Myth Buster!

Students like a teacher who is with it and can relate to them as a peer.

I remember the principal of the school where I did my practice teaching thirty years ago reminding me that the students have friends; they do not need me to be their friend—they need me to be their teacher. That means compassion, wisdom, and experience on my part, but I do not need to be their buddy.

Beth Ann Willstrop
Grades 9–12
English and Reading
San Antonio, Texas

Let students, parents, and administrators know you are professional through dress, words, and deeds.

Plan what you will wear on the first day to look your professional best. You will feel more confident, and those you encounter will make judgments about your professionalism based solely on your looks, rightly or wrongly, since they have no other data. Consider what message you want to send to others and let that be a guiding principle of how you dress.

Balance professional dress with comfort.

Whereas some veterans suggest a dressy dress or suit and tie on the first day, most stress comfort. You will have to take into consideration climate, school norms, and grade level as well as your own personal taste. Sitting on the floor or handling paints and paste may dictate very casual clothing or, better yet, a smock that suits you. Think about your poor feet, too! Wear comfortable shoes!

It's okay to be a little playful.

Wearing subject-related clothing shows you have a sense of playfulness while still being professional. This might include a tie with global themes or a dress with a book pattern. Science teachers may wear a lab coat. You can accessorize with scarves or pins to advertise your subject area. One elementary teacher I know wears various

Teacher Talks . . .

My first principal walked into my classroom one afternoon and took a good look at me and told me sternly that she wanted to see me after school. I spent the rest of that afternoon anticipating what job I could get after she fired me. At 3:30 I went to the office and waited to see her. She came out moments later and said, "Oh, I thought you were wearing culottes. I see it is only a pleated dress." That's the way it was back then. No pants, ever!

Ellen Kronowitz
Former Third Grade Teacher
Springfield Gardens, New York

Figure 7.2

Lab coat

School-themed sweater

 *Myth Buster!*

How a teacher dresses is not important.

The kids notice everything about you. My high school students commented on every aspect of my clothes, nails, shoes, hair. Teachers are idols until they prove themselves otherwise. Don't try to look like your students. It rings false for them. They don't want another peer because they are struggling with peer relation-ships as it is and you can be the bell-wether of fine fashion for them. Keep the sweats in your gym bag. Dress comfortably but do dress up. I always feel better about myself when I look my best.

Dottie Bailey
Speech Therapist/Teacher
Colton, California

"cool" socks with her outfits. Her students always look to see what unique socks she is wearing that day. Another has a sweater for major holidays. In high school, especially, don't overdue the playfulness lest you be considered just plain weird or "dorky."

Establishing Rapport with Your Students

The first days and weeks of school are the time to establish an authentic connection with your students. At the same time you are presenting yourself as a businesslike professional, it is not inconsistent to convey to your students that you are an approachable human being who is genuinely interested in them. The open communication channel begins with your very first words.

The first words are the hardest.

You can no doubt remember your first public speaking experience. It may have been the first time you made a speech, read a poem aloud, stood before your class to read a passage, or participated in a play or debate. You probably felt like you would freeze up or run off to hide. The reality is that you are well prepared to address your first class. Your students will likely not remember what you said first, but because it is of primary concern to new teachers, here are some common introductions:

- **The Welcomers** attempt to make the student feel right at home and set a positive tone at the outset.

   "Good Morning. I know we are going to have a good year and lots of fun."

   "Hi, I'm so glad to see all of you. We are going to have a super year."

   "Welcome to Chemistry. It's not as hard as people think."

   "Welcome to geometry class. See these models? You will make them this year."

Student Says . . .

Teachers shouldn't use very loud voices because it can sound rude and is disrespectful to the class. And it is important for teachers to say "please" and "thank you" to the kids.

Erik
Grade 5
Brookline, Massachusetts

I teach 600 students "general music" in two different schools. Parents often comment how music with me is their child's favorite subject. I have found the way to success is:

1. Know their names
2. Bring a lot of energy to the classroom
3. Focus on making it fun
4. Be silly

An enthusiastic approach is the only way! And get plenty of rest the night before!

Kevin White
Music Teacher
Charlottesville, Virginia

■ **The Introducers** get right to the point and launch into a formal introduction of the classroom personnel.

> "I'm Mrs._____, your _____ teacher, and this is Ms._____, our aide, who will help you also."

> "I'm Mr._____ and here are Boris and Natasha, our classroom pet rats."

■ **The Managers** put classroom management, rules, and discipline right out there and convey the expectation that the class will be well organized and well behaved.

> "The line is very straight, and I appreciate how quietly everyone entered the room."

> "Pick up your nametag and take a seat."

■ **Other Unique First Words** are offered by teachers who share their values, ideals and/or enthusiasm with their students.

> "I'm happy and excited to be your teacher."

> "Mistakes are permitted in this class."

Secondary students may not remember what you said first, but they will be evaluating you on the "cool" and professional scales. Younger students may express their concerns differently, but all students will be more concerned with the issues that directly affect them than they are with your first words. Homework load, the difficulty of subject matter, your grading practices, and discipline policy are all concerns that matter on that first day. Deep inside, however, students of any age are curious about your personal life, and you should share something with them.

It is most appropriate to be called by your last name preceded by Mr., Mrs., or Ms.

These are the customary titles and they convey professional respect. Many middle and high school teachers call on their students using Mr. or Miss/Ms. and the students' last names to convey mutual respect. Some primary teachers use only a last initial or first name preceded by a title if their name is especially hard to pronounce. In all cases, write your name on the chalkboard and pronounce it with your students. During attendance, students can easily learn your name by responding to your salutation, "Good morning, Juan" with "Good morning, Mrs. Matsumoto."

A little disclosure goes a long way.

Tell your students something about your personal life and professional background. The majority of teachers commonly tell their students about their family, pets, hobbies, why they love

Apply It!

Introduce yourself with an Autobiography Poem and then have the students follow suit. This would make a great initial bulletin board, along with photos of each student.

First Name	Ellen
3 Traits	Funny, loving, friendly
Relative of	Wife of Gary
Who loves ...	Family, friends, and horses
Who feels ...	fortunate
Who fears ...	losing loved ones
Who needs ...	a kind word
Who gives ...	a helping hand
Who would like to see (3) ...	peace, clean air, no hunger
Resident of ...	Redlands
Last Name	Kronowitz

Apply It!

Convey your educational beliefs to your students with a survival sack or small manila envelope that contains items such as these:

Rubber band	To remind them to be flexible
Paperclip	To remind them to stay connected to the class community
Eraser	To remind them that everyone makes mistakes
Sticky note	To remind them to stick to the goal when things get tough
Penny	To remind them they are valued
Hershey's Hug	To remind them that we all need hugs
Lifesaver candy	To remind them you are there to help
One Homework Pass	Mistakes are permitted
A noodle	Use your noodle

Survival Kit

teaching, why they became a teacher in the first place, and any apparent physical disabilities. Some teachers decorate a biographical poster with photos of family, pets, favorite hobbies, sports, foods, and so on. You might bring in 5 objects that will serve as props as you tell about yourself. My objects would be an album of family photos, a horseshoe or horse figurine, a swim cap and goggles, a map with places I've traveled to circled, and a book I am currently reading.

Even minimal self-disclosure (the type and name of your pet, your favorite hobby) will ease the tension, satisfy curiosity, and bring you down to earth

and make you more approachable. Consider the activity in the Apply It! above to communicate your philosophy and put your students at ease. You can substitute items to reflect your grade level.

Create Your Own Unique Way of Breaking the Ice

Generally, you're safe if you take one from every category in this acronym: WISHES—Welcome, Introduction, Share Hopes, and Establish Standards. This is your formula for a good start on the first day.

Apply It!

How will you welcome your students on that first day? How will you introduce yourself? What hopes will you share with the class? What standards will you emphasize? Jot down a few ideas.

Welcome _____

Introduction _____

Share _____

Hopes _____

Establish _____

Standards _____

Avoid It!

Your students are not your friends, and you can convey your role as teacher by your dress, demeanor, behavior, and words on the first days and weeks of school. The clothing and words you choose will often determine how much respect and status your students accord you. Facial piercing and tattoos may be acceptable in some circles, but remove piercings and cover tattoos as best you can during the work week.

We could learn a lot from crayons; some are sharp, some are pretty, some are dull, while others bright, some have weird names, but they all have learned to live together in the same box.

Anonymous

The most important single ingredient in the formula of success is knowing how to get along with people.

Teddy Roosevelt

Chapter **8**

How Do I Learn My Students' Names and How Do They Learn Each Other's Names?

Effectiveness Essentials

■ Knowing students' names is a powerful way of validating them.

■ There are a variety of grade-appropriate devices to help everyone to learn names quickly.

Make a Concerted Effort to Learn Your Students' Names as Soon as You Can

This is a powerful way to connect with your students and acknowledge them personally. It requires concentration and extra effort, but it can be done. Always check the pronunciation. All students should have the option of going by a nickname or shortened version.

Knowing students' names is a powerful way of validating them.

There is no greater compliment to a student than calling him or her by name at the end of the first day. You can associate the names with faces from school photos. In many districts, individual photos are taken at the time of the class picture, and they are attached to the permanent record cards. Take time to make the name-face association before school starts. Students will be shocked and pleased to be recognized. Or, buy an inexpensive digital camera and take the photos yourself.

Using Nametags and Nameplates. Nametags and nameplates are very popular aids for learning names. Teachers place them on desks or on the front of desks, pin them on the children's clothing, or string them around primary youngsters' necks (upside down so children can read them when they look down) (see Figure 8.1). Students can make their own nametags or nameplates. Overcome the reluctance of secondary students to wear nametags by explaining that they are common in the workplace. Your school may

Figure 8.1

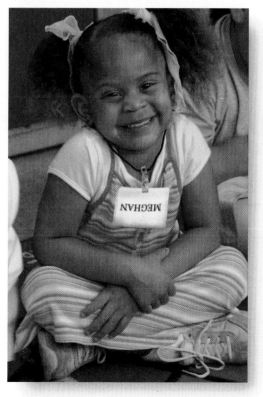

Apply It!

You can use a digital camera and take instant pictures of the students, table by table or individually. Writing the names below the faces will help you remember who's who, and you can memorize the photos. Once the photos have served their purpose as memory aids, you can use them to create a Welcome Back bulletin board bearing a subject/grade level-relevant caption. Or, you can attach the photos to your seating chart to help you associate names and faces when you have multiple sets of students.

require teachers to wear nametags, and that will support your request.

Using the Seating Chart. One of the most useful devices for learning students' names is the seating chart. You can get a jump on the process by having the blank chart or map ready to go (see Figure 8.2). The names just have to be filled in when you take attendance or look at the nametags. You can attach small digital images or write in some distinguishing characteristic such as "spiked hair" or "wears bright red glasses." Do not hesitate to ask students to identify themselves before responding. They will appreciate your attempts to learn their names.

Student Stars

Figure 8.2

David

Jamaal   Karen

Moira   Tony

Kanye   Yen

Lisa   Leslie

Liu   Erik

Help Everyone to Learn Each Other's Names

There are also a variety of grade-appropriate devices to help everyone to learn names quickly. It's important for you to know your students, but it is just as important for them to get to know one another as individuals. This decreases the likelihood of fights and arguments. Here are some additional suggestions from veterans.

Primary Grades, K–1

The teacher holds up name cards, and the children recognize their names, retrieve the cards, and place them in the designated spot. The teacher can call the names as well at the beginning,

but should encourage recognition solely by visual cues early in the year.

Intermediate Grades, 2–3

Students introduce themselves to the class. They can be given some guidelines and time constraints:

1. Tell us your name.
2. Tell us something about your family and pets.
3. What do you do after school?
4. What are your favorite sports?

Or, review alphabetical order by having children come up in small groups and alphabetize themselves, using their tags or cards.

A child who is "It" leaves the room and is assigned a partner in the room. When the child who is "It" returns, he or she must ask questions to find out who the partner is:

> Is my partner a girl or a boy?
>
> Is my partner in the first row?
>
> Does my partner have long hair?
>
> Is my partner wearing blue?

Students can interview a partner, following a set of guidelines, and then introduce the partner to the rest of the class. Guidelines can be distributed or derived by the class.

1. Partner's favorite and/or least favorite subject in school
2. Partner's career goals
3. Partner's pets
4. Partner's favorite sports or hobbies
5. Partner's favorite foods

Upper Grades 4–6

The Scavenger Hunt Game. Students have to find someone in the class who corresponds to one of the descriptions provided and then they put that student's initials next to the description on a prewritten grid. Figure 8.3 shows what this might look like.

Figure 8.3

Find Your Classmate

who hates pizza	who plays the drums	whose favorite color is purple	who has ridden a horse	who owns more than three pets
who can do a magic trick	who has lived in another state	who has a library card	who has lived in another country	who has a five-letter name
who speaks two languages	who wants to be a teacher	who has a birthday in September **RW**	who has a skateboard	who snowboards **BM**
who is wearing blue shoes **JTC**	who has a reptile as a pet	who has snorkeled	who plays soccer	who plays tennis
who likes spinach	who has two sisters	who is wearing a ring	who is wearing a necklace **RW**	who has a green backpack

All Grades Including Secondary

The Name Game. Each person introduces all the others preceding, going around the room or up and down the rows in the following manner:

Maria: I'm Maria.

Jason: This is Maria; I'm Jason.

Eric: This is Maria, Jason; and I'm Eric.

Isabella: This is Maria, Jason, Eric; and I'm Isabella.

Timelines. Divide an 11 × 14 sheet of construction paper in half the long way and have each student divide his or her strip into six equal parts (fraction review). In each segment students illustrate a significant event in their life, e.g, born, started school, moved to a new house, etc. They share these in class, a few each day during the first week of school. Figure 8.4 shows a sample.

Adjectives. Have your students describe themselves to the class using only three adjectives. You should model the exercise first.

Cooperative Groups. Have your students get into small groups and discuss their favorite music group, sport, movie star, TV program, etc. They will need to answer the questions about commonalities and differences (see Figure 8.5). This will help them learn about one another and begin to form a community.

What do group members have in common?

Where are the main differences?

What 3 things can you say about your group?

Figure 8.4

Teacher Talks . . .

In one of my grad classes I kept calling Debra "Marjorie," although they looked nothing alike. I was so focused on not doing it, that I did it repeatedly. Each time, I apologized profusely remembering how I felt when my mother frequently called me by my sister's name.

Ellen Kronowitz
Author

Figure 8.5

Student Names	Music	Movie	Food	Sports

Interviews. Students can generate interview questions and then interview and introduce a partner to the rest of the class. Or, you can provide interview forms with items like these:

My hero or heroine is _____

Why?_____

My career goal _____

My favorite subjects _____

My least favorite subjects _____

My pet peeve is _____

I am known for _____

I laugh when _____

I would like to know more about _____

_____

Something I excel at _____

Three words to describe me are _____

Something I want to get better at _____

_____

You don't want to spend a great deal of time on introductions that first period of the first day, but some of these simple ice breakers will create a cooperative climate in which students feel they have gotten to know at least one other student in the class.

Avoid It!

Getting to the end of the semester or the year without knowing who is who

Mispronouncing names

Confusing one student with another

Chapter 9

How Do I Establish Rules and Discipline the First Day?

No one is ever old enough to know better.

Holbrook Jackson,
English journalist

Effectiveness Essentials

- Be aware that your students will be judging your management style.
- Ascertain what the school norms are regarding discipline and rules.
- Good rules cannot be arbitrary.
- Good rules are understandable by everyone and sensitive to all students.
- Good rules respect and accommodate students with special needs.
- Good rules don't create more work for the teacher.
- Strictly enforce the rules the first day and in the weeks ahead.
- Communicate the rules to parents as soon as possible.
- Impress students with your seriousness about compliance with established rules.

Students Will Be Judging Your Management Style of the Class on the First Day

There will be anywhere from 20–40 pairs of eyes staring at you, and although they will never appear more angelic, beware! They will be watching and waiting to assess your "toughness" or "easiness." While they are at their best and paying close attention to your words and deeds, it is your time to make a firm stand about your standards and expectations. All but the kindergarteners have great experience sizing up their teachers that first day, and with each year their "skills" in this area improve. By their senior year, they are experts. You are one in a line of teachers they have scrutinized and judged at first glance. You need to pass the rule-making test with flying colors.

Ascertain What the School Norms Are Regarding Discipline and Rules

Your discipline plan must conform to those norms. Don't reinvent the wheel. How can you learn what the norms are? First, speak with your principal or resource teachers about the generic school and district rules with regard to discipline. Check out the website where the discipline policy is often posted and read the district/school policy manual. Ask colleagues what their rules are and how they abide by the generic and district rules. After learning about school and district

Apply It!

Think back to a teacher you respected. What personal attributes made you want to come to class? What were his or her management strategies? What happened when kids misbehaved? Now think about the opposite teacher whom no one respected or listened to. What personal attributes did he or she exhibit? What were this teacher's management strategies? What conclusions can you draw from this comparison?

policy regarding discipline, experienced teachers report setting rules on the first day of school. Common practices include:

- Eliciting classroom rules from the students.
- Ranking the rules with your students and selecting a maximum of five.
- Telling the students that as school progresses they can add or delete rules.
- Stating rules positively, e.g., *Raise hands* rather than *No calling out*.

The challenge secondary school teachers face results from the multiple sets of rules other teachers may set forth, often dictated by the subject matter. This can be confusing to your students. That is why, in secondary school, it is essential that you determine what the district and school givens are before you go it alone with your own rules. Here are some typical secondary school rules gleaned from high school teachers:

1. Obey all school rules.
2. Be in your seat when the bell rings.
3. Bring all required materials, books, and homework to class.
4. Raise your hand to speak, and be an attentive listener.
5. Be responsible and respectful.
6. Plagiarism and cheating result in failure.

Students in high school want to know the rules and the consequences for not adhering to them up front. In other words, they may not care what the rules are; they just want to know what the penalties are for not following them. Stating the rules and consequences on that first day will put the decision making in their hands.

Seven Principles Should Guide Your Rule Making That First Day

These principles are ones found in most discipline guides and they will serve you well as you consider your own rules, whether you allow your students to derive them or you write them

Student Says . . .

On the first day of school, the teacher goes over the rules and regulations.

Holland
Age 15, Tenth Grade
Redlands, California

yourself. It is key to remember that an elementary classroom is like a family, and since the students are with you all day, the rules you derive or set down can be reinforced all day long. In middle and high school, the rules may be different from class to class, depending on the subject matter. That is why it is essential that there be a generic set of rules for all to add to if need be. So again, check out what essential rules the district and school prescribe.

1. Good rules tend to be needed, fair, applied equally, consistently enforceable, age appropriate, reasonable, and respectful.

Any rules you impose on your students or ones they derive themselves with your assistance should meet these criteria. The most common rules in classrooms are listed below:

1. Respect rights and property of others.
2. Follow directions.
3. Work quietly in the classroom.
4. Be a good listener.
5. Raise hands to speak or leave seat.

Apply It!

Before you begin your rule-making discussion, ask your students to close their eyes and imagine what it would be like to have a classroom with no rules. List the pros and cons on the board. Ask them which list is more likely to help them learn. Once they recognize the need for rules, you can ask them to identify 5 rules that would make for a good classroom community. In middle and high school, ask your students what additions they would make to the generic district/school rules to enable them to remain safe, for example, in a science lab. Or, to best use their time in an art class or gym class or any other specific discipline. They can do this in groups and additional subject-specific rules can be gleaned from the group efforts.

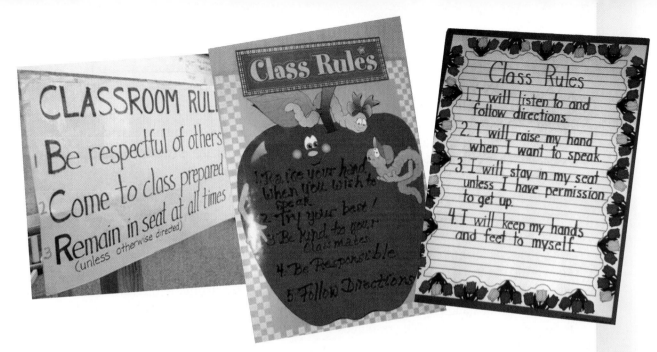

Rules in Plain Sight

Chapter 9   How Do I Establish Rules and Discipline the First Day?

One year I decided to do something different. The first day of class I told the sixth graders there would be no rules until we found a need for them. After three days of chaos and my nagging, and worse, I had them come to the class meeting space and we talked about how things were going. Everyone, including me, worked on a list of problems that we noticed with no rules in place. They recognized the need for rules and came up with two: "Clean up the mess you make" and "Be responsible." Although I would not recommend this exercise in anarchy to novice teachers, you might consider leading your students in a guided fantasy about a class with no rules.

2. Good rules are understandable to non-native speakers and are sensitive to cultural norms.

Make sure that you translate as necessary all rules for the students and their parents. The translation website http://www.babelfish.altavista.com will serve you well. Rules

Teacher Talks . . .

As a sixth grade teacher, I posted the following as the sole guiding principle:

When I am responsible, I will have a good day. When I am irresponsible, I will pay the consequences.

And below this rule were the following words:

Whatever you believe about yourself, you will become.

*Art Gallardo
Former Sixth Grade Teacher
Principal
San Bernardino, California*

should be posted in a prominent place in the room. In their book, *Management Strategies for Culturally Diverse Classrooms,* Johns and Espinoza (1996) provide a multicultural frame of reference for discipline matters. Examples include: Asian cultures value saving face and indirect communication so you may not want to engage in public and direct confrontation. Some African Americans and Hispanics are taught not to make direct eye contact as a sign of respect to elders, and so the teacher who says, "Look at me," may interpret failure to do so as disrespect. Johns and Espinoza's book is one of a number of valuable resources you will need to read to prepare yourself to appropriately deal with diverse student populations.

3. Good rules respect and accommodate students with special needs.

You will have students in your class who may not be physically or emotionally able to comply with your rules. For example, a student with Tourette's syndrome will be unable to keep from making uncontrollable utterances and even cursing. Students with physical disabilities may not be able to raise

Apply It!

Another way to drive home the need for rules is to make up a list of age-appropriate "silly" rules and discuss what is wrong with each one. Once your students identify what is wrong with each rule, they can turn it around and use the opposites as criteria by which to judge their own rules. Some examples follow:

Rule	Weakness	A good rule is ...
Only boys get bathroom passes	Not equal	Equal for everyone
No sneezing in class	Not possible	Possible
Late students have detention all year	Too harsh	Fair
Be nice	Vague	Specific

hands before speaking. Help your students realize that each one of us is special in some way and we need to be considerate of those who are allowed some leeway on some rules.

4. Good rules don't create more work for the teacher.

Your plan should be easy to administer. That is, you need to make sure that you are not overwhelmed with counting points, doling out candy, or punishing rule breakers during your recess or lunch period. Students who break a rule should be asked to tell you which rule they ignored or forgot. In this way they learn to monitor their own behavior. If you prominently display the rules and go over them as needed, perhaps even every day at the beginning of the year or semester, you will make your students more responsible. You will learn more about this in Unit 4, Positive Discipline.

5. Strictly enforce the rules the first day and in the weeks ahead.

Rules need to be indelibly written in the minds of your students. Catch all infractions immediately, restate the

⊘ *Myth Buster!*

Rules stifle creativity and self-direction.

Nonsense! Kids thrive in an environment where they feel safe. Kids often test structure and limits as a way to check to see if the boundaries are still in place. In a structured environment, kids can express themselves while all moving in the same direction.

Jason Paytas
Fourth Grade Teacher
Arcata, California

rule, check for understanding, and liberally praise students for following the rules. Adopt this motto, "It's easier to ease off than it is to crack down." Have the students memorize the rules. For example, in elementary grades, call out the number of the rule and have students respond with the rule or an example of someone obeying or disobeying the rule. In middle and high school, the rules should be written in their notebooks or binders, highlighted on the syllabus, enlarged on a poster, or tacked to the bulletin board.

Teacher Talks . . .

I write a list of "Classroom Manners and Expectations." I include things like, "I will say thank-you when I am given a gift or a piece of candy for a test." I explain it would be taken back if they "forget their manners." They will raise their hand and wait to be called on if they want to share something. If they don't observe these expectations, a point will be taken off of their behavior and classroom preparation grade. I explain how important it is for them to help each other if someone is confused, or struggling, or doesn't understand. I print out two copies for each student, which I sign. I hold a classroom meeting, explaining this will be a written, signed agreement between all of us, and I require that they sign it too. I keep a copy, and they keep the second copy in their binders. I emphasize that if any of them "forget their manners or classroom

(continued on following page)

expectations," I will stop the class, and we will review them again.

In a very short time, my students start to change. They start to demonstrate a desire to become well mannered young ladies and gentleman. They change from a class into a respectful, caring community.

The most wonderful and touching moment came this past week, when one of my students baked and decorated a birthday cake for one of her classmates. The recipient asked to make a speech. She said, "Thank-you for baking me a birthday cake. No other student has ever done something this thoughtful for me before. Last year when I was in fifth grade I didn't have any friends, now I do. Thank-you."

My wonderful, loving, caring students burst into applause, and one young man, (one of my "tough boys") said, "That made me cry, Ms. Wasserman." It doesn't get any better than that.

Laurie Wasserman
Learning Disabilities
National Board Certified Teacher
Medford, Massachusetts

Apply It!

Students are apt to be more cooperative if they have a hand in making the rules. You can combine creativity and rule making by asking students in groups to come up with 5 rules they think will lead to a productive learning environment. Each group writes their 5 rules on a chart they will hang up in the room. Then the charts are compared and commonalities are circled in red marker. The most effective rules, agreed upon by students and teacher, become the rules of the classroom as long as they are consistent with school rules and district policy. Facilitate group work by posing some key questions like these:

Describe a classroom, free from distractions and disruptions, where all students can learn.

What rules would you need to maintain this productive classroom learning environment?

Are your rules fair to everyone, enforceable, reasonable, and respectful?

Are your rules stated in positive terms?

Condense your rules to five essential ones that cover the bases.

6. Communicate the rules to parents as soon as possible.

On the first day, most teachers send a note home to parents (in translation if needed) explaining the classroom rules or they have the students rewrite the rules for their parents to sign. Parents need to know the ground rules so they can help you out. Middle and high school teachers include this information in the syllabus or student handbook, but it would be useful to send out a letter regarding rules that will not get lost in all the other information handbooks and syllabi contain. Should infractions occur, parents will have been forewarned about rules and will more likely accept the news that their youngster or teen has broken one.

Classroom Artifacts

Dear Parent or Guardian,

Thank you for sharing _____ with me this school year. I will do my best to help _____ reach his or her full potential. In order to have a safe, secure, productive learning environment, we have written these classroom rules:

1. Respect rights and property of others.
2. Follow directions.
3. Work quietly in the classroom.
4. Be a good listener.
5. Raise hands to speak or leave seat.

I know the students will work hard to follow the rules they developed. At school, I will encourage them in their efforts at self-control. If I need your help at home, I will be in touch with you by phone or note. If you have any questions or wish to speak with me, I can be reached at the school (phone number) between 8:00 and 8:30 a.m. and during recess (10:00-10:15 or 2:15-2:30). If these times are inconvenient for you, please leave a message and I'll return your call as soon as possible. You can reach me by e-mail at _____ @ yahoo.com. I look forward to working with you during the coming school year.

Sincerely,
Name
Grade   Room   School

Please keep the letter and return the signature portion by the end of the week in the envelope provided.
- -
I have read this letter and we will support the rules regarding behavior.

Parent or Guardian's Signature _____ Phone _____ E-mail _____

Student's signature _____

Comment, Questions, or Conference Request:

Teacher Talks . . .

High school students are just taller elementary school students. Don't be fooled by their size. I have to repeat the rules so often that first week of school, I feel like I am back teaching elementary school again. On the other hand, high school students devise more devious methods of circumventing the rules and invent more creative excuses for not following them than my former elementary students.

Anonymous

7. Impress students in word, behavior, and overall demeanor that you are serious about compliance with established rules.

Thirty pairs of eyes will be watching you the first time that a student breaks one of the established rules. Although you need to respond, make sure your response is measured and firm, rather than over the top. Point to the rules you have established and ask which one has just been broken. Tell them to "make a better choice." Let them know you will not belabor the infraction by moving on quickly and continuing instruction. The key is to make sure that the students realize at that moment that you say what you mean and mean what you say.

Avoid It!

Do not make rules that are:

Unenforceable	"No talking in class"
Harsh	"No homework, week of detention"
Too numerous	More than 5 rules
Unclear or vague	"Dress appropriately"
Unfair	"Late on bus—stay after school"
Too time consuming to enforce	"No candy in school"
Too negative	"Don't hit anyone"—rather—"Keep hands to self"

Unit 2 Checklist

Preplanning for First Day Checklist

For more information go to:

Planning

- [ ] Did I overplan and include "doable" homework? — Chapters 4, 5
- [ ] Are my activities motivating? — Chapter 5

Materials

- [ ] Do I have all materials I will need WITH me? — Chapter 5
- [ ] Do I have enough textbooks and furniture? — Chapters 5, 6

Classroom Environment

- [ ] Is my name and schedule on the chalkboard? — Chapter 5
- [ ] Are bulletin boards ready to go? — Chapters 5, 10
- [ ] Do I have the routines set in my mind? — Unit 3
- [ ] Is my furniture arrangement consistent with my instructional goals? — Chapter 6
- [ ] Have I decided on a seat-selection method? — Chapter 6
- [ ] Have I identified and accommodated my student with special needs and ELL students? — Chapter 6

Rapport with Students

- [ ] Is there a welcoming atmosphere in the room? — Chapter 10
- [ ] Have I decided how to break the ice? — Chapter 7
- [ ] Have I determined a method for learning names? — Chapter 8

Rules and Regulations

- [ ] Do I have a way to establish rules that conforms to district and school policies? — Chapter 9
- [ ] Are my rules easily communicated to students and parents? — Chapter 9
- [ ] Is my plan age-appropriate and flexible enough to accommodate all students' needs? — Chapter 9

And Most Important

- [ ] Will students give a positive first-day report back home? — Unit 2
- [ ] Will they look forward to returning to school on the second day? — Unit 2

Further Reading: Books About the First Days of School

Charles, C. M., & Senter, G. W. (2004). *Elementary classroom management,* 4th ed. Boston: Allyn and Bacon. The authors provide essential advice for organizing and managing and elementary classroom. They include information within the context of the standards-based movement and *No Child Left Behind.*

Emmer, E. T., Evertson, C. M., & Worsham, M. E. (2005). *Classroom management for middle and high school teachers,* 7th ed. Boston: Allyn and Bacon. The authors communicate 25 years of experience-based research including planning instruction, setting up the secondary classroom, establishing rules and procedures, and much more. The authors encourage teachers to embrace the challenge of teaching diverse students and those with special needs.

Evertson. C. M., Emmer, E. T., & Worsham, M. E. (2005). *Classroom management for elementary teachers,* 7th ed. Boston: Allyn and Bacon. The authors provide practical and experience-based suggestions for organizing the elementary school classroom, including communicating with students, planning, managing behavior, organizing the classroom, establishing rules and procedures, and much more.

Kronowitz, E. (2004). *Your first year of teaching and beyond,* 4th ed. Boston: Allyn and Bacon. This text addresses the concerns of first-year and novice teachers, including classroom organization, the first day, discipline, communicating with parents, working with colleagues and your principal, getting to know the school and community, and balancing a professional and personal life.

Schell, L., & Burden, P. (1992). *Countdown to the first day: NEA checklist series.* Washington, DC: National Education Association. This is a checklist of tasks teachers should accomplish leading up to and including the first day of school. Although it is not newly published, it remains relevant.

First Day of School Websites

Babel Fish Translation
http://babelfish.altavista.com/
This website enables you to translate up to 150 words of the most common languages into any of those same languages, including Chinese, Spanish, French, Korean, Italian, Greek, German.

Varied Teacher-Oriented Ideas for the First Days and Beyond
http://atozteacherstuff.com/
At this general website, you will find ideas for starting off the school year, thematic units on every conceivable topic, lesson plans, worksheets, teacher-tested ideas, online chat rooms for teachers, and much more.

A Teacher Network
http://teachers.net
At this generic website, you will find free printable worksheets, chat rooms, web tools, lesson plans, job listings, articles, and links to other sites for teachers.

Middle School Teacher Resources
http://www.middleweb.com/
This website is geared to the middle school teacher and includes ideas for the first day of school, chat rooms, articles on middle school reform, book reviews, and links to other useful sites.

Grades 7–12 Website
http://712educators.about.com/
This is a website geared to the middle and high school educator. You can access articles, lesson plans, teaching tips, curriculum ideas, and teaching strategies.

Education World at Your Fingertips
http://www.education-world.com/
This is a website for all teachers at all levels and administrators. You will find lesson plans, articles, technology updates, discussion forums, and much more. It is a website that you can enjoy browsing as well as searching for specific topics.

Unit 3

Classroom Organization and Management

Chapter 10

How Do I Accessorize the Classroom with Bulletin Boards and Extras?

Effectiveness Essentials

- Classrooms reflect the personality and instructional style of the teacher and the needs of students.

- Setting up and arranging the furniture is your first and most important task.

- Arrange for some private spaces and a quiet reading area.

- Decorating the space creates a unique, stimulating environment.

- Bulletin boards deliver very powerful nonverbal messages to your students.

- Design and construct some of your bulletin boards before school starts.

Classrooms reflect the personality and instructional style of the teacher, as well as the needs of the students. As you walk around your school, you will see that no two classrooms look exactly alike. Even when teachers at the same grade level collaborate in planning, the individual rooms still reflect the personality of each teacher and the needs of the particular group of students. Your room environment speaks volumes, not only to your students, but to their parents, the principal, other staff members, and other students around the school. We get quick impressions when we visit our friends' homes, our doctors' offices, and new restaurants. Décor counts! Make yours appealing and inviting.

Create a Physical Space Conducive to Learning

It's time to call upon your "inner classroom interior decorator" because that richly decorated space you were shown during any prior visits now has bare walls and the furniture arranged helter-skelter. Confront the work involved with the underlying motivation to create an organized, efficient, attractive home away from home for both you and your students. You are creating a space that gives them the best opportunities to learn.

Setting Up and Arranging the Furniture is Your First and the Most Important Task

You should already have a well-developed plan for arranging the furniture after reading the first two units of this handbook. Pretend it's moving day at your own house and arrange the furniture according to your plan, and keep rearranging it until you feel it's workable. Put on your oldest clothes and try out the various arrangements at school, sampling every seat to assure visibility. You may need to allow space for some of these areas: computers, library, teacher/small-group instruction, aide work station, art center, listening center, writing center, storage, overhead projector, screens, etc.

Arrange for some private spaces and a quiet reading area.

In primary classrooms, a refrigerator box can become a hideaway after some windows and a door are cut into it and

Teacher Talks . . .

Don't do this! Every afternoon before leaving the classroom in a laboratory school at a major university the students, 4th, 5th, and 6th graders, moved all the furniture out into the hallway. Then, each morning we planned the day and only brought in the furniture we needed. If we were painting large murals, we left all the furniture in the hallway. If we were taking tests, we brought in all the tables and chairs. This plan did not sit well with the fire department or the university administrators. The principle was a good one—use furniture functionally, but the implementation was a disaster. So we just learned to move furniture within the room to meet our instructional needs.

Ellen Kronowitz
Laboratory School Teacher
Columbia University
New York City 1972–1976

A Welcoming Library

the entire thing is painted. For older students, bring in an umbrella-type folding tent. Or, use a table covered with an overhanging cloth. Middle and high school students welcome private study carrels.

If your principal permits, build yourself a loft for reading. If you can't do this or don't know how, you might bring in an old mattress and cover it with a pretty floral sheet and use it for a reading area. One resourceful teacher I know uses an old-fashioned bathtub

filled with pillows for a special reading space. Bring in a small inflatable pool or rubber dinghy for the same purpose. Display magazines on a magazine rack or a narrow shelf. Recycle the older magazines into art or language arts projects.

Keep your room arrangement dynamic.

At the outset, you can arrange your desks in rows for maximum control and then you can relax and create a more open environment as the school year progresses. You can relocate the library area to another part of the room. You can change where the pet is located to keep interest high and boredom low. Every few months, surprise the class with an all-new room arrangement. Of course, this depends a great deal on what the space of your room will allow.

Apply It!

Take some graph paper and add to your furniture arrangement the other centers and spaces that you define as needed. This will be your blueprint. See Figure 10.1 for an example.

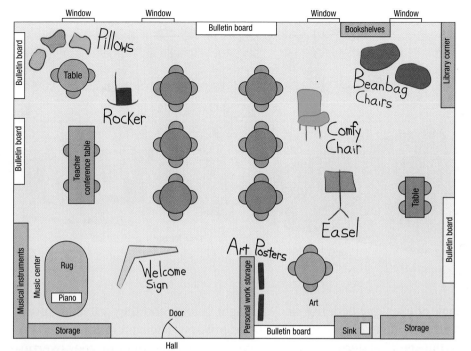

Figure 10.1
Classroom Blueprint

Decorating the Space Is Your Next Challenge

Think of the walls, windows, ceilings, and bookshelves as canvases for your artistry.

Accessories create a unique, stimulating environment.

You can jazz up your classroom with the addition of some thrift store or yard sale items. Beanbag chairs, carpets or carpet remnants, a small sofa, and, perhaps, a discarded lamp or two will create a warm and homey atmosphere. Reading lamps rest the eyes from the fluorescent lights and can calm students. These items are particularly useful in a library corner separated from the rest of the room. After all, how many of you read while seated in a straight-back chair with your feet flat on the floor?

A classroom designed for learning

Sit right down and read

Pet iguana

A fish tank or even one beta fish or a goldfish will provide endless entertainment for the students during their free time. Hang a bird feeder outside the window to encourage feathered friends. Students love to take care of living things, and the care of the plants and animals can be assigned to a monitor. During my elementary teaching years my students cared for rats, hamsters, a tortoise named Yurtle, tadpoles that developed into frogs, and assorted fish.

Hannah (1984) reports that when students are asked about their ideal classroom, they prefer to sit up high (lofts) or low (floor); they like pretty, bright colors; and they value comfort and privacy. Their preferences need to be considered in light of your overriding responsibility for creating an environment that reflects and supports your educational goals and teaching style. Leave some leeway for student input on room accessories, ornamentation, and even pets.

The décor can deliver very powerful nonverbal messages to your students.

You and your students spend approximately 30 hours each week in the classroom, and an aesthetically pleasing environment can do much to stimulate the senses and teach at the same time. The physical environment is the first thing students and observers notice about a classroom, and you want yours to deliver the message that exciting and sound instruction is going on there. Before you utter the first word on that first day of school, you will have delivered your message nonverbally to students through your attention to the door and the walls of your classroom.

Bulletin boards that focus interest on students—a "Star of the Week" board and a "Good Work" board—tell them they are important. A "Helper's Chart" tells them they will share in the responsibilities for their classroom with you. In primary grades, the calendar and weather chart will let students know you provide the security of routines they are used to. A subject-matter bulletin board clues them into the mysteries that will be unraveled as the year progresses. A word wall makes them more independent as they master the basics of literacy. Labels on all the objects in the room and the cardinal directions posted on corresponding walls will let primary students and English language learners feel confident that they will learn to read these markers soon.

Even at the high school level, bulletin boards can be used as a way to showcase the talents of the students who enter your room, whether it be classroom work or announcements of upcoming extracurricular events, such as games of school teams, concerts, plays, or contests. Such displays send the message to your students that you know what they're involved in and you know what is going on in school.

From the very first moment—at the doorstep—you can greet them with a door sign that says:

Welcome to My Stars, with digital photos and/or names on star shapes

Fall into _____ Grade, with names on leaves

Future Nobel Prize Winners Inside

Look Who's Mixing It Up in Chemistry, with names or digital photos on cut-out flasks

Welcome to the Ancient World

Strike a balance between excitement and quiet, restful places. Looking at the four walls is the only respite students have from their daily work. Create warm, bright spaces that instruct and motivate, but don't overdo it. Veteran teachers caution you not to overstimulate the senses of your students.

Teacher Talks . . .

I don't like putting up a lot of professionally made materials; they reflect what you can buy. I prefer to cut 3.5 inch strips of colored paper and have the students write their names, alphabet, math problems, definitions . . . on them and use them as bulletin board borders. These reflect student learning and their environment. By having their work displayed, there is pride in all of us in the final product.

Kris Ungerer
Kindergarten
Riverside, California

Teacher Talks . . .

Keep up current work and display all levels so students know what kind of work you expect from them. Do not just display A and B work examples. You can cut out names from work that is not as exceptional so as to not embarrass students. Do not overstimulate students with too much to look at in the room. Keep it interesting and neat.

Barbara Arient
Grades 9–12
Special Education, Moderate/Severe
San Bernardino, California

Welcome to Our Class

Our Best Work

Design and construct some of your bulletin boards before school starts.

Some teachers purchase or order from catalogs a great deal of prepackaged material, including bulletin board borders; others use available materials so they can draw or construct their own. You can copy and then make transparencies of images, and then project them onto the wall using an overhead projector if you feel you can't draw. It's a less expensive solution than buying a multitude of materials that will stay up only a few short weeks.

Careful lettering will tell your students you are precise and want them to take pride in their work. Bright colors will tell them you have a vibrant and exciting program planned. Mounting pictures on black paper creates contrast on bright bulletin boards and gives depth to your creations. Die-cut presses, available in many districts, turn out borders and bulletin board letters with no fuss and no bother.

Maintain a fresh look for your bulletin boards. Try out some different ideas for bulletin board backgrounds instead of the likely-to-fade butcher paper.

- Fabric of all sorts
- Wallpaper
- Wrapping paper
- Newspaper /comics section
- Burlap
- Indoor/outdoor carpeting

Instead of buying packaged borders, consider these ideas other teachers have suggested:

- Wide wire ribbon
- Photos of the students
- Old greeting cards/calendar pages
- Old CDs in the computer center
- Laminated gift wrap strips
- Newspaper cartoon strips
- Paint sample cards from home improvement stores
- Number lines/rulers
- Monopoly money

Suggestions for Secondary Schools

The Kottlers (1998) suggest that in secondary schools, bulletin boards serve nine purposes. These are: information giving, rule reminders, demonstrations, motivation, stimulation, student work display, teacher interests, reinforcement, and entertainment. The same could be said for elementary schools.

Teachers at the middle and high school levels suggest the following bulletin boards:

- Lists of assignments
- Standards
- Calendar
- Inspirational sayings
- Student work
- Motivational posters
- Rules
- Current curriculum topics
- School news/booster activities

Apply It!

For each of the nine purposes shown in Figure 10.2, jot down some age- and subject-appropriate ideas for classroom bulletin boards. Some examples have been provided.

Figure 10.2
Purposeful Bulletin Board Ideas

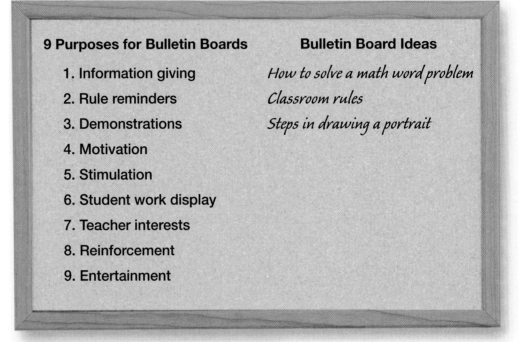

9 Purposes for Bulletin Boards

1. Information giving
2. Rule reminders
3. Demonstrations
4. Motivation
5. Stimulation
6. Student work display
7. Teacher interests
8. Reinforcement
9. Entertainment

Bulletin Board Ideas

How to solve a math word problem

Classroom rules

Steps in drawing a portrait

Ten More Bulletin Board Ideas

1. **Birthday Board.** This is a listing of all students' birthdays by month. In secondary schools, the teacher passes around a calendar and has each student note his or her birthday. This can be celebrated with a card from the teacher or a small gift.

2. **Tooth Fairy Report.** In the primary grades, a bulletin board marks the loss of each tooth. A large cutout tooth for each month lists the name and date of each event. Students enjoy marking these important milestones in their lives.

3. **Star(s) of the Week.** Highlighted students decorate the board with photos, hobbies, work, or whatever they choose.

I sat in a fourth grade classroom recently and checked out the walls. This is what I saw:

- Focus wall for academic standards
- A calendar
- Pledge of Allegiance and pressed American Flag
- Current events bulletin board
- Globe and maps
- Cursive alphabet
- "How to Treat Others" poster
- Rules for Homework poster
  1. Leave time.
  2. Take home what you need.
  3. Find a quiet place.
  4. Follow directions.
  5. Ask for help.
  6. Keep your homework in the same place.
  7. Return it to school on time.
- Class procedures
- Class rules
- Daily schedule
- Friendly letter format
- Homophone, antonym, and synonym charts

- Helper's chart
- Helping verbs chart
- Outline of math chapter on a graphic web
- Star of the week
- Subject matter bulletin boards
- Poems on posters
- Free time chart
- Getting help chart
- Class photos
- Inspirational sayings
- Huge ruler in centimeters
- Parts of speech poster
- Screen
- Teacher information board with lunch menus, bus schedules, bell schedules, school map, various notices
- Parts of a folktale poster
- Teacher-made curtains geared to the social studies theme
- Book jackets
- A huge bulletin board with an individual space for each student's work

4. **Baby Picture—Guess Who?** Students at all grade levels can bring in a baby picture, which is then posted on a bulletin board with number identification only. A contest can be held after two weeks to see who has correctly identified the most classmates and the teacher.

5. **Student Self-portraits or Silhouettes.** These are described in Chapter 5 as suggested activities for the first day of school.

6. **Teacher Autobiography.** A bulletin board introducing the teacher is also suggested in Chapter 7. You might include photos, samples of your hobbies, a favorite poem, or other information about you.

7. **Encouragement to Read.** Book jackets make an effective display. Some teachers use the bookworm idea and encourage students to read a book and add a segment to the worm.

8. **Current Events.** Another suggested theme is current events at the school, local, national, and international levels. "Nose for News," "News Roundup," or "News Hound" banners can evoke charming, simple drawings or cutouts done by you using an opaque projector.

9. **Instructional Boards.** These boards either introduce some concept or provide an overview or preview of some content area. Primary teachers use color, shape, or alphabet bulletin boards, while middle or high school teachers might highlight the

Apply It!

"Google" classroom bulletin boards and start collecting ideas. Or, use the websites listed at the end of this unit for bulletin board ideas.

first unit or theme. An overview of the semester or year can be attractively depicted under a headline, *Preview of Chemistry,* with a glitzy movie poster format.

10. **Individual Bulletin Board Spaces.** Many teachers solve bulletin board worries by dividing the largest wall in the classroom into equal sections, one for each student. This can be done with colorful yarn. Inside the rectangles, each student displays his or her best work, a photo, a favorite item from home, an art project or a creative writing assignment. The display can be changed according to a schedule or when the student decides to display some other aspect of his or her life at home or at school.

Whatever your initial bulletin boards turn out to be, make sure they are neatly lettered; thoughtfully arranged; have attractive, bright-colored backgrounds; and can be read from all parts of the room. Finally, consider using the space overhead for displaying student work. Wires strung across the room enable you to hang student artwork from the wires with paper clips.

Emmer et al. (2003) have some terrific suggestions for rovers or "floaters," teachers who move from room to room either because of year-round schedules or because their secondary school necessitates such an arrangement. Their suggestions include: conferring with the teachers who share your room, using the overhead more than the chalkboard for obvious reasons, establishing your own small spaces on bulletin boards and shelves, and using a rolling cart or a luggage cart.

Avoid It!

Avoid spending money on prepackaged bulletin boards when the students will benefit from creating bulletin boards with you. Do not allow your boards to become dog-eared, faded, and tattered.

A student wants some kind of undisrupted routine or rhythm. He seems to want a predictable, orderly world.

Abraham Maslow

Chapter **11**

How Do I Establish and Maintain Routines for Entrances/Exits, Beginning and Ending the Day?

Effectiveness Essentials

■ Routines in the classroom enable the teacher and the class to function smoothly and provide the safety and security students need.

■ The way in which students enter the room sets the tone for how the day will go.

■ Establish a procedure for what you expect your students to do when they enter the room.

■ Ingrain an exit procedure so when a real emergency occurs, everyone will get out safely and quickly.

■ Normally, the day should begin in the same way every day and should include many rituals.

■ The end of the day needs to be planned for as carefully as every other part of the day.

Routines Serve a Vital Function

Because they are habitual and can be performed automatically, routines set our minds free for more creative and critical thinking activities. While one part of our brain mechanically performs our routines in the morning, the remainder is free to plan the day's activities, consider problems, and anticipate whatever challenges await us.

Humans are creatures of habit and adhere to certain routines and procedures throughout the day.

When my alarm goes off, it sets in motion a unique and regimented set of procedures for meeting my day. Almost with eyes closed I perform the daily rituals, day in and day out, in the same order without fail. If I lose a half hour, some of my daily rituals have to go. Either the cats don't get any petting, or I can't have fresh-brewed coffee. I can't read the morning headlines, or I can't do my workout tape. In short, my day gets off to a bad start.

Routines in the classroom will enable you to provide the stability, safety, and security your students need.

The more stability there is in the classroom, the less likely it is that disruptions will occur. If certain activities or procedures are learned and practiced in rote fashion, the time saved and effort spared can be used for more stimulating instructional activities and events. Routines create order, and when the basic operation of your classroom is under control, you and the students will feel less stressed. In this chapter and the ones that follow you will learn about routines for:

- Entering and exiting the classroom
- Beginning and ending the day
- Materials storage and distribution
- Bathroom and water fountain permission
- Movement within the room
- Getting help
- Hand raising
- Noise control
- Free time
- Collection, distribution, and labeling of papers
- Instructional management

Teacher Talks . . .

The best piece of advice I can give to teachers is something I learned my first year of teaching fifth grade. Routine is a MUST. Students need to know what's going on to feel involved and important. The more the kids know the routine, the more able they are to help when the teacher is out or conflicts arise. My kids practice everything (lining up, changing classes, packing up to go home) the first week of school. We literally hold drills to practice these things.

I write the next day's schedule on the board at the end of every day. I show the kids how to look in my plan book and write up our activities. They have been able to write up the daily schedule when I am absent. They enjoy this routine and thrive on it. They try to be the first to ask me to "write the schedule." It makes them feel important and involved. After all, if kids aren't actively involved they will actively try to create trouble!

Laurel Garner
Fifth Grade
Duluth, Georgia

When students act confused or unsure of what to do or how to do it, it's a good sign that you have to think through or create another routine or procedure.

Entrances and Exits

The beginnings or endings of any endeavor are important bookends for what comes in between. Although technically your interest is in what happens in between, paying attention to the entrances and exits will serve you well.

The way in which students enter the room sets the tone for how the day will go.

Meeting your students at the door helps you establish your presence and allows you to greet each one individually. This is the perfect time to say something positive to each student. It may simply be "Good morning" (in student's native language as appropriate) or "I like your new haircut" or "That's a neat sweater." At the high school level, this can be a fine time to acknowledge accomplishments from the night before, such as "Nice game last night" or "I heard the math club trounced their opponents."

Have your students form lines outside the classroom prior to entering.

Although school rules may be more relaxed, lines diminish pushing and shoving and discourage barreling into the room. Lines also help to make a smooth transition from socializing outside to work inside the classroom. These same procedures can be followed during any entrance into the room, whether from recess, physical education, or another part of the building. Students can be shown how to line up (not by gender because of Title IX regulations), and this expectation is most easily imprinted when it applies to all situations involving entrances into the room. Although this is most readily enforced in elementary and middle school, at the high school level the same purpose is served by meeting your students at the door,

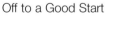

Off to a Good Start

where you can more easily monitor and assure an orderly entrance.

Establish a procedure for what you expect your students to do when they enter the room.

Turn off all lights when you leave the room and establish the turning on of the lights as a signal that the next activity is about to begin. Or, better yet, have an activity on the desks or on the board for your students to do as soon as they enter the room in the morning or after breaks. Some teachers have students write in their journals first thing in the morning and read their books first thing after lunch. These alternatives give you

Figure 11.1
Pocket Chart

Apply It!

What can you have your students do in the first few minutes of school or for the first few minutes of the period? This should be an ongoing assignment that has both a management and an instructional purpose.

a few minutes to collect your thoughts, especially in the morning and after lunch, when clerical tasks may command your attention.

For middle and high school students, use entrance and exit routines that are customary in your school, but be sure your students enter your room ready to learn. Every moment counts in a short period. You don't want to waste half the period quieting rowdy students—and one way of avoiding this is insisting on an orderly entrance.

Design the quickest method to take attendance in high school so as not to waste time. If

Teacher Talks . . .

During my first month of teaching in my first year, the school at which I taught had a lap-running fundraiser. As our P.E. activity that day we went out to practice running. I decided to take the classroom wall clock out with us so the students could easily see how long it took. When we returned to the classroom, I noticed a stony silence coming from the other classrooms. Apparently, the clock had stopped and it wasn't until another teacher noticed my students that I realized that my entire class had missed their buses to go home.

Heidi Thompson
First Grade teacher
Yucaipa, California

Student Says . . .

Question: How does your teacher dismiss the class? *She tells us to put our heads on our desk. Whichever table is the quietest goes first.*

Walker
Age 7.5, Second Grade
Redlands, California

kindergarten students can turn name cards over in a pocket chart and take their own attendance, then middle and high school students can do the same. For each period have a sign-in sheet or have a seating chart that is on a clipboard that students must sign in on. Write your seating charts in erasable pen. Seats will change. You can count on it! You may choose to call roll each and every day to help you learn the names, but after awhile, you can simply scan the room and see who is missing. Keep a tardy list at the door that late students must sign.

Teachers suggest dismissing by table or row, with the quietest one leading the pack.

Combining the group dismissal with the line is another alternative. By table, students line up for P.E., recess, lunch, library, assembly, or final dismissal. Transitions are unstable times in a classroom. No matter what the grade level, the more structure you give to the situation, the more likely it is that safety and low noise level will prevail. This is true especially when the exit from the room is required for simulated (or real) emergencies such as fire drills. In large gatherings, such as assemblies or rallies in high school, there is usually an established order of dismissal. Find out what it is and take note.

You can dismiss by some clothing attribute: students wearing stripes or red tops, white tennis shoes or a sweater, for example. This is not only a good way to have students line up for dismissal, it also provides a non-threatening way to teach basic concepts to English language learners. In secondary classrooms, you don't have the luxury of a slow dismissal because it is essential that students get to their next class on time. You need to establish a quick method such as dismissing by those rows or tables that are packed up and ready to go.

Ingrain an exit procedure so when a real emergency occurs, everyone will get out safely and quickly.

Make sure your students know the signals and frequently practice the procedures used in your school for emergency situations. Even if your school does not require it, it is best to have a copy of the class roster accessible so you can grab it in case of emergency and count heads immediately. Carefully review and reinforce these procedures in the first days and weeks of school and then intermittently after that.

When moving around the school with your class, walk in the middle, not at the front. When you lead the line, the students at the back of the line will create their own party. When you bring up the rear, the students in the front will get away from you. Give clear directions about stopping points along the way. For example, "Stop at the water fountain or stop in front of the office and wait for me." Line leaders should be responsible for following your directions.

Beginning and Ending the Day

Students of all ages enjoy the safety and predictability of morning and end-of-the-day routines. How important are these routines? Try an experiment and "forget" something on purpose. You will experience for yourself the uproar that ensues! Students will let you know if you have forgotten something. They expect certain things to happen in a certain order.

In middle and high school, homeroom teachers are responsible for beginning the day and implementing the routines, such as attendance taking, collection of monies, announcements, etc., that elementary teachers are solely responsible for. However, the beginning of each period in secondary school requires planning and order on your part. And the last moments of the period or the class are key to orderly dismissal and everyone getting to their next destination.

The day normally begins in the same way every day and includes many rituals.

These may include:

- Collection of money, permission slips
- Attendance, pupil counts
- Flag salute and song
- Announcements
- Homework collection
- Explanation of the day's schedule or period agenda and the standards that will be addressed
- Birthdays, tooth fairy update, calendar, weather, etc. in primary classrooms
- Sharing, current events, or a classroom meeting
- Journal writing

Middle and high school teachers should have a routine for what students do upon entering that is appropriate to your subject area.

Beginning the Day
In this clip, the teacher talks about how each routine at the beginning of the day serves a distinct purpose. After watching the video, make a list of all the things you must do at the start of the day, prioritize them, and make a cheat sheet so beginning the day rituals become standardized.

Question: How does your teacher end the day? *At the end of the day when our desk is clean, she tells us to pack up.*

David
Age 11, Sixth Grade
Satellite Beach, Florida

Apply It!

A pleasant way to end each day is the compliment activity. Randomly distribute the nametags, cards, or sticks you use to call on students (Chapter 13). Everyone in turn compliments the student whose name they receive. Thus, everyone gives and gets a compliment. For example, John gets Steve's stick or card and says, "I would like to compliment Steve for. . . ." Steve says "Thank you" and then gives the next compliment to the person whose name he has been given. And so on. In this way, the students leave school with a positive outlook for the next day.

Closure is important at the end of the day.

Use the last 5–10 minutes for a quick review of the day's activities with your students, discussing what they learned or enjoyed most that day. Present an exciting preview of the next day. Use the time for clearing off tables, cleaning out desks, tidying up the room, and making sure that all papers and notices that need to go home are distributed. Set a timer or use an alarm clock to remind you and the students that it is time to clean up. Buses run on schedules, and they can't wait for students to clean up after an art lesson. Add a special, individualized, and positive comment to as many students as time allows as you dismiss them.

Many of the same routines for ending the day also pertain to ending the period in middle and high schools. You can set a timer, and when it rings, have

Five Ideas for Beginning the Period

1. Copy the period outline from the board into your notes.
2. Write a question that comes to mind when you read the period standards or objectives.
3. Summarize yesterday's notes into a paragraph.
4. Fill out a feedback form for yesterday's session (Figure 11.2).
5. Make yourself a set of flashcards based on what you learned the previous day.

Figure 11.2

Period Evaluation

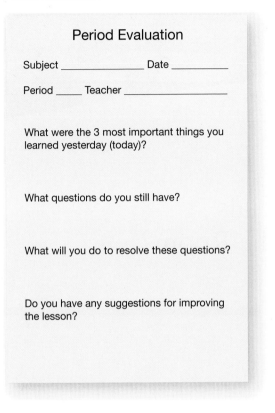

Period Evaluation

Subject _____ Date _____

Period _____ Teacher _____

What were the 3 most important things you learned yesterday (today)?

What questions do you still have?

What will you do to resolve these questions?

Do you have any suggestions for improving the lesson?

the students clean up, gather their papers, make sure they have copied the homework, summarize the lesson, review the homework, and tell the students what to bring the next day. If you have time, you can ask them to describe what was most interesting, tell you what idea was completely new to them, ask any remaining questions, predict what they will learn the next period, etc. Remember that **you** signal the end of the period—**not** the bell. In high school, the last period teacher, especially at the end of the week, has the biggest challenge of corralling the students who are antsy to get to after school jobs, practices, pep rallies, games, or just get out. You will need to plan accordingly for those last 10 minutes of the final period of the day and the week.

Teacher Talks . . .

Regardless of how your day has gone, before students leave, give positive affirmations either to the whole class or to individuals. Students leave the classroom with positive feelings and will be happy to start a new day tomorrow.

Marsha Moyer
Fifth Grade
San Bernardino, California

Avoid It!

Among the errors to be avoided at the beginning of the year are:

Letting infractions slide because you are too busy

Not taking enough time to check for understanding of the routines

Introducing too many routines at once

Thinking that your students don't need to practice

*For every minute
spent in organiz-
ing, an hour is
earned.*

Anonymous

Chapter **12**

How Do I Move Materials
and Students Around the Room?

Effectiveness Essentials

■ Establish which materials may be accessed by students and set up distribution and collection procedures.

■ Determine a respectful policy for dealing with violations of rules and procedures.

■ Establish routines for purposeful out-of-seat activities such as pencil sharpening, etc.

By now, you are well on your way to becoming a logistics expert. You will need to establish just a few more routines for materials distribution, bathroom and water fountain privileges, and movement around the room. In the next chapter, you will learn about instructional routines.

Materials and Equipment

Schools are not yet paperless environments. There is so much teacher "stuff" in classrooms that needs to be accessed and monitored, and distributed and collected efficiently. Student "stuff" in desks, in cubbies, on hooks, or in lockers presents yet another organizational challenge.

Establish what materials may be accessed by students.

The teacher's desk and file cabinet or special supply shelf should be off-limits to the students unless they have your permission. Similarly, their cubbies, desks, and coat hooks are their private spaces. Shared paper supplies should be pointed out during your room environment orientation, and you need to be clear about how these supplies are to be distributed. Will your students be allowed, for example, to get whatever papers they need when they need them; will monitors hand out papers; or will you pass the papers out yourself to individuals or to monitors?

In most high schools and middle schools, lockers are assigned to all students. In some schools where the privilege has been abused, students must carry all of their books with them all day. Ouch! You should emphasize that personal lockers are off-limits to other students out of respect for privacy and that students should not share lockers or their lock combinations. Since lockers and contents are joint student and school district property, the courts have consistently ruled that administrators may search lockers based on "reasonable suspicion." Check out what constitutes reasonable suspicion for locker and other searches in your district. Tell your students that inappropriate pictures or photos on the outside or inside of lockers are not acceptable.

Establish procedures for materials distribution and collection.

Will monitors collect papers, or will you collect them? Will you have a central collection tray that individuals can use when they finish their work? How will students get pencils, crayons,

Teacher Talks . . .

We are "Garner's Gators" and we have a "Gator turn-in box." It's a large wooden bookcase (sponge painted with gators) and each section is labeled. The kids know to turn in their work to the "Gator turn-in box." They like to say the name aloud and it helps them associate our name with their work.

My fifth graders know the importance of organization. They are immersed with organization from day one of school. We spend the first two days organizing and color coding our materials—books, folders, materials, coats, backpacks, etc. Blue social studies book goes with blue folder and notebook, red science book goes with red folder and notebook, etc. I even have them help me color code the art supply cabinet. They have learned to do this on their own and will sometimes come up with an organization system that we can all use!

Laurel Garner
Fifth Grade
Duluth, Georgia

*Use a computer program to collect
and keep track of grades and
turned in materials.*

Barbara Arient
Grades 9–12
Special Education, Moderate/Severe
San Bernardino, California

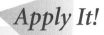

Apply It!

Create a worksheet such as the one
shown in Figure 12.1, adding other
materials as needed, to get a handle
on how to organize and distribute
your supplies. This activity will help
you make some decisions about
materials location and distribution.

scissors, and paste? Will these items
be on the desks or at a central location? Will students be allowed to
come up at will to get what they need,
or will supplies be distributed by you
or by a monitor?

Bathroom and Water Fountain

You have been planning out routines
and procedures at your desk for two
hours, drinking lots of water, tea, or
coffee, and all of a sudden your blad-
der reminds you that you have to
establish some biology-related rules
for bathroom and water fountain use.
Accidents are common in primary
grades, and your rules should take this
into account. At secondary levels, at
certain times of the month, the girls
may need to use the bathroom, NOW!
Every student now and then has an
emergency. Water is key to health,
and you need to achieve a balance
between intake and output!

Figure 12.1
Location and
Distribution
Chart

Supplies	Location		Distribution	
	Each Desk	Central Location	Monitor	Teacher
1. Paper				
2. Pencils				
3. Rulers				
4.				
5.				
6.				
7.				
8.				

Establish a fair and equitable policy for bathroom breaks.

Recesses, lunch, and between periods are the specified times for bathroom breaks. However, realistically, you may have to deviate from these norms and establish some bathroom rules because students have special needs and nature does not always adhere to schedules. Before creating your own rules about bathroom usage during class time, ask colleagues or department heads what the school norms are. You do not want to deviate from them.

Most teachers use a pass system. Only two students at a time (different genders) are allowed out of the room so that they do not fool around in the restroom with a friend. Some teachers fashion large passes out of wooden blocks. Others suggest that since the pass often ends up on the floor of the restroom, you should consider passes on lanyards or bracelet passes. Make sure your name and/or room number is on the pass, that there are only two of them, and that students understand these procedures:

- They should not leave during instructional time or when directions are being given.
- They must wait until a pass is available.
- They must keep all restrooms neat and tidy for others.
- They must leave and return without disturbing others.

Bathroom Passes

Students who abuse your bathroom policy should be dealt with individually so as not to cause embarrassment. After an incident, and periodically thereafter, review bathroom rules without mentioning specific offenders. In my experience, the less fuss you make about the bathroom policy, the less likely it is that students will use passes when they really don't need to.

Here are some other teacher suggestions. You can combine any number of them to meet your grade-level needs:

1. Assess a penalty for leaving the room during instruction. Students may have to stay in for five minutes or give up earned tickets or reward "bucks" to leave the room.

2. Give each student three bathroom passes for the semester. When they use them up, that's it!

3. Teach your students to use American Sign Language to signal that they need to use the restroom. The sign is the one for the letter T. Make a fist and insert the thumb between the index and middle finger and move it side to side. This will be a silent signal that will not disturb others. See Figure 12.2.

4. Require students to leave a placeholder on their desks when they need to use the restroom. This lets you know who is out of the room and why, especially in large classes where a visual reminder may be needed. See Figure 12.3.

5. Limit the number of times a student may sign out to the restroom in a week and require students to record their comings and goings in a log or on a timesheet.

Figure 12.2
ASL Sign for Toilet

Although some of these suggestions may sound harsh, you do not want your students to miss valuable instruction, especially in light of two recesses and a lunch break in elementary school and time between periods in secondary schools. In special cases, you can bend the rule.

Remind kindergarten parents to make sure boys and girls know how to undo their belts or, better yet, encourage parents to consider elastic waist pants. In kindergarten, look for signs of imminent bathroom need. By the time these busy folks in kindergarten raise their hands, it is sometimes too late.

Water access is not as necessary as bathroom breaks.

Water is always available at recess and at passing times. When fountains are in the room, you may choose to allow students to drink as they require liquid nourishment, but beware! Since there is a direct connection between drinking and bathroom requests, you may be adding to your own management problems if you provide access to water all day, even within the room. A compromise would involve water lineup after transitions into the

Figure 12.3
Placards to Put on Tables
When Students Leave the Room

room for those who need it. On very hot days, in very hot classrooms, you can always suspend the rules or allow students to have individual water bottles at their desks. When you buy the water in pint bottles in bulk you can affix name labels and have students refill them, assuring equal access.

In high school, depending on the rules, students carry big, bulky water bottles and drink from them all period long. You can make a rule that allows one in-class water bottle break during class on very hot days. Since the periods are so short, you are not committing the misdemeanor of student dehydration or water deprivation. They can drink before and after class.

Teacher Talks . . .

Because I teach kindergarten, and there is no bathroom in my room, I send pairs of students to the bathroom at one time. That way, if one gets stuck in the bathroom because the door is heavy, there are two people to try to open the door. Also, an added benefit—they tell on each other immediately upon re-entry if either was naughty.

Kris Ungerer
Kindergarten
Riverside, California

NOTES

Movement within the Room

Your students, especially the energetic ones in elementary school, need teacher-sanctioned opportunities to stretch and amble. Secondary students move about between classes, but the elementary students need to move about periodically, too.

Structured Movement

You can structure periodic in-class exercise routines. There are several excellent DVDs that feature classroom-appropriate controlled exercise routines. When you provide the opportunity for exercise, fewer students are likely to make their own individual opportunities, which can disrupt and cause delays. In middle school or the upper grades, after establishing a signal such as a bell for returning to work, schedule periodic five-minute mini-breaks to enable this peer-dependent group to socialize.

Managing Pencil Sharpening

The constant grinding noise of a sharpener can grate on the ears and disrupt instruction. The extreme position some teachers hold is that all broken pencils and wastebasket material must be held until specified times, usually early morning and after lunch. Better yet, have a supply of pencils at each table in a coffee can. One table leader is responsible for sharpening them at the start of the day. During the day, students can exchange their broken pencils for a sharpened one.

Access to the Wastebasket

You can't totally eliminate the need to get rid of dirty tissues or paper scraps. Equip each table cluster with a cheap plastic wastebasket from a bargain store and have the students dispose of their refuse without leaving their seats.

Moving to Groups

If your classroom is typical, you will need to establish routines for moving to groups. No matter what the grade level is, when your students work in groups, you must provide clear instruction about the groups they are to work in, even posting the groups, so there is no confusion and the transition to groups is quick. To ease transitions from groups to seat work to activity, you will need to make two charts, one listing the names of all members of each group and another that signals what activity each group is engaged in. A wheel arrangement or pocket chart works very well.

You can make a rotation chart by listing the centers down one side and the students who will be at each center on the right side. Use Velcro or magnetic tape to attach the names or even laminated digital photos of your students. See Figure 12.4.

Another popular device is the rotation wheel. Cut out two large circles. Divide the outer circle into your centers and the inner circle into groups. You will also need a chart of who belongs in each group. Just turn

Figure 12.4
Center Rotation Chart

Teacher	Karen, Paul, Laticia, Jacob
Teacher/Aide	Linda, Len, Don, Juan
Spelling	Maria, Liz, Jake, Eric
Writing	Bella, Sue, John, Steve
Reading Games	Paul, Gary, Donna, Jan
Computer	Niki, Allen, Rachel
Listening	Ruby, Denny, Ryan, Jason
Library	Sam, David, Elena, Juanita

Avoid It!

Strike a balance between a strict and rigid policy for bathroom privileges. You do not want to humiliate your students, and sometimes there is a real emergency. Don't adopt a policy you can't enforce or one that is so inflexible that you will be hard pressed to explain away accidents to parents and administrators, not to mention the students.

Figure 12.5
Center Rotation Wheel

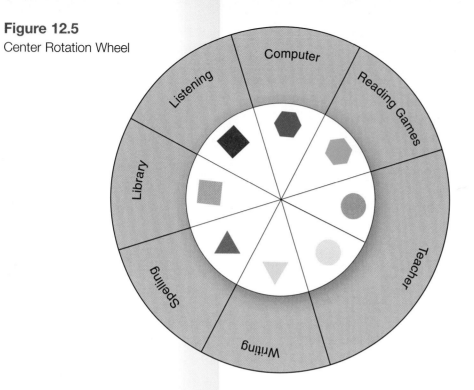

Figure 12.6
Groups and Symbols Chart

Karen, Paul, Laticia, Jacob	⬤
Linda, Len, Don, Juan	⬤
Maria, Liz, Jake, Eric	▲
Bella, Sue, John, Steve	▲
Paul, Gary, Donna, Jan	⬡
Niki, Allen, Rachel	⬡
Ruby, Denny, Ryan, Jason	◼
Sam, David, Elena, Juanita	◼

the wheel to show where each group should be. See Figures 12.5 and 12.6.

When you have established your schedule, set up a procedure for changing to another group efficiently and quietly. Some teachers use a timer, others a bell, and many simply announce that it's time for a change.

You will want to post rules for working in groups. Consider these:

1. Help each other.
2. Share and take turns.
3. Praise each other.
4. Talk quietly.
5. Evaluate how the group worked.

Chapter 13

What Instructional Routines Will I Need?

Effectiveness Essentials

- Good discipline is dependent on effective instructional management.

- Teachers learn many routines by trial and error, common sense, or observation of other teachers.

- Establish and rehearse procedures at the very start for how your students can get help when you are busy.

- The best way to abate noise and chatter is to differentiate among whispering, talking, and silence.

- Specify the acceptable noise level for any one activity beforehand.

- Be consistent about hand raising and avoid questions that elicit choral responses.

- Use a system for calling on students that assures equity.

- Limit disruptions by establishing a Free Time policy.

- Schools, grade levels, and teams often decide to have uniform labeling of papers.

- Determine how you will collect and redistribute homework and assignments.

Teachers learn many routines by trial and error, common sense, or observation of other teachers. One teacher reported, "stumbling into what worked best." A *reliable* student assisted one new teacher by recounting how they did things last year. You may be thinking that a tactical operations degree would be a useful supplement to a teaching credential after reading about routines. In fact, logistics are a major factor in any complex endeavor, but especially in teaching. There are still a few more routines to consider, and they apply to instruction.

Effective Instructional Management

With a central tenet that "good discipline is dependent on effective instructional management," Jacob Kounin (1977) developed a set of principles for instructional management. His work will be discussed in greater detail in Unit 4, Chapter 18, but because these principles are so important, they are briefly noted here.

Ripple Effect

This occurs when a teacher corrects or praises one student and it influences other students to shape up or correct misbehaviors to earn the same praise: "See how quietly Table 1 is waiting for instructions." All other tables come to attention with hands folded.

Withitness

Withitness is defined as having eyes in back of your head or being aware of the entire class at all times. Before you begin, make sure all eyes are on you and keep scanning the room for potential disruptions.

Group Alerting

Keep everyone on task and make every class member accountable for responding. Using name cards or sticks (described on page 122) is a great way of applying this concept.

Satiation

Satiation occurs as boredom sets in or when the students have had enough. Leave them wanting more.

Overlappingness

This concept is defined as the ability to attend to two activities at once—for example, walking over to a student who is playing with a puzzle or phone arcade game and confiscating it without missing an instructional beat.

Pacing and Transitions

Teachers should be aware when lessons have gone on for too long. Transitions between activities should be smooth and include closure as well as an introduction to what is coming next.

Instructional Routines

The more you can routinize the procedures that support your instruction, the more smoothly the instructional period or day will go. You won't have to ask yourself every day, for example, "Now how will I collect papers today?" It will be automatic, as will the other instructional support routines in this section.

Routines are only as effective as their constant reinforcement. So, as you consider each and every routine that follows, apply these principles:

1. Begin on the first day to establish the procedures that will be in use the whole year or semester.
2. Be very specific about how you want things done.
3. Have the students practice each procedure until they get it right.
4. Liberally compliment students when they follow procedures.
5. Reteach the routines and quickly deal with deviations from established procedures. For example, "I hear a good answer, but I won't call on anyone who doesn't raise his or her hand."
6. Give rational reasons for each routine as it is introduced.

Help Needed

You need to establish how your students can get help when you are busy. I found it frustrating to have students tugging at my sleeve when I was involved in a lively discussion during a small-group session. Secondary students will just sit there with raised hands or find more "amusing" things to do when they are stuck and you are busy. Clearly explain the objective, encourage procedural questions, ask one student to repeat the directions, write all assignments on the board, identify alternative sources of help, and provide something meaningful for students to do when

Teacher Talks . . .

The best advice I can give a new teacher is to forget teaching academics for the first week or two, especially in the younger grades. What needs to be focused on is modeling, modeling, modeling, and then some more modeling! After routines and expectations are in place, then the academics will happen. Time can now be spent on teaching and having fun instead of constant interruptions for behavior or the "What am I supposed to do now?" questions! Happy teaching!!!

Shirley Byassee
Grade 3
Colorado Springs, Colorado

(continued on facing page)

their work is completed. Then you can really enjoy and profitably use the time spent in small-group instruction. Create a *When I Need Help Chart* and select your own age-appropriate alternatives from this list:

- Ask the monitor of the day.
- Ask a cross-age tutor.
- Ask one of the volunteer parents.
- Do what you can and skip the hard parts.
- Use the word wall, instructional charts, spelling journal, dictionary, or thesaurus.
- Whisper to a neighbor for help.
- Consult appendices in your text for formulae or conversions.
- Consult maps in your text.

When students need your help and you are unavailable, two systems seem to work better than raising hands. The first involves the "take-a-number" method. To facilitate service, many businesses use preprinted numbers to serve customers. Prepare a duplicate set of numbers on cards or laundry tags or Post-Its™. When students need help, they take a number from the pad or a laundry tag from a hook and go on to something else while they wait. You simply call out the numbers in order

or put the duplicate numbers up on a hook one at a time. Students then come up to your desk when they see or hear their number. This works very well and provides a first-come, first-served, fair method of getting help. See Figure 13.1.

Since a raised hand can get very tired, an alternative method is to give each student a red and green Lego block or Unifix cube. When help is needed, the red cube or block is placed on top of the green one. At all other times, the green is on top. You can see this easily and the student can keep on working until you get there. This has

Figure 13.1

Duplicate numbers on Post-Its™ or Laundry Tags

worked so well for so many of my student teachers that I encourage you to try it. I have made these red/green signaling devices out of toilet paper rolls with red masking tape on one end and green on the other. The blocks can be used in the computer lab as they fit nicely on top of a computer. See Figure 13.2.

One teacher wears a sign that says, "Please see me later" when she is involved in small-group instruction and wants to discourage interruptions. She points to the *I Need Help Chart* when students come up to her. This may sound extreme, but you are actually establishing independence and making it more likely that students will solve the problem themselves, learn to rely on peers for instruction, or discover the virtue of patience. If too many of your students are baffled, you need to reteach the material to the entire class or work with a small ad hoc group.

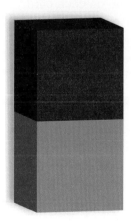

Figure 13.2
Help Needed Blocks

Noise Control

The best way to abate noise and chatter is to differentiate among whispering, talking, and silence. This is a useful distinction to make, because total silence is hard to maintain during an entire day. Try it yourself sometime! Using a homemade cardboard traffic light can help control the noise level—green signifying talking, yellow for whispering, and red for silence. See Figures 13.3 and 13.4. Have your students practice differentiating between whispering and talking. You can make a game of this. Have them say their names with their voice and then whisper their names, using only their breath. Teachers usually have a signal for total silence, like lights off, a bell, or a hand signal, and allow whispering at all other times.

Specify the acceptable noise level for each activity beforehand. Be realistic about how much silence can be expected in the classroom. If you teach your students to whisper, you will have a quiet classroom—not a silent classroom, but a quiet one. One teacher puts a doll in a basket and announces that the baby is sleeping. Another cautions students not to awaken the rabbit (stuffed animal or real classroom pet). Still another cautions that the canary is getting nervous.

are writing or read something while students are reading. This will also cut down on attention-getting behaviors that masquerade as interminable questions.

Ellen Kronowitz,
Student Teacher Supervisor
Redlands, California

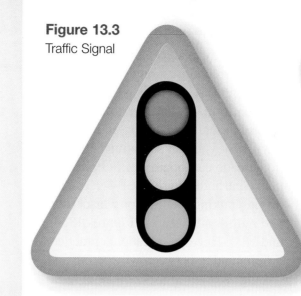

Figure 13.3
Traffic Signal

Figure 13.4
Noise Level Circles

Student Says . . .

Question: How does your teacher get the class's attention?
She says "5-4-3, Eyes On Me"

> Walker
> *Age 7.5, Second Grade*
> *Redlands, California*

These techniques work well, even with older students.

Hand Raising

Be consistent about hand raising and avoid questions that elicit choral responses. Called-out responses or questions frustrate beginning teachers. Preface your questions with, "Raise your hand and tell us . . ." Always compliment and encourage students who remember to raise hands, especially at the beginning of the year. During a dynamic discussion, debate, or brainstorming activity, you can always suspend the rules.

No matter what level, consider using a system for calling on students that assures equity. With young students, teachers might write the names of students on sticks and place these in a coffee can. These craft sticks or tongue depressors are chosen on a random basis and removed from the can until the can is empty (everyone has had a turn). The can is then refilled with the sticks, and so on. Another teacher uses a deck of cards and writes a student's name on each card. The cards are used in the same way as the sticks, but are more compact and more age-appropriate for intermediate grades and secondary students. See Figures 13.5 and 13.6.

Free Time

To cut down on disruption when students finish quickly, you need to have a Free Time policy. Note that if your students are finishing too quickly, it may be evidence that the work is too easy or insufficient in volume. Establish a routine for what your students do when they finish work, and post this on a bulletin board in plain view. Some suggestions include:

- Read a book.
- Play a game quietly.
- Take a puzzle and work it out.
- Work on some other unfinished project.
- Make up a crossword puzzle or acrostic.
- Work at the computer.
- Play with class pets, clean cages, and feed them.
- Help others with their work or with learning English.
- Listen to a story using headphones.
- Tidy up your desk.
- Review your portfolio.

Labeling Papers

Schools, grade levels, departments, and teams often decide to have uniform labeling of papers. Check with your colleagues to see what the norm is. In general, you will most likely need student name, date, subject, and, for secondary students, the period and your name on each paper for easy

Figure 13.5
Playing Cards

identification when the papers get mixed up. Color coding the papers by period is very useful. Use a different color copy paper for each period. Middle and high school teachers will

Apply It!

What are some age-appropriate ideas for your Free Time poster? Take into consideration your subject area and age group. Design some extension or reinforcement activities. Consider that most students love game formats, extra computer time, and creative curriculum applications. Jot down your grade and subject-specific ideas for later transfer to a poster.

Figure 13.6
Can with Name Sticks

Teacher Talks . . .

Students put their work at the end of the table, all headings going one way, and one student brings it up. The reasoning is it's neat and only a few people are moving around the room at time, which works well in classroom management.

Kris Ungerer
Kindergarten
Riverside, California

need to add some additional routines for setting up a notebook, labeling assignments, turning in projects, making up assignments, going to lockers, storing backpacks, etc.

Collection and Distribution of Papers

You need to consider how you will collect and redistribute homework and assignments. In order to maintain privacy, you might assign everyone a random number and set up your grade book with these numbers. In that way, you can have a student monitor put the papers in numerical order for you and you will know immediately whose assignment is missing. When the papers are returned, students can look for their numbers and not invade anyone else's privacy when they look through the folder. You may want to have an in and an out box in a convenient location. Some teachers have student mailboxes for return of papers.

Apply It!

Brainstorm all the other possible routines and procedures that you may need and that have not been covered, given your subject or grade level. Think back to your observation, student teaching, or own experience in school. List as many situations as you can that may necessitate other routines or procedures.

Avoid It!

Don't introduce all routines at once, especially on the first day. For example, movement to and from centers need not be discussed right off. However, bathroom routines are a priority the first day. Don't stick with routines if they are not working for you or are no longer needed. Don't be afraid to encourage students to suggest better ways of doing things.

Don't encourage "learned helplessness" by jumping up every time you see a student who needs help. Provide clear directions, check for understanding, elicit questions, and then let the students do some self-help before you intervene.

Chapter 14

How Can I Engage Students in Operating the Classroom?

Great discoveries

and improvements

invariably involve

the cooperation of

many minds.

Alexander Graham Bell

Effectiveness Essentials

- Many of your routines can be handled through delegation of authority.

- Make sure that your second language learners and students with special needs participate fully in monitorial duties.

- Rule setting, voting, and planning events create cohesion.

- Display a suggestion box in your classroom and encourage students to suggest improvements to any aspect of classroom life.

- Create a class identity through a logo, class mascot, class motto, class emblem, or class coat of arms.

- Read all you can and talk with experienced teachers about how they establish routines and procedures to create a cohesive classroom community.

From the first day of school I tell my students that our classroom is their daytime home. Involving the students in the classroom setup and bulletin board decorating is only a part of keeping the classroom orderly and making all students feel as if they belong. They are always ready to show off their new writing or works in a clean, nicely decorated classroom.

Loretta Gomez
Fourth Grade
San Bernardino, California

Good managers know how to delegate authority. Teachers who want to delegate can use monitors to manage a great many of the routines of classroom life. Besides reducing your own role as manager, you are enabling students, through the monitor or helper system you set up, to assume responsibility, gain independence, enhance self-concept, and practice leadership skills.

Types of Monitors

Think up as many jobs as you can, so every student feels a responsibility for maintenance of the classroom community. Below is a list of some possible jobs. Most teachers rotate these jobs on a weekly or semimonthly basis:

Messenger Service	Flag Bearer
Paper Passer	Calendar Changer
Pencil Sharpener	Librarian
Homework Handler	Clean Team
Sports Equipment Supervisor	▪ chairs
Board Eraser	▪ sink
Pet Caretaker	▪ floor
Gardener	▪ wastebasket
Doorperson	▪ shelves
Lunch Counter	5–8 Table Leaders
Snack Server	Unofficial Teaching Assistant

Some high schools give students credit for being a teaching assistant or TA. What do they do? You need to check with your department head, but often TAs run errands, make copies, and give you administrative support that doesn't compromise the privacy of your students.

Although you may not need all the monitors listed above, the opportunity is there for more than half the students to be involved in running the classroom at any one time. Use this list when deciding on monitors. You can make badges for

Figure 14.1
Monitor Visor and Monitor Badge

your monitors or create paper visors with job titles on them for your elementary students. Certificates of appreciation for a job well done will be welcomed by your students and their parents. See Figure 14.1.

Include English language learners fully in monitorial duties.

This will help them feel a part of the social fabric of the classroom and assist them in gaining a sense of belonging and acceptance vital to their self-esteem. Embrace this motto as well: Less work for teacher and more independence and responsibility for students.

Include students with special needs in all leadership and monitorial roles.

Give students with special needs the opportunity to engage a student assistant to help them with tasks that are challenging for their given disability. Never assume that they cannot perform the task.

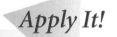

Apply It!

Make a subject- and age-appropriate list of monitors that would be useful in your classroom.

Assigning Monitors

Most teachers rotate jobs on a weekly or semimonthly basis, with the changing of the guard usually occurring on Monday. Your students should sample each job throughout the course of the year; alternative methods of assignment, with pros and cons, follow.

Volunteering

Students volunteer for positions, but this method may discourage shy students from participating.

Lottery

Each student's name is on a craft stick in a can or on a card in a fishbowl. As names are chosen, the student gets to choose the job he or she would like to

We All Help

do. Once the names have been drawn, they are removed from the lottery until all students have had a turn. This provides randomization with equal access. However, favorite jobs may be taken first.

Class List

The names are taken in order from a class list displayed on the bulletin board. Clothespins with the job titles are attached to the chart in order next to the name of the person. The clothespins are moved down a notch each week so everyone gets to sample each job. This is the fairest method I know of. Table leaders are rotated weekly as well and fall into a separate category. See Figure 14.2.

Figure 14.2

Class List with Jobs Titles on Clothespins

Names	Jobs
Steve	MESSENGER
Maria	GARDENER
Juan	BOARD CLEANER
Leticia	SNACKS
Kathy	LIBRARIAN
Sam	PENCILS
Karen	PET

Reward

Some teachers attach monitorial positions to good behavior. This system discriminates against the poorly behaved student who just may need the chance to exercise some responsibility in order to change his or her behavior. This student never gets the opportunity in the reward system.

Predetermined Schedule

Each week, the teacher selects students for each job and makes sure everyone has an opportunity. Although this may assure the "right person for the job," it takes the choice of position out of the students' hands.

Elections

Some teachers hold elections for class officers or leaders—some using very sophisticated ways, simulating the election process in our democracy, including nominations, campaigns, and secret ballot elections. This can become a popularity contest and we all know how it feels to be on the losing end.

Application

Some teachers simulate the entire job-hunting process. This is a good time to teach youngsters how to fill out a simplified application, write a cover

Figure 14.3
Class Job Application

Class Job Application

Name _____

Applying for _____

Why I want this job _____

My Qualifications _____

Signature _____

Date _____

letter, and even make up a résumé. A student committee can interview each prospective job applicant and select the most experienced and qualified student for each job. See Figure 14.3.

Other Opportunities for Creating a Cohesive Classroom Community

You are with your students almost as many hours Monday–Friday as you are with close family members, unless you don't sleep at all. The same is true for your students in elementary and middle school. Your class can

We had pet hamsters. It made me feel very responsible to help take care of them and other stuff.

Erik
Grade 5
Brookline, Massachusetts

become a sort of family that cares about and supports one another. A cohesive classroom community will provide a sense of belonging that you students desperately need. In high school, the allegiance is to the peer group and to the school as a whole. But you can still encourage a sense of community with any number of activities.

The most essential way of engaging your class as a community is the rule-setting activity.

Let your students have a say in rule making. From the first day, if they are involved in setting the rules, it is more likely they will buy into and follow them.

Have your students vote on everything that involves them.

For example, I was helping prepare students for a global festival. We were going to eat falafel and learn a traditional dance. I had the students vote on which they wanted to do first, even though I suspected the outcome. We counted the votes and proceeded to cook and eat. No surprise, but the students had a say in an outcome that neither the teacher nor I held strong

opinions about. Of course, there are some things that are solely determined by you, but when it comes to which of two books to read aloud or which story should be in the listening center, let them have a say.

Have your students plan events with you.

If there is to be a winter festival, sit in a circle and discuss what the options are before putting them to a vote. If you are planning a toy drive for the holidays, give them a voice in planning and decision making. If they are making baskets for the needy, have them decide what items should be included. If you are sending disaster relief, let students decide on the nature of the fundraiser.

Display a suggestion box in your classroom and let students make suggestions to improve any aspect of classroom life.

A suggestion box empowers your students to participate in the life of the classroom and express opinions that they may hesitate to communicate openly. It also is a way to encourage good citizenship in our participatory democracy.

Suggestion Box

Create a class identity through a logo, class mascot, class motto, class emblem, and class coat of arms.

One year, when Charles Schultz's *Snoopy* was popular with my students, we named the classroom after his birthplace, the "Daisy Hill Puppy Farm." Secondary students can enjoy a sense of cohesion through team-building activities. They can engage in friendly competitions to design a class logo or motto. See Figure 14.4. They can design bulletin boards in teams. They can compete in instructional games and contests. They can vie to have the most innovative suggestion for improving the class.

Read all you can and talk with experienced teachers about how they establish routines and procedures to create a cohesive classroom community. Although the tasks described in this unit may seem a bit overwhelming at first, the time and effort you expend at the beginning will allow you the freedom to enjoy and exercise your primary function—instruction.

Figure 14.4
Sample Class Mascot

Avoid It!

Avoid choosing only your "teacher's pets" or the most well-behaved students for the classroom jobs. The student who never gets chosen for special recognition is probably the one you should choose. This could mark a turning point in the student's behavior and/or attitude toward school. Make sure everyone has an equally vital role in classroom functioning.

Never trust a computer you can't throw out a window.

Steve Wozniak,
co-founder Apple Computers

The Internet is a giant international network of intelligent, informed computer enthusiasts, by which I mean, "people without lives." We don't care. We have each other....

Dave Barry,
humorist

Chapter 15

How Do I Manage Technology in My Classroom?

Effectiveness Essentials

- Many of the students in your class have a better handle on technology than you do.
- Your computer can ease the burden of some of your most time-consuming teacher tasks.
- Your computer can support your curricular and personal objectives.
- All learners can benefit from the use of technology.
- In one-or-two-computer classrooms, teachers use the computer as one of many learning centers to which students rotate.
- Projection devices enable you to conduct whole-group lessons with word-processing programs, simulations, or educational games.
- Students can work in groups at the computer during center time or on a rotating schedule that provides equal time and access.
- Develop a rotation schedule for the computer(s) in your classroom and appoint a monitor.
- Be sure to preview and evaluate every software program you use.

If your life is similar to mine, you probably have experience with technological advances such as pagers, cell phones, digital cameras, CD players, ATMs, copiers, fax machines, online card catalogs, virtual reality games, handheld personal organizers, i-Pods, MP3 players, electronic portfolios, and online university courses—the list could go on and on.

Not one of these was available when I started teaching. The electric typewriter was my word processor, vinyl records provided my music, and the hand-cranked ditto machine that turned my fingers blue was my copier.

Many of the students in your class have a better handle on technology than you do. Not only can they set the time on the VCR to something other than a blinking 12:00, TiVo and DVRs are now their staples. They play X-Box games with speed and accuracy. Use the survey in the Apply It! box to find out exactly how much technology expertise your students have.

Managing the Use of Technology for Education
In this video clip, the narrator discusses technology as but one of many tools a teacher can use. Time management and acceptable use policies are discussed as well. After viewing the clip, discuss ways that technology can be used to support your curriculum and develop a list of rules for computer use in your classroom. Describe an instance in which using books or community resources might be more time-efficient.

Apply It!

Conduct or adapt a student survey like this one.

Do you have a computer at home? Yes ☐ No ☐ laptop ☐ desktop ☐ PC ☐ Mac ☐

What peripherals do you have on your computer?

   CD burner ☐ DVD drive ☐ speakers ☐ digital camera ☐ other _____

What computer programs do you use? _____

What Internet sites are your favorites? _____

Do you use e-mail? Yes ☐ No ☐

What is your e-mail address for our class listserv? _____ *(optional)*

How many hours per day do you work on your computer? _____

Do you download and pay for music for your own use? Yes ☐ No ☐

What game boxes do you have? _____

What games do you play? _____

Handhelds, Computers, iPods

Using Technology to Enhance Teaching

Technology is one loyal classroom assistant that doesn't earn a salary. It will save you time, that rare and valuable commodity in the busy classroom. Technology supports your curricular and personal objectives and augments instruction to meet the needs of ALL students, including English language learners and students with special needs.

Computers are teacher time savers.

Your computer can actually ease the burdens of some of your most time-consuming teacher tasks. These include record keeping; parent communications; planning and locating resources to support your curricular objectives; and locating activities and resources to meet individual differences, particularly of students with special needs. Think of your computer as a robot at your beck and call—a tool that serves and doesn't dictate your needs.

25 Teacher Time Savers Provided by Your Computer

1. Managing electronic portfolios
2. Researching content or finding lesson plans and thematic units hot off the web
3. Generating tests
4. Making PowerPoint presentations and slide shows for your students
5. Locating and/or constructing curriculum-related games, crossword puzzles, word searches, worksheets
6. Creating an address book for your various periods and e-mailing students and/or parents through the period listservs if your students have e-mail access at home
7. Creating a course overview using Blackboard, a course management system, http://www.blackboard.com
8. Finding unique graphic organizers of all sorts
9. Accessing and evaluating websites for student research
10. Creating certificates, homework passes, thank you notes, lesson plan templates
11. Creating scavenger hunts and webquests
12. Downloading photos and clipart and other graphics for stationery and bulletin boards
13. Finding thoughtful and inspiring quotations for your class
14. Networking with teachers who are engaged in similar projects
15. Previewing a fieldtrip site
16. Downloading game formats such as *Jeopardy*
17. Taking an online course to improve your skills or meet further certification requirements
18. Designing your own business cards
19. Locating conferences and or proposing a workshop or session
20. Reading online newspapers and magazines
21. Designing a class website. (This website will take you through the process: http://www.edzone.net/%7Emwestern/101.html/)
22. Keeping track of student assignments and grading using spreadsheets or software programs such as E-Z Grader©, or Gradekeeper©, or Gradebusters©
23. Creating and updating a substitute teacher file
24. Downloading e-books
25. SHOPPING ONLINE ☺

Teacher Talks . . .

Student daily reporters contribute to our website blog that highlights the events of the day. These reporters take pictures to go along with their writing to create an authentic article. The blog offers the students and me a record of their writing improvement. Parents and other visitors enjoy reading the blog to learn about what we do at school, and also to see how much the student writing improves over the course of the year. The website offers an authentic audience for my developing writers.

Each student has access to a handheld computer all day, every day. We use Palm Tungsten E handhelds and Palm wireless keyboards for word processing, concept mapping, basic math skills, video presentations, and more. Whether they are used for ten

(continued on facing page)

30 Student Instructional Uses for the Computer

1. Supporting and extending curriculum through motivational software
2. Facilitating cooperative learning, socialization, and English language acquisition when one computer is used as a shared tool
3. Connecting your class with others across the country or the world to share information—as "key" pals
4. Researching using tools such as multimedia encyclopedias, CD-ROMs, and the web
5. Providing problem-solving opportunities through simulations
6. Encouraging the use of information databases
7. Facilitating communication skills by enabling student participation in forums for students such as Student-sphere, Hilites, Kidlink, and Ednet
8. Promoting writing and desktop publishing
9. Printing a map of your town or of places you are studying
10. Viewing live webcams of volcanoes, animals, the space station, etc.
11. Visiting a museum
12. Using drill and practice games
13. Touring the White House, Senate, House of Representatives, National Archives
14. Creating spreadsheets for math and science
15. Utilizing digital photography applications
16. Reading e-books on line
17. Creating timelines
18. Playing subject-matter games such as *Jeopardy* with a PowerPoint template you can create by going to http://www.graves.k12.ky.us/tech/jeopardy_instructions.htm (see Figure 15.1) or playing "Homeworkopoly," a game format you can download at www.teachnet.com/homeworkopoly/
19. Downloading clip art and graphics to illustrate stories
20. Creating PowerPoint projects/slide shows in cooperative groups
21. Creating thematic webs with Kidspiration or Inspiration©
22. Taking a virtual fieldtrip
23. Going on a scavenger hunt or webquest
24. Researching an author or historical figure
25. Preparing current events reports with online newspapers
26. Using an online thesaurus or dictionary
27. Getting help with homework
28. Printing maps/directions for real or simulated journeys
29. Sending one another e-cards or postcards
30. Downloading free educational games

Apply It!

Highlight 15–20 activities from the list on page 136 that you would like your students to engage in. Then turn those items into a survey for your students. Ask students to rate each one on a scale from 1 to 3:

   3 Very Interesting   2 Interesting   1 I know how to do this already

Start with those activities that receive the highest rating. Secondary students can do the data analysis for you.

Your computer can support your curricular and personal objectives.

On page 139 are 25 things your plastic and metallic servant can do to meet your instructional and personal productivity goals. On the facing page are 30 student uses of computers.

As in all things, your students with special needs must have equal access to technology.

It is not expected that you go it alone. Collaboration with the special educators at your site is key. They will know of the adaptive technologies that fit your students' needs. Adaptations may be as simple as using the largest fonts in word processing or as complex as voice recognition software. As soon as you identify your students with special needs, arrange a meeting to go over their IEPs and determine what, if any, technology adaptations are needed.

Figure 15.1

Jeopardy Board

Category Heading	Category Heading	Category Heading	Category Heading	Category Heading
100	100	100	100	100
200	200	200	200	200
300	300	300	300	300
400	400	400	400	400
500	500	500	500	500

minutes a day or three hours, these handhelds are integrated into our curriculum and have helped to increase student learning and engagement.

Matt Villasana
Shepard Elementary Fourth Grade
Columbia, Missouri

Visit us at Studio Four:
www.columbia.k12.mo.us/she/mvillasa

An Adaptive Keyboard

In this video clip, a student with a physical disability uses a word prediction/synthesizer program to type on the adaptive keyboard.

Word Processing

In this video clip, a student with use of one hand is empowered by using a word-processing program to express her thoughts about and feelings of isolation.

After watching these two clips, discuss how the students with special needs are accommodated and talk about the benefits of inclusion in technology.

English language learners can use audio devices to help facilitate language acquisition.

Books can be downloaded from http://www.audible.com to MP3 players or iPods. As the students hear as well as read the book, they can follow the flow of language, hear how difficult words are pronounced, and go back as many times as they need to.

A Reporter Writes . . .

iPod-Enhanced Reading a Hit

C.L. Lopez
Staff Writer
San Bernardino Sun
10/13/2005
Excerpted with permission

REDLANDS. Silence enveloped the classroom.

Students listened raptly as pet mongoose Rikki-tikki-tavi fought a battle to the death with Nag, the cobra.

Rikki-tikki-tavi won, as the 19th-century story was brought to life on a 21st-century device for the 15 children in Linda Bomar's seventh-grade English class at Clement Middle School.

. . . The widely publicized iPod is the latest alternative to books on tapes or compact discs. Since its arrival at Clement, pupils are finding it easier to tune in to the audio versions of books and stories.

The children listen to the stories through earphones as they read it from the book. It gives each student the power to move at his or her own pace, moving ahead or going back to listen again to an earlier segment or skip around in the story, something that is awkward to do on a tape or CD.

. . . The iPod also allows the pupil to learn the pronunciation of difficult words as they are read by actors, professional storytellers and sometimes by the author.

Gearing Up for Integrating Technology

You do not need some rare, innate technology gene. You can learn more about technology through effort, trial and error, inservices, networking with colleagues, technology journals, and visiting technology websites. You may feel overwhelmed just by reading this chapter. The way I control my anxiety is by taking one step at a time when I have

time and typing in keywords or phrases in a search engine such as *Google* (http://www.google.com). Type the term in the search region, and away you go. At *Google,* you can also click on images and get pictures of anything you put in the search region.

Evaluating Software Programs

You need to preview and evaluate every software program you use. There

10 Steps to Computer Confidence and Competence

1. Survey your classroom, school computer lab, or district resource center to see what hardware is available to you.

   Computers in classroom? How many?

   Computers in lab? How many?

   CD Rom drive

   VCR

   Palm handhelds

   Clicker technology

   AlphaSmarts

   P.C. Tablets

   iPods or MP3 players

   T.V. and connector to computer

   Digital cameras

   Scanner

   LCD projection device

   Digital or regular camcorder

   Internet access

   Mobile computer labs

   Wireless technology

   Other

2. Survey the resources for the preceding hardware, such as software programs of all sorts including interactive books, skills programs, word processing, graphics and art

(continued on following page)

statistics

From the NEA (2003) Regarding
Teacher Access to Technologies

Teachers with access at their
worksite to the following:

Computers	94%
Videocassette recorder	91%
T.V. Monitor	87%
Computers with CD drives	87%
Standard software	87%
Internet	86%
E-mail	85%

programs, databases, spreadsheets, simulations, etc.

3. Next, commit some time to teacher utility programs so you can see immediate benefits. *Teachers Tool Kit* (Hi Tech of Santa Cruz), for example, enables you to design word searches, word scrambles, and multiple-choice tests. *Grade Busters* (Jay Klein Products), is an example of an easy-to-use database for recordkeeping and grading. A program such as *The Print Shop Deluxe* (EdMark) or *Kid Pix* (Broderbund) can help you design fliers, invitations, bulletin board banners, and awards. Suggested software for beginning computer users who have money to spend can be found in a variety of educational catalogs.

4. Inform yourself step by step as the need arises. When I needed to communicate with colleagues from home, I learned how to set up my e-mail and read messages from home. Saving time and energy can be a terrific source of motivation for learning new things.

5. Ask for help from teachers and tech savvy students at your school.

6. Plan to enroll in a technology course, workshop, or inservice seminar.

7. Attend a technology conference or sessions at teacher conferences that focus on technology applications to your subject matter.

8. Join a computer users group and swap public-domain software. Computer Using Educators (CUE), http://www.cue.org, can point you to a local group.

9. Teacher magazines such as *Instructor* or *Teaching K-8* often include ideas for using your computer effectively, and specialized computer magazines, such as *Technology & Learning* (Subscription Department, P.O. Box 5052, Vandalia, OH 45377) or http:// www.techlearning.com, supply lesson plans and teaching strategies, even on managing the one-computer classroom.

10. Finally, take every opportunity to play around on the computer yourself. There are many resource directories of websites specifically geared to teachers who want to integrate technology. Many of the websites have prepackaged time-saving lesson plans that you can adapt.

Apply It!

Go to the search engine, http://www.google.com and choose a topic to research. Insert the topic keywords into the search region and see what comes up. Then search for images you can download related to the topic. Next time, type in your topic followed by these terms, one at a time: lesson plans, units, webquests, scavenger hunt, virtual field trips, games, simulations, books. You will be shocked at how efficiently your computer can help you create a unit of instruction. If you are really adept at using search engines, try your hand at creating at least two slides for a PowerPoint presentation in a content area.

are some terrific software programs on the market. Some are not so good. Ask yourself these questions when you are assessing software:

✓ Does the program support and expand the educational goals you have set?

✓ Is the program attention grabbing as well as instructionally sound?

✓ Are activities developmentally appropriate?

✓ Does the program have open-ended opportunities so that students can reuse it?

✓ Are there several levels of increasing difficulty?

✓ Is the program student friendly and easy to use?

✓ Does the program give immediate feedback in a positive way?

✓ Can the program be run without sound so the noise does not disturb the class?

Managing the Computer-Assisted Classroom

The main question teachers have about computers in the classroom, once they have some basic knowledge of their operation and applications, is, "How do I manage computer-assisted instruction with 30 or more students and only one, or maybe two or three computers if I am very lucky?"

Use the computer as one of many learning centers to which students rotate.

The program is demonstrated to everyone in the class using a connector to the VCR or an overhead projection device such as a P.C. Viewer. Then the students rotate to the center in groups of two to work on the activities. Aides, parent volunteers, and cross-age tutors can help you manage computer-assisted instruction in the lower grades.

Projection devices enable you to conduct whole-group lessons with word-processing programs, simulations, or educational games.

Students take turns suggesting the next sentence, editing documents, or volunteering answers while the whole class watches the screen.

Students can work in groups at the computer during center time or on a rotating schedule that provides equal time and access.

Two or three students can work together on a simulation or educational game. Start slowly with peer tutoring, or by matching a computer-using student with a novice. These sessions may be structured as cooperative learning sessions with rules, specified tasks, and group interdependence assured through the assignment of specific roles: the facilitator who seeks everyone's input, the keyboarder who inputs the data, and the recorder who summarizes the steps and results on paper. These roles will shift each time. Here are some tips:

1. Focus on one curriculum area at a time.
2. Choose a program that enhances instruction in that area.
3. Learn the program thoroughly yourself and diagnose any potential difficulties.
4. Teach this program to a few students, who can then teach it to others.

Avoid It!

Viruses are a serious issue. To avoid contamination, make sure that students do not insert disks from home into the class computer. Make sure that the computers are covered and that someone who has been trained to do so uses computer wipes to clean the screens and the keyboard. This can be one of your classroom monitorial duties. You might also establish a routine of washing hands before computer use to avoid a sticky keyboard. At the end of the week, make sure you check computers for any inappropriate content entries and for temporary files and caches that are no longer needed.

Develop a rotation schedule for the computer(s) in your classroom and appoint a monitor.

This classroom "tekkie" sees to it that the rotation schedule is followed and that each student on the list gets his or her allotted computer time.

Devise a routine to allow equity in access to computers.

Identify students who have personal computers at home. You may want to provide more classroom computer access to those who do not. Here are some ways to ensure equity in computer usage:

1. *A pocket chart with names on cut-out apples.* When a student completes his or her work, the apple is turned and the next one on the list has a turn.

2. *A clothespin chart divided down the middle into "waiting" and "completed" sections.* When the students go to the computer in order, they move their name clothespin from "waiting" to "completed."

3. *Post a class list and have students check off their turns.* You will also need to decide if and how you will time students. A kitchen timer works well, as does dividing the day into segments and assigning students to segments based on their access chart.

Figures 15.2
Computer Access Chart

4. *Use Popsicle sticks or a deck of playing cards* to draw names for computer time and exhaust the sticks or cards before starting over.
5. *Assign students numbers* as in a bakery or at the post office and let the students know whose turn it is by their assigned number.
6. *Rotate students in pairs* on to the computer during learning center time.

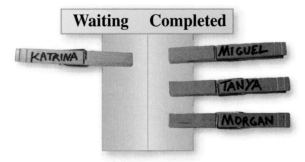

Figure 15.3
"Waiting" and "Completed" Chart
with Names on Clothespins

Unit 3 Checklist

Classroom Organization and Management Checklist	For more information go to:
☐ Is my arrangement conducive to my instructional plan?	Chapter 10
☐ Have I decided on bulletin boards and accessories?	Chapter 10
☐ Can I see everyone and can they see me?	Chapter 10
☐ Have I established routines for entrances, exits, beginning and ending the day or period?	Chapter 11
☐ Do I have routines for materials, movement around the room, bathroom, and water fountain?	Chapter 12
☐ Have I decided on instructional routines?	Chapter 13
☐ Have I decided on monitors and how to select them?	Chapter 14
☐ Have I designed activities to promote cohesion?	Chapter 14
☐ Have I conducted a survey of the hardware available?	Chapter 15
☐ Have I checked the availability of standards-based/curriculum appropriate software?	Chapter 15

Further Readings: Books about Classroom Organization and Management

Bitter, G. G., & Pierson, M. E. (2004). *Using technology in the classroom* (6th ed.). Boston: Allyn & Bacon. This book is for teachers who want to know more about integrating technology into the classroom. It has up-to-date and comprehensive information about using the Internet, suggested educational websites, new technology tools, and much more.

Diffily, D., & Sassman, C. (2004). *Teaching effective classroom routines.* New York: Scholastic. This book describes how to create spaces conducive to good management and discipline and covers the routines that will help the day flow smoothly.

Nations, S., & Boyett, S. (2002). *So much stuff, so little space, creating and managing the learner centered classroom.* Gainesville, FL: Maupin House Press. This book is for the K–5 teacher and provides many ideas and tips for keeping track of supplies, lesson plans and paperwork, student information, and a great deal more.

Rominger, L., Packard, S., & Elkin, N. (2001). *Your first year as a high school teacher.* New York: Three Rivers Press. This book has good information about setting up your classroom, making rules, and other important tips for the first-year high school teacher. This is a very practical guide written by experienced high school teachers.

Williams, J. (2000). *How to manage your middle school classroom.* Westminster, CA: Teacher Created Materials. This is a very practical and easy-to-use guide for the middle school teacher, and covers most aspects of classroom organization and management. It includes ready-to-use forms and a great many easy-to-follow guidelines.

Classroom Organization and Technology Websites

Bulletin Board Ideas

http://www.kimskorner4teacherstalk.com/ classmanagement/bulletinboards.html

http://schooldiscovery.com/schrockguide/ bulletin/index/html

http://www.teachnet.com/how-to/décor/ bboards

These websites have classroom management and bulletin board ideas

Virtual Field Trips

http://www.theteachersguide.com/virtualtours.html

This is one of many virtual fieldtrip websites you can visit. It will give you an idea of what is available.

Museum Resources

http://americanart.si.edu/index2.cfm	American Art Museum at the Smithsonian
http://www.metmuseum.org	Metropolitan Museum of Art
http://www.exploratorium.edu/	Exploratorium, San Francisco
http://www.mnh.si.edu/Museum	Natural History Museum at the Smithsonian

These and many other museum websites are available to you and your students. These are some of my favorites.

Keypal/e-pal sites

http://www.bconnex.net/~kidworld/keypals4.htm

http://www.worldkids.net/clubs/kci

http://www.eduplace.com/projects/keypals.html

http://www.mightymedia.com/keypals

http://www.gaggle.net

These sites will enable your students to interact across the world with others their age.

Technology Center at Education World

http://www.educationworld.com/a_tech/

At this location, you will find articles, tips on blogging, techtorials, webquests, technology lesson plans, technology tools, tips of the week and more.

The International Society for Technology in Education

http://www.iste.org/

The International Society for Technology in Education (ISTE®) provides leadership to improve technology teaching K–12. There are a great many resources and links on this website.

Unit 4

Positive Discipline

Unit 4
Positive Discipline

It is our continuing love for our children that makes us want them to become all they can be, and their continuing love for us that helps them accept healthy discipline—from us and eventually from themselves.

Fred Rogers (Mr. Rogers)

Chapter **16**

What Are the Main Views of Changing Behavior?

Effectiveness Essentials

- Even experienced teachers are concerned about discipline.

- Most teachers combine elements of many approaches to discipline.

- Most approaches fall into two camps: the behavior modification camp and the logical consequences camp.

- In behavior modification systems, incentives or rewards and penalties are imposed by the teacher to modify behavior extrinsically.

- In logical consequence approaches, encouragement is the alternative to praise and logical consequences are the alternative to punishment.

- Logical consequences are always related to the offense, reasonable, and respectful.

- Teachers need to provide all students with opportunities to experience success.

Even experienced teachers are concerned about discipline. In fact, teachers are more fearful of the D word than are students. There has been a proliferation of discipline models in recent years and the subject can get very confusing. But it's important to put discipline into the context of the entire educational experience. In addition to studying subject matter and acquiring academic skills, school is a place for students to learn the lifelong skills of self-discipline and accepting responsibility for their actions.

- **Safety.** Students need to feel physically safe, emotionally secure, and free from threat and intimidation both inside the classroom and outside. School may be the safest place in their lives.

- **Limits.** Students need to abide by limits and learn what is appropriate and inappropriate behavior. This is the other side of the safety issue. To ensure an environment that is safe for everyone, each student must conform to appropriate behavior standards.

- **Acceptance.** Students need and desire the approval of others. When they behave in a socially acceptable manner, they will earn acceptance from others and feel a sense of belonging in the classroom.

Apply It!

Take a few minutes to think about reasons to support the need for discipline and order in the classroom. Then compare your answers to those that follow.

- **Self-Esteem.** Self-esteem needs closely follow those of acceptance (Maslow, 1987). Students who can control their behavior will gain a sense of mastery and will feel competent and respected in their classroom community. Feeling competent in one area of life can help shore up poor self-esteem in other areas.

- **Learning.** Your students have both the need to reach their potential and the right to an orderly classroom environment free from distractions, interruptions, and behavioral disruptions that interfere with their learning.

- **Responsibility.** Students need to learn that for every action there is a logical and sometimes equal reaction. Taking responsibility for one's actions is a cornerstone of democratic society.

- **Democratic Training.** In a workable discipline system, students learn

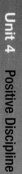

about democratic principles and concepts such as:

1. One person, one vote
2. Rule of law
3. Self-responsibility
4. The rule of the majority, with respect for minority views
5. Consequences for actions against the greater good
6. Individual freedoms balanced against the common good
7. Respect for all, regardless of viewpoint

How did your own list compare?

Most teachers combine elements of many approaches to discipline. You have probably read a great deal about approaches to discipline, and if not, I would urge you to spend time reading some of the books or visiting the websites that are listed at the end of this unit. Before you adopt any one system, spend some time clarifying your own beliefs about discipline.

Apply It!

Take some time to work through this Discipline Clarification Activity. Rank-order these positions vis-à-vis discipline from 1 to 7, with 1 being the position most like your own.

_____ I'll figure out discipline as I go along.

_____ I believe in counseling individuals about their behavior.

_____ Students should participate in making rules and solving classroom problems.

_____ Discipline entails helping students make good choices.

_____ Students should experience the logical consequences of their behavior.

_____ Students respond best to rewards and punishment.

_____ A classroom is a dictatorship and I make the rules.

It was probably hard for you to rank these statements, as most teachers are eclectic in their beliefs and practice walking the thin line between a laissez-faire approach and total authoritarianism. In between you will find statements reflecting common approaches to discipline. Most approaches fall into two camps: the behavior modification camp and the logical consequences camp. These two divergent viewpoints for changing behavior can be compared and contrasted. Other systems derive from the two approaches, and they will be mentioned where they apply.

Behavior Modification: Incentives and Penalties

A prominent psychiatrist and expert on discipline (William Glasser) remarked in a speech that if Pavlov had experimented with cats instead of dogs, his behavior reinforcement theories would have been long forgotten. I have two cats, so I know that Glasser was probably right. But Pavlov didn't use cats and behavior modification techniques are very much in vogue in schools today.

In behavior modification systems, incentives or rewards and penalties are imposed by teachers to modify behavior extrinsically. After the rules are handed down (or, in some instances, established with your students) and then practiced, an intricate system of rewards and penalties is initiated. Canter's work in assertive discipline (2001) and Jones' work (1992, 2000) are examples of systems based on rewards and penalties. One reward Jones suggests is Preferred Activity Time (P.A.T.), in which teachers use a stopwatch to either subtract or add free time minutes. If students take away teaching minutes through misbehavior or inattention, then they are docked free time minutes. Some of the other positive rewards that teachers use for appropriate behavior are listed at the right.

We all respond to positive rewards. For adults, it may be a certificate of appreciation, a bonus, or a sincere, "You did a great job." For students, a homework pass, a trinket, or a certificate also work wonders to shape positive behavior. And not just in elementary school.

I recently visited a classroom that had a token economy in place. Students earn tickets (raffle type available at office supply stores in rolls) for positive on-task behaviors. They write their names on the tickets, and at the end of the week, a drawing is held and those whose names are drawn get to choose something from the treasure chest that contains a variety of items. The small and inexpensive items are greatly valued by the students and the system works very effectively, especially because tickets are given to students who are "caught doing the right thing."

Positive Rewards

Elementary
Individual
Certificates
Special activities
Stickers, small gifts
Food
Homework exemption
Verbal praise
Honor Roll

Whole Class
Popcorn parties
Field trip
Extra P.E. time
Ice cream party
Special cooking activity
Verbal praise
Preferred Activity Time (Jones)

Middle and High School
Individual
Computer Time
Recognition certificates
Fast-food coupons
Homework passes
Gel pens, key chains
Posters

Whole Class
Activities the students enjoy
Free time

Earn Tickets

What's Inside?

Choose a Prize

Student Says . . .

When the class misbehaves we have to put our heads down for a couple of minutes. Some teachers make us sit out some minutes of recess.

Kurt
Age 8, Third Grade
Plano, Texas

Rewards can be earned individually, in groups, or as a whole class.

Designing a record-keeping system is fairly easy; maintaining it is difficult. Teachers make a chart of students' names and attach stars, move pushpins, or color in the spaces when students earn points. If the record keeping is done by groups at a table, the entire table is listed and points accrue when all the students at the table are doing the right thing. Some teachers run the system by total class behavior and add marbles or popcorn kernels to a jar when everyone is behaving appropriately. A

Avoid It!

Incentive programs take time, and you must be consistent and fair in using them. Students will clamor for points and keep you on your toes if you forget. Beware of addicting your students to rewards. Otherwise it will be hard to tell if they have really internalized controls or are simply behaving in anticipation of material rewards. If the purpose of discipline is ultimately self-control, you may be acting counterproductively by relying too much on extrinsic motivation. The management of these systems may cause more disruption in your class than the behaviors they were designed to correct in the first place.

Myth Buster!

Rewards aren't needed in high school. That age group is above it.

High school students want to be treated like adults, but they are still children at heart. Athletics is tied to grades for high school students. This is used as a huge reward for many students who would not try if grades weren't tied to sports. I still have students who ask if we are having a Holiday or Halloween party. Fridays in my classroom we still have P.A.T. (Preferred activity time), where the students earn points for free time (on time, positive attitude, completing work, respectful behavior, staying in seat). They need 20/25 (5 points per day X 5) to get P.A.T. My students really look forward to this, and if there is a change in schedule, they want to know when they will have it.

Devon Van Dam
High School English, Government, Special Day Classes
McKinleyville, California

full jar means a popcorn party or special treat. Some teachers announce the number of points or marbles to be earned before each activity begins.

On the flip side of the rewards system are the various penalties that teachers assess for infractions of the rules.

When this happens, depending on the system, students gather negative checks on the board or on a teacher's clipboard that translate into ever more negative consequences. These may include staying in for recess, staying after school, going to the principal's office, carrying a note home, or missing favorite activities.

Figure 16.1
Behavior Modification Daily Accounting

Teacher Talks . . .

I had a student in class who was constantly in trouble during the day and after school in extended day (an after school day care program). I devised a system of rewards with the approval of his parents whereby he was awarded from 1–5 points by me after consulting with my student teacher, aide, and recess personnel and 1–5 points by his extended day worker each day for a possible total of 50 points for the five days of school. I print out the tickets on purple paper and date them in advance. His parents know to ask for the purple ticket. At the end of the week, if he had accumulated > 45 points his reward was to go out to dinner at his favorite restaurant. If he received < 35 his favorite activity (Nintendo) was denied him for the weekend. From 35–45 was a neutral zone and there was neither a reward nor a penalty. Now he usually accumulates > 45 points but never less than 35. A success story!

Jason Paytas, First Grade
Arcata, California

My teacher finds fun ways for us to work together . . . each of us has an envelope with colored cards inside. Each color has the following special meaning: yellow = doing well, orange = a warning, green = extra homework, blue = miss recess, pink = phone call home. We get points for the days when the whole class has yellow cards. When we have enough points we get to have a party.

Erin
Age 8, Third Grade
Glenview, Illinois

Penalties in middle and high school may include detention, isolation, fines, and suspension, combined with parental notification. You will be expected to follow the referral procedures and be in line with the other staff members in identifying those behaviors that mandate suspension as punishment. In California, a student can be suspended for infractions that seem unimaginable and unlikely, but they happen.

Classroom Artifacts

California Education Code with Reasons for Suspensions from A-Q 48900.

A pupil may not be suspended from school or recommended for expulsion, unless the superintendent or the principal of the school in which the pupil is enrolled determines that the pupil has committed an act as defined pursuant to any of subdivisions (a) to (q), inclusive:

(a) (1) Caused, attempted to cause, or threatened to cause physical injury to another person.
   (2) Willfully used force or violence upon the person of another, except in self-defense.
(b) Possessed, sold, or otherwise furnished any firearm, knife, explosive, or other dangerous object. . . .
(c) Unlawfully possessed, used, sold, or otherwise furnished, or been under the influence of, any controlled substance. . . .
(d) Unlawfully offered, arranged, or negotiated to sell any controlled substance. . . .
(e) Committed or attempted to commit robbery or extortion.
(f) Caused or attempted to cause damage to school property or private property.

(g) Stolen or attempted to steal school property or private property.
(h) Possessed or used tobacco, or any products containing tobacco or nicotine products. . . .
(i) Committed an obscene act or engaged in habitual profanity or vulgarity.
(j) Unlawfully possessed or unlawfully offered, arranged, or negotiated to sell any drug paraphernalia. . . .
(k) Disrupted school activities or otherwise willfully defied the valid authority of supervisors, teachers, administrators, school officials, or other school personnel engaged in the performance of their duties.
(l) Knowingly received stolen school property or private property.
(m) Possessed an imitation firearm.

(n) Committed or attempted to commit a sexual assault....

(o) Harassed, threatened, or intimidated a pupil who is a complaining witness or a witness in a school disciplinary proceeding....

(p) Unlawfully offered, arranged to sell, negotiated to sell, or sold the prescription drug Soma.

(q) Engaged in, or attempted to engage in, hazing....

Denying preferred activities or meting out punishment has a downside.

Although punishment may stop the behavior immediately, Nelsen (2000) cautions that in the long haul, punishment results in the four R's: revenge, resentment, rebellion, and retreat. One

Figure 16.2

Pocket Chart with Color-Coded Cards

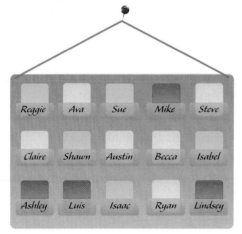

teacher has reversed the pocket chart suggested by Lee Canter and associates from ever-increasing color-coded negative cards to ever-increasing positive ones. She flips the card when the student or group is doing the "right thing." The first color stands for good, the second for great, the third for excellent. Special rewards are given to those who reach excellent. This turn-around on ever-increasing negatives to ever-increasing positives has had a profound effect on the climate of the classroom (see Figure 16.2).

Encouragement and Logical Consequences

Encouragement is offered by Dreikurs and others (1998) as an alternative to praise. Encouragement means that you don't have to be 100% perfect. It means you have made progress along the way and that progress is noted and

statistics

The National Center for Education Statistics (2004) reports that:

- Between 1993 and 2003, the percentage of students in grades 9–12 who were involved in a fight on school property dropped from 16% to 13%.

- Between 1993 and 2003, the percentage of 9–12-year-olds who reported carrying a weapon on the school site within the past 30 days declined from 12% to 6%.

- In 2003, 12% of students in the 12–18 age range reported that derogatory words (related to religion, disability, gender, sexual orientation, race, ethnicity) had been used against them.

- Student bullying is one of the most frequently reported discipline problems at school: 26% of elementary schools, 43% of middle schools, and 25% of high schools reported problems with bullying in 1999–2000.

- In general, ethnic minority students report more fear at school. However, reports of feeling afraid have declined in all groups.

I tell my students that when they wake up each morning and come to school, they spend six to seven hours with me, which is usually more time than they spend with their parents. They may be in the same house with them, but that does not mean that they spend time with them. After all, they are busy with homework, outdoor time, TV time, phone time, etc. I told them that they should therefore think of me as their mom away from home. My job was to teach them, comfort them, encourage them, and yes discipline them as needed. However, my most important job was to love them so that they could put away all other thoughts and prepare to learn. I have no losers in my class. They should therefore consider me their mom away from home. Over the years many of my

(continued on facing page)

supported. Encouragement gives you the will to continue on the right path. Praise suggests completion, approval for a job well done or an achievement.

Dreikurs believes that all students want to be recognized and to feel that they belong. His model is based on mutual respect, encouragement, and taking responsibility. It is a model that seeks to encourage good citizenship when no one is looking. Students do the right thing because it is the right thing to do as opposed to students who do the right thing because they are intimidated by the fear of getting caught. Some people drive at 80 miles per hour until they see the flashing lights. Others drive at a safe speed all the time because it is the reasonable and responsible thing to do.

Teachers need to provide all students, and especially the discouraged ones, with opportunities to experience success.

Dreikurs believes that students can be made responsible for their behavior as they experience the "logical consequences" of that behavior. Praise is easily showered upon those who suc-

ceed, but those who have not yet succeeded also need encouragement. Encouraging the small steps on the way to success is as important as completing a whole task. If a misbehaving student is a discouraged student, as Dreikurs and colleagues (1998) assert, then the teacher's goal is not to give false praise that the student knows is not deserved but rather to help him or her achieve small victories through encouragement. Some ways of encouraging students include:

- Recognizing effort as opposed to success

- Pointing out helpful contributions

- Highlighting the improvements you observe

- Assigning special jobs that your student can succeed in

- Having your student share a special interest or talent with the class

- Asking students to assist others who need help

- Displaying the student's work

- Demonstrating in word and deed that you believe in him or her

Apply It!

Encouraging statements build upon strengths and minimize errors. Encouraging statements focus on the activity, not the end result. Identify the following statements as either encouragement (E) or praise (P). If they are praise statements, turn them into encouragement:

1. You have taken a good deal of care with your handwriting. Now, work harder on your spelling. P/E

2. That's a difficult question, but I am sure you will figure out the answer. I'll give you a hint. P/E

3. You are the smartest science student I ever had. P/E

4. You are a terrific athlete. P/E

5. Your help giving out the papers was much appreciated. P/E

6. Today you raised your hand to answer questions most of the time. P/E

7. You are the greatest helper in the class. P/E

8. You worked quietly during language arts time today. P/E

9. Take another look at your computation to find a small error. P/E

10. Super duper job on that! P/E

(Answers: Encouragement 1, 2, 5, 6, 8, 9; Praise 3, 4, 7, 10)

Your encouraging words might include:

> Don't give up. I know you can figure it out.
> You have improved in . . .
> Let's try it together.
> You do a good job of . . .
> You can help me by . . .
> I'm sure you can straighten this out.

students slip up and call me mom in the classroom. I tell them that is all right because I love them all as if they are my own and consider it an honor.

Sandra Stiles
Sixth–Eighth Grade Reading Remediation
Sarasota, Florida

As seen on
http://www.LessonPlansPage.com

Just as encouragement is an alternative to praise, logical consequences are an alternative to punishment.

Whereas punishment is applied by an outsider and may be generic (miss recess, call to parent, visit to principal or dean), in the logical consequences approach (Dreikurs, 1998), the student experiences the natural or logical consequences of his or her

Apply It!

For each of these mini-case studies, speculate how teachers would use each of the approaches (behavior modification and logical consequences) to address the problem behavior:

Case 1 Susan doesn't complete any assignment and/or homework and doesn't seem to care very much. She dawdles and daydreams and feels no compunction to finish her work.

Case 2 John is relatively quiet, never raises his hand, and is mostly invisible and not motivated at all. He seems withdrawn and depressed at times but he doesn't really cause any disturbance.

Case 3 Liz is the class clown. She mugs and makes funny noises during instructional time.

Case 4 Sandy is the class bully, pushing and shoving in line and threatening to beat up students on the way home.

own behavior and the consequence is not generic. The consequence is always related to the offense. For example, a student who trashes her textbook needs to share with someone else until restitution is made. A student who is abusive to a classmate may have to write a letter of apology. A student who is disrespectful in the library is denied access to library books that week.

Logical consequences are always related to the offense, reasonable, and respectful.

A student who writes graffiti on the bathroom wall cleans it up during recess. A student who fights on the playground sits on the bench for a day or two. A student who spills the paint mops it up. Students are usually given the choice between stopping the misbehavior or accepting the logical consequence. Logical consequences are never humiliating, and they teach students about responsibility and the relationship between actions and consequences. Remember to use the phrase "make a better choice" before you try anything else.

To implement the strategy, follow these steps:

1. Make behavioral expectations clear.
2. Make clear the logical consequences of not meeting the behavioral expectations.
3. Base your relationship on trust and respect.
4. Identify misdirected behaviors and problem solve with the student.
5. Encourage students instead of always praising them.

Avoid It!

I recently compiled a list of penalties teachers use. Here are some of the most severe punishments:

I keep a cell phone on my desk and have the misbehaving kid call home on the spot.

I add or take away the letters that spell QUIET. If they are all erased, the class gets no free time.

I make the "bad kids" sit in the middle of the circle.

I saw my mentor teacher construct a faux dungeon complete with paper shackles.

Chapter **17**

What Are Some Causes of Misbehavior?

People's behavior makes sense if you think about it in terms of their goals, needs, and motives.

Thomas Mann,
German novelist and essayist

All human actions have one or more of these seven causes: chance, nature, compulsion, habit, reason, passion, and desire.

Aristotle

Effectiveness Essentials

- You can prevent discipline problems by looking for underlying causes and dealing with them.
- Disruptive behavior results from four misdirected goals.
- Look for root causes when students exhibit extreme behaviors or affect and get them help.

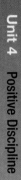

The best way to deal with discipline problems is to prevent them from happening in the first place. Marzano, Marzano, and Pickering (2003) analyzed more than 100 studies to identify five principles that underpin effective classroom management. These are rule setting; appropriate and timely disciplinary interventions; positive student–teacher relationships; a teacher's positive or "can do" mental set; and student cooperation in maintaining the positive learning environment. Classroom management is under your control. It is how you do business in your classroom, and the five principles Marzano and colleagues offer will make you an effective manager and prevent many of your discipline problems.

Not all discipline problems can be averted by effective classroom management, however. After you are sure that your classroom management is based on Marzano and colleagues' principles and you are still having difficulty with some of your students, it's time to look at the students and become a detective in addition to being a good manager.

Be Aware of Underlying Causes of Misbehavior

To prevent discipline problems, look for underlying causes of misbehavior and deal with them before they break out into more serious, attention-seeking behavior. Dreikurs and others (1998) tell us that all behavior is related to goals we are seeking. The primary goals we all seek are to belong and to feel significant. A misbehaving student is a discouraged student who, when thwarted from seeking these primary goals, substitutes four mistaken goals: attention, power, revenge, and assumed inadequacy.

You need to be a good detective and find the mistaken goal, so that students' behavior can be redirected (primarily through encouragement, mutual respect, and understanding) to return to the original goals. You have three clues to go on:

1. The recognition reflex. This is a student's smile that gives it away when you seek and get permission from the student to guess why he or she is behaving this way.
2. Your visceral reaction to the misbehavior. This is how the teacher feels when the behavior occurs.
3. What the student does when told to cease and desist.

Attention

Johnny is tapping his pencil and teacher says, "Please stop tapping your pencil." Johnny stops for a minute or two and starts humming. Janice tips back in her chair and rocks back and forth. The teacher, afraid she will tumble and hit her head, tells her to sit up straight and stop. She does and resumes in short order. Attention-getting behaviors say, "Look at me."

An attention-seeking student irritates or annoys you, and when told to stop, he or she ceases and then resumes or substitutes another attention-getting behavior. These behaviors are directed at the teacher or other classmates. Although they are not that serious, if they are not dealt with, they progress into more serious problem behaviors. Instead of asking the student to stop, try saying, "Could it be that you want to have my attention now?" or "Could it be that you are finished and want to move on to something else?" The student's smile will tell you that you hit the nail on the head.

Remedies include spending special time with the student; redirecting the behavior; ignoring the behavior; imposing a consequence that is related, respectful, and reasonable; and presenting choices to the student (Nelsen,

Apply It!

Try framing some choices for these behaviors. "Make a choice, either _____ or _____."

a. talking to neighbors
b. calling out
c. forgetting homework
d. getting out of seat and walking around
e. combing hair or sprucing up in class
f. coming to class late
g. engaging in name calling

2000). A now-retired kindergarten teacher was often heard to tell her block-throwing students, "Either you share and play nicely or you will have to leave the block center. Make a better choice," and they did. The language of making choices is key to teaching your students about being responsible for the decisions they make, both now and in the future.

Other terminology is "make a different choice," or "make a better choice." Or, "either you (fill in the expected behavior) _____ or (fill in the consequence) _____."

Ready to Launch

No Talking

Working Together
to Solve a Problem

Power

Lynn is defiant. "No one tells me what I can and cannot do. I don't have to play by the rules, not at home, not at school." This is the tug-of-war student who challenges your every directive. A power-seeking student intimidates you and, when told to stop, may passively resist or defy you even more. This is the "You can't make me" kind of misdirected goal. First, cool off and arrange a time to meet with the student. Remedies include withdrawing from the situation, cooling off first, problem solving with the student, redirecting the student's power needs, focusing on what you will do instead of what you will make the student do, and scheduling special time with the student (Nelsen, 2000).

Think of a student you encountered with a serious power issue. Write down a dialog for a conversation you might have had with him or her using the ten-step process in the Apply It! on page 167.

Revenge

Pat will get revenge on you for forcing him to back down in a confrontation. He has lost the battle but tries to win the war. He is saying to himself,

Apply It!

In a non-confrontational conversation, follow these ten steps:

1. Begin by telling the student all the positives you see (talents, skills).

2. Describe the negative behavior in question.

3. Seek verification from the student and accept no excuses. Just ask, "Is this happening?"

4. Encourage the student to list the "costs" of continuing the behavior. List them on paper.

5. Encourage the student to talk about the benefits of desisting. List them on paper.

6. Compare the two lists and discuss which list is more productive.

7. Brainstorm together what better choices the student could make.

8. Offer assistance to the student.

9. Sign a contract indicating what each of you will do to make the better choice a reality.

10. Revisit the issue after a week's time by asking, "How's it going? Have you fulfilled your part of the contract? Have I?" Revise the contract if need be.

Teacher Talks . . .

One student continued to misbehave during a lesson so I sent him to the back of the classroom to stand for a time-out. Unfortunately, the fire extinguisher was housed at the back of the classroom too. The student proceeded to pick up the fire extinguisher and spray it all around the classroom! The room was filled with white dust and sand. I immediately removed the class from the room so we could breathe. Needless to say, that was the last time I ever used time-out. I restructured my entire discipline plan.

Dion Clark
Former sixth grade teacher
High School Vice-Principal
San Bernardino, California

"I will have the last laugh." You may find your tires slashed in the parking lot or a nasty anonymous note on your desk. You may be accused of hitting, pinching, or even worse by the parents who unwittingly buy into the revenge scenario.

A revenge-seeking student hurts your feelings and, when asked to stop, is destructive or spiteful. Remedies include allowing a cooling-off period, engaging in problem solving with the student, giving encouragement, and scheduling special time with the student (Nelsen, 2000). The same ten steps can be followed for this student, although serious revenge takers might need to be seen by the principal or school counselor if they have caused serious damage, either verbally or to your property.

Assumed Inadequacy

I had a student whom I will call Alex. His response to every threat, every bribe, every entreaty, every punishment was, "I don't care." And he didn't. One day, three classes were watching a current film that was the culminating activity for a literature unit. I said, "Either you respect the other kids and watch the film silently or you will have to sit in the office." His response, "I don't care." "You don't care?" I asked. "No, I don't want to watch this film anyway." So I marched him to the office where he sat for the rest of the film.

I have often regretted how I handled it because I knew how much attention Alex craved, but like many decisions we make as teachers, it seemed like the best thing to do at the time. I couldn't let him disrupt the enjoyment of the other students. However, I knew that inside there was a boy craving attention that he had all but given up on receiving. I should have asked him to be a film critic who could report back to the class on how well the film followed the book.

A student whose goal is assumed inadequacy makes *you* feel inadequate because you don't know how to reach him or her. You can't break through the wall of seeming indifference or passivity. The student remains unre-

ceptive when confronted. Remedies include making success incremental, training the student in what to do, using encouragement, not giving up, and arranging for special time with the student (Nelsen, 2000).

Nelsen (2000) presents a very clear and concise discussion of the work of Dreikurs and of Glasser. You may want to read more about them either in Nelsen's interpreted version or in the original works listed at the end of the chapter.

This is but one framework for understanding your students' underlying motivation to misbehave. You need not accept it fully, but try in general to see things from the student's point of view. Ask yourself, "Why is the student doing this?" Make some good guesses. Instead of just meting out punishment, which works only in the short haul and may build up long-term resentment in students, stop and think about probable causes or motives. Your hypotheses may be incorrect some of the time, but there is a possibility that some of your theories may be tested out and even proven. You gain much more by canceling out a negative with a positive solution than by doubling the negativity by assessing an immediate penalty.

You need not be a fully certified counselor, but you could initiate a conversation with an observation and open question like, "You seem to be bothered (angry, sad, upset, concerned, distressed, etc.). Would you like to talk about it?" JUST LISTEN. You can reflect back the content and feelings articulated by the student and ask some probing questions. Be sure to let the student know that people are there to help, and if you feel you are in over your head, a referral to a school counselor is appropriate. Always speak respectfully.

Symptoms of More Serious Behaviors

The physical and emotional changes of teenagers present a particular challenge for those of you teaching at that level. Allow angry students to write about their feelings instead of taking them out on someone else. You may ask them to role-play and express the other person's point of view and vice versa. Use these techniques with all ages.

Some of the behaviors you might see have a basis in these hormone surges, but some of them are more serious. For more persistent or serious misbehaviors, you should immediately notify your counselor or administrator. You are not alone in dealing with serious behaviors. Your school counselor will be able to tell you if there is a behavior management plan in place, or she may provide information previously gathered on the student.

Check the discipline policy manual to see if the behavior is grounds for expulsion or suspension. This is important information to have at your fingertips, so all students can be held to the same account for these serious behaviors. Although the following list is far from complete, especially symptomatic behaviors to look for are:

- Anger
- Withdrawal
- Procrastination
- Lateness
- Bullying
- Defiance
- Clowning around
- Moodiness
- Abusive language
- Threats to do violence
- Threatening clothing and gang insignia
- Absences and excessive tardiness
- Signs of physical or mental abuse
- Depression
- Suicidal writings, comments, or drawings that depict suicide
- Violent drawings
- Any extreme changes in behavior
- Threats to other students
- Manic behavior

Watch It! video

Behavior Disorder
In this video clip, interventions are discussed for the difficult behavior of one student over the course of several grades. After watching the video clip, consider which mistaken goal is at work and what you might have done if you were "Nick's" teacher. This will give you an opportunity to contemplate the kind of interventions you would undertake in cases similar to this.

statistics

According to the National Center for Educational Statistics (2004):

- 1,922 children (ages 5–19) committed suicide away from school in the 2000 calendar year.

- In 2003, 21% of students (12–18) reported street gang activity in their schools.

- In 2003, 5% of students in grades 9–12 reported having at least one alcoholic drink and 6% reported using marijuana at school during the previous thirty days.

- In 2003, 29% of students in these same grades reported that someone had offered, sold, or given them an illegal drug on school property in the last year.

When you take the time to talk with your students, you may discover the root causes that underlie these symptoms and obvious manifestations. When these symptoms become apparent, confer with the appropriate resource person: principal, nurse, school counselor, social worker, school psychologist, or community worker. It is not unusual to find students in your class with serious attention-deficit/hyperactivity syndromes, students with a parent(s) who are in jail, homeless students, students living in group homes, students on probation, or students with a history of family violence and abuse. When you notice symptoms of these and other root causes, the best way to approach a student is to say, "I notice that you seem preoccupied (sad, angry, depressed, moody, etc.). Do you want to talk about it with me or with the counselor? We have support and resources here at school. We can help."

Avoid It!

Some discipline plans require that you assess penalties swiftly and immediately and "take no nonsense." I would caution you to look a bit more deeply before you act. Kids are like icebergs. You can't see what's underneath the surface without teacher sonar. You may be the one person who takes an interest and who can get to the bottom of the problem. A kind word, an understanding look, a nonjudgmental attitude just may unlock a closed door and make a difference in a student's life.

Avoid confrontations in front of the entire class. Conduct your discussions in private. You want to avoid having a student either lose face or strongly resist to show how tough he or she is in front of peers. Public humiliation is never an appropriate professional response.

Avoid going it alone. There are many resources at your site and at the district level to help you figure out appropriate interventions.

Chapter 18

How Can I Prevent Discipline Problems Before They Start?

Prevention is better than cure.

Proverb

No method nor discipline can supersede the necessity of being forever on the alert.

Henry David Thoreau
American poet, lecturer and essayist

Effectiveness Essentials

■ Good teaching and organized, efficient classroom management will help to solve or prevent many discipline problems.

■ Students learn best in a comfortable classroom environment.

■ Some causes of behavior disruptions are related to instruction.

■ Orderly procedures facilitate the smoother operation of all activities within the classroom.

■ Adhering to Kounin's principles of good teaching during instructional time can cut down on potential disruptions.

Good teaching and organized, efficient classroom management will help to solve or prevent many discipline problems from occurring in the first place. WHY? Because we all respond and react to the situation at hand, and the more you "control" the variables of instruction, including the physical arrangement of the classroom, the less likely it is that you will have to "control" or discipline the students. So, it's best to start with a look at the context in which problems arise. That is effective classroom management!

The Physical Environment

Students learn best in a comfortable classroom environment. Paying attention to these parameters may increase the likelihood that students will attend to their learning tasks with minimum distraction and disruption:

- A well-ventilated room
- Glare-free lighting
- Colorful and informative bulletin boards
- A clean and orderly room
- Private spaces for students to get away from it all
- Visibility from all areas of the room for you and the pupils
- Compatible seatmates
- A teaching style conducive to your furniture arrangement

Attractive Classrooms

Meeting Individual Differences

Some causes of behavior disruptions are related to instruction and you can do something about this by recognizing that for some students, the assignments are not consistent with their abilities. These include the inability to do the work, sheer boredom, lack of challenging assignments, and expectations that are too high. Counter these possibilities by recognizing each student's uniqueness. Unmet instructional needs may cause your students to engage in attention-getting behavior that undermines your classroom control. Here are some ideas for meeting instructional needs.

Differentiated Assignments

Make sure each student can succeed at the tasks you assign. This may necessitate rewriting some assignments, tape-recording assignments, or providing more challenging work for the advanced learner.

Grouping

Individual needs can also be met by grouping according to specific needs, abilities, and interests, when appropriate. Students with special needs should be seated with students who are considerate and willing to help out. This will be discussed further in Unit 6.

Choices and Decisions

Students' individual differences may also be met by providing choices whenever possible—in creative writing topics, in art assignments, in P.E. games, and in seating.

Realistic Expectations

One of the ways to determine if your expectations are too high or too low is to put yourself in your students' place. Make revisions whenever you have the sense that you wouldn't be able to complete the assignment if you were in the students' shoes.

Capitalizing on Interests

Finding out what motivates each student and gearing instruction around common interests will accomplish two goals. First, you will capture students' attention more easily, and, second, you will convey the message that you care about your

NOTES

Apply It!

At the beginning of the year, have your students tell you what's in and what's out in their popular culture. Prepare an inventory with fill-in items such as these:

Favorite pop music stars	What we are shopping for
Favorite county music stars	What we like as gifts
Favorite hip hop music stars	What we like to eat
Favorite movie stars	Favorite computer games
Favorite movies	Favorite electronic devices
Favorite books	Favorite spectator sport
Favorite television programs	Favorite store in town

students. Developing rapport with your students is easy if you are honest, sincere, and genuine with them. Conduct an interest inventory (see the Apply It! feature). Using current fads as themes in your instruction may just be the spark you need to keep students involved and out of trouble.

Planning

Thorough and well-formulated planning will help you cut down on potential disruptions. If your planning allows for every student to succeed, you are maximizing your chances for effective discipline. It is far better to underestimate your students' abilities during the first few days than it is to go over their heads. The worst thing that can happen is that they will feel successful!

Meaningful Activities

Plan worthwhile and meaningful activities to cut down on behavioral problems. Design motivating lessons that hook the students at the outset. Let your students know the purpose or objective of the lesson and point out which curriculum standards are being addressed. Use a variety of media and technology in your instruction and vary your teaching strategies. Plan a balance among individual work, cooperative learning in groups, and teacher-directed instruction in order to create

Engagement equals no time to misbehave

Chapter 18 How Can I Prevent Discipline Problems Before They Start?

variety and to maintain involvement and interest.

Procedures

Orderly procedures facilitate the smoother operation of all activities within the classroom. Make sure you have gone through the lesson in your mind as well as written it on paper so you can anticipate any skipped steps or procedures that potentially will sandbag your lesson. Make sure materials are at the ready. If you have to go back to a cabinet to get supplies, you will interrupt the flow and undermine your lesson.

Student Engagement

Engage your students and increase on-task behavior. Create a list of "things to do" for students who complete their work quickly. These activities must be rewarding in some way. Making more work the reward for early completion soon will lose its appeal. Students who are wise to your scheme will slow down and even avoid finishing in the allotted time.

"Sponge" Activities

Use "sponge" activities to reduce down time. It's hard to think on your feet if you have an extra few minutes after you complete a lesson. Sponge activities are so named because they absorb the extra few minutes. If you don't have something to keep students actively involved, they may create their own diversions, ones you may not approve of. Sponges should relate to your curriculum, call for oral responses, and require no preparation on your part. Whether you teach at elementary or secondary level, ready-made "sponge"

Classroom Management

A teacher demonstrates how active learning can reduce and prevent management problems. After viewing the clip, choose a teacher-directed lesson you have presented and turn it into an active learning lesson.

Student Says . . .

When my teacher gets upset at the class, she yells, "be quiet" and does not say anything until everyone stops talking.

Adam
Age 8, Third Grade
Lexington, North Carolina

172

activities can serve as good concept reviews, or even non-graded quizzes. Make a "quiz show" out of the sponge activities. Some ideas for sponges are listed below:

- Name things that come in pairs
- List one country for each letter of the alphabet
- Name things that fly
- Name solid geometry figures
- Name characters in Romeo and Juliet
- Name the constellations
- Name rights guaranteed in the Bill of Rights
- Name the impressionists
- Name the Greek/Roman gods and goddesses
- Name the states in alphabetical order
- Name presidents in chronological order

Apply It!

Given your grade level or subject matter, list at least ten sponge ideas you could use to soak up extra time.

Things to Do When You Are Finished

Instruction

During instructional time, you can cut down on potential disruptions by adhering to principles of good teaching. Although good instruction cannot guarantee good discipline at all times, you can reduce potential problems by considering the possibility that a strong link exists between the two. It is even more important to minimize disruptions through effective classroom management or preventive discipline in middle and high school when the periods are so short. Time is of the essence in all grades, but in secondary school you don't want to spend the whole period settling the class down or trying to get their attention. In *Discipline and Group Management in Classrooms*, Jacob Kounin (1977) identified the following principles of good instruction.

Students Focus Before a Lesson Starts

Focus Attention

Before beginning any lesson, make sure the students are looking at you and that you have everyone's undivided attention. If you begin while students are talking or inattentive, the situation can only get worse. Keeping the group alerted involves encouraging individual and unison responses and not calling on someone before you ask the questions; otherwise, the other 32 will tune out. Calling on students randomly with name sticks or a deck of individualized cards is one way of keeping them on their toes.

Over-dwelling

Make sure that lessons proceed at a steady clip. If you allow yourself to be distracted or slowed down, the delays will enable minor disruptions to erupt like mini-wildfires. Be careful of *over-dwelling* and *fragmentation*. A teacher engaging in over-dwelling is spending too much time on directions, irrelevant details, or the physical props of the lesson. A teacher engaged in fragmentation divides the lesson into too many unnecessary steps or procedures or has each student do something individually when a group or the entire class could do it more efficiently all at once.

Withitness

Observe and be alert during all presentations. Kounin (1977) invented the term *withitness* to describe teachers who have eyes in the back of their heads. Maintain eye contact with each student and move around the room. Pretend you are a bat hovering over the room with everyone under your wing. Students of all ages are less likely to act out when they feel they are in direct contact with you.

Teacher Talks . . .

My students in high school English classes would always notice when I changed the color of my nail polish and similar details of my dress and accessories. However, in order to focus their attention on the subject matter I often had to resort to dropping the metal wastebasket from the height of my desk.

Dottie Bailey
Speech and English Teacher
Colton, California

Students often feel teachers have eyes in the back of their heads. . . . Sometimes they need to!

Variety and Group Alerting

Vary the lesson formats, the group size, the media, and the materials. To keep everyone involved, ask stimulating and sometimes unpredictable questions. Use "every pupil response" techniques whenever possible, as these allow everyone to be involved in responding at the same time. They enable you to diagnose on the spot who understands the lesson and who doesn't, saving you hours of grading written work. Engage students by asking them to:

Say it aloud

Use a finger signal (thumbs up or down, for example)

Display responses on individual sets of flash cards, chalkboards, or white boards

Respond when their names are pulled from a bundle of ice cream sticks or a deck of cards

Overlappingness

Practice multi-tasking or "overlappingness." Kounin's (1977) term *overlappingness,* a key to effective classroom management, refers to a teacher's ability to handle two or more things at the same time. An example would be walking over to a student who is tapping his or her pencil while still conducting the lesson, or checking a paper while working with a small math group and not missing a beat.

Smooth Transitions

Avoid *dangles, flip-flops, thrusts,* and *truncations. Dangles* and *flip-flops* occur when the teacher leaves one activity dangling or hanging, goes on to another, and returns once again to the initial activity. *Thrusts* occur when a teacher barrels into an activity without attention to pupil readiness. *Truncations* occur when a teacher aborts an activity and never returns to it. These erratic instructional shifts baffle students, and when students are confused, they may turn off and amuse themselves in inappropriate ways.

Know When to Stop

Terminate lessons that have gone on too long. Know when your students have reached their saturation point, and attempt to bring closure to the lesson before that time. Always leave students asking for more.

Check for Understanding

Before dismissing a group after a teacher-directed activity, make sure your students know what to do next. This can be accomplished by asking someone to summarize both the lesson's content and the directions for seatwork or follow-up. Always ask if anyone has any questions about what to do next. Do not give in to students who persist in asking interminable questions after you have answered them time and time again. Just tell them to "pretend" they know the answer. They will probably quit stalling and get to work. It's also helpful to model concentrating on a task by writing a letter to a friend during their writing assignment or reading silently a book of your choice while they are reading.

Emotional Objectivity

Emotional objectivity, along with "withitness," according to Marzano (2003), is a key construct of an effective classroom management plan. Emotional objectivity requires that no matter how upset you may be with a student, you continue to interact in a business-like manner. If you are perceived as overreacting or biased, the offender will blame you for being "prejudiced" or "making a big deal out of nothing" instead of taking responsibility. When assessing a penalty or consequence, you need to be firm and clear without apologizing to or feeling sorry for the student. Focus on the behavior and the causes instead of personalizing the behavior as an attack on you, identifying with the student, or seeing the fault as your own. Anticipate which students might act out and then purposely talk yourself into positive expectations for the day or period.

Avoid It!

During the first weeks of school, do not worry about how much you are teaching; rather, focus on preventive discipline and classroom management. The instruction will come soon enough in a well-managed classroom.

Teacher Talks . . .

Classroom management starts with discipline. To discipline, you have to show that you care about the child. You must discipline with love. Be tough. Stick to your classroom rules. Model these rules. If a rule is broken, there must be consequences. Apply the appropriate consequences. Always discipline with a hug afterward. Look the child in the eyes and tell him that you care about him. Make sure he knows that you still care about him; you were just disappointed in his behavior. You are tough on him because you care. You will always care about him. That is discipline with love. A classroom cannot function without it.

Laurel Garner
Fifth Grade
Chattahoochee Elementary School
Duluth, Georgia

As seen on
http://www.LessonPlansPage.com

If I want to be

great I have to

win the victory

over myself . . .

self-discipline.

President Harry S. Truman

Chapter 19

What Teacher Behaviors Lead to a Positive Classroom Climate?

Effectiveness Essentials

- Establish a warm, calming, neat classroom climate.

- There are many ways to create a positive classroom climate.

- Model respect in order to establish a democratic classroom community.

- Show that you respect all students and value diversity through everything you do in the classroom.

The tone you set for your class is often referred to as "climate." No matter where you live, try to establish a climate more like Florida in February and less like Chicago. The most attractive, well-designed room will lose its attraction if an icy, frozen, and rigid climate prevails. Establishing a warm, calming, neat classroom climate comes naturally to most teachers. Conveying a positive and enthusiastic attitude toward your students may alleviate many behavior problems before they begin (Marzano, 2003). Marzano and colleagues cite teacher–student relationships as key to effective classroom management. This means that teachers should have equal parts of dominance (leading and in control of the class) and cooperation (willingness to take a personal interest in students and in the class as a whole).

A Baker's Dozen: Thirteen Ways to Create a Positive Classroom Climate

Think about how you greet dinner guests at your home. You meet and greet everyone, show them around, and make sure they are comfortable. You circulate among your guests and make introductions so that no one feels left out. On a less personal level, you want to make your students feel welcome in the shared space of the classroom. There are many ways to establish a warm, welcoming classroom climate.

1. Smile when appropriate.

When I started teaching, there were no discipline gurus to rely on and barely any guidebooks on discipline. The

Which teacher is more open to students?

Teacher Talks . . .

Have clear, simple and concise rules. Limit to 2 to 5 in your room. I chose (1) Be respectful; (2) Follow school rules; (3) Do your best work; (4) No food or drinks. They are somewhat positive and broad enough to encompass my needs in the classroom. I also verbally go over the definitions with the students and constantly review them. I send home a syllabus to be signed by the parents which includes a little more detail of the rules that are posted in my room and my contact information if they have any questions.

*Barbara Arient
Grades 9–12
Special Education, Moderate/Severe
San Bernardino, California*

conventional wisdom was "Don't smile until Christmas." The notion of the stern-faced schoolmarm of the nineteenth century prevailed. Students were to be intimidated by a stern manner. Think back on your own experiences in school. Were there teachers you were afraid of because of their dour demeanors?

More importantly, did you ever take advantage of teachers just because they had pleasant looks on their faces? The answer is probably, no. Smiling when you greet your students tells them you are glad to see them. Adopt a business-like, yet friendly demeanor, the middle ground between the back-slapping, chummy teacher and the stern, prune-face one.

2. Move around the classroom in physical proximity to all students.

University students typically take seats in the back of the room, far from me. Pity the poor latecomers who have to be up close and personal to the teacher. However, your students are usually not in the back by choice, and you need to make proximity a conscious effort. Most teachers talk to and walk to the middle of the class and across the front. Be

aware that the students in the back need closeness to you as well. Keep moving around the room as much as possible.

I was observing a student teacher read a story to her kindergarten class and could see the big picture. It was quite entertaining from my vantage point in the back, watching the kindergarteners in the back row who couldn't see and couldn't be seen by the student teacher. Some were conducting beauty parlor, braiding one another's hair. Others were making faces or lying down. They couldn't see the action, so they made some of their own. They were quite surprised and embarrassed when they turned around and saw me watching them. They shaped up immediately. The student teacher could have

Move to All Sections of the Classroom

walked around with the book or alternatively had the first row of students sitting directly on the rug, the next row kneeling above them, and the third row standing so everyone could see.

3. Maintain an open body posture.

Would you rather approach a principal who has her arms folded in front of her chest or one who extends a hand and greets you? Would you feel better about debriefing your lesson with a supervisor who sits across from you or next to you? These are two examples of opposite positions regarding body language. Whole books have been written about body language and nonverbal messages the body conveys. Be more aware of yours so that students and

Closed Body Posture

What Messages Do These Two Postures Send?

Open Body Posture

Teacher Talks . . .

I once read that the way to make friends and keep them is to say something genuinely kind each day. It takes time to develop the habit. It sounds corny to say, "I love your shoes, I wish I could wear them!" But, you'd never expect the grin you get from a comment like that. I try to focus on their work. And when a student takes pride in her work, it fosters intrinsic goals to continue working well.

Kris Ungerer
Kindergarten
Riverside, California

parents perceive you as open rather than self-protective. Come out from behind your desk. Walk among your students with your hands at your side instead of folded in front of you. Sit next to your students when you are counseling them, not across from them.

4. Listen attentively to what students say.

With 30-plus students, it is hard to find time to listen to their personal stories, especially when they are tugging on your sleeve, saying, "Teacher, teacher." But you want to let them know that you are interested in them. Some ways you can include personal sharing during the school day might include having students sign up to tell you personal stories, maybe five minutes total per day. Or, you might allow students in middle and high school to share news at the beginning of the period. Display

a suggestion box and encourage students to recommend alternative procedures or assignment options. Beware! Young students like to tattle on classmates and you don't have the time to referee all the squabbles. Instead, have them write out their grievances and deposit them in a "tattle tales" mailbox made from a shoebox (see Figure 19.1).

5. Share appropriate personal stories about yourself or your experiences.

I always participate in introductions the first day of class. Students often come up to me to share pictures of their horses when they find out I have two of my own. I award a small prize to the first student who guesses where I was born, not too difficult as I maintain my Brooklyn accent. I share my teaching mishaps and successes throughout the years. I have also asked

Figure 19.1
Cardboard Mailbox
Labeled *Tattle Tales*
and *Suggestion Box*

students to make some reasonable guesses about me (my family, house, pets, interests, hobbies, genre of books I read, music tastes, etc.), and at the end of the day I tell them which ones were accurate. This would be a fun activity for middle and high school students as well. In the younger grades, I avoid the guessing game and directly tell something about myself and my family, pets, hobbies, etc.

Apply It!

Think about what you will tell your students about yourself. Will you use any props such as photos or other objects? Will you make it into a guessing game?

6. Say something complimentary to each student each day.

Compliments are key to a positive classroom climate. You can give compliments during every exit from and entrance into the classroom. You can give compliments as you walk around the room. You can make a "compliment tree," a multi-branched

Star of the Week

Teacher Talks . . .

Besides knowing the subject matter really well, a good teacher must give his students the confidence to succeed. Praising your students goes a long way in giving them confidence and the feeling of wanting to learn. If a student did not do well on a particular day, I could always find something to praise. It could be something like, "That's a nice sweater" or "Your haircut looks very nice," etc. Naturally, a good teacher should have good discipline in his or her class. The discipline should be firm but fair.

Gordon MacDonald
High School Band Teacher
Montvale, New Jersey

Apply It!

Recall that in Chapter 13 I suggested using sticks or a deck of playing cards to help you call on all students. Use these sticks or cards to call on students for end of the day or period compliments. Mark each student's name on a card or a stick. Each day, distribute the cards or sticks randomly. Start with the first student who says, "I want to compliment _____ for _____." The compliments should be a strong point or a positive attribute. Each student gives and gets one compliment. Collect the cards or sticks and distribute them randomly each day. This is an effective way of alerting students to others' strengths.

dead tree limb secured in a planter from which students hang paper apples with written compliments for or from their peers.

Some teachers have a *Student of the Week* bulletin board. I would recommend a bulletin board divided into fourths so students don't have to wait so long for their turn. Their digital photo is posted along with special objects, awards, certificates, etc. The class gets to compliment the student of the week while the teacher writes down the comments. The comments are posted as well.

A teacher of students with special needs was concerned that his students found it difficult to be positive toward one another, so he devised a clever plan. He decorated soup cans with colorful sleeves, one for each of his ten students. At the end of the day, each student was given nine tokens to distribute in the cans of those students who had been nice or with whom they had gotten along during the day. The tokens were tallied at the end of the week, and the top five MVPs (most valued people) got to use the limited number of study carrels for the following week. Within weeks, his students were able to see the glimmerings of "what goes around comes around" and their behavior improved.

A Classroom Meeting

7. Conduct classroom meetings.

Consider conducting morning meetings in a circle to give the class or homeroom a sense of belonging and cohesiveness. In some desk arrangements, this may be difficult, but the students can at least move their chairs so that everyone can see everyone else or sit on their desks for the meeting. The topics might be current events, sharing, plans for the day, organizing an event, the latest school buzz, compliment time, or story time or show-and-tell for young ones.

8. Use teaching strategies and seating arrangements to create a sense of belonging.

Cooperative learning strategies will break down isolation in a classroom and encourage a group identity. If students are also seated in table groups, they will have a "home base." Naming the groups will also encourage a group feeling. The names can reflect the curriculum, e.g., planets, Native American tribes, rainforest animals, famous artists, etc.

Teacher Talks . . .

When sharing stories about what we did over the weekend, a first grader said his family took their horse to another house to get bred. Then, with a very serious and somewhat confused look on his face, he continued, "I guess there is some sort of bread that, when a horse eats it, it makes them have babies." It was all I could do not to laugh out loud. I clenched my teeth and moved on to the next student. As she was sharing her story about going to her grandmother's or something, there were many perplexed looks on the other little faces around the room. I have a feeling there were some interesting dinner table conversations that night.

Jason Paytas
Former First Grade and now Fourth Grade Teacher
Arcata, California

183

Student Says . . .

My perspective of a good teacher is one with lots of enthusiasm and lots of energy for learning, keeping us kids excited and being there for us when we need help. I think it's important for teachers to accept the way we are as individuals and treat us all equally.

Kira
Age 11,
Sixth Grade
Arcata, California

9. Allow students choices.

You can encourage a warm classroom community feeling by letting students make simple choices that are important to them but inconsequential to you, such as which of two songs to sing, which game to play during physical education, or which poem to read aloud. It is important that students feel their opinions are valued and validated.

10. Call each student by name.

Your name defines you, and it is important that you call on your students using their names. This should be easy if you are using the sticks and card method described in Chapter 13. Your seating chart will cue you into student names in middle and high schools. Monitor how often you call on students by making ticks on your seating chart, ensuring that your questions are evenly distributed.

11. Include self-concept activities as part of your everyday program.

Take some time to include self-concept activities in your day. Many are subject-matter-oriented, such as personal time-lines for math, self-portraits for art, or writing an ad for yourself for language arts. Or, use a story starter or sentence stem each period or day for journal writing such as:

> My proudest moment . . .
> The greatest gift I ever received . . .
> Wishes for my life . . .
> The happiest time of my life . . .
> My biggest strength . . .

12. Play calming background music.

Playing calming music such as New Age or classical music as students enter the room will calm them down and create a soothing environment for learning. Some say this activates the brain. Some teachers use room freshener to activate the senses as well.

13. Display interesting artifacts and student work around the room.

In addition to displaying student work and projects, think of ways to make your room more visually appealing and homelike. Some teachers hang curtains. Some have plants or a fish tank. Others purchase exotic items from discount stores, museum shops, or flea markets. You may have items around your house, from your travels, or from import stores that are visually appropriate for classroom life. Change these around from time to time.

Artifacts Spark Student Interest

Respect and Responsibility

Modeling respect in your classroom is the most important thing you can do to establish a classroom community based on democratic values. How does the teacher model respect? The students will be watching your every word and deed. So . . .

1. Aspire to rate high on the "fairness" quotient.
2. Treat everyone as equally as you can.
3. Deal with confrontations privately.
4. Respect students' private spaces.
5. Show respect for all students and value diversity through the pictures on your walls, the books you choose to read, and the lessons you plan.
6. Give the student(s) an opportunity to make things right before you resort to punishment.

Classroom Meetings

In democratic classrooms, students are encouraged to monitor and enforce the rules. Marzano (2003) cites students' responsibility for classroom management as one of his five research-based constructs of effective classroom management. The classroom meeting has many purposes, e.g., planning together, talking about current issues, and discussing curriculum topics. But it is also a key channel for optimizing student involvement in and responsibility for classroom management. William Glasser (1975, 1998), the originator of the classroom meeting, believes that students can

Teaching Respect

A teacher uses *The Rainbow Fish* (1992) to teach students how to respect one another by sharing. After viewing the clip, how does the teacher model respect for her students? What developmentally appropriate activity can you devise to teach the concept of sharing to older students?

Social Skills

A conflict resolution team solves problems on the playground. After viewing the clip, what is the teacher's role and what skills do the students model? What are the four rules that are key to conflict management?

control themselves if their needs for survival, approval, love, power, fun, and freedom are met. Survival needs are up to the family and society, but the other needs can be met in the classroom setting when you lighten up, have some fun, provide love and approval, and enable students to have a say in how things are run.

The teacher's role is to help students make positive choices, and one vehicle for this is the classroom meeting. Jane Nelsen (2000) has simplified Glasser's work on the classroom meeting by suggesting that entire class or individual conflicts be handled in class meetings, and the initiator can be the teacher or the students. Everyone sits in a tight circle, and although it is the teacher's role to facilitate the discussion, it is the students' role to make the value judgments and analyze the costs and benefits of continuing or desisting. Students brainstorm and evaluate the effectiveness of the proposed solutions to right the wrong, and after a solution is agreed upon, everyone commits to it. It is the act of problem solving itself that is important, not the efficacy of any one solution.

In secondary school, the classroom meeting is even more effective because

Apply It!

Post a sign like this: *The 3 R's— Respect, Responsibility, Reliability.* Discuss what each would look like when practiced. Then divide your class into six groups. Two groups write a list of ten behaviors that show respect, two groups do the same for responsibility, and two groups tackle the concept of reliability. Share with the whole class after the groups complete their work.

teenagers are capable of abstract thinking and can better analyze and evaluate solutions. Then again, during classroom meetings, middle and high school students are more likely to be intolerant and forceful in their opinions. Because the classroom meeting is an age-appropriate forum for them to practice analytical and critical thinking skills, you will have to make a concerted effort to have them listen to one another. Use an egg timer to allow each one to have his or her say and then relinquish the soapbox. You will have to choose the issues care-

Simplified Steps for a Classroom Meeting

1. Compliment circle or some positive activity to heighten class cohesion.
2. Expose the problem.
3. Seek verification that the problem exists.
   a. No excuses
   b. No blame
   c. No individuals singled out
4. Discuss the costs of continuing in the behavior.
5. Discuss the benefits of desisting.
6. Make a value judgment about whether the costs outweigh the benefits.
7. Ask students to offer solutions and evaluate them.
8. Set the course of action and ask students to commit (often in writing) to follow it.
9. Have a follow-up meeting to assess the effectiveness of the solution.
10. Recycle the steps if necessary.

fully, given the time constraints. Most one-issue meetings can be compressed into 20 to 30 minutes.

You can be a hero to your students whether they tell you or not. The highest compliment you will receive may be, "I want to be a teacher when I grow up." It won't be because you taught the causes of the Civil War or because you taught them two-digit division. It will be because you sent them forward as confident, positive, secure, respectful, and competent citizens in our diverse nation.

Avoid It!

Having a bad day is not an option for teachers. Leave your problems at home. Your students will expect some consistency in your mood and the way you respond to them. Students require some stability in the teacher–student relationship and if you are grouchy one day and happy the next, your reliability is at risk and you may lose their trust.

When a teacher

calls a boy by his

entire name it

means trouble.

Mark Twain

Chapter **20**

What Are Some Nonverbal Strategies to Maintain Order and Some Responses to Avoid?

Effectiveness Essentials

- You can deal with minor infractions and distractions nonverbally without disrupting the entire class or instructional sequence.

- Effective nonverbal body language consists of teacher gestures, body posture, facial expressions, eye contact, and proximity control.

- Dealing with every minor infraction takes away from valuable instructional time.

- Students from generational poverty may have different ways of interpreting events.

- Serious acts need to be treated differently from rule-breaking behaviors.

- Deal with serious discipline problems without overreacting when provoked.

- Avoid becoming obsessed with classroom discipline to the exclusion of instruction.

Nonverbal and Low-Key Interventions

You can deal with minor infractions and distractions nonverbally without disrupting the entire class or instructional sequence. Effective nonverbal body language consists of teacher gestures, body posture, facial expressions, eye contact, and proximity. The ten suggestions that follow have no money-back guarantee that all misbehaviors can be handled without sacrificing instructional time. But try them first before resorting to harsher penalties or consequences.

Sign Language

Students can learn some simple signs in American Sign Language (ASL) to alert you to a need, and you can use signs to convey nonverbal messages without disturbing the class. Also, when students use this valuable communication tool, they may develop an interest in acquiring more signs. See Apply It! for ways to access ASL online or scan the library's catalog.

The Look

Establishing eye contact with the offender and staring until the behavior diminishes works for some teachers. Jones (1992, 2000) advocates this practice, along with other nonverbal interventions. Remember that cultural norms may disallow the student from looking directly back at you.

Physical Proximity

Walking toward the offender will usually stop the behavior. You may need to move closer to the student and stand nearby. The increasing invasion of the student's space will usually

Teacher Talks . . .

Years ago I had to learn some American sign language including the alphabet, because I was temporarily assigned a partially deaf student. Since then I've incorporated the use of some sign language to quietly communicate back and forth with my students, thus not disturbing the whole class. We communicate things like water, bathroom, recess time, lunchtime, concentrate/focus read, write, sit down, etc. The students seem to enjoy learning the alphabet and other signs.

Gabe Aguilar
Sixth Grade
San Bernardino, California

Apply It!

Go to a website such as http://www.masterstech-home.com/ASLDict.html, or any dictionary of basic ASL terms and access signs for bathroom, water, quiet, and sit down. See Figure 20.1. I accessed the sign for water simply by clicking on images in http://www.google.com and typing in "American Sign Language Water." Access these terms and five others you may need in your classroom.

Figure 20.1
Sign for Water

Figure 20.2
Signal

cause him or her to desist. A hand on the desk as you pass is also effective, if moving to the edge of the desk hasn't achieved the desired outcome. You may want to learn more about nonverbal limit setting by reading the work of Jones (1992, 2000). Jones uses nonverbal body language, incentives, and individual help to motivate on-task behavior and stop off-task behaviors such as talking and general goofing around. The end result is more time-on-task and, thus, more teaching and learning time. Here are some examples:

Jack and Steve are talking during a lesson. The teacher can

1. Make eye contact and let them know they are being watched.
2. Give a shake of the head while maintaining eye contact.
3. Hold up a hand, palm outward, signaling stop.
4. Move toward the offenders.
5. Stand next to the offenders.
6. Put hand on desk of offenders.
7. Look right at them and glare.

Jones also believes in incentive or reward systems that include group and individual rewards, and free time that is earned for favorite activities. A stopwatch is employed to gauge on-task versus nonproductive work. Students earn minutes for on-task behavior or lose minutes for preferred activity time (P.A.T.). It takes teacher commitment to use the stopwatch technique consistently. Jones advocates quick and efficient individual help when students are stuck.

Signals

Signals can be established ahead of time with individuals. A finger to your cheek tells John you see what he is doing and want him to stop. This helps John save face, because the pre-established signal is private. Signals that work in general are a shake of the head, the raising of the eyebrows, a quick arc of the finger.

Enlisting Cooperation

You can nip the misbehavior in the bud by enlisting the student's aid for some small task relevant to the lesson. You might ask the culprit to erase the board or pass out materials. Whatever the job, both you and the offender will know why he or she has been chosen, and you still won't miss a beat in your instruction.

Questioning

Posing a question to the student who has just started to act out can redirect his or her attention to the task. Make sure it is a question that can be answered easily, as your goal is not to embarrass the student but to channel his or her attention in a productive way. If you feel the student cannot answer the question, have him or her select someone whose hand is raised to supply the answer.

The Encouraging Moment

When you observe a potential offender doing something right or trying to do the right thing, offer praise. You are better off waiting for the moment when you get your chance to turn a student in the direction of success. Strike when the iron is hot and encourage your student.

"See Me" Cards

You can duplicate cards that you can unobtrusively place on a student's desk that say something equivalent to "See Me." You may also have a place for students to write in why they think they received the card and what a better choice would have been. (See Figure 20.3.)

Delayed Reaction

Rather than interrupt the flow of instruction, simply and firmly tell the student in question that you wish to speak to him or her at the end of the lesson. This invitation to a private conference, only one sentence in length, may cause the student to shape up, negating the need for a long conference. The delayed reaction also gives you a

Figure 20.3
See Me Card

See Me Card

Why?

_____

_____

_____

A better choice would have been

_____

_____

_____

Name _____
Date _____

Student Helps Teacher

chance to cool off and consider an appropriate response. Nelsen (2000) suggests that this cooling off is most important when you are angry or frustrated and are likely to exacerbate the situation by responding in kind to the student's discouraged behavior.

Role Playing or Letter Writing

When there is a dispute, it's often useful for students to write out their angry feelings or express their point of view on paper. In the case of the upset student, writing it out is a more positive way of diminishing strong feelings. In a dispute, the two students can exchange their papers and read each other's description of the events leading up to the altercation. Sometimes I have put the two students on opposite sides of me and ask each to tell what happened from the other's point of view. This helps them to understand, if not empathize, with the other student and thus ameliorate the conflict.

Social Class Determines Reactions

Based on her research, Ruby Payne (2005) suggests there are hidden rules that govern what students experience at school and how they react to discipline. Students from generational (inherited) poverty, the middle class, and wealthy classes interpret events differently when it comes to behavior and consequences. The driving forces that motivate decision making for individuals of each group differ considerably and influence their responses. Table 20.1 delineates these differences and provides an

Table 20.1 How Social Class Determines Reactions

Socioeconomic Class	Driving Forces	Response to Conflict
Generational Poverty	survival, relationships, and entertainment	physical fighting
Middle Class	work and achievement	verbal aggression
Wealthy	social, financial, and political connections	social inclusion or exclusion or by legal means

example of each group's perspective on something; in this example, resolving a conflict.

Before you can change the behaviors, it is important first to understand the hidden rules and help students understand that they may have to adopt different rules or adapt their behaviors to survive in work environments where other rules apply.

Beyond Rule Breaking: Crossing the Line

Serious acts need to be treated differently from rule-breaking behaviors or the manifestations of mistaken or misdirected goals. The most serious, unlawful offenses need to be dealt with swiftly according to your district's policy that derives from your state education code or laws governing education.

It is possible that one or more of your students will be suspended or expelled from school because they have crossed the line. As you read the offenses that are grounds for suspension in the "Classrooms Artifacts" feature in Chapter 16, you may have been surprised that such a listing exists and is necessary at all. It is best to know what may be considered grounds for suspension.

Many schools use a referral process. In middle and high school, since you only see the "culprit" for one or two periods, it is hard to follow up. Before you encounter your first severe behavior problem, find out what the policy is for serious infractions in your middle or high school and the steps you must take.

Students in middle and high school may take their offenses to a higher level. Behaviors that should concern you include fighting, name-calling, stealing, cheating, plagiarism, destruction of property, constant defiance, bullying, refusal to work, profane language, and threats of violence, among others. There are no tried-and-true recipes for dealing with these behaviors either, but certain general principles obtain:

1. Except when students are in danger, it is best to deal with serious infractions when you are calmer and better able to act in a rational manner.

2. Keep detailed records (anecdotal) of the student's behavior with dates, descriptions of behavior, and your response. Detailed anecdotal records will be helpful when discussing the problem and seeking solutions with school personnel or with parents.

Teacher Talks . . .

Being in a foul mood one day, I sent four kids to the principal for minor infractions. After school I was called in and given valuable guidance. When you send a student out of the room you are seen as having less power. Not sending students to the office also keeps principals happy because you are not lining their office with students. On average I send only 1 student to the office per year, and then, it's only one time; sometimes I don't send any at all. Try to bring the student that's bothering you the most, closest to you. Your proximity often times brings the student in line.

Kris Ungerer
Fifth Grade
San Bernardino, California
Currently Kindergarten
Riverside, California

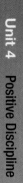

Parent-Teacher
Conference

3. When you suspect that a student will persist in the inappropriate behavior, ask for help early on. By using resource persons available to you at the school or district level, you are demonstrating that you are resourceful, not incapable. Most schools have a Student Study Team (SST), which is a group of professionals who work to solve behavioral and other problems. These teams generally are composed of the school psychologist, special education resource teachers, classroom teachers, and the principal. It's best to devise some long-range plans or strategies by enlisting the aid of the SST, your principal, school or district psychologist, counselor, special education resource teacher, and the student's parents.

4. Other, more experienced teachers can help as well, especially those who have encountered the student in earlier grades.

Parent/Guardian Conferences

After speaking with the principal and the school or district counselor, enlist the aid of your student's parents or guardians. It is important for you to regard the conference or any contact with parents as a two-way communication channel. You have certain information and they have certain information. Adding your experience at school to the parents'/guardians' experience at home makes shared problem solving possible. That should be your message to parents.

Make your first contacts by phone, and if you need to, initiate a conference. Use an interpreter as needed and make sure one is available during the conference. The parents/guardians should already have a great deal of information from your prior contacts. During the conference follow these six steps:

1. Make the parents or guardians comfortable. Say something positive about their son/daughter.

2. Describe the inappropriate behavior, using anecdotal data. Watch for overreactions by the parents or guardians and head them off.

3. Stress to the parents or guardians that their son/daughter is capable of behaving and has many positive attributes despite his or her negative behavior.

4. Elicit data from parents' or guardians' insights about their son's/daughter's attitude toward school, the student's behavior at home, how inappropriate behavior is dealt with at home, and what the parents or guardians see as possible causes of misbehavior at school.

5. Devise a plan together that is grounded in encouragement and logical consequences and does not run counter to cultural norms.

6. Follow up and inform parents or guardians about their son's/daughter's progress.

Responses to Avoid

The hardest part of dealing with discipline problems of the more serious kind is repressing some of the very human responses that serious offenses provoke. If there is ever a time to put on your angel's wings and sit under a halo, it's when a serious offense occurs in your classroom. A calm, cool manner on the part of the teacher will not only disarm the offender but also soothe the other students, who may be as upset as you are. What follows are various responses to avoid. Experienced teachers know that it is impossible to avoid all of them. But they try.

Holding a Grudge

When the behavior has been dealt with, try to wipe the slate clean and forgive and forget. Begin each day anew. As one teacher phrased it, "Never let the sun go down on your anger."

Taking It Personally

Separate yourself from the situation and realize that the behavior is symptomatic of some disturbance within your student and doesn't necessarily reflect his or her attitude toward you. This may require that you schedule frequent pep talks with yourself.

Everyone Suffers

It simply isn't fair to apply consequences to the entire class because a few of your charges are misbehaving. Discriminate between the offenders and the nonoffenders and go on with business as usual.

Ejection from the Room/Time Out

It is illegal in many districts to place your students outside the room unsupervised. Even if it is not, it is still not a good solution. Students will simply fool around in the halls or on the playground. You can be sure they won't stay where you put them. Avoid sending them to another classroom or to the principal except in rare instances. Not only does this burden the other teachers and the principal, but also if you exercise this option too frequently, your actions may send a message to your class and to your

statistics

According to the MetLife Survey of the American Teacher: Transitions and the Role of Supportive Relationships (2004–2005), 68% of students considered the statement "My school only contacts parents when there is a problem with their child" to be "mostly true."

"Thinking Chair"

administrator that you cannot deal with misbehavior. Try to tough it out and deal with problems in your own classroom. Use a "thinking chair" for the young set and an isolated study carrel for older students.

Physical Contact

Corporal punishment is defined as punishment upon the body, and it is banned in many states. Although you may be driven to distraction, never grab, pinch, or hit your students. They will magnify some of the slightest restraining techniques, and you need to protect yourself from irate parents and even a lawsuit. Also, you don't want to model a physical response to the rest of the class, as you are hoping to extinguish this kind of behavior in them.

Equally, in this day and age, a harmless touch, hand on the shoulder, pat on the back, hug, or any other positive physical contact may result in claims of sexual harassment. You have to be aware of the consequences of touching a student, no matter how harmless the intent.

Humiliation

Included in this category of don'ts is sarcasm, nagging, requiring the wear-

> I will not talk in class. I will not talk in class. I will not talk in class. I will not talk in class. I will not talk in class. I will not talk in class. I will not talk in class. I will not talk in class. I will not talk in class. I will not talk in class. I will not talk in class. I will not talk in class. I will not talk in class. I will not talk in class. I will not talk in class.

ing of a dunce hat, having the student stand in a corner, or imposing other public embarrassment. Your students need to save face, and if you can talk with the offender privately, you are denying him or her an audience for further defiance or face-saving entrenchment of the negative behavior.

More Work

Writing sentences 25 times or more or doing extra work may not change the behavior. Rather, it may negatively associate work, which should be intrinsically pleasurable, with punishment.

Threats You Can't/Won't Carry Out

You will lose your credibility if you back down, so avoid this by thinking

196

Apply It!

Consider the following fifteen classroom behaviors that vary in degree from minor to serious. Use all of the resources in this unit to brainstorm: possible causes and possible solutions whether through behavior modification, logical consequences, parent conferences, nonverbal interventions, or a combination approach. It's better to pre-plan possible interventions before they actually occur! Devise a plan for dealing with these situations at your potential or current grade level:

1. A student constantly rocks back and forth in her seat.

2. A student uses a racial epithet to you or another student.

3. A student says to the teacher, "You have bad breath."

4. A student destroys property of another student.

5. A student never brings her homework to class.

6. A student taps his pencil on the desk constantly.

7. A student says, "I don't care."

8. A student says, "You can't make me."

9. A student shoves another student in line.

10. A student won't share materials during a project.

11. A student brings a weapon to class.

12. A student throws objects at another student.

13. A student gets out of his seat and walks around the room.

14. A student makes fun of another student.

15. Make up one you have experienced.

_____

statistics

According to Linda Starr (2002) writing in *Education World*:

- Corporal punishment in public schools is legal in Alabama, Arizona, Arkansas, Colorado, Delaware, Florida, Georgia, Idaho, Indiana, Kansas, Kentucky, Louisiana, Mississippi, Missouri, New Mexico, North Carolina, Ohio, Oklahoma, Pennsylvania, South Carolina, Tennessee, Texas, and Wyoming.

- Black students comprise 17 percent of the U.S. student population; yet blacks are on the receiving end of 37 percent of the physical punishments administered.

- White students make up 63 percent of the student population and receive 55 percent of the corporal punishments.

- Schools are the only institutions in the United States in which striking another person is legal, including prisons, mental hospitals, and the military.

- Every industrialized country in the world except the United States, five Canadian provinces, and one Australian state prohibits corporal punishment in schools.

carefully about consequences before you announce them. Try withdrawing from the situation and establish a cooling-off period. Find a way out for both of you to win if you are in a standoff situation. Simply saying, "I am choosing to let that go

If we are ever to turn toward a kindlier society and a safer world, a revulsion against the physical punishment of children would be a good place to start.

Dr. Benjamin Spock

this time, John, although I expect that you will not be fighting on the playground again," allows you both an easy out, and you are still in control of the situation by making the choice. Or, have your student choose between desisting and the logical consequence that pertains.

Apply It!

Now it is your turn to synthesize all you have read in this unit and in Chapter 9 and articulate your own comprehensive plan for discipline. Write a letter to parents articulating your plan and the philosophy underlying that plan.

Avoid It!

Try not to become obsessed with classroom discipline matters. If you stop and try to deal with every misdemeanor in the classroom, you will never get any teaching done. There are times when it is best to just let it go. If you can't deal with it in using the strategies described above, and if it is minor enough, then choose the unwritten discipline strategy and just let it go.

Although discipline is essential, it is only one component of effective instruction. If you are too focused on discipline and too concerned about control, you may not attempt some of the more active learning, inquiry, and cooperative learning strategies. Don't play it too safe and opt for a quiet classroom as your highest value.

If you make an error in judgment, you have the opportunity to recoup your losses the next day. Your students will be very forgiving and flexible. If you've been too lax, then tighten the discipline the next day. If you've been too harsh, then lighten up. Trust yourself and your intuition. Your experience, the experiences of colleagues, and the students themselves will help you figure out what works and doesn't work for you.

Unit 4 Checklist

Positive Discipline Checklist	For more information go to:
☐ Do I have a method for establishing rules that conforms to district/school policy?	Chapter 9
☐ Are my rules easily communicated to parents?	Chapter 9
☐ Does my discipline plan accommodate all students?	Chapter 9
☐ Have I checked for understanding of the rules and been consistent in enforcing them?	Chapter 9
☐ Am I looking for causes of the misbehavior?	Chapter 17
☐ Does my classroom environment promote good classroom management?	Chapter 18
☐ Do I follow Kounin's classroom management principles?	Chapter 18
☐ Am I promoting a positive classroom climate?	Chapter 19
☐ Have I examined and understood the school and district policies for serious offenses?	Chapters 16, 20
☐ Have I ascertained the makeup of the SST at my site?	Chapter 20

Further Reading: Positive Discipline

Canter, L., & Canter, M. (2001). *Assertive discipline* (3rd ed.). Santa Monica, CA: National Educational Services. This book is a step-by-step approach to implementing Assertive Discipline. The 3rd edition balances a caring environment with a carefully structured classroom environment.

Charles, C.M. *Essentials of effective discipline* (2002). Boston: Allyn and Bacon. Written in a teacher-friendly style, this book offers practical advice on encouraging positive behavior and attitudes and dealing effectively with misbehavior. There are many strategies and useful tips emphasizing positive communication and cooperation.

Charles, C.M., & Senter, G. (2004). *Building classroom discipline* (8th ed.). Boston: Allyn and Bacon. This text presents 18 models of discipline that have a solid theoretical base. The readers are challenged to synthesize models that meet their needs or situations from the variety presented in order to develop a comprehensive discipline system that works.

Jones, F. (2000). *Tools for teaching*. Santa Cruz, CA: Fred Jones & Associates. This is a down-to-earth, practical guide that trains teachers in specific skills enabling them to deal with a wide variety of management issues.

Nelsen, J. et al. (2001). *Positive discipline : A teacher's guide A–Z* (2nd revised ed.). New York: Three Rivers Press. This book first introduces the concepts that inspire the positive discipline approach and then discusses more than 100 possible discipline and behavioral topics and solutions.

Nelsen, J. et al. (2000). *Positive discipline in the classroom* (3rd rev. ed.). New York: Three Rivers Press. This is a thorough explanation of positive discipline concepts with specific recommendations for implementing classroom meetings. The logical consequences approach is compared to behavior modification, and the four misdirected goals and how to identify them are covered.

Thompson, J. (1998). *Discipline survival kit for the secondary teacher*. San Francisco: Jossey-Bass. This guide to discipline in secondary school emphasizes positive techniques to manage individual and group behavior. It includes tips on preventive measures and dealing with discipline challenges. Many helpful forms are included.

Informative Websites

American Sign Language Dictionary
http://www.masterstech-home.com/ASLDICT.html
This is a comprehensive sign language dictionary. Click on the letter of the word you are searching for and you can search for signs for your classroom management needs.

Jane Nelsen /Positive Discipline
http://www.positivediscipline.com
This is the official positive discipline website with tips for teachers and parents, resources, articles, materials, and books to implement the approach.

Fred Jones
http://www.fredjones.com
This is the official Fred Jones website where you can find articles, tips, and products.

Canter and Associates
http://www.canter.net
This is the official Canter Associates website. Here, you can access books and materials, find tips, enroll in professional development courses, and register to obtain free resources.

Education World
http://www.educationworld.com/
This site contains excellent articles on classroom management and discipline issues. Be sure to register for and then access their free message boards, which contain valuable tips from teachers. The message board for classroom management is very informative.

Unit 5

Planning and Organizing Subject Matter

All states and schools will have challenging and clear standards of achievement and accountability for all children, and effective strategies for reaching those standards.

U.S. Dept. of Education

A man who does not plan long ahead will find trouble right at his door.

Confucius

Chapter **21**

How Do I Align Standards and Fit Everything In?

Effectiveness Essentials

- Goals 2000 and No Child Left Behind have changed forever the way you and your fellow educators look at curriculum, instruction, and assessment.

- A standards-based curriculum combined with the No Child Left Behind mandate can set uniformly high expectations for all students, provide educational equity, and make clear statements to parents, teachers, and students of what will be learned.

- The first step in long-range curriculum planning is to become familiar with the standards and expectations of your district for your grade level or subject matter.

- Think of planning as a continuum from the general to the specific or from your state standards to your daily plans.

- Mapping out your year, month by month, can help you fit in everything and avoid feeling overwhelmed when you look at the curriculum materials and the standards documents in your district.

When I began teaching, I was given a stack of curriculum materials, along with a class list, record book, and key to the teachers' rest room. Included in the curriculum materials were various guides (one each for social studies, science, and language arts). Inside each guide were the goals, content, and topics to be taught, suggested learning activities for each topic, and a bibliography of print resources that I could turn to if I ever had time. Math and reading curricula consisted of what the teacher's edition of the texts told me to teach, and art consisted of activities taken from *Instructor* magazine or borrowed from other teachers. Music and P.E. were hit-or-miss affairs. Each weekend I brought home curriculum guidebooks and manuals, and I labored to fit topics into little boxes in a weekly planning book. I hoped I was teaching what my third graders needed to know. But I always had my doubts! You see, I started teaching before there were the guidelines that exist today. There were no state standards, no benchmarks along the way, and no standardized assessments to measure just how much my students had learned. I had to rely on my teacher-made tests and judgment.

Then and Now

Of all the responsibilities that a new teacher has, none is less practiced during student teaching than curriculum planning. The period between the completion of your credential program and your first teaching assignment is the time to reflect on what your curriculum will be during your first years of teaching. All planning must be based on more than just your own desires for what you would *like* to teach. It must incorporate the requirements of national, state, and local interests, as well as the needs of your individual students.

Standards-Based Planning

Two acts of Congress have changed forever the way you and your fellow educators must look at curriculum, instruction, and assessment. They present challenges and opportunities that dictate how you do business in your classroom. These two acts established a system of state-mandated standards, along with accountability to ensure that all students meet them, regardless of any mitigating factors. Both acts have completely changed how teachers today plan for the upcoming academic year.

Goals 2000

Goals 2000 jump-started the standards-based school accountability movement. Standards-based education requires that educators explicitly identify what students must know and be able to do. Goals 2000 supported comprehensive state- and district-wide coordination and implementation of programs focused on improving student achievement of state standards.

Under Goals 2000, standardized tests were given once per year. But they weren't always tied to the standards. As a result, there was inconsistency from district to district, and state to state. Then, Congress spoke again with one voice to ensure that every child should be educated to his or her full potential and dictated standards-based testing to ensure accountability with the *No Child Left Behind Act* of 2001.

No Child Left Behind

The No Child Left Behind (NCLB) *Act* of 2001 increases the educators' accountability for student performance. Federal monies are now tied to those student performances. Under NCLB, states, districts, and schools that demonstrate improved achievement will be rewarded. On the other hand, schools that continually fail to meet set performance levels are sanctioned. Parents and communities will know how well their children are performing on annual state reading and math assessments in grades 3–8, and schools are held accountable for their effectiveness. Read about specific provisions of NCLB at http://www.ed.gov/nclb/landing.jhtml

A standards-based curriculum combined with the *No Child Left*

Four Pillars of NCLB

1. Stronger accountability for results
2. Flexibility for states and communities in how they use federal education funds
3. Determining and implementing research-driven educational methods and programs
4. More choices for parents

Basic Tenets of Goals 2000

1. All children in America will start school ready to learn.
2. The high school graduation rate will increase to at least 90 percent.
3. All students will leave grades 4, 8, and 12 having demonstrated competency over challenging subject matter including English, mathematics, science, foreign languages, civics and government, economics, the arts, history, and geography, and every school in America will ensure that all students learn to use their minds well, so they may be prepared for responsible citizenship, further learning, and productive employment in our nation's modern economy.
4. United States students will be first in the world in mathematics and science achievement.
5. Every adult American will be literate and will possess the knowledge and skills necessary to compete in a global economy and exercise the rights and responsibilities of citizenship.
6. Every school in the United States will be free of drugs, violence, and the unauthorized presence of firearms and alcohol, and will offer a disciplined environment conducive to learning.
7. The nation's teaching force will have access to programs for the continued improvement of their professional skills and the opportunity to acquire the knowledge and skills needed to instruct and prepare all American students for the next century.
8. Every school will promote partnerships that will increase parental involvement and participation in promoting the social, emotional, and academic growth of children. (1994)

> ## Congress Says . . .
>
> *On January 8, 2002, President George Bush signed into law the No Child Left Behind Act, "An act to close the achievement gap with accountability, flexibility, and choice, so that no child is left behind. Be it enacted by the Senate and House of Representatives of the United States of America in Congress assembled."*

Behind mandate can set uniformly high expectations for all students; provide educational equity; and make clear statements to parents, teachers, and students of what will be learned. In addition, this curriculum enables teachers and administrators to develop assessments directly related to the standards instead of relying solely on standardized achievement tests. You will read more about assessment and accountability under NCLB in Unit 7.

Schools and districts that don't meet their yearly improvement targets face intense scrutiny and potential repercussions. Often, school scores and

Watch It! video

Planning for Instruction
Two teachers plan a unit on civilization for secondary students. After viewing the video, write out the steps these teachers used in planning. Were any steps missing? How useful are graphic organizers in planning?

district scores are published in the newspaper, and low scores or a lack of improvement can even lead to a principal's ouster or a takeover of the district by the state department of education. Schools also face the possibility of cutbacks in federal and state monies.

Before school begins, you will need to engage in long-term planning within the framework of both NCLB and Goals 2000. During student teaching, your supervising teacher basically set the curriculum. Although you may have had some responsibility for designing units of study, an invisible structure was set up long before you arrived on the scene. Now it's your responsibility.

Long-Range Planning: The Year at a Glance

Although it is impossible to plan down to the last detail until you have actually come face-to-face with your students, you can use the time between student teaching and the beginning of the school year to sketch out a curriculum to ease some of the panic typically felt as opening day draws near.

Why do you need to plan ahead? In addition to alleviating butterflies, you need to plan because:

1. You will increasingly be required to meet the expectations of the two major legislative mandates.
2. You don't want your students to miss out on necessary material on which they will be tested.
3. A well-thought-out curriculum, geared toward the needs, interests, and abilities of the students will alleviate many discipline problems.
4. Your district may have imposed a pacing schedule you are required to follow.
5. Planning will make you more confident and encourage you to learn new material and gather your resources and materials.

Becoming Familiar with Standards

There are multiple levels and sources of standards. Standards usually originate in professional organizations such as National Council for the Social Studies or National Council of Teachers of Mathematics. Then, the state education departments look at them and adapt or adopt them as their own. Finally, at the school district level, curriculum and instruction personnel further refine the standards so they can be allocated to grade levels and into courses.

The first step in long-range curriculum planning is to become familiar with the standards and expectations of your district for your grade level or subject matter. Collect all documents that are relevant, such as lists of state standards, benchmarks, pacing schedules, state frameworks, district standards, and teachers' manuals.

How do you get hold of these? The most practical way is to visit the school as soon as you receive your assignment and pick up all relevant materials. The website www.education-world.com/ standards/ enables you to access standards by state or by subject matter for all subjects and grade levels.

The more familiar you are with the upcoming curriculum, and especially the performance standards, the more comfortable and creative you can be in planning an overview of the year's instruction. After looking at this material, you may feel overwhelmed. How are you going to plan lessons in all curriculum areas, given $22\frac{1}{2}$ hours or so of instructional time per week? This one question alone provides a substantial challenge to the first-year teacher (see Figure 21.1).

Student Teacher Talks . . .

My first year worry is that I'll be given a classroom full of children, and not know what to do. I know how to handle discipline problems, I know what to expect from parents, and whom to talk to in case of problems. What I don't know is what to teach! I have been observing, learning, and asking questions, but the one thing that I still don't know is what to teach. Where do teachers get their ideas for themes or units? Do they take them right out of the Frameworks? Do they borrow from other teachers? How and when will I be given the golden key of knowledge? I am set for the first couple of weeks, but my biggest fear is that after that, my lessons will be boring and not have a lot of substance because no one has ever taught me what to teach.

Laura Graham
Credential Candidate
Ontario, California

Figure 21.1
Working with Standards

Standards from the Professional Organizations:
*Examples: National Council for the Social Studies
International Reading Association
National Science Teachers Association
Association for the Advancement of Health Education
National Association for Sport and Physical Education*

State interpretations of national organization standards

Textbook Influence

District interpretations of state standards

Figure 21.2
Nested Planning

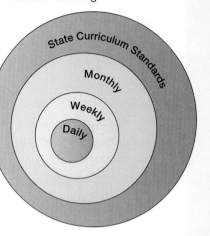

Clothespins
Point to the
Day's Standards

Math Standards Board

Planning as a Continuum

Think of planning as a continuum from the general to the specific or from your state standards to the daily plans you follow every day in your classroom (see Figure 21.2).

1. Know the curriculum and standards.
2. Divide it all among the months of the school year so it all gets done.
3. Develop themes for each month from which weekly plans will be made.
4. Develop weekly plans.
5. Develop daily plans.

Generally, you will find standards in all of the following curricular areas. The websites for all of these areas are listed in Chapter 38.

- English Language Arts
- Mathematics
- Science
- Social Science
- Physical Development and Health
- Fine Arts
- Foreign Languages

Managing Standards

At the middle and high school level, standards can be managed more easily because teachers only have one or two subject areas, and within a discipline, such as math, the standards are similar even though the course name may be different. The real challenge is somehow dealing with the voluminous standards at the elementary level for each of the multiple subjects you teach. It has been suggested that it would take a ten-hour day to achieve all of the standards assigned to a grade level. In my local school district, the third grade math standards break down as follows: 20 number sense standards; 9 algebra and functions standards; 12 measurement and geometry standards; 5 statistics, data analysis and probability standards; and 14 mathematical reasoning standards. And math is just one of the multiple subjects an elementary teacher must address.

You may feel overwhelmed when you look at the curriculum materials and the standards documents in your new district. Some of them may not be clearly written in plain teacher talk. How will you manage all of them? If you are an elementary school teacher, many of the "essential" standards will be emphasized in your planning documents. These are the key standards that will be tested. You may be given a curriculum sequence to follow and/or a pacing guide to assist you. Also, turn to mentors, buddies, and support personnel to help you identify the critical standards.

In middle school, you will probably plan with others in your team because of block scheduling. The veterans on the team will be of great assistance to you as you plan a cohesive unit of study that addresses standards across the curriculum. At the high school level, your department colleagues may have already highlighted the essential standards.

statistics

According to the U.S. Department of Education (http://www.ed.gov/)

- The average number of school days in the United States is 180 versus 204 internationally. The length of the school day is longer, with approximately 5.5 hours of instructional time daily and 1000 hours annually (Florian, 1999).

- According to a study conducted by Marzano and Kendall (1998), one of the problems facing American educators is that too many standards have been identified. Based on their conservative estimates, it "could take as much as 22 years of schooling to adequately cover all of the content identified in the standards."

Implementing a Standards-based Curriculum

1. First, take a deep breath.

2. If you cover each standard in each curriculum area separately, you will go batty.

3. You will see that standards are generally arranged hierarchically.

4. There are some essential standards (generally the 1.0, 2.0), followed by many sub-standards under these items (e.g., 1.1, 1.2, 1.3).

5. Focus on the essential standards and you will see that the sub-standards add up to the larger one.

6. When your students are having trouble meeting the major standard heading, you need to look at the sub-headings in your standards documents and pinpoint exactly where the problem lies.

7. Start with one curriculum area at a time (only a few for those lucky middle and high school teachers).

8. Lay out the standards in shortened form on a big piece of chart paper like the one in Figure 21.3. Use your own shorthand.

9. Then, begin to look for any commonalities among the subject areas. For example, critical thinking standards such as "compares and contrasts" or "evaluates" may overlap in your curriculum.

10. Use a highlighter to accent those that you may be able to combine. Use another color highlighter to mark those that you find essential or that you have been told are essential because they appear on benchmark exams.

Figure 21.3

Example of Overlapping Standards in Two Curriculum Areas for Grade 6: Partial Listing

Language Arts Standards

**2.0 Reading Comprehension
(Focus on Informational Materials)**

2.1 Identify the structural features of popular media (e.g., newspapers, magazines, online information) and use the features to obtain information.

2.2 Analyze text that uses the compare-and-contrast organizational pattern.

Comprehension and Analysis of Grade-Level-Appropriate Text

2.3 Connect and clarify main ideas by identifying their relationships to other sources and related topics.

2.4 Clarify an understanding of texts by creating outlines, logical notes, summaries, or reports.

3.0 Literary Response and Analysis

Students read and respond to historically or culturally significant works of literature that reflect and enhance their studies of history and social science. They clarify the ideas and connect them to other literary works. The selections in Recommended Literature, Kindergarten Through Grade Twelve illustrate the quality and complexity of the materials to be read by students.

Structural Features of Literature

3.1 Identify the forms of fiction and describe the major characteristics of each form.

Narrative Analysis of Grade-Level-Appropriate Text

3.2 Analyze the effect of the qualities of the character (e.g., courage or cowardice, ambition or laziness) on the plot and the resolution of the conflict.

3.3 Analyze the influence of setting on the problem and its resolution.

3.4 Define how tone or meaning is conveyed in poetry through word choice, figurative language, sentence structure, line length, punctuation, rhythm, repetition, and rhyme.

Social Studies Standards

6.4 Students analyze the geographic, political, economic, religious, and social structures of the early civilizations of Ancient Greece.

1. Discuss the connections between geography and the development of city-states in the region of the Aegean Sea, including patterns of trade and commerce among Greek city-states and within the wider Mediterranean region.

2. Trace the transition from tyranny and oligarchy to early democratic forms of government and back to dictatorship in ancient Greece, including the significance of the invention of the idea of citizenship (e.g., from Pericles' *Funeral Oration*).

3. State the key differences between Athenian, or direct, democracy and representative democracy.

4. Explain the significance of Greek mythology to the everyday life of people in the region and how Greek literature continues to permeate our literature and language today, drawing from Greek mythology and epics, such as Homer's *Iliad* and *Odyssey,* and from Aesop's *Fables.*

5. Outline the founding, expansion, and political organization of the Persian Empire.

6. Compare and contrast life in Athens and Sparta, with emphasis on their roles in the Persian and Peloponnesian Wars.

Apply It!

If you are a middle or high school teacher, access the standards for one subject area and lay them out on the matrix. If you are an elementary teacher, you will need to follow the suggestions for all your subjects, but especially the ones that have benchmark assessments, and, even more important, those that are tested at the state level.

Look to Colleagues. The teachers in the grades below you and above you have very similar standards, just at a lower or higher level. Therefore, it would be very useful to look at the grade-level standards above and below your grade so you can see that key standards, topics, and skills are revisited throughout the grades. When you have done this, you will know how much you have to cover, and knowing the range is better than being caught up short at the end of the year or semester.

Look to Textbooks. Increasingly, the textbooks you are using identify the standards that are addressed. In some reading texts, standards are integrated, although there is no fully developed text that incorporates all of the standards in all of the curriculum areas for your grade level. That is up to you! Your resource teachers, principals, mentors, beginning teacher support team, curriculum coordinators, and new teacher in-service providers will help you navigate the sea of standards.

Curriculum Mapping

The next step is to map out your year on a different piece of paper—this time, month by month (see Figure 21.4). This will be a visual indication to you that you can fit it all in. You will need to pace your instruction according to your students' needs, interests, and abilities, but even a rough sketch of the entire year will be helpful, especially if you think about combining the essential standards into bigger units of instruction.

Avoid It!

Do not be afraid to ask for assistance with the daunting task of long-range planning. Even the most experienced teachers are in uncharted waters because of standards-based instructional mandates. You can all work it out together. Help is available!

Teacher Talks . . .

If you try and teach every individual standard, you will go crazy. Instead, choose topics you are required to teach and review all your standards in light of that choice. You will begin to see opportunities to incorporate the essential standards from most curriculum areas into your unit of study. The little bits and pieces are really steps along the way to the big picture, so focus on the essential standards and the bits and pieces will fall into place.

Jason Paytas
Fourth Grade
Arcata, California

Figure 21.4

Partial Sixth Grade Curriculum Map in Self-Contained Classroom by Month

	Topics	Target Standards and Skills	Assessments	Activities/Resources/Technology
September	Ancient Civilizations—Egypt Reading for Information Topography of Egypt Writing Coherent Essays	**Language Arts** Students write clear, coherent, and focused essays. The writing exhibits students' awareness of the audience and purpose. Essays contain formal introductions, supporting evidence, and conclusions. Students progress through the stages of the writing process as needed. **Social Studies** Students analyze the geographic, political, economic, religious, and social structures of Egypt. **Math—Pyramids** 1.0 Students deepen their understanding of the measurement of plane and solid shapes and use this understanding to solve problems—creating a pyramid to scale. **Science** Topography is reshaped by the weathering of rock and soil and by the transportation and deposition of sediment. As a basis for understanding this concept: Nile River **Arts** 3.0 Understanding the Historical Contributions and Cultural Dimensions of the Visual Arts	Writing rubric Group Project on selected aspect of Egyptian culture Written tests on Egypt Map of Nile and explanation of importance to Egyptian life Building a Pyramid to scale	Videos from *National Geographic* and PBS Word processing of reports on Egypt Print resources, including textbook Virtual tour of Egypt Hieroglyphic stamps Wall painting in Egyptian style Cooperative learning on Egyptian culture
Oct.	Ancient Civilizations—Ancient Hebrews			
Nov.	Ancient Civilizations—Greece			
Dec.				

Unit 5
Planning and Organizing Subject Matter

Chapter 22

How Do I Write Unit, Weekly, Daily, and Lesson Plans?

It pays to plan ahead. It wasn't raining when Noah built the ark.

Anonymous

Effectiveness Essentials

- Plans are a thinking map that sets an endpoint and steps along the way to reach the goal.

- There are at least two types of units: the teaching unit and the resource unit.

- The first-year teacher should approach curriculum integration slowly, with only one or two curriculum areas at first.

- Consider various levels of thinking in your planning, your questioning during lessons, and your designing of assignments (Bloom's Taxonomy).

- Some states and/or districts mandate the number of minutes for each school subject.

- District regulations and principal expectations vary when it comes to format and detail in lesson plans.

- Lesson plans should accommodate the diverse needs of students in your classroom, including English language learners and students with special needs.

Your well-thought-out plans will be your security blanket during the first weeks of school and beyond. Careful planning does not mean that the resulting plans are indelible and rigid. They can and will change! But plan you must.

Plans will give you the confidence to step into your classroom as a well-prepared professional who is ready to make adjustments as you get to know your students. Your instruction will ultimately result from the dynamic interaction between your plans and the needs, interests, and readiness of your students. This chapter will enable you to translate your long-term plan into manageable unit, weekly, and daily lesson plans.

Unit Planning

Unit-based instruction is an option for those of you who wish to spend time thinking about curriculum delivery before the first day of school. Rather than following the manual for each separate subject area, unit-based instruction allows you to cluster some topics/standards into larger chunks of instruction (units) that enable you to cover multiple standards in several curriculum areas at the same time.

Although unit planning is time-consuming and challenging, it can save you countless hours of preparation later. You will have more fun and your students will experience less curricular fragmentation. Even student teachers, as busy as they are, appreciate the rewards of unit-based instruction.

Once you have some idea of what you must teach, or the curriculum givens, sketch out a very brief beginning unit in social studies, science, literature, or whatever your area of instruction might be. Having one beginning unit roughly sketched out will enable you to start the year with confidence. For elementary school, consider a literature-based unit built around a favorite book you can secure in multiple copies from the book room or favorite student book club. If you teach a specific subject area in middle school or high school, map out your first introductory unit to the subject. Ultimately, this unit can ease the burden of that first week of school until your roster is set and you have all your teaching texts and materials.

Types of Units

There are basically two types of units, the teaching unit and the resource unit. The teaching unit is much more specific than the resource unit. As you read this section, think about which type would best meet your needs and those of your students.

The teaching unit consists of a set of separate lesson plans that are all related to one topic and targeted to a specific group of students based on their needs, interests, and abilities. The teaching unit may include lesson plans in many or all curriculum areas. A unit on Mexico, for example, might include standards-based lesson plans for writing a letter to pen pals (language), designing bark paintings (art), learning a Mexican dance (physical education), counting in Spanish (math), and making tacos (math and cooking).

The resource unit is more general than the teaching unit and can be adapted for any grade level. It is a compendium of ideas for teaching a particular topic through an integrated curriculum. The resource unit consists of a rationale, content outline, set of goals, brief descriptions of learning activities, evaluation, and bibliography. The activities span many curriculum areas, and you may need to expand lesson plans that are directed to a particular group of students in order to implement the unit.

Resource units challenge your creativity, and the out-of-the-box thinking required to implement them is so much fun. When you have a handle on the standards and skills that you must teach, the resource unit provides creative outlets for you and your students. Also, because they are not as specific as teaching units, they can be shared among colleagues who can adapt them easily to their own group of students.

Designing a Resource or Teaching Unit

The steps to designing a resource unit are easier to implement than you may think, especially as a novice teacher. But if you follow this framework, you will experience the joy of seeing all of the disparate curriculum pieces elegantly melded into a whole unit.

Choose a topic based on the standards for your grade or subject area. Ask veteran teachers to share any subject or grade-appropriate units. Brainstorm with colleagues about topics and available resources. Excellent sources for units are the interests or cultural backgrounds of your students provided they coincide with the standards. A mini unit on cultures in your room might be an appropriate way for students to share and shine. A mini

Apply It!

Sentence stems are effective tools for gathering information about prior knowledge. If the topic is the Civil War, you might write on the board, "When I think of The Civil War. . . ." or, "What I want to know about Abraham Lincoln is. . . ." Similarly, you might put up two very large charts and have students brainstorm together: What do they already know, and what do they really want to learn about the topic? If you begin the unit by addressing students' initial questions first, you will hook them in to study the rest (see Figure 22.1).

unit on a literary work that has recently been made into a movie might hook students into English criticism.

Before you go any further with the topic you ultimately decide on, try it out on your audience to see what they already know, what they want to know, and what their level of interest in the topic is.

The next step is to find out about the topic if you are not already familiar enough with it to make your content outline. One of the major benefits of teaching is the opportunity to learn new things as you are conducting your unit research. Many gaps in my own education were filled in as I prepared for teaching. Begin with a good print or CD-ROM encyclopedia. Then, search the Internet to amass information on your chosen topic.

Immerse yourself in the content by visiting libraries and checking out student-level books on the topic. In the interest of time, I found that if I went to texts and nonfiction accounts geared toward students, I would find the material already predigested and written in a language that both they and I could readily understand.

Figure 22.1

The Beginning of a KWL Chart (Ogle, 1986)

ABRAHAM LINCOLN AND THE CIVIL WAR

What I Know	What I Want to Know
• The Civil War was between the North and the South	• Which were the Northern and which were the Southern states?
• Slavery was an issue	• How many soldiers died?
• Lincoln was President	• What were the causes of the Civil War?
• Lincoln was shot	
• He has a monument in Washington	

Finally, sit down with a big piece of butcher paper and think of all the exciting ways you can carry through this unit. Make a web or map of your tentative ideas or simply write them all down and categorize them according to the curriculum areas that seem most dominant. If your topic derives from social studies or science, think back on all the ideas pertaining to language arts and art that might be germane. If your topic derives from literature, think of all the other curriculum areas, including language arts, that might pertain to the unit (see Figure 22.2).

Adapting the Unit

Only when the resource unit is adapted to a particular group of students through specific and complete lesson plans does it become more

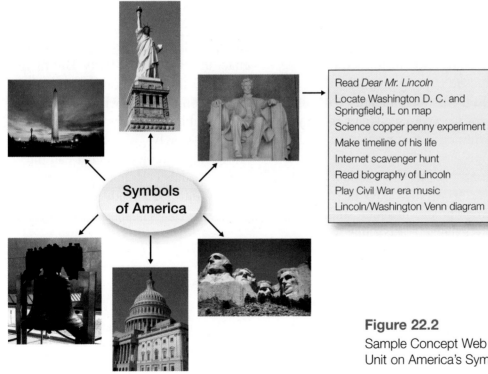

Read *Dear Mr. Lincoln*
Locate Washington D. C. and Springfield, IL on map
Science copper penny experiment
Make timeline of his life
Internet scavenger hunt
Read biography of Lincoln
Play Civil War era music
Lincoln/Washington Venn diagram

Symbols of America

Figure 22.2
Sample Concept Web for Unit on America's Symbols

focused. Use some of the sheltered English techniques (see Chapter 29) when planning your unit activities if you are working with non-native English speakers who are literate in their primary language. These strategies include good teaching techniques such as hands-on activities, use of visuals, cooperative learning, and similar projects. Students with special needs, including the gifted, should have differentiated assignments and activities built into the unit.

Curriculum Integration within Units

After you have brainstormed the activities to carry through the unit, go back to the list of standards you outlined for the year (see Chapter 21). You will notice that many of them fit right in. Let's say you are designing a self-concept unit. Your students need to write, so why not have them write autobiographies? In social studies, you are expected, according to the year-at-a glance, to teach about timelines and to construct one, so why not begin the process with personal time lines? Although this is a case of the tail wagging the dog, you will not be the first or the last teacher to design your unit plans this way. Always keep in mind that students learn best when the material is meaningful to them.

The first-year elementary teacher should approach curriculum integration slowly, with only one or two curriculum areas at first. As a beginner who is unfamiliar with the curriculum for the grade level, you can try to integrate where possible and move at your own pace toward making other curriculum connections. For example, you can start by incorporating language arts, art, and music into a social studies unit on the American Revolution by having the students make era flags, sing popular revolutionary songs, and enact the Boston Tea Party. But there are some skills and concepts that defy integration, and you will feel more comfortable easing into integrated teaching slowly.

A single-subject teacher can integrate art, music, drama, math, and writing into the already set curriculum

Apply It!

At this point, you may want to sketch out a unit that would be appropriate for a grade level or subject you may be teaching. See Figure 22.3.

Figure 22.3
Unit Planning Worksheet

Chapter 22   How Do I Write Unit, Weekly, Daily, and Lesson Plans?

UNIT PLANNING WORKSHEET

Insert activities for curriculum areas if you are an elementary teacher. If you are a secondary teacher, use the circles for specific lesson ideas.

Topic: Insects   **Grade:** 3   **Subject:** Science

STANDARDS: Life Sciences Grade 3
Adaptations in physical structure or behavior may improve an organism's chance for survival. As a basis for understanding this concept:

a.   Students know plants and animals have structures that serve different functions in growth, survival, and reproduction.

b.   Students know examples of diverse life forms in different environments, such as oceans, deserts, tundra, forests, grasslands, and wetlands.

c.   Students know living things cause changes in the environment in which they live: Some of these changes are detrimental to the organism or other organisms, and some are beneficial.

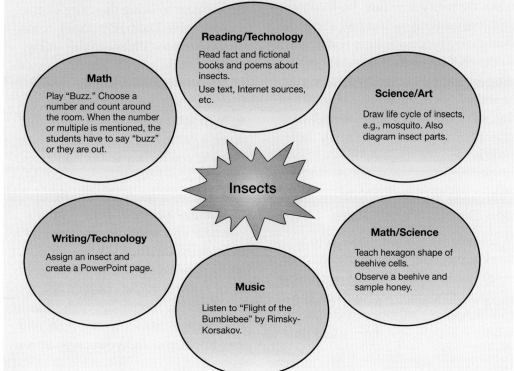

Reading/Technology

Read fact and fictional books and poems about insects.
Use text, Internet sources, etc.

Math

Play "Buzz." Choose a number and count around the room. When the number or multiple is mentioned, the students have to say "buzz" or they are out.

Science/Art

Draw life cycle of insects, e.g., mosquito. Also diagram insect parts.

Insects

Writing/Technology

Assign an insect and create a PowerPoint page.

Music

Listen to "Flight of the Bumblebee" by Rimsky-Korsakov.

Math/Science

Teach hexagon shape of beehive cells.
Observe a beehive and sample honey.

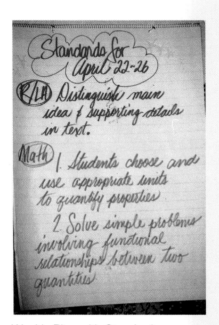

Weekly Plan with Standards

in history, science, or math without having to worry about absolute coverage of the integrated subject standards.

A beginning teacher at any level would not be expected to teach the curriculum in an integrated fashion during the school year or semester. In fact, it is just as much of a burden to force integration of curriculum as it is to teach each curriculum area separately.

Weekly Plans

It is easier to plan for the short haul when the entire structure, both content and organization, is laid out, even though this process is time-consuming. In the end, however, time spent planning for the big picture will save you countless hours on Sunday night when you sit down with a blank weekly plan book and have to fill in all those little boxes.

Planning within School and District Parameters

When you sit down to write your weekly schedule, you want to have as much information about the parameters of your scheduling decisions as you can. School organization, the master school schedule, and curriculum time allotments and order will all influence the decisions you make about how your week will look. It's better to know at the beginning what the limitations will be to avoid constant changes in your schedule from unforeseen events.

But there will be unanticipated events nevertheless, and you need to be flexible and aware of what other teachers may be planning so you can coordinate. For example, you may come to school one day armed with a full day of plans, only to discover that a colleague has arranged for the fire department to bring their fire engine and adorable Dalmatian, Spot, to the playground to talk about fire safety. Or, in middle school, a special assembly may be called when the mayor makes an unscheduled appearance. In high school, the pep rally for that week's game may disrupt all of your plans if you have a last period class. Or, you may have shortened periods that day to equalize the lost time.

Obtain a copy of your district's calendar and schedule, and transfer it to your own master calendar or personal organizer. Include holidays, open houses, parent conferences, testing dates, in-service days, and special school- and district-wide events that will affect you and your class. Pencil in the big sports events, homecoming, etc., so you can anticipate a heightened level of excitement. Then, when you write up your weekly schedule, you can see if there are days or time slots in which you have to adjust your instructional planning. Use Post-it™ type notes on your plans or in your plan book to indicate which lessons were shortened or abandoned altogether and need to be readdressed.

Holidays, or lack thereof for long periods of time, present another scheduling challenge. When a break is coming up, your students will need something extra special to keep their attention on class work and away from holiday plans. Conversely, during the long periods between vacations, you also will need to perk up weary students and energize yourself to keep them motivated.

Create a Master Schedule. On a master weekly schedule, write down the school schedule for a typical week. Include the times for lunch, preparation periods, assemblies, library, computer lab, and so forth. Then, make a list of activities that will pull out some of your students, such as speech, band, lunch monitors, resource teacher, or the counselor.

You don't want to schedule major new content lessons during these times if doing so can be avoided. Fill in these weekly givens on a schedule. Then you can duplicate these masters with key, immutable times already filled in. The blank spaces are yours! You may feel as though the entire week is taken up with special functions, but so it is in a comprehensive elementary or secondary school where extracurricular, monitorial duties, and pull-out programs round out the educational experience.

It is not unusual for states and/or districts to mandate the number of minutes for each school subject in elementary grades. You need to find out as soon as you can the time allotments for each subject area and if there is any prescribed order to the day.

Planning Oversight. District regulations and principal expectations vary when it comes to how much detail you are expected to include in your plans. Some principals collect the plans every week and look through each and every square. Others ask only that the plans be available in a prominent place on your desk. Principals and mentors will provide you invaluable feedback about your planning. They

> **Vice Principal Talks . . .**
>
> *When I do my daily walk-throughs of classrooms, the first thing I look for is the lesson plan book. A lesson plan is like a blueprint for a great masterpiece. I want to see the groundwork. Teachers put a lot of time and effort into creating lesson plans; I absolutely want to see them!*
>
> *Dion Clark*
> *Vice Principal*
> *Sierra High School*
> *San Bernardino, California*

may ask you to shorten or lengthen your plans and/or suggest alternative activities and resources you might consider.

It is important to ascertain the principal's planning expectations as soon as you find yourself with a teaching job. You want to get off on the right foot by providing your site administrator with the degree of specificity she or he expects to see in your plan book. If you have done your month-at-a-glance exercise, then it should not be too difficult to divide by four and make up your weekly plans. The most typical format is the weekly schedule, or the more detailed weekly plan. Keep your plans in a loose-leaf notebook so you can rearrange them as needed and add supporting materials easily.

Planning for Higher Levels of Thinking

Make sure you are considering various levels of thinking as you plan, ask questions during lessons, and design assignments. Bloom's taxonomy (1964) is a very well established guide.

Planning for Diversity

As your planning becomes more specific, make sure that you are attempt-

Apply It!

Select one of the lesson plans you have written in one of your classes and write at least two questions at each level of Bloom's taxonomy. Although you may not have the levels exactly right, it doesn't matter as long as your questions are varied, involve different thought processes, and require responses beyond "yes" and "no" or simple recall.

Avoid It!

A temptation you should resist when writing your weekly plan is to teach the entire year's curriculum in a week or a day. Instead, plan incrementally, that is, in bite-sized, easily digestible pieces.

ing to meet the diverse needs of students in your classroom. Davidman and Davidman (2001) demonstrate how most lessons, activities, and units can be transformed to reflect the diversity in your classroom. At the point where you are translating your long-term and midrange planning into actual classroom instruction, you need to think about how you will differentiate learning. Consult Chapter 28 in Unit 6 if differentiated learning is an unfamiliar term.

Accommodating Learning Styles

Keep in mind that students generally learn best from hands-on, concrete experiences and that Gardner's (1993) theory of multiple intelligences implies accommodations to the learning styles of your pupils. He originally identified

Bloom's Taxonomy

Level	Thinking Skill	Example	Outcome Verbs
Knowledge	factual or recall level	Name the Great Lakes.	define; describe; identify; label; list; match; name; read; record; reproduce; select; state
Comprehension	understanding	Explain the water cycle in your own words. Summarize the story we just read. Describe the political cartoon.	classify; cite; convert; describe; discuss; estimate; explain; generalize; give examples; make sense of; paraphrase; restate (in own words); summarize; trace; understand
Application	transfer of info to a new situation	How would the story change if it happened here? Try out some new problems with this formula.	administer; articulate, assess; chart; collect; compute; construct; determine; develop; discover; extend; implement; include; predict; prepare; produce; project; provide; relate; report; show; solve; transfer; use
Analysis	classification, compare/contrast	How is *Romeo and Juliet* like *West Side Story*? Put these rock specimens into groups that have common characteristics and name the groups.	correlate; diagram; differentiate; discriminate; distinguish; focus; illustrate; infer; limit; outline; point out; prioritize; recognize; separate; subdivide
Synthesis	creative or original response	Draw a portrait in the style of Picasso. Write a new ending for the story.	adapt; anticipate; categorize; collaborate; combine; communicate; compare; compile; contrast; formulate; integrate; model; modify; rearrange; reconstruct; reorganize; revise
Evaluation	a judgment based on criteria	Was Goldielocks justified in entering the bears' house and eating porridge, breaking their chair, and sleeping in the bed? Why or why not?	appraise; compare and contrast; conclude; critique; decide; defend; interpret; judge; justify; reframe; support

NOTES

Chapter 22   How Do I Write Unit, Weekly, Daily, and Lesson Plans?

Intelligence	Strength	Examples
Linguistic	sensitive to word meanings and order, verbal	writers, playwrights
Logical-mathematical	thinks abstractly, logical	mathematicians
Spatial	thinks in pictures, images, and metaphors	architects, artists
Musical	learns through musical patterns	composers, dancers
Kinesthetic	uses body and movement in learning	athletes, dancers
Interpersonal	understands others	politicians, therapists
Intrapersonal	operates in sync with emotions	poets, novelists
Naturalistic	uses the natural environment to learn	environmentalist

seven intelligences that can operate independently of one another. In 1999, Gardner added an eighth intelligence: naturalistic. The implications for teaching may be that since your students can be intelligent in many modes, instruction might be modified to develop and nurture individualistic, natural proclivities. You will have a more in-depth discussion of the intelligences in Chapter 28.

Daily Plans and Lesson Plans

A lesson plan is a kind of thinking map that sets an endpoint and designates steps along the way to reach the goal. It is for you more than for the students because you want to help them get from here to there in an efficient way, while enjoying the activities along the route. If you were traveling across the country by car to a friend's wedding but didn't have a map, you might have quite an adventure wandering hither and yon. On the other hand, you might miss all the great sights along the way and the wedding as well!

Classroom Artifacts

(As seen on http://www.LessonPlansPage.com)

Abby Volmer, a literacy coach at Odessa Middle School in Missouri, shares an example of a Unit Plan that accommodates all learners.

Unit Plan—Accommodating Multiple Intelligences
Title—Capitalization—Direct Quotes
Multiple Intelligences Activities and Instructional Strategies

Verbal/Linguistic

Instruction Circle the Sage—Have 6 people who know the rules for capitalizing direct quotes stand at different points of the room. Teams split and gather around sages to hear info. They go back to teams and share and compare. (Interpersonal)

Activity Write a dialogue between two fictional characters. (Be sure to use before, after, and interrupting quotes.) Highlight the capitals in direct quotes. (Intrapersonal)

Logical/Mathematical

Instruction After "Circle the Sage," students look at sheets and decide on rules for capitalizing direct quotes. (Interpersonal)

Activity Read a dialogue page and highlight the capitals in the direct quotes. Graph how many times the direct quote was used and capitalized either before/after/or interrupting the quote.

Visual/Spatial

Instruction Cut and paste direct quotes in three categories (before, after, and interrupting).

Activity Create a cartoon strip that uses capitals in direct quotes. (Be sure to include before, after, and interrupting quotes.)

Musical/Rhythmic

Instruction Background music during "Circle the Sage."

Activity Create rules sung to the tune of "Twinkle, Twinkle Little Star."

Bodily/Kinesthetic

Instruction Students stand each time they are to capitalize when the word is spoken. (Whole Group)

Activity Create either a dance or an exercise (movement) routine that would go with the direct quotes.

Naturalist

Activity Create a conversation that might occur between a predator animal and a prey animal. Somehow represent the animals with pictures, posters, puppets, etc. (Intrapersonal)

Interpersonal

Activity Same as verbal/linguistic, but have two people carry on a conversation on paper using capitals in direct quotes.

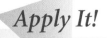

Apply It!

Select a project that you are planning to assign to students. Let's say the topic is Westward Expansion. Think of alternative ways students can meet the requirement using Gardner's multiple intelligences. For example, if a subtopic is the life of a cowboy, students can write an essay; make a display of cowboy tools; play and analyze cowboy songs; write a play that exposes the feelings of cowboys; make maps of the major cattle routes; make a graph that depicts the rise and fall of cowboys in the West; write a diary of ranch life; write a poem, etc. This allows students to capitalize on their strengths and also to see the variety of responses that others come up with.

Topic _____

Assignment Choices

1. Linguistic
2. Logical-mathematical
3. Spatial
4. Musical

5. Kinesthetic
6. Interpersonal
7. Intrapersonal
8. (Naturalistic)

Essential Elements of a Lesson Plan

Once you get the hang of writing lesson plans, you will notice they consist of three essential elements: objectives that derive from the standards, procedures, and evaluation.

1. Objectives that derive from the standards   Where do I want to go?
2. Procedures (including materials)   How will I get there?
3. Evaluation   How will I know when I arrive?

District and School Expectations

How detailed your daily lesson plans need to be depends on your department/school and/or district requirements. Certain lessons require more detailed planning than others. Those that need extra planning include art, science experiments, social studies simulations, new physical education (P.E.) games and skills, and any other lessons that introduce a skill or concept unfamiliar to your students. Many a lesson has self-destructed because the procedures weren't clear in the teacher's mind, the teacher hadn't thought through the organizational pattern, or the teacher hadn't anticipated all the materials that would be needed. Write individual lesson plans on forms you are familiar with from your student teaching days or use the generic lesson plan form in Figure 22.4.

Lesson plans will allay your anxiety as well as provide a substantive instructional guide to a substitute or administrator who takes over your class in an emergency. The lesson plans help the substitute get on the same page as you, and you don't lose as much time as a result of your own absence as you might if you didn't have the plans carefully written out. Use your weekly plan book to sketch in those lessons that are review or routine, such as spelling tests or math drill, or are clearly outlined in the various manuals. But make sure to indicate on your daily plans those lessons that clearly necessitate a more detailed instructional map for you to follow.

Ⓧ *Myth Buster!*

Principals never look at plan books.

I have asked my staff to put a plan book in front of me as soon as practicable when they see me come into the classroom in "observation mode," which in my case means "computer in hand." (Tenured teachers get two observations a year and non-tenured teachers get four.) Then I can see what was planned for the lesson and (hopefully) understand better what was intended and the depth of thought that went into it. I also ask for the first week's plan the Friday before school starts and for a half-year lesson sequence (major topics) at the beginning of the year and again in January. The hope is that teachers will look toward the big picture—the essential questions—of their subject and how they can be answered during the course of the year.

Dr. Virginia S. Newlin, NBCT
Principal
Rock Hall Middle School
Rock Hall, Maryland

statistics

The MetLife Survey of the American Teacher: Transitions and the Role of Supportive Relationships (2004–2005) reported on the frequency of a principal's observation of new teachers:

	Elementary	Secondary
A few times a week or more	35%	28%
A few times a month	45%	51%
A few times a semester	13%	14%
A few times a year	7%	6%

Figure 22.4

Generic Lesson Plan Format

Teacher _____ Subject _____ Time Requirements _____	
Grade Level _____ Period _____ Date _____	
Content Standards	(List the standards that are being addressed in the lesson plan.)
Prerequisites	(This is the prior knowledge requisite for success.)
Instructional Objectives	(These are derived from the standards and tempered by the students' prior knowledge.)
Adaptations	(These are accommodations for English language learners and students with special needs, including the gifted.)
Materials	(All specialized equipment and materials are listed here.)
Motivation	(This is a description of how you will engage the students.)
Procedures	(List the steps in the lesson.)
Assessment/Evaluation	(This describes how you will determine the extent to which students have attained the instructional objectives.)
Follow-up Activities	(These are indications of how to reinforce and extend this lesson, including homework, assignments, and projects.)
Reflection	(What went well, what adaptations should you make next time, and what needs to be re-taught as a result of the assessment?)

Format for Lesson Plans

You may want to use the 5E lesson plan (BSCS, 1997) for discovery lessons. The steps include

Phase	Teacher Role
1 Engage	Motivate or capture the students' interest.
2 Explore	Enable the students to engage in a hands-on experience or experiment.
3 Explain	Introduce formal concepts and vocabulary.
4 Elaborate	Go into greater detail using the concept in different contexts.
5 Evaluate	Assess students' learning.

Or you might prefer the popular seven-step lesson plan developed by Madeleine Hunter (R. Hunter, 2004), which prescribes the following seven stages:

Phase	Teacher Role
Anticipatory Set	motivates, focuses attention of students
Statement of Objectives	tells students what they will accomplish
Instructional Input	explains, lectures, demonstrates, gives instructions
Modeling	demonstrates, shows
Check for Understanding	watches faces, ask questions, asks for summary
Guided Practice	guides and corrects students as they practice
Independent Practice	monitors students as they work on their own

Organizing Your Lesson Plans

Duplicate whatever forms you plan on using or mix and match forms as appropriate, with the key headings you need already in place. Then, it is just a matter of filling in the blanks. Keep the plans in a loose-leaf folder.

Write your plans in pencil because they will change! Develop a code for identifying what was adequately covered, what needs to be re-taught, and what never got taught because of interruptions or a special assembly. You also might want to identify those activities that didn't work, those that were great fun, and those that needed more time. Use symbols or differently colored check marks as you review the previous week's plan before you begin the following one. Post-it™ notes or flags are also very popular with teachers. Affix them to your plan book to help you remember what needs review, what needs total re-teaching, what didn't get taught, and so forth. If you create a system that works for you, you will save yourself a great deal of time trying to remember whether you taught an activity and how well it went.

Classroom Artifacts

(As seen on http://www.LessonPlansPage.com)

Elizabeth Hodgson, a K–5 science teacher, and Rachel Vogelpohl Meyen, a fourth grade teacher, both from Durham, North Carolina, share an example of a lesson plan that accommodates learners through multiple intelligences. This plan also demonstrates integration of social studies, language arts, and technology standards and team planning. The codes are mine and illustrate how you can mark your plans or code your plan book to remind you of where you stand vis-à-vis your plans. Notice that the standards are the same as the objectives.

Ran out of time ←   *They liked this activity* ♥   *Need to return to this* ●

Topic: North Carolina
Curriculum Areas: Social Studies, Language Arts, Computers/Internet
Grade Level: 4

Standards/Objectives

Social Studies

2.03 Describe the similarities and differences among people of North Carolina, past and present.
3.02 Identify people, symbols, events, and documents associated with North Carolina's history.
5.02 Describe traditional art, music, and craft forms in North Carolina.

English Language Arts

4.02 Use oral and written language to: present information and ideas in a clear, concise manner, discuss, interview, solve problems, and make decisions.
4.07 Compose fiction, nonfiction, poetry, and drama using self-selected and assigned topics and forms (e.g., personal and imaginative narratives, research reports, diaries, journals, logs, rules, instructions).
5.07 Use established criteria to edit for language conventions and format.

Technology

3.01 Create, format, save, and print a
      word-processed document.

Materials:

- Pencil
- Paper
- Computer with Microsoft Word software
- Tape recorder
- Blank tapes

Activities:

Diary Entry Writing Continued

Students should finish creating their
diary entries. They will continue to utilize their chosen medium from the day
before. ♥

Publishing Diary Entries

Upon the completion of their writing,
students should edit, save, print (rewrite
or retell) their entries, depending on
their chosen medium. The students
should complete their entries by the
time the presentations are scheduled to
begin, though presentations should continue, with all students presenting their
material, even if they have not fully
completed their editing process.

Diary Entry Presentation ←

Group children (approximately eight to
a group) so that one member of each
Web Quest group is in each of the new,
larger groups. Each student will read or
play his/her diary entry for the group.
At the end, each group will vote on one
entry to be shared with the entire class.

Present the chosen entries to the class,
and allow the students to ask and
answer questions and comment.

KWHL Chart ⭘

Move the students' attention back to the
original KWHL chart. Add information
to the "learned" column, and then begin
a discussion and analysis of the mis-
conception the students may have originally had about North Carolina's
history of slavery and the Underground
Railroad.

Multiple Intelligences:

Verbal/Linguistic: (reading, discussing students' diary entries, presenting those
entries to class)

Intrapersonal: (creation of own diary entry)

Interpersonal: (communicating/sharing
entries in groups)

Note: Activity also appeals to auditory
(listening to and discussing diary presentations) learners.

Assessment:

Assessment of students' diary entry, using
the *diary-writing rubric.*

Affective assessment of *students' reflections* on the unit content, the teaching
strategies employed, and their general
interest levels will also be completed at
this point.

Figure 22.5

Lesson Plan Template

Benefits of using the Lesson Plan template

Keeping lesson plans in this way allows for consistency and easy transfer of assignments into the Makeup Work and Substitute Lesson templates. It is also a way for administrators to check and assimilate plans "at a glance."

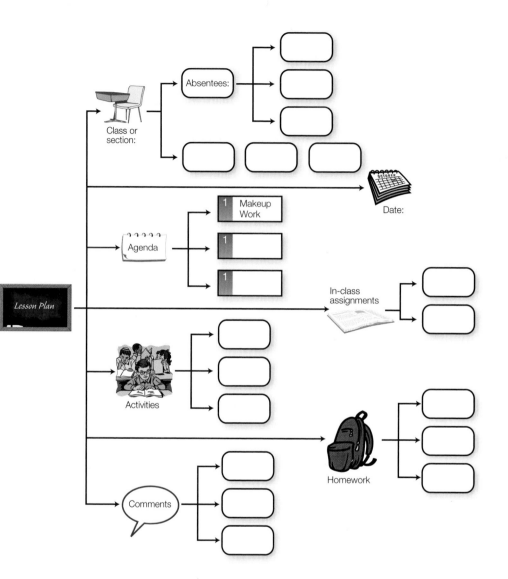

The Software program *Inspiration* has some excellent planning forms that will enable you to just fill in the blanks and print them out. Many schools utilize this software and it is popular with students of all ages, even the young ones who have their own version called *Kidspiration*. *Kidspiration* enables young children to design thematic webs using pictures and symbols, even if they cannot read or write fluently. Consult the website http://www.inspiration.com and the example of one such lesson planning template in Figure 22.5.

Avoid It!

Teachers generally feel overwhelmed by writing so many plans, especially for an elementary class. Don't think of the time it takes. Think about the time it saves down the road for the current and upcoming years! You may choose to share your plans, use them again, or post them on one of the lesson plan websites cited at the end of this unit. If you are assigned the same grade level or the same subjects to teach in middle school or high school, you will have plans in your binder ready for some tweaking, but you won't have to start from scratch. Your subsequent years will be easier because you have committed your plans to paper and have kept them. Also, think about what would happen if you don't take the time! Winging it is for the birds!

The most common planning mistakes to avoid are:
- Lesson objectives that do not specify a measurable or observable student outcome
- Assessments that are not linked or do not measure the specific behavior indicated in the objective
- Not collecting enough information about student readiness
- Activities that are not directly related to helping the students achieve the desired goal or objective
- Too much busy work and/or very time-consuming projects that lack substance

*The best things
in life are free.*

American Proverb

Chapter **23**

How Do I Gather Materials and Resources to Support My Instruction?

Effectiveness Essentials

■ Conduct an inventory of materials provided by the school, district, and resource centers.

■ Carefully screen the materials you select for any gender, racial, ethnic, cultural, or age stereotypes and bias.

■ Identify sources (including parents) of free materials, supplies, services, and field trips in your school community.

■ Be resourceful and creative when it comes to securing teaching materials and supplies so you don't spend your own money needlessly.

Before you arrive

After you stocked your room

Visit your storage rooms ASAP

Unfortunately, as with most public and private organizations today, our nations' schools find themselves feeling the squeeze of budget cuts. This squeeze often filters down to each individual teacher. At the beginning of the school year, in a "worst-case" scenario, you may arrive to find an empty room with four bare walls and nothing but tables and chairs and a teacher's desk. Classrooms you have observed or student taught in are chock-full of materials and supplies, and the resource centers and supply and storage rooms are veritable candy stores of resources, instructional materials, and supplies. But beware, on your first day of teaching, the cupboards in your classroom may be bare! And while you will likely have

some materials to get started with, even in the best situations, the materials provided may not be as voluminous as you might prefer. Therefore, all teachers have to become resourceful and creative. This chapter will help you gather, order, buy, and use materials wisely.

Locating Resources and Supplies

An instructional resource is somebody or something that can be used as a source of information or help. Resources might include models for science, maps, globes, kits, DVDs, computer hardware and software, or human resources in the school or community. There are multiple resources available to you, and you just have to

Teacher Talks . . .

On that fateful day in February I got a phone call at 3:30 p.m. from my soon-to-be principal offering me my first job. They would be creating a new kindergarten class due to over-flow and I would be the teacher starting tomorrow! I rushed over to the school with eight hours of wak-ing time before 24 kids would arrive. The room was bare—no tables, chairs, nor wall decoration. I quickly made friends with the other kindergarten teachers—begged and borrowed chairs, tables, minimal materials, and was ready to go at 8:30 the next morning.

Jan Christian
First Grade
San Bernardino, California

ask for them. Supplies are those tools that enable you and your students to conduct business. Included are the crayons, pencils, paper, paste, rulers, bulletin board border, art supplies, scissors, etc. The materials you use in your classroom can be found or obtained in a number of places.

Your School Site

Your school site is the first place to search out resources and supplies. You can ask for help from the principal, the resource specialist, the assistant principal, or one of the other teachers. They will be able to tell you where instructional materials, kits, media, and technology are located and how to secure what you need. They also can help you conduct an inventory of supplies provided by the school. You will need to conduct an extensive survey to establish what is provided so that you will know what you need to obtain elsewhere. Check with grade-level or same-subject colleagues for resources and supplies. Contrary to some myths, teachers do share.

The District Office

Your next stop, after you have surveyed the resources at school, is your district's resource centers. Does your

district have a media center from which you can borrow a digital camera, a digital video camera, or an LCD projector? Does the instructional materials resource center have that skeleton you have been seeking for biology class or the model of a volcano? Is there a curriculum library with instructional kits, idea books, and prepackaged units tied to the standards? These centers are repositories for instructional resources shared across schools, and it is important to determine the location of this gold mine, whatever name it goes by in your district. Make sure to ask about procedures for borrowing materials from the district, length of time they may be kept, and whether they can be renewed.

Survey all print and non-print media, and carefully screen the materials you select for any gender, racial, ethnic, cultural, or age stereotypes and bias. Choose materials that reflect the diversity in schools and a modern world view. Survey videos, videodiscs, computer software, DVDs, photographs, cassettes, posters, and other non-print materials that relate to your grade level or subject matter standards. The resource center personnel will help you identify resources, given your subject matter and standards.

Myth Buster!

Teachers like to keep materials and ideas to themselves.

In my experience of thirty years as a classroom teacher I know that teachers like to share. Teachers are very creative people and the more ideas we hear, the better we are able to adapt them to our own situations. I hear an idea and it sends me off in thousand different directions. I may not be able to come up with the original idea but I can spin off from other teachers. When another teacher asks for ideas or materials from me, I feel complimented. It makes me feel that I am pretty good, after all! Conferences are the way that teachers share all of their ideas. Every conference you go to, you write down all of the ideas and can't wait to get back to your own classroom to try them out.

Hester Turpin
Reading Specialist
District Resource Literacy Teacher
Colton, California

Other Institutional Resources

Consider other, often overlooked sources of free instructional resources: public and university libraries and local museums. Universities are resources for special equipment in science or social studies. Public libraries have large selections of videos, DVDs, and books for your standards-based units. Museums lend displays and kits to schools and often have a cadre of docents who bring everything from snakes to Native American artifacts to your classroom.

Apply It!

In your staff room, initiate a sharing system for instructional materials and/or supplies. A colleague who has what is requested simply signs the appropriate space, and the initiator now knows whom to contact (see Figure 23.1). Items are crossed out as the orders are filled. Use a chalkboard so items can be erased easily.

Figure 23.1

Sharing System among Colleagues

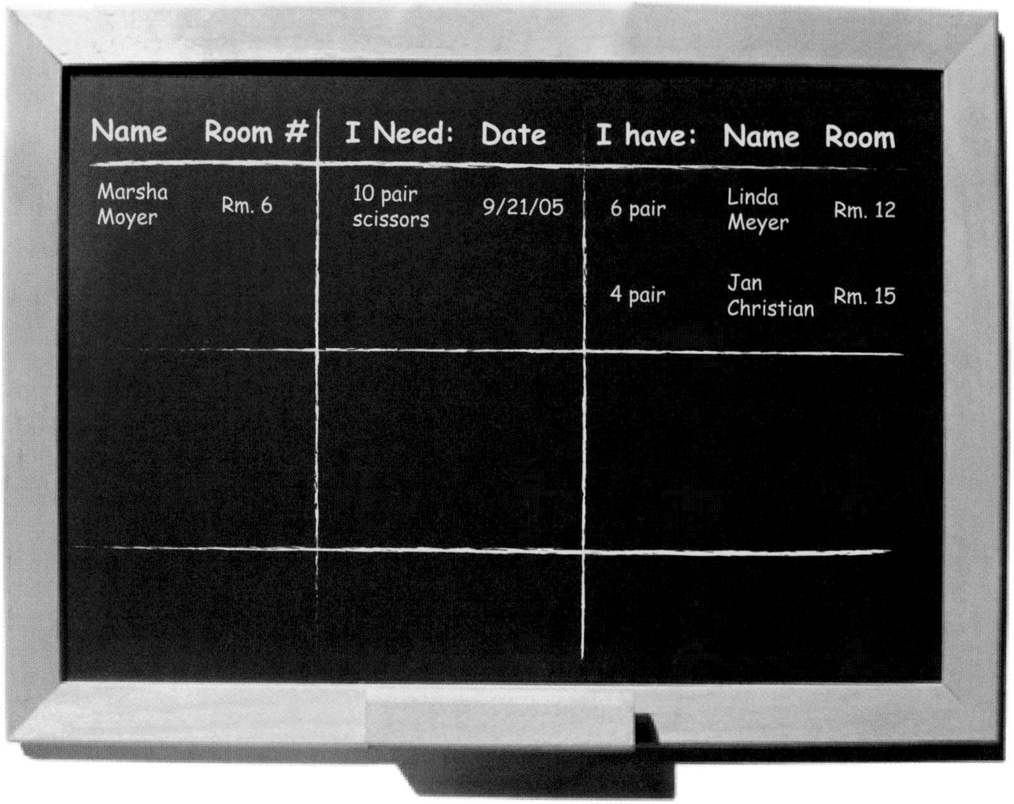

Name	Room #	I Need:	Date	I have:	Name	Room
Marsha Moyer	Rm. 6	10 pair scissors	9/21/05	6 pair	Linda Meyer	Rm. 12
				4 pair	Jan Christian	Rm. 15

Parents as Sources

The parents of students in your class are another source of supplies. Many schools send home a suggested supplies list by grade level (see Figure 23.2). Some school districts and schools post their lists on the school's website.

In addition, parents can collect cost-free supplies for class use. Large-size ice cream vats, the type used at multiflavor-type stores, make wonderful storage cubicles when piled up on one another. Shoe boxes or milk cartons with the front ends cut out suit a

Figure 23.2

School Supply Lists

Kindergarten/Grade 1	Grade Three	Grade Four, Five, Six	Grade Eight
white glue or stick	white glue or stick	white glue or stick	2 or 3 inch 3-ring binder w/dividers (Science—stays in class)
crayons	crayons/colored pencils	crayons/colored pencils	1 or 1.5 inch 3-ring binder w/dividers (Math)
pencils	pencils	pencils	5 subject ("big") spiral notebook (World Geography)
scissors	scissors	scissors	200–400 sheets of loose leaf paper
pocket folders	pocket folders	pocket folders	Several one-subject spiral notebooks
composition notebook (hardback black and white)	composition notebook (hardback black and white) or spiral notebooks or binder	composition notebook (hardback black and white) or spiral notebooks or binder	1 composition book (English)
towel/rest mat	loose leaf paper	loose leaf paper	1 dozen or more #2 pencils
tissues	tissues	tissues	1 bag of pens (blue or black)
supply box	supply box	supply box	1 box of colored pencils
ruler: cm. and inches	pens	pens	1 box of markers
	ruler: cm. and inches	ruler: cm. and inches	1 glue stick
	highlighters	highlighters	1 calculator
	index cards	index cards	1 protractor
		protractor	1 protractor (to keep at home)
		backpack to carry items	2 boxes of tissues for classrooms
		day planner/organizer	

Figure 23.3

Cubbies from Ice Cream Vats

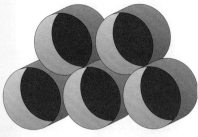

Figure 23.4

Folder Storage from Cereal Boxes

similar purpose, as do wine cartons when the cross pieces are left intact. Large-size cereal or soap powder boxes, when cut on the bias, make sturdy file boxes, book holders, and paper caddies (see Figures 23.3 and 23.4). Duplicate (translate as appropriate) your own list of needed containers

Student Supplies for High School and Elementary School

and send the list home to parents/guardians with a polite cover letter, samples of which are shown in the Classroom Artifacts on the next page. Here are a few suggestions:

Item	Container Needed
Paste	Film cans
Pencils/pens	Orange juice/coffee cans
Math manipulatives or word banks	Margarine containers
Scissors/paint brushes/rulers	Coffee cans
Paint containers	Orange juice cans
Paint mixing	Margarine containers
File folders, magazines, paper storage	Cardboard boxes, cereal and soap powder boxes
Planters	Milk containers cut down
Cooking bowls	Margarine containers/milk containers
Assorted materials	Styrofoam trays
Storage cubicles	Ice cream vats, milk cartons

And don't forget that parents can serve as good resources, too. Parents with jobs that tie into your instruction can be guest speakers. Or perhaps they can serve as good connections for obtaining needed resources.

Apply It!

Compose a letter that can go home the first week of school requesting materials and supplies unique to your subject matter and standards-based instructional needs.

Ordering Materials Wisely

Policies regarding the ordering of instructional materials and supplies differ greatly from district to district, and from school to school. Usually, your principal will outline the ordering procedures at the first staff meeting. Information of this sort can also be obtained from the department head, staff members, the policy manual if one exists, the school secretary, the resource specialist, or the

Classroom Artifacts

Dear Parent or Guardian,

We are setting up a classroom store to help us learn to add and subtract money. Will you please save, wash, and smooth the rough edges of cans of all varieties. Please leave the labels intact. We can also use empty food boxes and plastic containers. Please send the empties to school with your child during the first week in November, and please make sure to stop by toward the end of the week to see us operating our store. We thank you for your help.

Sincerely,
Mrs. Jan Garcia and Class 2-1
Parkville School

Dear Parents:

We are trying to gather a supply of art materials to use all year long. Please look through the list and send to school any that you have available during the month of September. We thank you in advance for helping us to make art more exciting.

scraps of fabric	wallpaper remnants	wooden spools
old shirts for smocks	film cans for paste	shelving remnants
yarn	bottle caps	egg cartons
newspapers for papier-mache	margarine containers	cardboard remnants
cotton batting	wood scraps	brown paper bags
juice cans for paint containers	coffee cans for brushes	toilet paper rolls
	greeting card fronts	corrugated cardboard

Please pack like items together in a brown paper bag and label the bag as to its contents. This will make sorting materials easier. We thank you for your cooperation.

Sincerely,
Mr. Mark Horowitz
Art Teacher
Bridgeport Middle School

Apply It!

Your own ordering priorities will depend on how well endowed your school is, how much you can gather from other sources, and your own needs. Begin to list the items you would order if you could. These should be items not readily available from other sources. You can always add to your list or remove any items you happen to obtain elsewhere.

grapevine. It is important for you to know how monies are allocated.

1. Are all teachers allotted a sum, solely for their own use?
2. Does the school principal rank your requests, along with all others, alone or with the help of a school committee?
3. Is the budget so limited that resources are doled out as long as they last?

If you gain support from co-workers and approach your administrator with a specified need, a list of instructional materials that will meet the need, the exact cost of such materials, and a list of colleagues eager to share the materials purchased, you have a better chance of having your request granted. Your principal may set forth criteria for ordering wisely, but here are three criteria that might help you obtain what you need:

1. Ordered items should help meet individual differences.
2. Ordered items should be non-consumable.
3. Ordered items should be sturdy, long lasting, and adaptable.

Sample items that meet these three tests of durability include:

- multicultural materials
- computer software
- globes, maps, atlases
- tapes, CDs, DVDs, and videos
- manipulative materials
- supplementary reading books
- science equipment
- teacher resource or idea books
- lab coats
- storage and file cabinets
- bookshelves
- science and social studies kits
- simulations and educational games
- almanacs, thesauruses, dictionaries, other reference books

Going the Extra Mile for Materials

As an aspiring school supplies "pack rat," consider some outside sources of free and inexpensive instructional materials. If you are like most beginning teachers, your salary precludes excessive spending and there is no reason to spend hard-earned dollars when there are many no- or low-cost options. Start with freebies and move into sources of inexpensive materials later.

Freebie Guides

Although "freebie" guides are far from free themselves, they do contain a wealth of materials for teachers that more than makes up for the initial investment. You might suggest ordering one of each title for the school professional library or resource room. These are usually paperbacks with titles such as *Elementary Teachers' Guide to FREE Curriculum Materials, Middle School Teachers' Guide to FREE Curriculum Materials,* and *Secondary Teachers' Guide to FREE Curriculum Materials.* These titles are available from Educators Progress Service, Inc. online at http://www.freeteachingaids.com/

Apply It!

Have your students practice business letter form, handwriting, grammar, and spelling by selecting a needed item and writing a letter requesting it as your representative. They can also write for innumerable items listed in their own freebie guide, *Free Stuff for Kids* (2001).

Book Clubs and Free Books

Free books for your classroom can be slowly amassed by encouraging your students to subscribe to pupil book clubs, if district policy allows this. Some districts may not want to burden you with the extra responsibility for collecting monies, or they may feel that economically disadvantaged students will be left out. Usually, given a certain quantity ordered, the teacher can select a specified number of titles free. This may seem like a small reward, but the books do pile up and they are free and current. Less current titles can be obtained from public libraries, which often cull their collections to make room for new titles. Inexpensive trade books can be found at swap meets, garage sales, and used-book stores.

The Local Community

No matter where you teach or at what level, you need to examine your local community for ideas to enhance your classroom instruction.

Source for Supplies. If you are searching for a real bounty of assorted free supplies and materials, look to all the various commercial establishments in and around your neighborhood. Many of the large office supply stores have set up special programs to help schools obtain supplies. Shoppers can earmark a specific school, and a portion of the receipts are donated to that school. Find out if businesses in your area have set up programs such as this. Also, feel free to ask about educators' discounts where you shop. My local chain bookstore offers teachers discounts and so do other local businesses. You should always ask.

Your students can be excellent scavengers for freebies and you can give them a list of needed materials that they can easily find and save at home or gather in the neighborhood. It will teach them a great deal about recycling opportunities in their very own homes.

Here are just a few examples of what a superb scrounger can obtain:

Rug companies	Sample books for art projects
	Remnants to define areas
	Foam for stuffing projects
Wallpaper stores	Sample books for art projects
	Remnants to cover bulletin boards
Supermarkets	Cardboard cartons and boxes
	Styrofoam trays
	Plastic berry baskets
	Seasonal displays
	Old magazines
Lumberyard	Scrap wood
	Dowels for puppets
	Wood curls for class pets
Notions store	Buttons, sequins, glitter, yarn, tape, trimmings, needles, thread
Shoe repair shop	Scraps of leather, laces
Ice cream stores	3-gallon ice cream vats for storage
Cleaners	Wire hangers, plastic bags for clay projects
Copy/print shops	Paper of all colors, shapes
Tile companies	Scraps of mosaic tile for art projects
Garages/auto repair	Wheels, tires, assorted junk for construction
Telephone company	Colored wire, telephones on loan
Florists	Wire, foam blocks, tissue paper
Travel agencies	Travel posters, brochures

Apply It!

Check through your local community directory and Yellow Pages. Identify your own potential sources. The first time you ask, you will be embarrassed. The second time, you will be ill at ease. By the third inquiry, you will be a pro, reinforced by the positive responses you most probably will receive. Start your own scrounging directory and keep adding to it. List the establishment, the address, telephone number, and items received. Your students can write thank-you notes for each donation.

Local Field Trips. Your school community can also be a source of free field trips to support instructional goals. These off-the-beaten-path field trips often require no buses, no money, and no bother. It's good for business, excellent public relations, and, most of all, stimulating for both the tour guides and the student tourists. Here are a few examples of unusual, free field trips that can be arranged through local business establishments in my area:

Fast-food restaurant—Tour of the operation	Recycling plant—Tour
A florist—Students are taught to make a corsage	Veterinary clinic—Tour
Tortilla factory—Students sample and see how tortillas are made	Western Union office—Tour and explanation of telegram delivery
County courthouse—Tour including courtroom; visit to a trial in progress	City Hall—Tour including City Council when in session
Dairy—Tour of milking facility	Bank—Tour of operations
Newspaper—Tour of newspaper facility	Stables—Tour and presentation on care of horses
Radio station—Tour	Pizzeria—Tour and demonstration of pizza-making process
Post Office—Tour of facility	Police station—Tour, often including fingerprinting
Medical center—Tour	
Yardage store—Tour, including discussion of different fabrics	Fire department—Tour
Bakery—Tour	Sheriff's helicopter—Tour and demonstration
Grocery chain—Tour	

Teacher Talks . . .

When I wanted the students to work in small groups in order to write or chart activities, I needed something they could use beside paper. I went to a home improvement store and bought two large shower boards. They cut each large board into six smaller pieces (they are a nice size), I now have twelve good sized white boards for the students to use. When the students work in small groups, they each use a different dry erase marker on the board. They are great for small group activities such as Venn diagrams, character listings, math and science. They are quite handy when the teacher is working with small groups and needs something to use besides paper and pencil. The students love using them and they are really motivating.

Ivania Martin
Former Fourth Grade Teacher
Benicio, California

Apply It!

Explore the free field trip options surrounding your school. I included only generic names in my list because the same services may not be available from a different branch of the same international or national chain in your area. Start your own directory of free, local field trips. Begin with your friends or neighbors. Is one neighbor an optometrist? Ask if you can tour the office with your class. Does another work in a local hospital? Arrange a visit. Does another work in a bank? Get behind the scenes. Friends and relatives will be very understanding, as will local professionals and business people. A thank-you card or gift from the class will be much appreciated by those who offer their services and time as tour guides. What better way is there for incorporating career education into your curriculum? Share these sources with your colleagues. Get a school-wide directory going.

At the Fire Station

Teacher Stores and Campus Stores

Many teachers spend money at local teachers' supply stores. If you have saved money by following the suggestions in this chapter, you can be a bit extravagant and feel comfortable doing so! You can probably find out from a colleague the name of the supply store frequented by most teachers in your area. These stores are to teachers what candy stores are to kids.

Middle and high school teachers should add any instructional resources and supplies that directly relate to their subject areas. In addition, you may want to consider ordering or buying more file folders, Post-it™ notes, index cards, and dry erase markers. Look for teen-oriented posters and rewards. Use your funds sparingly here and make sure that items you are purchasing cannot be obtained free with a little ingenuity. Most often they can be!

Some middle and high schools have campus stores where students may purchase needed items. Encourage secondary students to purchase student planners so they can organize their assignments.

On a Field Trip

Bargains at Discount and Warehouse Mega-Stores

Other sources of inexpensive supplies are the various discount and warehouse stores in your neighborhood. These are the bottom-line stores, the bargain hunter's paradise, and the ultimate in cost cutting. Here, trade books for students may cost $.99, as opposed to $8.50. Art supplies and food items may be bought in bulk at a fraction of the regular cost. Remember to shop for school supplies as you shop for large items for yourself. Look for the least expensive items that will hold up with constant use.

Recycled Merchandise

Garage sales, thrift stores, swap meets, bazaars, and auctions are sources of inexpensive materials and low-cost treasures. Teachers find perfectly good chairs, tables, lamps, plants, and rugs at these venues. You can accessorize your classroom with recycled items that are as good as new. My house is furnished with cast-offs, but they are called antiques!

Buy what you need, buy what you anticipate needing, but remember that free is possible, preferable, and more gratifying. Organize your materials in large, colorful, and well-marked boxes so you can keep the clutter to a minimum at home and at school.

Students need planning tools too.

Avoid It!

Don't be too concerned about not having everything you want during those first days and weeks of school. You will gather materials slowly, and pretty soon you will be competitive with the other pack rats at your school. Remember that in ancient Greece, Socrates did pretty well without a fully stocked classroom—in fact, without a classroom at all!

I am not authorized to fire substitute teachers.

Bart Simpson,
cartoon character

Chapter **24**

How Do I Plan for Classroom Aides and Substitutes?

Effectiveness Essentials

- Instructional aides can offer both clerical and instructional support in your classroom.

- Many teacher assistants work extensively with students with special needs.

- Your aide should spend as much time as possible working directly with students.

- Establish a good working relationship with your aide and clearly define his or her role and responsibilities.

- Clearly communicate your classroom systems, procedures, and instructional strategies.

- The more information your substitute has about your class, general procedures, and schedule, the better this person will handle the other ambiguities.

- Provide the substitute with clear lesson plans and alternative motivating activities that you know your students enjoy.

- Talk to your class about the role of the substitute teacher and the need to respect him or her.

Working with an Instructional Aide

When a classroom or instructional aide is assigned to your classroom, you may feel anxious and delighted at the same time. You are delighted that you will have the additional help, but also you are likely to feel a little nervous about what to do with this extra person in light of your own concerns about beginning the school year.

The Role of the Instructional Aide

Instructional aides, sometimes called *para-educators* or *paraprofessionals,* offer you clerical and instructional support in your classroom. Their assistance affords you additional time for planning and teaching. The best para-educators enjoy working with students from diverse backgrounds. They are expected to follow your directions for individual and small group instruction and to handle discipline with the same patience and sense of fairness that you do.

Many teacher assistants work extensively with students with special needs. As more and more schools follow the inclusion model—that is, integrating special education students into general education classrooms—your para-educator is essential in helping you provide the extra assistance and ensure the successful inclusion of students with special needs.

Bilingual instructional aides also provide extra attention to your English language learners. They can communicate with parents, help your students transition to English, and assist you in establishing links with the community.

Instructional aides in secondary schools often specialize in a certain subject, such as math or science. They may assist with special projects; prepare

Let's plan together

Two times the assistance

> ## A Preschool Aide Talks . . .

I've learned from my work with children with special needs to always have a backup plan, and that changing focus mid-lesson is not only necessary sometimes but okay, too. Coming back to a lesson can be great, especially if there was a physical break in the meantime, i.e., drop the counting game to make a train with the children and march around the room before picking up the counting game again. It is surprising how often children's attention improves.

I've learned that an understandable and reliable routine helps students and teachers. Of course, flexibility is important, but flexibility within a predictable routine works best.

Sarah Dominick
Preschool aide
Autistic preschoolers
Stockholm, Maine

Aides can help in many subject areas.

materials and equipment; design and implement special exhibits; or set up a science experiment in a lab. A knowledgeable technology aide can lend support in the computer lab or in individual classrooms with hardware or software issues.

Preparing to Work with an Aide

Before working with an aide, ask some policy questions about traditional paraprofessional duties at your school site. Aides may talk among themselves, and you don't want to miss the mark with too little or too much initial responsibility. Find out:

1. How many hours per day/days per week your aide will be in your classroom.
2. What legal constraints exist vis-à-vis a paraprofessional's responsibilities in the classroom.
3. What duties aides traditionally perform in your school.
4. What the other teachers at your grade level do with their aides.

Avoid It!

Williams and Snipper (1990) caution that if teachers ask the bilingual aide to work with English learners exclusively, especially without giving the aide any direction or instruction, your students' academic development may suffer. Furthermore, the non-native speakers may feel abandoned by the teacher and feel inferior to the other students who have the "teacher's" attention.

Have your aide spend as much of his or her time as possible working with students. Veterans were asked what roles and responsibilities aides or paraprofessionals generally assume in the classroom. Their responses follow:

- reading with small groups
- assisting individuals during seat work
- conducting drills in small groups
- reinforcing and reviewing reading and math skills
- tutoring individuals/providing enrichment
- overseeing learning center activities
- taking dictation for stories
- assisting students with the computer
- monitoring activities
- correcting papers
- entering grades
- updating records
- filing
- repairing books
- restocking from supply closet
- changing bulletin boards
- preparing materials for lessons
- running off and collating copies
- binding student's stories into books
- laminating materials for class use
- using your lesson plans to differentiate instruction
- supervising students in the cafeteria and hallways
- setting up equipment
- preparing instructional materials

An Aide Talks to Teachers . . .

It is important to keep in mind that you, as the teacher, need to be flexible in working with your aides. People have their own personalities. Therefore, there is room for conflict. Just remember that you need to give and take throughout the time you work together. Dictatorships will not work.

*C. Francine Apacible
Classroom Bilingual Aide
Hillside School
San Bernardino, California*

Orienting Your Aide

The other pair of eyes, ears, and hands will be a bonus in so many ways if you are approachable, flexible, clear, organized, and appreciative. The aide will be just as nervous as you are, and as a team you can make the most of the instructional time in the classroom. Your students will be the beneficiaries.

1. The first step in establishing a good working relationship with your aide involves getting to know this individual as a person. If possible, before school starts, set aside a time to talk face-to-face about your mutual prior experience working with students, your philosophies of education, attitudes toward discipline, and skills you both bring to the classroom.

statistics

According to the Bureau of Labor Statistics (2004):

Teacher assistants held almost 1.3 million jobs in 2002.

Approximately 4 in 10 teacher assistants work part time.

Median annual earnings of teacher assistants in 2002 were $18,660.

Nearly 3 out of 4 teacher assistants work in public preschool and elementary schools.

2. Determine what the role and responsibilities of the paraprofessional will be and write them down. Blank schedules, one per week, that clearly outline your aide's duties day-by-day, time slot by time slot can be very helpful in delineating these tasks.

3. Establish an ongoing time during each week to sit down and plan for the following week. Charles and Senter (2005) suggest that you include a discussion of professionalism in your orientation, incorporating such items as appropriate dress, demeanor, promptness, dependability, and avoidance of gossip.

4. Discuss your record-keeping system and orient the aide to your marking procedures and to the instructional materials he or she may be using. Supply a duplicate set of manuals if they are available. Provide a workstation for your aide and a place to store clothing and personal items. Post your aide's name up on the door and chalkboard alongside your own. Make clear to your students that your aide is there as a second teacher and will enforce the same rules and discipline system.

5. Communicate appreciation to your aide frequently and in novel ways. Some teachers present aides with small gifts, award certificates, or recognition luncheons (Figure 24.1).

Figure 24.1

Appreciation

Certificate of Appreciation
Awarded to

_____

For Outstanding Service in B3

Teacher and Students

Coaching Your Aide

Offer suggestions regarding motivating activities and game formats, every-pupil response techniques, positive discipline strategies, questioning techniques. If you are working in a special education full-inclusion classroom or simply with a mainstreamed population, your aide will prove to be that second pair of eyes, hands, and ears that you will desperately need. Provide coaching in the following areas and others as needed:

- Technology and software applications
- Questioning and feedback strategies
- Motivational techniques and building on students' prior knowledge
- Game formats for drill and practice
- Every-pupil response techniques
- Your discipline plan and positive desist techniques
- The elements of lesson planning
- Facilitation of cooperative groups
- Shortcuts for checking student work
- The purpose and organization of student portfolios

Preparing for Substitute Teachers

The substitute teacher is a valued member of a classroom team, a pinch hitter in emergencies. The brave substitute may be unfamiliar with the school, the class, the grade level, the materials, and the content. In addition to all the ambiguity that goes along with the position, 30 plus students sometimes mistake the arrival of a substitute for party time. I have seen students who act like angels with their own teachers suddenly demoralize substitutes.

Avoid It!

Although your aide may have more school experience and be older than you are, remember that you earned your credential. Stay calm and allay fears of being watched and judged. When you relax and maintain open communication channels with your aide, you'll find that two heads will accomplish far more than one. As your relationship with your aide deepens, you'll wonder how you ever managed or could manage alone.

You need to be of assistance to substitutes to make their service to you and your class more effective. The substitute may be called in at the last minute, and you want to ensure that learning takes place in your absence. You don't want to have to pick up the pieces when you return to school, nor do you want to stay at home with the flu feeling guilty about what might be going on in your absence. There are a few guidelines that you can follow and certain preparations you can make. After that, sit at home, sniffle, and hope for the best.

Teacher Talks . . .

I leave great substitute teacher plans and I never labor over them for hours the night before. During the third or fourth week of school, after I have figured out the kids and we have established our procedures, I write my sub plans. They are in generic format that I will use for 90% of the days that I am absent. All of the subjects and routines are explicitly typed out. I include every detail of what we are accustomed to, things that only the students and I know out of habit because we are there. I leave space to highlight the particulars that change from day to day, like the title of the read-aloud book, the math work that we are on, or special events.

The night before the sub comes, I write in the order of the schedule and highlight the priorities. It leaves me confident that a new sub knows exactly what to

(continued on facing page)

The Substitute Folder

The more information your substitute has about your class, the procedures, and schedule, the better this person will handle the other ambiguities. This information needs to be in concise form because the substitute may arrive five minutes before class and will not have much time to prepare. Have a red or bright-colored folder clearly marked for substitutes so they can find it without calling out the bloodhounds. That folder should contain the following data.

- **Multiple Copies of Your Class List.** On it the substitute can make notations of all sorts and check off the homework.

- **Seating Chart.** A seating chart will help the substitute learn the names or at least call on your students with ease. The seating chart will also help the substitute quickly catch those who decide to pull a switcheroo and sit with a friend for the day.

- **School Map.** Provide a map of the school site for the substitute so that she or he can easily find key school locations. You might circle key locations in red to be even more helpful.

- **Class Schedule and Comings and Goings.** Provide a general class schedule and schedule of out-of-room activities. Be sure to include days and

Figure 24.2
Substitute Folder

times. There is often much confusion about comings and goings, and 35 voices expressing conflicting accounts of when they have library time can be most distressing to an already harried substitute.

- **Summary of Your Administrative Duties by Day.** Substitutes are expected to follow your schedule exactly, but they need to know what your extra school duties are so they can cover for you. You may have to change this schedule monthly, since your duties will change from month to month.

- **Discipline and Organization.** You want to provide some information to your substitute about your discipline plan. Include in your substitute folder the letter regarding discipline that you sent home to parents.

- **Bus Information in Concise Form.** You want to make sure that everyone gets on the right bus at the right time in your absence.
- **Buddy Teachers, Aides, and Volunteer Schedules.** Provide your substitute with the name and room number of a buddy teacher, the name of your aide and the aide's hours, the schedule of any expected volunteers for the day, and the names of three students who can be counted on to give accurate and up-to-the-minute information about classroom life in general.
- **Notations about Students with Special Needs.** Provide information about students with special needs. Some may need to see the nurse for medication or diabetic testing. Others may have adaptive P.E. Still others may have modified work programs and different behavior standards.

Lesson Plans and Bags of Tricks

When you know in advance that you will need a substitute, you can leave up-to-the-minute lesson plans and review work for the class. You can write your plans with the substitute in mind and have all the materials at hand and ready to go. Some teachers, even in an emergency, will quickly write up-to-the-minute plans and send

them to school with a friend or spouse that morning.

The lesson plans that you have already formulated should always be written in a form that would enable any reasonable person to decipher them and then teach from them. In addition, include in your substitute folder many review sheets and activities for any possible emergency, and update the material every two weeks or so just in case.

Leave the substitute a box or bag of motivating activities that you know your students enjoy. Experienced substitutes have learned to bring their own bags of tricks, but if you provide your own, tailor-made to your class, you will be several steps ahead (see Figure 24.3).

Respect for Substitutes

Talk to your class about the role of the substitute teacher and how that person is really an emergency teacher

expect, and yet I have spent the same amount of time planning that I normally do. The final special feature: I tell the sub to be very strict so that I get a warm welcome when I return.

Sarah Barten
Third Grade
Desert Sands, California

Student Says . . .

When we have an inexperienced substitute teacher, the class goes nuts. The students know they can get away with it because the subs act like big kids. When we have a sub who knows the ropes, students try to get away with it but they don't succeed. The students can tell who is strict and who isn't in five minutes. Experienced subs act like professionals.

Natalie Gibbs
Age 17, Twelfth Grade
Yucaipa, CA

I had the worst case of the flu and spent the longest time preparing substitute plans and arranging my classroom so everything would be in perfect order when the substitute arrived. The next morning my school secretary phoned me ten minutes before the bell. I thought that perhaps the plans weren't good enough. It turns out I had actually forgotten to call in for a sub!

McKayla Beach
Eighth Grade, Social Studies
Palm Springs, California

Figure 24.3
Resources for Substitute Teacher

who saves the day for learning. Discuss specific ways the class can make it easier for this pinch hitter and write them on a list. If your classroom discipline policy is based on a premise of self-responsibility, it is more likely that your students will not take too much advantage of the situation. Should you get a negative report upon your return, despite all of your preventive measures, you can impose a logical consequence, such as requiring the

culprits to write the substitute a letter of apology or bringing the whole issue up during a class meeting.

It is very important at the secondary level to instill respect for substitute teachers. These students are quite aware that the sub is vulnerable to their monkey business. Discuss in a meeting with students why you will be absent, rules of behavior, and positive and negative consequences depending on the report you receive from the substitute.

Apply It!

Start collecting materials for your substitute folder as soon as possible.

Avoid It!

Don't let any mistreatment of substitute teachers go unnoticed. The work you do to instill respect for substitutes will long be remembered and appreciated by future substitutes in your classroom.

Unit 5 Checklist

Planning and Organizing Subject Matter Checklist	**For more information go to:**
☐ Have I obtained all relevant planning documents?	Chapter 21
☐ Have I identified, with the help of others, the essential standards?	Chapter 21
☐ Have I set out a long-term plan?	Chapter 22
☐ Have I consulted with other teachers about the preferred style of lesson plans and when they are reviewed?	Chapter 22
☐ Have I bought a plan book and/or organized a notebook to collect my lesson plans?	Chapter 22
☐ Are my plans taking individual differences into account?	Chapters 22, 28, 29
☐ Have I conducted a school, district, and community survey of resources and supplies?	Chapter 23
☐ Have I made a list of basics or essentials to request from parents?	Chapter 23
☐ Have I planned for an instructional aide if one is assigned?	Chapter 24
☐ Have I organized a substitute folder and bag of tricks?	Chapter 24

Further Reading: Planning for Substitutes and Aides

Herbst, J., & Hillam, C., Illus. (2002). *The substitute teacher's organizer: A comprehensive resource to make every teaching assignment a success.* Huntington Beach, CA: Creative Teaching Press. Included in this resource are forms and ideas to create a substitute teacher binder that will help organize the materials that make a substitute's day easier.

Morgan, J., & Ashbaker, B.Y. (2001). *A teacher's guide to working with paraeducators and other classroom aides.* Alexandria, VA: Association for Supervision and Curriculum Development. This book offers advice and activities that facilitate communication between you and your aide. It focuses on how to find time to effectively work with and supervise your aide.

Seeman, C., & Hofstrand, S. (1998). *Super sub: A must have handbook for substitute teachers.* Parsippany, NJ: Pearson Learning. This handbook was written by an experienced mother-daughter team of teachers and includes in three sections: tools and advice, actual sub plans in eight areas including lists of supplies for a "bag of tricks," and sponge activities.

Selected Websites for Lesson Plans and Lesson Planning Tips

Ed Helper
http://www.edhelper.com
This website was created by teachers and features lesson plans by subject matter, webquests, free worksheets, a gradebook, puzzle maker, units, high school skills, and much more.

FREE (Federal Resources for Educational Excellence)
www.ed.gov/free
This website provides links to all educational resources from the federal government. All subject areas are covered, and secondary teachers will find it very useful.

Public Broadcasting Teacher Source
www.pbs.org/teachersource
This website features PBS teacher resources by subject and curriculum ideas across grade levels. More than 3,000 lesson plans and activities are available to you.

Discovery Channel School
http://school.discovery.com/schoolhome.html
Lesson plans, teaching tools, and streaming video make this a very valuable resource for teachers of all grade levels.

The Lesson Plans Page
www.lessonplanspage.com/
Free lesson plans in all subject areas for all grade levels are included. They are well organized by subject matter and grade level. Science projects and inspirational stories are additional features.

Websites for Information on Standards

Developing Educational Standards
http://edStandards.org
This valuable website enables you to download standards by state and by subject matter.

Department of Education
http://www.ed.gov
Here you will find the updated information on No Child Left Behind, standards, statistics, and educational resources.

Unit 6

Engaging
All Learners

Unit 6
Engaging
All Learners

If you accept the expectations of others, especially negative ones, then you never will change the outcome.

Michael Jordan

A master can tell you what he expects of you. A teacher, though, awakens your own expectations.

Patricia Neal, *actress*

Chapter **25**

How Do I Communicate Positive Expectations to My Students?

Effectiveness Essentials

- High classroom and school-wide expectations can and do affect student achievement and attitudes.

- A *self-fulfilling prophecy* occurs when an initial perception of a situation or performance creates behaviors that makes the original impression come true.

- Teachers play a critical role in helping students develop positive outlooks about themselves by creating a positive classroom atmosphere.

There was no question in my house that my sister and I would go to college. It was an expectation, reinforced from the time I was very young. I am sure that you have had similar experiences in your life. Either someone set the bar very high and you succeeded in jumping over it or you were told, "No, that's not possible." When told that you could not do something, you may have either given up or tried to prove the naysayer wrong.

The Self-Fulfilling Prophecy

High classroom and school-wide expectations can and do affect student achievement and attitudes. A key finding of effective schools research confirms that high expectations are a critical element for success. In effective schools, high expectations are communicated through policies and practices that focus on academic goals. For example, when schools raise their academic qualifications for student athletes, some students may feel unfairly targeted, but ultimately they can choose to adjust and work harder to meet the higher academic qualifications.

The general consensus is that a strong relationship exists between what we believe about students and what they can achieve. This is also known as a *self-fulfilling prophecy*. A self-fulfilling prophecy occurs when an initial perception of a situation or performance creates behaviors that make the original impression come true. Educators and the public in general have come to believe that the self-fulfilling prophecy is real and that both high and low expectations can affect student achievement. Consider the following hypothetical examples.

Let's say a student transfers into your math class from another high school and her records are late in arriving. You assume she is at grade level and make no accommodations in her program. You expect from her what you expect from all other students and she performs up to speed. When her records arrive, you are surprised to find out that she is a student with special needs who is part of the special education math inclusion program. Was she misdiagnosed originally? Did she appreciate the challenge and rise to the occasion to meet your higher expectations?

On the other side, the brother of a student you had two years ago arrives in your sixth grade class. You wrongly assume he is as disruptive as his older brother was. You seat him away from all the other students, praise him less than other students for the same positive responses and behaviors, and discipline him more harshly for ordinary offenses. Pretty soon you will have a behavior problem on your hands, one of your own making!

Early Evidence

In their 1968 study, *Pygmalion in the Classroom,* Robert Rosenthal and Lenore Jacobson were the first to suggest that teachers' expectations have a tremendous effect on student achievement. The purpose of the study was to test the hypothesis that teacher behaviors and the resulting student outcomes could be influenced by the expectations of the teachers. Rosenthal and Jacobson predicted that when teachers were informed that certain students had more intellectual potential than others, the teachers might behave in ways that supported this expectation, which would then affect student scores on IQ tests.

In their study, two groups of students in grades 1–6 were evenly matched for intelligence. Teachers were given fabricated information about the learning potential of one group, the experimental group. Teachers were told that testing results showed these students to be on the verge of a rapid

surge in intellectual development. Because teachers believed this assertion to be true, they challenged them more than they did students in the control group who were, in fact, no different intellectually. At the end of the experiment, the students in the experimental group, especially those in the early grades, displayed higher achievement on IQ tests than the students in the control group. The results led the researchers to suggest that the high expectations teachers set for the experimental group and the teacher behaviors those expectations generated were responsible for the unusual growth.

The Process

What parents and teachers believe and act upon make an indelible impression on kids. The positive expectations as well as the negative ones or the expectations that are left unsaid all leave their mark.

Good (1987) describes the process by which teacher expectations affect student outcomes. See Figure 25.1 for the circular process in graphic form.

1. At the beginning of school, the teacher makes positive or negative judgments about expectations for student behavior and achievement from attributes

Figure 25.1
Self-Fulfilling Prophecy

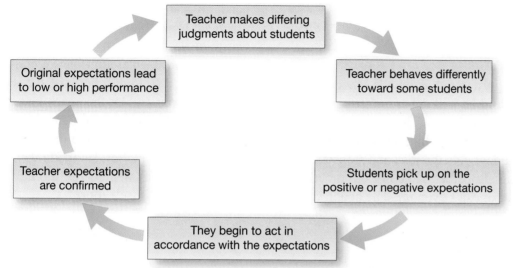

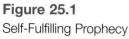

such as gender, socioeconomic level, appearance, race, culture, language ability, etc. *(The math teacher believes boys are better at math than girls.)*

2. The teacher acts on those set attitudes toward some of the students based on preconceived notions about their race, socioeconomic level, gender, etc. *(The math teacher calls on boys more, or heaps more praise on the boys' responses.)*

3. The teacher's behavior communicates to the students his or her expectations for academic performance or behavior.

(Girls feel intimidated by being called on less and they stop trying. They begin to feel that they won't succeed in math, whereas boys are encouraged by all the attention and praise they receive.)

4. When the teacher's behavior toward the student(s) continues over time and is consistent, and if students do not actively resist or change it, their self-esteem, performance, and other behaviors begin to conform to the teacher's initial impression. *(The girls don't try as hard, stop listening in class, and lose interest. They stop raising their hands. Their grades begin to suffer.)*

5. The students' behavior then reinforces the teacher's perceptions and the students conform even more to what has been expected. *(The girls' lower grades confirm the math teacher's initial perceptions.)*

A diminutive middle school student is told he will never make the varsity basketball team. The coach ignores him and doesn't let him play very often. The student gets the idea and stops practicing altogether. He comes to practice, but doesn't even try. The coach thinks to himself, "I knew it." And the boy doesn't make the team. On the other hand, my son, relatively short in stature, practiced basketball from the time he was three years old with a toddler-sized hoop. He shot basket after basket and when he went to high school, he threw his heart into it and let the coach know through attitude and performance that varsity ball was his goal and that his height wouldn't matter. He made the team. Is he more talented? Or did he just believe in himself more?

Apply It!

Think of a situation that you have been involved in where the original judgment either led to a positive or negative self-fulfilling prophecy. You can choose any of these factors, which often create self-fulfilling prophecies, or use any other factor that has led to positive or negative judgments.

Factors	Examples of Preconceived Positive and Negative Judgments That May Lead to Self-Fulfilling Prophecies
Gender	Girls are more compliant and boys more resistant.
Race/Ethnicity	Asians excel at science and math.
Socioeconomic status	Poor students don't have the means to go to college.
Grooming/Clothing	Boys who wear dark clothing are menacing.
School location (urban)	Violence is prevalent in urban classrooms.
Negative comments	Olivia's former teacher says that she is defiant.
Reading ability	Girls are better readers than boys.

Researched-based Practices for Conveying Positive Expectations

Being aware of any of your preconceived perceptions that are based on unfounded and unsupported evidence is a very important way that you can self-regulate and avoid negative self-fulfilling prophecies that will impede students' achievement. Conversely, when you focus on positive expectations, convey your belief that students will succeed, and structure learning to ensure success, your students will rise to the challenge. Recent research has provided guidelines for conveying positive expectations in a proactive way.

Adhere to Standards

Adhere to standards without changing the expectations for your students based on prior achievement data or other teachers' opinions. Good (1987) suggests that goals be established without reference to prior achievement data that may set the bar too low. Take with a grain of salt other teachers' judgments about your students' learning potential. Find out for yourself where your students are vis-à-vis the standards. Don't lower the bar. Instead, communicate to your students in word and deed that they can and will achieve the standards and/or pass the exit exams.

Specify Objectives

Set objectives that are not too specific. Marzano and colleagues (2001) caution that when objectives are too specific or stated as behavioral objectives (measurable outcome, criteria, and conditions), the students may tune out the rest of the information while they narrowly focus on the stated objective. The goals, therefore, should be specific without being constraining and should allow students to adapt them to meet their own instructional needs. For example, an objective such as "students will name the planets" may cause the students to focus on memorizing them without regard to a more holistic understanding of the relationship of the planets to one another and to the sun.

Provide Effective Feedback

There are four types of feedback that teachers make use of: positive feedback (*Great!*), negative feedback (*No, that's not right*), neutral feedback (*restating the response or saying something noncommittal such as "okay"*), and corrective feedback (*providing the*

NOTES

Chapter 25   How Do I Communicate Positive Expectations to My Students?

Teacher Talks . . .

I got a new homeroom class. I was kind of dreading it because a lot of teachers had been complaining about what a rough group they are. I thought, "Oh God, can I handle this?" So I started preparing for the new class by asking our Dean of Students what the kids needed and which ones I had to keep my eye on. She spoke about one student who was failing on purpose because he wanted to live with his father who lives in a different state.

After meeting my homeroom I thought, "They aren't so bad! In fact, they're better than my first homeroom."

All special areas teachers have to spend 25 minutes out of 90 on FCAT preparation. I was working with the kids explaining how to read arithmetic questions. Then I called out some numbers to let them do some examples. The one who had been purposefully failing last

(continued on facing page)

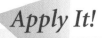

Apply It!

Here are some incorrect responses you might receive in class and corresponding corrective feedback for two of them. How will you respond to the remainder?

Student Response	Teacher Corrective Feedback
There are 300 bones in the adult human body.	Actually 300 in kids, and 206 in adults
You spell assessment, A-S-S-E-S-M-E-N-T	Try again with another *s* added.
There are 6 glasses in a quart.	_____
The President has the power to declare war.	_____
The square root of 144 is 14.	_____
The capital of New York is New York City.	_____

correct answer). Neutral feedback is effective when you want to promote multiple responses from your students. Corrective feedback puts students back on the right track and should be timely and specific to the response (Marzano et al., 2001). Tell students where they have gone right or wrong instead of just responding, "That's not right," or "Great!"

Teach Belief in Effort

Teach your students to believe in the value of effort. This means that you can provide encouragement for the little steps along the way to success, giving the E for Effort! Too little recognition is given for student efforts, according to Marzano et al., (2001), and students need to be made aware that efforts pay off. Very often, students do not see the big picture and give up when they make the slightest misstep. Your job is to stress again and again that mistakes are permitted; make a poster to that effect to hang over the chalkboard. Respond to errors with either corrective feedback or comments such as, "Let me help you fix that," or "Together we can figure this out." Have them recite this mantra every day, *What I believe about myself will affect how I perform and how successful I will be in school and in life.*

Provide Recognition

Provide recognition and dispel the notion that rewards decrease intrinsic motivation. Recognition should be given in non-tangible form, whenever possible, and be tied to attainment of performance standards, according to Marzano et al. (2001). That means you can dispense certificates, coupons, good job stamps, stickers, and even treats or small prizes. These motivate students and reinforce the idea that there are rewards for a job well done or for sincere efforts along the way. Students will bask in the recognition, and the benefits in terms of self-worth and confidence are enormous.

Guard Your Instructional Time

Protect every minute of your instructional time. Time on task without disruptions will communicate positive expectations to your students. And positive expectations will convey to your students that they will succeed. When you make every minute count, you are more likely to have students focused on the instruction without distractions. Strong school policies regarding lateness and absence will only increase the perception that school is important and that students need to be there in mind and body (Cotton, 1990).

Promote Literacy

Emphasize the importance of reading. Cotton (1990) reports that written policies regarding the amount of time spent on reading instruction daily, using a single reading series to maintain continuity, frequent free reading periods, and assigning homework which emphasizes reading will convey positive expectations. Reading is key to all learning and the emphasis, time, and importance you allot to literacy, whatever subject you teach, will pay dividends in terms of student self-esteem.

Stress the Importance of Achievement Now and Later

Emphasize to your students the importance of academic achievement now and later in life. Some schools set minimal acceptable levels of achievement to qualify for participation in extracurricular activities and sports and notify parents when expectations aren't met (Cotton, 1990). There are too few students who believe that they can actually go to college. It is your challenge to make

semester and another student kept raising their hands and answering questions correctly!

So during planning, I wrote them positive notes home to encourage the efforts in them and their classmates. The one who had been failing was so excited when I talked to him and gave him his letter that he almost started to cry. He said, "I wish that I had you as my teacher last semester. You are the first one who has ever written my mother a positive note." At the end of study hall, he thanked me once again for the letter. I could tell that this is going to turn his year around. I know that this student will do great this semester even though he misses his father and wants to live with him. I could see it in his face. So often, teachers see the classification of their students rather than their potential. Too often, they see the negatives and not the positives. One positive thing can turn a student's lifetime of negatives around. The reward is awesome!

Jennifer A. Ponsart
Music Director
Four Corners Charter School
Davenport, Florida

(As seen on http://www.LessonPlansPage.com)

Apply It!

Go to *www.Biography.com* and select some short biographies that show how people overcame initial difficulties to succeed later in life.

them believe they can do it and show them the baby steps along the way.

Take Responsibility

Take responsibility for the achievement of your students. Staff members who hold high expectations for themselves and for student performance are more likely to convey the message to students that they will succeed. Catch yourself when you want to play the blame game. Although there may be some valid reasons for students' earlier failures, big and small, it is your responsibility to take each student where he or she is and move them forward. There is no greater compliment than a successful outcome that a student attributes to you.

Intervene Right Away

Intercede immediately when students need help. When students are having difficulty understanding a concept or demonstrating a skill, find out where the problem is and re-teach in a different way, since the first way didn't work and merely repeating the same lesson will not help. Students have a variety of learning styles, and if you take into account the work of Howard Gardner, explained more fully in Chapters 22 and 28, you can offer the students alterna-

tive activities to meet the objectives you have set. Alternatively, cooperative learning groups, described in Chapter 27, are effective for students to help one another figure a problem out with minimal teacher intervention.

Connect Learning to Personal Experience

I remember someone telling me that you don't need to design dazzling enticements to motivate your students. Rather, just ask your students what they know, feel, or have experienced vis-à-vis a topic. The way to hook students into learning is to relate the topic to their experience or teach those subtopics that most interest them first.

Use the KWL strategy (Ogle, 1986) that requires a chart with three columns, What I Know, What I Want to Know, and later What I Learned. KWL is one specific strategy you can use to relate new material to prior experience and motivate your students to inquire more deeply. The students love to fill in the first column with all that they know from prior experiences or instruction. As they activate their prior knowledge, they are motivated to learn about what they don't yet know or understand. Questions beget

Figure 25.2

Connecting to Personal Experience

K	W	L
What I Know about Penguins	**What I Want to Know about Penguins**	**What I Learned about Penguins**
They are birds.	*How big are they?*	*They walk long distances.*
They live in cold places.	*Do they fly?*	*Males sit on the eggs.*

questions. Or, use sentence stems like this one, "When I think about democracy . . ." or "The questions that come to mind about the Civil War are. . . ." See Figure 25.2 for an example.

Use Heterogeneous Grouping and Cooperative Learning

Utilize heterogeneous grouping and cooperative learning activities. These strategies maximize students' strengths and minimize weaknesses. Everyone must pull together to succeed. *Either we all sink or we all swim.* The students help one another to accomplish the task and the individual tasks are designed to play to each student's strength. Although the students are assigned individual tasks, there is group accountability for completion of the

assignment, use of social conventions, and often one group grade. See Chapter 27 for more about setting up and managing cooperative learning groups.

Incorporate Diverse Learning Strategies and Problem Solving

Use diverse learning strategies and problem-solving tasks that have more than one answer. Stress to your students that they differ in their skills, abilities, talents, and approaches to learning. Make time for your students to examine one another's products, performances, solutions to problems, art works, etc. This creates an atmosphere in which all students are equally valued, and no one is better or worse, just

Student Says . . .

My social studies and science teachers are good at assigning special projects that we complete and then report on to the entire class. I think this is a good way to learn because you have to know the material well enough to be able to tell the entire class about the project. I like special projects best when it's a sharing of information instead of a competitive situation. I think I usually learn a lot from listening to other students talk about their projects.

Kathleen
Age 14, Ninth Grade
Glenview, Illinois

Apply It!

Have your students create slogans, bumper stickers, badges, logos, tee shirts, etc., that communicate high expectations. These can be acronyms such as TOPS—Together Optimizing Pupil Success or slogans such as Reach for the Stars!

Dare to Dream

Reach for the Stars!

Myth Buster!

Teaching is not a performance and you are not an actor.

We were learning about the American Revolution in my fourth grade classroom one year and I could tell that my inner city children were not getting it. They looked perplexed when we read about Paul Revere, Minutemen, and the Stamp Act, so I got creative! I told them about Paul Revere while pretending to ride my "horse" all over the classroom. Then they timed me as I "jumped out of bed" and "got dressed" as a Minuteman because the Red Coats were coming. They were delighted when I hopped up on one leg to

get my boots on and nearly fell over in the process! It also took bringing in props and acting out all the various taxations, while rapping about "no taxation without representation" and the "bling-bling doesn't belong to the king-king" for my children to finally understand this piece of history. It may have looked crazy to anyone else, but it took acting out the Revolution to make it real to my students.

Kim Bridgers
Fourth Grade
Hermitage, Tennessee

different. You will be pleasantly surprised when you break out of the *pour and store* mold and encourage creative responses or alternative solutions to problems. The students will be encouraged that diverse thinking and alternative responses are valued.

You CAN Do It!

Establish a Positive Classroom Climate

Create a warm, friendly, and encouraging classroom climate. You will not compromise your authority when you show true concern for your students, act a little goofy, or do anything to help them learn, however silly it may look to others. You can return to Unit 4, Chapter 19 for suggestions.

Increase Your Wait Time

Allow students time to think before you expect an answer. Some students are quick on the draw, but others are more reflective. The fast responders can wait a little to allow the reflective responders to get a chance. You will encourage more student responses when you increase your wait time. The result will be greater participation and better responses (Rowe, 1972; Stahl, 1990). Wait at least three seconds before calling on a student, but the longer, the better. Count: 1 chimpanzee, 2 chimpanzees, 3 chimpanzees, 4 chimpanzees, 5 chimpanzees. That's about 5 seconds. Try it out!

Avoid It!

Avoid differentiating your high-expectation students from your low-expectation students by:

- Calling on and waiting longer for responses from high-expectation students than low-expectation students.

- Praising high-expectation students more and criticizing low-expectation students more.

- Seating low-expectation students in the back of the room farther away from you.

- Giving less feedback and encouragement to low-expectation students.

- Giving low-expectation students fewer opportunities to learn new material than high-expectation students.

- Listening to lunchroom gossip about your students.

- Giving less stimulating assignments to low-expectation students.

statistics

These following statistics illustrate the need to promote positive expectations and thus increase college attendance by all students, but especially by low SES students.

According to the National Center for Education Statistics (2006) Conditions of Education http://nces.ed.gov/programs/coe/2006/section3/indicator23

- In 2004, some 51 percent of low-socio-economic status (SES) twelfth-graders expected to earn a bachelor's degree or attend graduate school, compared with 66 percent of middle-SES seniors and 87 percent of high-SES seniors.

- The 2002–2003 public high school graduation rate for the average freshman class four years earlier was 73.9 percent. The rate ranged from a low of 59.6 percent in the District of Columbia to a high of 87.0 percent in New Jersey.

Motivating At-Risk Students
Students in high school are motivated through the arts. After viewing the clip, write down what sorts of projects or programs would motivate your at-risk students.

I never teach my pupils; I only attempt to provide the conditions in which they can learn.

Albert Einstein

Chapter **26**

What Research-based Strategies Should I Consider?

Effectiveness Essentials

- It is only recently that teaching strategies have been put to the test of research.

- Some research-based strategies help students identify similarities and differences by comparing and contrasting material.

- Figures of speech have been proven to promote student creativity and to encourage student thinking.

- The use of graphic organizers has been proven to facilitate understanding.

- Advance organizers are general and higher order concepts to which students can attach new information.

During your credentialing process, you likely have gathered an array of ideas, strategies, activities, and methods that purport to teach the concepts and skills you need to teach. In addition, you can go into any teacher supply store or read teacher magazines and come up with creative new ways to teach. However, today, teaching strategies have been put to the test of research. In fact, No Child Left Behind mandates that research-based strategies be implemented in classrooms. This is a cornerstone of the legislation. No longer can teachers just rely on strategies that have always worked for them. Now, by NCLB mandate, the strategies teachers use must be proven by research to be effective. In this chapter, you will learn some well-researched strategies, some of which are demonstrated in the video clips included on the DVD that comes with this book.

In a nutshell, not only are these strategies based on research, but also they work because they actively engage students. These strategies require that students be connected to the material in ways that encourage their full participation. They are the opposite of passive lectures or demonstrations, although there is a place for those strategies in your repertoire as well. But if you want your students to be active learners and thoroughly engaged with the material, take a closer look at the video clips and the sample lessons that follow.

Comparing and Contrasting

The first group of strategies includes those that help students identify similarities and differences by comparing and contrasting. This skill is important at all levels and enables you to raise your students' thinking level beyond just knowledge and comprehension to analysis, the fourth level of Bloom's taxonomy described in Chapter 22. They can do this on a Venn diagram or in chart form. Figures 26.1 through 26.4 identify some simple charts and graphic organizers

Figures 26.1–26.4
Comparing and Contrasting

	Washington	Lincoln
Early Life		
Jobs		
Wars		
Successes		

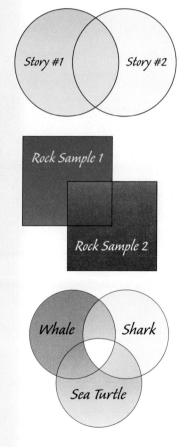

Graphic Organizer: Venn Diagram
A teacher demonstrates use of a Venn diagram in literature class. After viewing the clip, create a lesson using any of the graphic organizers to enable your students to make comparisons among two or more items in any subject area. Fill in the diagram yourself to ensure that your students can make the comparisons.

Animal Classification
Students sort pictures of animals in this elementary classification activity.

Apply It!

Think about how you would design a classification activity. In teaching about
(fill in your topic)
_____ you might provide each group of students with envelopes containing words on pieces of paper and ask them to make categories. Or, ask your students what they remember from a text segment, write all the words and phrases on the board, and then have them come up and use symbols to make categories. You can even play "Stump the Class" by having one student make a grouping and asking the rest of the class to guess the basis for the grouping. See Figures 26.5 and 26.6 for classification activities I have done with students, one on jobs in the community and one on Ancient Egypt.

Figure 26.5
Job Classification Activity

you can use to help students distinguish the similarities and differences among several items. An example of a Venn diagram lesson is provided in the video clip.

Sorting

Sorting is a strategy that encourages students to look for common elements or attributes and sort them into the correct pre-established categories. The student may be asked, for example, to sort rocks into metamorphic, igneous, or sedimentary after learning the characteristics of each. Or they might be asked in math to sort pictures into color categories, shape categories, or number categories.

Figure 26.6

Classification Activity

Baskets	Sandals	Priests ♥	Papyrus	Pyramid
Scribe ♥	Pharaoh ♥	Desert	Nile	Delta
Mummy	Drought	Polytheism	Anubis	Scarab
Flood	Ra	Giza	Tut	Sphinx
Rosetta Stone	Farmer ♥	Tomb	Howard Carter	Artisan ♥
Valley of the Kings	Wall Painting	Hieroglyphics	Rafts	Book of the Dead

KEY: ♥ = Jobs in Ancient Egypt

Classifying

Classifying is a similar strategy that enables students to form their own concepts, given just the data. This is a slightly higher order thinking strategy because the teacher does not provide the categories. The items to be classified may be actual items, pictorial representations, or words.

Figures of Speech

The use of certain figures of speech is another research-proven strategy that you may find useful in your practice. For example, Marzano, Pickering, and Pollack (2001) suggest that using metaphoric examples is yet another means of helping your students recognize similarities and differences. Joyce and Weil (2003) explain the use of figures of speech or metaphors in a teaching strategy called *Synectics*.

The use of figurative language can enliven learning by suggesting mental images that motivate and facilitate creative thinking. Three common figures of speech teachers use in the classroom to make materials more easily understood are similes, metaphors, and analogies.

Similes

A *simile* is a figure of speech that makes a comparison between two unlike things using the words *like* or *as*. "He acts like a couch potato" or "she is as silly as a goose." Here are some ways to formulate curriculum-based similes:

A. Simple comparison of two seemingly unlike specific things

How is the heart like a pump?

How is a volcano like a pimple?

How is a cell like a factory?

How is a teacher like a conductor?

B. A comparison of a category from which students choose an item to compare to a specific concept

What fruit or vegetable is most like you? Why?

What food is most like a diverse classroom? Why?

What amusement park ride is most like life? Why?

C. Comparison of abstract specific to a concrete specific on some attribute

Which is greener, jealousy or grass? Why?

Which is thinner, an excuse or a piece of string? Why?

Which is sweeter, a homecoming or a candy bar? Why?

Which is denser, fog or an unwilling student? Why?

Metaphors

A *metaphor* is a comparison of two things using words that are not to be taken literally: "She is a fox," or "I'm drowning in work." Since they require a high level of abstract thinking, metaphors are perfect for your secondary students. You can give them metaphoric references in poetry and literature such as:

The fog comes in on little cat's feet—Carl Sandburg

The heart is a lonely hunter—Carson McCullers

Analogies

An *analogy* is a comparison of two things that contain some similarities. Analogies are used to help explain something or make it easier to understand. The following form of analogy is the most complex because these analogies require that students compare relationships. Because they require such abstract thinking, only the simplest should be used with younger students.

Cat: _____ as dog : puppy

paint : artist as _____ : potter

Hot : chili as _____ : ice cream

Barometer : _____ as thermometer : temperature

Humans : carbon dioxide as plants : _____

In all of these examples, **why** is the important question to ask.

For secondary students who are capable of abstract thinking, you might want to select examples from the Miller Analogies Test, a test used in graduate school admissions. Here are four examples from different subject areas. You can see the rest of the examples and test yourself at:
http://harcourtassessment.com/haiweb/Cultures/en-US/dotCom/milleranalogies/about/Sample+Analogies+and+Annotated+Answers.htm

---

1. VASE : AMPHORA as FLOWERS : _____
   a. wine   b. glass   c. leaves   d. grain

2. VINEGAR : _____ as ACETIC : CITRIC
   a. apple   b. oil   c. tea   d. lemon

3. CONSTITUTION : MAGNA CARTA as UNITED STATES : _____
   a. Pilgrims   b. Virginia   c. England   d. Rome

4. _____ : ACROPHOBIA as SPIDERS : ARACHNOPHOBIA
   a. water   b. crowds   c. noise   d. heights

Answers: 1a; 2d; 3c; 4d

Figure 26.7

Sequence Organizer

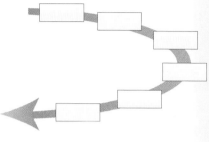

Figure 26.8

Cycle Graphic Organizer

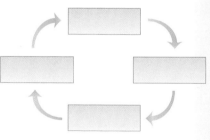

Graphic Organizers

The use of graphic organizers has been proven to facilitate understanding. Marzano, Pickering, and Pollack (2001) refer to them as non-linguistic representations. Some already have been explained in this chapter. Here are several formats for you to consider.

Sequence Charts

Sequence charts help students place events in order. They can be used for:

- time lines
- plot sequence
- steps in an experiment
- project procedures
- story boards
- steps in problem solving
- to give any sort of directions

Circular Charts

Circular charts can be used to help students visualize or depict cyclic events. Some ideas are:

- The water cycle
- The food chain
- The seasons

Concept Maps

Concept maps are another way to represent ideas in graphic form. *Kidspiration* and *Inspiration* (http://www.inspiration.com) are superb technological applications, but you can make webs on your board or on charts as well.

Figure 26.9

Concept Map

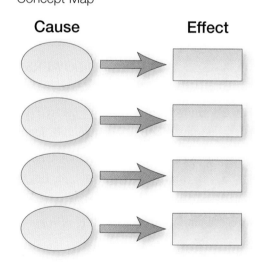

Figure 26.10
Large Wall Concept Map

Graphic Organizer: Mind Map
Students use mind mapping in cooperative learning groups in literature class. How would you use a mind map to teach a lesson in your area or at your grade level?

Advance Organizers

Advance organizers are general and higher order concepts to which students can attach new information. They are typically the first step in direct instruction strategies and provide a framework or scaffold upon which subsequent information is hung. In other words, the advance organizer is the "big picture," the large, important idea that is somewhat universal. Think of the advance organizer as the trunk of a tree. The sub-concepts branch out from the trunk and the supporting facts are the leaves on the branches.

Advanced organizers were first introduced as a teaching strategy by David Ausubel (1968) and have been shown by Marzano and his colleagues (2001) to be very effective in helping students to order or scaffold their learning. The use of advance organizers has been shown to improve levels of understanding and recall, especially when the material is difficult to understand or disorganized.

Hierarchical Structure

This strategy is the opposite of discovery learning. The advance organizer is presented first and explained up front. It can be in the form of a story, a personal narrative, or a graphic organizer and can involve previewing text

Apply It!

Create a direct instruction lesson using an advance organizer. Where will you find these "big ideas"? They are usually highlighted in your textbooks or manuals. Use a story, photos, skimming, or narratives to introduce the big ideas. You will see that being up front with the main ideas will enable students to latch on more quickly than they might have otherwise.

Student Says . . .

Good teachers direct the class with note taking, and I end up with good notes that really help me when I study for a test. My best learning happens when my teacher is good at explaining a concept, just doesn't make me memorize a lot of facts I'll forget, and allows me to be creative.

> Kathleen
> Age 14, Ninth Grade
> Glenview, Illinois

Apply It!

Design a partial outline for your subject area. Try it out on your students and notice their enthusiasm for filling it in by skimming or reading the text. The outline becomes a tool for studying. Apply all of these strategies in one instructional unit, along with the two research-based strategies that lend themselves to cooperative learning, which are discussed in the next chapter.

material through skimming, study guides, and partial outlines. After the organizer is presented, the students will have a cognitive ladder or on which to hang the details of the new material. The new material is presented in light of the advance organizer, so there is no discovery or guessing game involved in this direct instruction strategy.

Let's take the example of *cultural diffusion,* that is, the influence of one culture on another through the spread of ideas, products, or processes. This is the advance organizer or "big idea." I once taught a lesson to sixth graders

on how Greek culture influenced the Romans who followed them. I began by defining *cultural diffusion.* I showed students photos I had taken in China and Russia, which included several recognizable brands such as soft drinks, common brands of tennis shoes, and signs for our familiar fast food restaurants. Then, I asked them for examples of how other cultures have impacted our lifestyle. They gave me plenty of ideas—from food to music to clothing. At that point they were ready to learn how the concept of *cultural diffusion* was exemplified by the Greeks to the Romans.

Avoid It!

Avoid becoming set in your ways using any one strategy, over and over again, no matter how effective. The research-based strategies in this chapter and the others presented in the next chapter should give you a better equipped toolbox to meet the differing learning styles of your students. Vary your instructional strategies to avoid boredom.

Types of Advance Organizers

Being up front with students about what you are trying to convey can also be accomplished through study guides, teacher-prepared notes, and partial outlines. Study guides ask focused questions so students know what is important to study. Teacher-prepared notes present the material in an outline or framework so students can easily ascertain what is essential and what is not. A partial outline is very useful because it only gives away part of the information and the students must do some detective work to fill it in. A partial outline for ancient Greek architecture might look like this example in Figure 26.11.

Figure 26.11
Partial Outline

Parthenon

I. Rooms

    A. Pronos - front porch

    B. Naos - main room with statue of Athena

    C. _____ back room for offerings

II. _____ Column
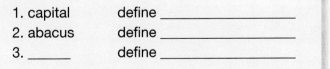
    (Name of Greek Column)

    A. Number of columns in Parthenon

        1. 8 at each end instead of the usual 6

        2. _____ on each side

        3.

    B. Parts of a Doric Column

        1. capital   define _____

        2. abacus   define _____

        3. _____   define _____

281

*Great discoveries and improvements invariably involve the **cooperation** of many minds. I may be given credit for having blazed the trail, but when I look at the subsequent developments I feel the credit is due to others rather than to myself.*

Alexander Graham Bell

Chapter 27

How Do I Combine Research-based Strategies with Cooperative Learning Groups?

Effectiveness Essentials

■ Many classroom activities lend themselves to cooperative learning.

■ Cooperative learning groups are heterogeneous groupings of students who work together to complete tasks while learning social skills that foster cooperation.

■ Two research-based strategies that can be conducted in cooperative learning group format are reciprocal teaching and problem solving.

An effective research-based strategy that works with many classroom activities is cooperative learning (Marzano et al., 2001). In particular, cooperative learning can facilitate learning in a multicultural classroom (Coelho, 1996) and can help second language learners (Johns & Espinoza, 1992). In this chapter, you will learn to structure cooperative learning activities and implement two research-based strategies that use the format: reciprocal teaching and problem-based learning. First, let's take a look at the basic principles of cooperative learning.

Principles of Cooperative Learning

Cooperative learning groups are heterogeneous groupings of students who work together to complete tasks while learning social skills that foster cooperation. Basic principles of cooperative learning include, but are not limited to the following:

- Optimal group size is three to five students according to most proponents.
- Each member of the group is an active participant.
- Membership in groups reflects heterogeneity with regard to ability, social class, gender, ethnicity, and language differences. In other words, cooperative learning groups reflect the real world.

- Cooperative groups foster interdependence among the members through the sharing of materials, group accountability, or individual contributions to one final product.
- Students practice social skills (for example, saying "please" and "thank you," using names, and making eye contact) in cooperative groups.
- Students are encouraged to solve their problems without teacher intervention.

Teachers who use cooperative learning begin with groups of three or four students. Some of the tasks students can work on in cooperative groups are: preparing research reports, with each member becoming an expert on a part of the topic; editing stories; creating a crossword puzzle; deciphering a word search; making a collage; playing matching games; conducting experiments; brainstorming; making a chart or graph; and solving a puzzle.

Cooperative Learning—Middle School
Students in a science lab work cooperatively and rotate to conduct experiments at several stations

Cooperative Learning—Elementary
A fifth grade teacher challenges her students to come up with story problems about fractions in cooperative groups.

After viewing one or both videos, what do you see as the advantages and disadvantages of the cooperative learning approach? Were the three pillars of cooperative learning—interdependence, accountability, and social or process skills—evident in the lesson?

Teacher Talks . . .

After input and a test on poetic devices and figurative language, I assign each student one poem. I group the poems by theme: love, death, war, nature, etc. Each group (4 or 5 in a group) discusses all the poems in their group to determine what theme they have in common. They also must decide how each poet treats the theme differently and come up with reasons why.

Then each group presents their poems and leads a class discussion. They are required to read their poems aloud and use some kind of visual aid. (One group wore berets and brought in real coffee for a coffeehouse setting.) After all groups are finished, each student writes a critical analysis of his/her poem.

When finished, each student has studied his or her own poem in great depth, the poems in his/her group in some depth, and all the other poems in the class briefly.

Susan Johnson
AP English and Language Arts
Richwood, West Virginia

(As seen on http://www.LessonPlansPage.com)

Positive Outcomes of Cooperative Learning

In cooperative groups, students can learn from one another while participating in ways that address their strengths. The value of the strategy for addressing diversity of all kinds cannot be overemphasized. Outcomes of cooperative learning may include:

- increased understanding of differences and diversity.
- increased self-esteem.
- increased problem solving and academic achievement.
- increased comfort with computer technology when computers are used.

Step-by-Step Successful Cooperative Learning

Many teachers fear that cooperative learning is a synonym for controlled chaos. They avoid the strategy because it appears so vague and unstructured. Some of you may have had a bad experience when you tried cooperative learning. I have simplified the steps in the process so you can feel more confident and give it a try.

Figure 27.1

Large Color Posters That Are Renamed for Each Task

Key:
Green = Check Capitals
Blue = Check Punctuation
Pink = Spelling Checker
Orange = Does it make sense?

1. First, decide on a task that can be divided evenly into three or four equal parts. An example would be story editing. The jobs might be Punctuation Editor, Capitalization Editor, Spelling Editor, and Overall Organization Editor. Clearly explain and demonstrate what each job is about.

2. Denote which jobs are which using color-coded posters and "tickets." You can change the key for different cooperative learning tasks each time, reusing the posters and tickets.

Figure 27.2

Color Tickets Coordinated to Tasks

3. Hand out the tickets to groups of four and have each student choose a color-coded ticket to the job they want. If they can't decide in three minutes, you will decide for them.

4. Set a time limit and announce a social skill, such as talking softly, saying please or thank you, sharing materials, calling one another by name, listening, etc.

5. Monitor the groups and check to see that the groups are using the skill.

6. Review with the students how things went, and have them fill out an evaluation of their participation, use of skill, etc.

7. Experiment with cooperative learning groups even though the class periods may be short. You can set aside time during several sessions and not feel you have to complete the task all in one sitting.

Figure 27.3
Cooperative Learning Feedback/Evaluation

Group Members _____

We worked well together   😊 ☹

We completed the task   😊 ☹

We used the social skill   😊 ☹

Next time we could improve by
_____
_____

Avoid It!

Avoid the use of generic jobs in your cooperative group planning. Some of the job titles I have heard include Harmonizer, Consultant, Facilitator, and Peacemaker, as well as the more common Materials Distributor, Recorder, and Reporter. The problem with these titles is that they don't pertain to each and every lesson, and that's why cooperative learning frustrates some teachers. Often, the only students who do the actual work are the recorder and reporter. The materials distributor is done at the beginning and the harmonizer harmonizes without having a real job.

Teacher Talks . . .

I had a very fractious, difficult class last year because everybody wanted to be the leader and nobody wanted to be a follower. Getting them to do anything together or to cooperate on projects was a nightmare. This year, I have a very compliant group of fifth graders who all want to be followers! They are most content to let ME be the leader and they follow along accordingly. When I had laryngitis a couple of weeks ago, I wrote on the board that I could not speak at all, and asked them if they would care to decorate our classroom bulletin board to illustrate our current reading book, "My Side of the Mountain." One hour later, their finished product was absolutely beautiful to behold, with NO help from me other than I had supplied the paper, scissors, staplers, etc. They worked beautifully together, said please and thank you, nobody fought, no harsh words were spoken, and the finished product is very creative and well done.

Shannon Vanderford, Fifth Grade
West Memphis, Arkansas

(As seen on http://www.LessonPlansPage.com)

Apply It!

Think of some activities that you normally use that might lend themselves to a cooperative learning format. Remember that the jobs should be equal. Use a pie chart to create the three, four, or five equal tasks that can be distributed among group members.

Figure 27.4
Pie Charts

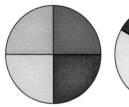

Reciprocal Teaching

A research-based strategy that can be conducted in a cooperative learning group format is reciprocal teaching. Palincsar (1984) describes reciprocal teaching as an instructional activity that requires a dialogue between teachers and students to facilitate comprehension of text. The dialogue is structured around four jobs, making it conducive to cooperative learning.

Reciprocal Teaching Jobs

Although one student leader can do all four jobs, with input from the group members, the leadership can be distributed equally as follows:

> The **Summarizer** summarizes what has been read with the help of the other students or teacher, if need be.
>
> The **Questioner** asks questions to help the group members better understand the passage.
>
> The **Clarifier** clarifies or asks others in the group to better explain what they mean.
>
> The **Predictor** leads the group in a discussion about what may happen next.

Suggested Steps in a Reciprocal Teaching Lesson

Reciprocal teaching lends itself to very clearly defined roles and procedures. In fact, it is so structured that you might try this strategy as your initiation into cooperative learning before you try anything more complex.

> 1. Group students (4 per group).
> 2. Identify students in each group for each of the four roles for the first round.
>   i.   summarizer
>   ii. questioner
>   iii. clarifier
>   iv. predictor
> 3. Students read _____ paragraphs and utilize note-taking strategies.
> 4. The Summarizer draws attention to the key ideas.
> 5. The Questioner poses questions regarding the selection.
> 6. The Clarifier addresses puzzling elements and tries to answer the questions that were posed.
> 7. The Predictor offers guesses about what comes next.
> 8. Repeat the process for the next _____ paragraphs, switching roles to the right or left.

Apply It!

Try out a reciprocal teaching lesson. Use your textbooks as the source of reading material. Model each step along the way before you set the students to the task. Use *PowerPoint* or the overhead projector to demonstrate how to approach the text material. Have your students read along with you. Act out each of the four roles yourself, modeling what kind of statements or questions each group member is likely to say or ask. Check for understanding by having your students work as a whole group to practice each role separately while you give them feedback. Then, let them get into their groups, assign a short text passage, set a time limit, and let them go for it. Monitor them and provide corrective feedback if needed. Debrief them and ask for suggestions on how to improve the process. If you need more information, refer to the references at the end of this chapter.

Problem Solving

The second research-based strategy that can be conducted in cooperative group format is problem solving. Other common names you have heard for these strategies are *inquiry, group investigation,* and what Marzano and colleagues (2001) call generating and testing hypotheses.

Inquiring Minds

Inquiry is the very opposite of listen-and-learn, or pour-and-store, methods of teaching. Rather, it engages students in a process of exploration that requires them to formulate questions and find answers leading to new understanding. The teacher becomes a facilitator instead of the all-knowing guru and is recast as a fellow inquirer or as a mentor or guide. This is a very important strategy for all grade levels. It involves all the steps in Bloom's taxonomy and provides opportunities for students to truly act as scientists or social scientists, exploring questions that they formulate and designing experiments or experiences to validate or negate their initial conceptions or understanding of any given problem.

Motivating through Problem-based Learning
Students in high school plan a project based at their local airport.

Math Strategies for Problem Solving
Elementary students are encouraged to use problem solving in math to determine average height.

After viewing one or both video clips, identify the advantages and disadvantages of using a problem-based approach. Would it be difficult for you as a first-year teacher to try problem-based teaching? Why or why not? Design a problem-based lesson plan. What will be your "hook"?

My fifth grade students built a model replica of the Wright Brothers' 1903 Flyer. The model weighed nearly 75 lbs. and measured 22 ft. by 10 ft. After immersing my students in appropriate literature about the Wright Brothers, I was able to introduce the scientific and mathematical components to the project. I instructed my students to use power tools correctly and responsibly and gave them step-by-step instruction on the construction itself. The students decided to paint the airplane red, white, and blue as a tribute to our great nation. My principal, who supported the project from the very beginning, has been my mentor and inspiration for such an undertaking. I proceeded with this project in a manner that would give her and her school recognition for her wonderful leadership and guidance. Any success, in my eyes, was a dedication to her for her

(continued on facing page)

Steps in Inquiry

Although they differ slightly from one another, generally the steps include:

1. A problem or puzzling situation to be solved or resolved
2. Generation of questions or hypotheses
3. An experiment to test hypotheses or study tasks or research to solve a problem
4. Independent and cooperative group research or experimentation
5. An analysis and interpretation of the data
6. A report of the conclusions

For example, I brought to my methods class a Japanese good luck figure called a *daruma,* as shown in the photo. I asked the students what they thought it was. We listed responses on the board. Then I asked what country or culture might have made it. We listed responses on the board. I asked how we could find out. The students listed several sources of information such as looking at art books and textbooks, asking people, querying members of the anthropology department, and going

Japanese Daruma Dolls for Good Fortune

to the campus museum, among others. I told the students that there was only one object and that I couldn't let it out of my sight. They proposed drawing it, and some photographed it with their digital phones and cameras. We decided that everyone would have the chance before class next time to show their drawings or photos to people they encountered. We organized cooperative groups of four to distribute the four questions that needed to be answered.

1. Is it a special person?
2. When and where was the first one made?
3. What is its purpose?
4. Where are they found in our community?

Excitement was high the next session as we compared answers. Several of the students brought darumas to class, and one student even made one from papier-mâché. Everyone in class had an idea for trying inquiry in their field experience, from a gnarled piece of ginger in kindergarten, to a photo of Confucius in sixth grade, to bringing in a dollar bill and exploring the meaning of the symbols on the reverse in a high school government class. We all learned this was a strategy that works with all ages.

Wright Brothers Airplane

Perry Lopez

Avoid It!

Avoid being too directive when students are tackling a problem. Part of the strategy involves them working things out for themselves. Intervene when necessary, but challenge them to figure problems out for themselves whenever possible.

generosity. I converted the classroom into a "mini museum" and added a puppet show, printing press, family tree, schematics table, raffle table (Wright Brothers Memorabilia), and an assembly line that recreated a small replica of the Flyer. My students became the hosts for other students, district representatives, and parents. My proud students demonstrated that they were able to achieve a high degree of critical thinking.

Perry Lopez
Fifth Grade
Bronx, New York

(As seen on http://www.LessonPlansPage.com)

We have become

not a melting pot

but a beautiful

mosaic.

Jimmy Carter

Chapter **28**

How Do I Differentiate Instruction to Meet the Needs of All Learners?

Effectiveness Essentials

- You will find that diverse classrooms are the rule rather than the exception.

- Howard Gardner has identified eight facets of intelligence.

- Differentiated learning describes a set of principles that enable you to meet the broad range of readiness, interests, abilities, talents, and skills in your classroom.

- The three components of instruction that can be modified are the content, the process, and the products.

Teaching is such a complex, unique profession that I can offer only one assurance in this book—you will have a perfectly successful year if all of your students are cloned from one individual of your choosing. I can make this offer knowing that at some time in the sci-fi future, I may have to pay out, but I feel confident at the moment.

Individual Differences

On that first day of school, the individual differences in your class will jump out at you. Gender and physical differences are only the tip of the iceberg. Beneath the surface are students from different socioeconomic strata; students who come from various family configurations; students with special needs, differing interests, and abilities; students with different cultural backgrounds, different languages, different learning styles, and different attitudes toward school. This is not a new phenomenon. Consider that in one-room schoolhouses of the past, teachers had a similar challenge.

Although the statistics in your school may differ from those in the statistics feature at the right, increasingly, you will find that diverse classrooms are the rule rather than the exception. You can look at this new population either as a daunting challenge or as an opportunity to stretch your skills and abilities in new directions while celebrating the multitude of unique individuals relying on you to guide and assess their progress fairly.

statistics

An Elementary School Snapshot

- The total school population is 850.
- 10 percent are African American.
- 44 percent are Latino.
- 4 percent are Native Americans, Pacific Islanders, and Asians.
- 42 percent are Anglo.
- 560 children are free-lunch recipients.
- 290 students are recipients of Aid for Families with Dependent Children (AFDC).
- 36 are identified as gifted.
- 193 are English language learners.
- 120 have individual education plans (IEPs).
- A special day class of students with learning disabilities is mainstreamed into "regular" classes for part of the day.
- Some children are homeless.

Diversity Now

statistics

One-fifth of U.S. children under age 18 either are immigrants or are members of an immigrant family (Coles, 2000).

Myth Buster!

We should always teach to the middle.

In reality, good teachers demonstrate enthusiasm for all students' ability levels. Our passion for our role as teachers is evident and contagious. Students respond to energetic and motivating instructors. While it is easier to prepare lessons for one general group, all students, regardless of ability, deserve high standards and equal representation. In California a teacher must expect the make-up of a class to include RSP (resource) students, English language learners, at-risk students, and non-readers. Identifying the needs of each individual not only ensures that students receive a quality education, but also upholds the integrity of the teacher. We are teachers of all students, not just a select few.

Ingrid Munsterman, Principal
Ruth Grimes Elementary School
Colton Joint Unified School District
Bloomington, California

The Theory of Multiple Intelligences

One way to understand how your students differ from each other and what each brings to the classroom is through Howard Gardner's theory of multiple intelligences. Gardner's work (1993, 2000) proposes that instead of a single, fixed intelligence, there are actually eight facets of intelligence. In other words, we are all smart, but in different ways. The exciting part of this theory is that teachers can organize learning to take into account the differing intelligences in the classroom.

Visual/Spatial

Students with visual/spatial intelligence excel at spatial relationships and learn visually. They enjoy drawing, creating, illustrating, and learning from photographs, videos, and other visual aids.

Verbal/Linguistic

Students who have strength in verbal/linguistic intelligence learn best through the language arts: reading, writing, speaking, and listening. These constitute the traditional methods of instruction.

Mathematical/Logical

Students who show evidence of mathematical/logical intelligence demonstrate skill with numbers and problem solving. They think abstractly and analytically. They do well when instruction is logically sequenced.

Bodily/Kinesthetic

Students who exhibit bodily/kinesthetic intelligence have good motor skills and are coordinated. They learn best through hands-on activity: games, movement, role-play, and building and manipulating things.

Musical/Rhythmic

Students who excel in musical/rhythmic intelligence learn through songs, patterns, rhythms, instruments, chants, listening to music, and other forms of musical expression.

Intrapersonal

Students who shine in intrapersonal intelligence are introspective and in touch with their feelings, values, and beliefs. They need time alone to reflect on their learning and how it relates to them.

Interpersonal

Students who demonstrate interpersonal intelligence are outgoing, sociable, and people-oriented, and they learn best working in groups or interacting with others.

Naturalist

Students whose forte is naturalist intelligence (added in 1996 to the original seven) demonstrate an ability to find patterns in the natural world and the plant and animal life therein. They learn best through classifying and visual discrimination activities, especially when environmental education is involved. Field trips and gardening are two activities they enjoy!

Multiple Intelligences
A first-grade teacher demonstrates and discusses how she uses multiple intelligences in a unit on simple machines.

After viewing the video clip, think of an upcoming unit for your grade level or subject matter. Create activities that tap into the multiple intelligences defined here. If you have difficulty, consult some of the works by Howard Gardner listed in the references at the end of this unit. Here are some online multiple intelligences inventories. It would be fun to take them yourself and then administer them to your students.

http://www.ldrc.ca/projects/miinventory/mitest.html

http://surfaquarium.com/MI/inventory.htm

Chapter 28 How Do I Differentiate Instruction to Meet the Needs of All Learners?

An Example

Imagine your class is studying desert environments. Here are some ideas for activities that would afford opportunities for students to activate the eight intelligences. You can provide your students with a contract that requires that they complete a certain number of activities, each representing a different intelligence to expand their repertoire.

Visual/Spatial

- Paint or draw a desert scene.
- Create a desert collage.
- Watch a video about the desert.
- Construct a desert diorama.

Verbal/Linguistic

- Read a factual book about the desert and write a book report.
- Write a coyote trickster tale after reading some examples.
- Create a desert crossword puzzle using desert vocabulary.
- Write a research report about a desert animal.

Mathematical/Logical

- Design and conduct as experiment to see how much water a small cactus plant needs.
- Classify and categorize the plants found in the desert.
- Locate three deserts on a U.S. map and specify the longitude and latitude of each.

- Make a graph of annual rainfall in 3 deserts: Gobi, Kalahari, and Sahara.

Bodily/Kinesthetic

- Pantomime desert animals and have the class guess what you are.
- Feel and describe desert plant specimens.
- Fill a bottle with colored sand that you have dyed in desert colors.
- Create a game or sport that can be played in the desert and teach it to the class.

Musical/Rhythmic

- Write a song or jingle about the desert.
- Listen to the theme music from "Lawrence of Arabia."
- Make a list of sounds you might hear at night in the desert.
- Write a rap about the desert.

Intrapersonal

- Describe how you would feel if you were stranded on a desert island and saw a ship in the distance.

- Should the desert tortoise be a protected animal? Why or why not?

- Write a poem about how the desert makes you feel.

- Would you rather live in the desert in a big house or by the sea in a small one?

Interpersonal

- Interview someone who has lived in or visited a desert to get his or her reactions to the experience.

- Debate: The desert tortoise should or should not be protected.

- Write a group report comparing three deserts: Gobi, Sahara, Kalahari.

- In a group, choose a desert and make a desert mural including plants, mammals, insects, birds, and reptiles.

Naturalist

- Make a collection of desert fauna and flora using pictures from the Internet.

- Sort the pictures into categories, as a scientist would do.

- Learn the scientific names of at least ten desert plants.

- Research Death Valley on the Internet through the National Park Service.

DESERT CONTRACT: Name _____

Choose 3 activities

Pantomime a desert animal	Create a desert diorama	Write a coyote trickster tale	Create a desert mural with 3 others
Listen to Lawrence of Arabia music	Classify desert plants	Learn the scientific names of 10 desert plants	Should the desert tortoise be protected?

Figure 28.1

Multiple Intelligences Sample Contract

Apply It!

If you feel very brave, you can design multiple-intelligence–based activity centers and require your students to choose centers with the directive that they do at least one activity in each center. Make color-coded folders with center names on them, and have students choose a folder and activities that correspond to strengths and/or intelligences that they want to develop. You can name your centers after famous people who exhibit the intelligences:

Shakespeare Center—Verbal/Linguistic

Einstein Center—Logical/ Mathematical

Paul McCartney Center—Musical/Rhythmic

Jacques Cousteau Center—Naturalist

Picasso Center—Visual/Spatial

Tiger Woods Center—Kinesthetic

Thoreau Center—Intrapersonal

Oprah Winfrey Center—Interpersonal

Differentiated Instruction

Differentiated learning describes a set of principles that enable you to meet the broad range of readiness, interests, abilities, talents, and skills in your classroom. The principles of differentiated instruction as articulated by Tomlinson (1999) provide another perspective on meeting the diverse needs of your students.

Core Knowledge

Teachers need to focus on the core knowledge of each subject area. The core knowledge can be the concepts, skills, and principles that are required of each student, and are also known as the essential standards.

Formative Assessment

Teachers need to continuously assess where students are vis-à-vis what they need to learn. The assessment involves not only readiness but also interests and how that student learns best. This is known as formative assessment.

Modifying Instructional Components

The three components of instruction that can be modified based on a teacher's ongoing assessment are the content, the process, and the products. You can modify content by choosing the way you "input" it. You can simplify for those who are

Figure 28.2

Differentiating Instruction Planning Form

Differentiating Instruction Planning Form

Curriculum/Subject Area _____

Standard(s) Addressed _____

Date _____

Period _____ Teacher _____

	Content Input	Process	Products
Student 1			
Student 2			
Student 3			
Student 4			
Student 5			

Strategies for Adapting Instruction
A language arts teacher adapts instruction for a student with a hearing impairment. After viewing the video clip, think about a particular lesson you have taught recently and adapt it for a low achiever, a high achiever, a student with a learning disability, a student with physical, emotional, or behavioral challenges, or any other student with special needs you are currently teaching. Use the template shown in Figure 28.2.

In my third year of teaching general music, I was given a class of children with cerebral palsy to teach. They were all kindergarten age. They were all in wheelchairs, except one. I think there were about 6 children all together. It was quite a challenge to come up with things they would enjoy and could feel success in accomplishing. One activity we did first thing was to warm up their voices. We would act like we were chewing food and humming at the same time. While they were doing that, they would move their arms up and down to the high and low of their voices. This was something all of them could do, except one . . . Aubrey. Her disability was more severe than the others. She could only make a couple of sounds to denote yes and no. She would sit and sometimes the teachers who brought the children would make

(continued on facing page)

not yet ready and enrich the content for those who have mastered it. Some ways of varying the "input" include using:

- varied level text material
- supplementary materials
- varied audio-visuals
- interest centers
- varied time allotments
- technology of all sorts
- varied instructional strategies
- cooperative learning
- varied community resources, such as speakers and field trips

Some of the ways you can modify the process are by helping students

make the learning experience relate to their needs and interests and by focusing attention on multiple intelligences.

You can make the material more meaningful (the process) when you include some of the strategies that were covered in this unit. These strategies include graphic organizers of all sorts, group investigation, classifying and sorting, cooperative learning, reciprocal teaching, advance organizers, and analogies and metaphors.

You can modify the product by designing product options for your students based on Gardner's theory of multiple intelligences or tiered assignments. Students can be given a list of options to show their mastery of the content and you can assess them based on predetermined criteria or rubrics.

Providing for Every Student

You will have students in your class who need extra support in one or more areas. Following are ways to modify lessons for higher and lower achievers and for students with unique challenges.

Students with Learning Difficulties

You can support your students with learning difficulties by teaching to their strengths and making some simple accommodations in your planning, instruction, and assignments. The following modifications are straightforward and easy to implement, requiring very little extra effort on your part.

- Allow time for plenty of practice.
- Conduct student-teacher conferences.
- Break assignments into smaller, manageable parts.
- Use peer tutors.
- Underline important directions, key words.
- Give shorter assignments, and allow more time for completion.
- Tape-record stories and use other technologies.
- Give immediate feedback and lots of encouragement.
- Use large type on worksheets.
- Keep directions simple, write them out, or give them orally.
- Provide many opportunities for success.
- Provide low-reading-level, high-interest reading material geared to the student's interests.
- Use visuals and manipulative materials when available.
- Use cooperative learning strategies.
- Watch for fatigue and boredom.

Higher Achieving Students Who Need Enrichment

It is also probable that you will have students in your class who excel in one or more areas, especially if you subscribe to the theory of multiple intelligences. For these students, more of the same is not acceptable.

- Encourage the reading of library books and perhaps totally individualize the reading and/or math program.
- Encourage individual research, construction, or science projects geared to the students' abilities and interests, for extra credit.
- Provide opportunities to sit in on special unit activities in other classes.
- Introduce new and challenging materials, games, puzzles, and brainteasers.
- Have individual conferences with the student to guide his or her progress.
- Encourage creative responses to stories (e.g., writing to the author, creating a play script from the story, etc.).
- Consider modifying assignments based on multiple intelligences.

her arms move while we were doing this activity and sometimes not.

One day, six months into the school year, we started our warm up as usual and as I looked around the room, and there was Aubrey, on her own, moving her arms up and down with the others. I pointed it out to the teachers and we were all very excited. That moment had a deep impact on my life as a teacher and a musician. And 19 years later it still inspires me.

Deborah Lichfield
Middle and High School Music
St Johns, Arizona

(As seen on http://www.LessonPlansPage.com)

statistics

- Nationally, 13 percent of public school students had a Special Education individualized education program (IEP) in 2001–2002.
- Among those states reporting students with IEPs, the proportion ranged from 10 percent in Colorado to 20 percent in Rhode Island.
- Specific learning disabilities, speech or language impairments, mental retardation, and emotional disturbance continued to account for the majority of students served (Report to Congress, 2002).

http://www.ed.gov/about/reports/annual/osep/2002/index.html

Teacher Talks . . .

Teaching isn't just about what you teach your students, it's also about what they teach you. When you choose to become a teacher, it brings you into a world of young people who, if you give them a chance, will open up their hearts, share their fears and loves, and make every day special. I have cried with a young woman who had anorexia; visited four kids who were all in mental hospitals at the same time and just wanted a candy bar, a teen magazine, and a hug; witnessed young women with hearing impairments learn to communicate with a grocery store cashier so that eventually they could shop independently; and watched middle school students celebrate "moving on" to high school with the confidence and poise of young men and women. I admit it, I cry every year when I see who they've become. I can't imagine doing anything else with my life.

Laurie Wasserman, Special Needs Teacher
Andrews Middle School
Medford, Massachusetts

(Quoted on www.EducationWorld.com)

Students with Special Physical, Emotional, or Behavioral Needs

Some students in your class may need some differentiated and/or individualized attention because they have special needs related to specific physical, emotional, or behavioral challenges. Individual differences may point to a need for further testing. If you suspect that a student is either gifted or has learning disabilities, notify your principal, who will outline for you the legal requirements for arranging more intensive testing by the school psychologist, nurse, or special education resource teacher. If you have student in your class with behavioral or physical challenges, you will have a great deal of help from the special education team.

An Example

I had a student with a hearing impairment in my methods class last year, and a student assistant was assigned to sign for him during class. I was very nervous about how I should modify my instruction. I consulted the Office of Students with Disabilities and they offered some simple guidelines such as using the board more, looking at the student when I was talking because he read lips, and writing out all directions for him. That quarter I did some of the best teaching I have ever done! The principles that guided me turned out to benefit all the students. If you are fortunate enough to have students with special needs in your class, seek advice and you will be the better teacher for the experience.

Avoid It!

Although the number of students in your classroom who fall within the norm may already overwhelm you, direct your attention to those who need your extra effort. Do not hesitate to seek out your resource teacher for suggestions and strategies that can be tailored to the students you have in mind.

Chapter **29**

What Are Effective Strategies for English Language Learners?

El que sabe dos lenguas, vale for dos. (He who knows two languages is worth double.)

Spanish maxim

Effectiveness Essentials

■ Principles of good instruction apply to English language learners.

■ Learning about new cultures and new languages is an exciting opportunity for you and your students.

■ Culture and language are inexorably linked, and, therefore, it is important to help English language learners maintain their own culture and language.

■ Multiculturalism should be an integral part of every day in your classroom.

■ Specially Designed Academic Instruction in English (SDAIE) presents grade-level appropriate content in English using special techniques.

■ Teachers are better prepared to facilitate the language development of second language learners than they realize.

■ Establish and maintain links with the parents of your English learners.

Diversity in Language and
Culture at All Grade Levels

statistics

- By 2050, nearly one-quarter of our population will be Hispanic. One in three members of the Latino population are under age 15—a number that only highlights the importance of education in this century (Riley, 2002).
- Our schools now serve 5.5 million students who do not speak English as their first language (Paige, 2004).
- In California, there were 1.5 million ELL service recipients (one-fourth of all students) in 2001–2002, while Texas reported more than half a million (one in seven students) receiving ELL services (Snyder & Hoffman, 2002).

Increasingly, you will find in your classroom students who are culturally and linguistically diverse. You may be feeling very unprepared as a novice to accommodate them.

Given the statistics shown in the box, it is inevitable that you will need to differentiate instruction for the English language learner as well as the other diverse students mentioned in Chapter 28.

Teaching English Language Learners

Principles of good instruction apply to the instruction of English language learners—the task is not as formidable as you may feel it is. Most principles suggest that hands-on, active learning strategies work well with students

learning English. There are a few accommodations that are specific to this group, however, that will be elucidated in this chapter.

You will be afforded an exciting opportunity to learn about new cultures and even new languages while seeking exciting and creative ways to differentiate instruction to meet the needs of your English language learners. Your ELL students will be a valuable resource in helping your entire class improve their English language skills and cross-cultural understanding.

Preparing Yourself

Teachers who have had the experience of learning a foreign language and also have an understanding of students' cultural backgrounds are better equipped to sustain their high academic perform-

Apply It!

Think back to a time when, in terms of language, you were on the outside looking in. It might have been in an immersion middle school language class, on a trip to a foreign country, or in conversation between friends who started speaking a different language and forgot you were there for a few minutes. Write a quick paragraph about how you felt as an outsider.

For me, it was a home stay in Japan, where not one of the family members spoke English, and I did not speak Japanese. We used dictionaries, pictures, signs, and drawings to communicate. Clearly, I was the student in the household, and I was sensitized to how it might feel to be a student in my class who spoke not a word of English.

Can You Read These?

ance according to Diaz-Rico & Weed (2006). The implications are clear. If you have had the opportunity to study a foreign language, you will be better prepared to work with your English learners. If you take the time to learn about the culture(s) represented in your classroom, you will be prepared to teach the students as well.

There are so many books, CDs, and kits available to help you learn a different language or improve your ability to converse in the language you studied in high school or college. Take the opportunity to learn some words or phrases. I recently saw a book series that promises that students can learn Spanish, French, Italian, or Chinese in just ten

minutes per day! I currently am improving my college Spanish in ten minutes per day. I challenge you to do the same.

Teaching Cultural Norms

Culture and language are inexorably linked. It is important to recognize that your students are learning a new culture as well as a new language. The cultural norms of English speakers differ from those in other cultures, and it is just as important to teach those cultural norms along with the language, as the Watch It! video clip explains.

It is important to help English language learners maintain their own culture and language. This not only benefits them but, even more so,

Watch It! video

The Importance of Culture
In this clip, the importance of teaching a new culture as well as the new language is emphasized. After viewing the clip, describe how you would support the cultural identity and self-esteem of your culturally and linguistically different students. How do you teach mainstream cultural norms without alienating students from their own cultural norms?

Everyone is welcome here.

benefits your native English speakers who can learn new words and customs as well. Decorate your room with photos, posters, books, and artifacts of the cultures in your classroom. Read-alouds should reflect the diversity of human experience. Crafts, music, foods, and games from all cultures should be highlighted in your curriculum whenever possible.

Specific ELL Strategies

Most English language learners will be in immersion and sheltered English classes or regular classes. Some English learners may be enrolled in bilingual classes taught by bilingual teachers or in dual language immersion classes, where a percentage of each day is spent learning in both languages and the classes are evenly

divided between English learners and native English speakers.

Sheltered English, also referred to as Specially Designed Academic Instruction in English (SDAIE), presents grade-level appropriate content in English using special techniques. In the immersion and SDAIE programs the language of instruction is English. The regular teacher, often inexperienced in effective practices for working with English learners, needs support to teach them successfully.

Teachers are better prepared to facilitate the language development of second language learners than they realize. According to Johns and Espinoza (1992), teachers often have an intuitive knowledge of the language learning process, which is a good start, when combined with a belief that students can learn.

Teaching Bilingual Students
Teachers discuss the importance of clarifying and explaining procedures through demonstrations and peer help. After viewing the video clip, list the techniques that the teachers used to facilitate students' comprehension of English. If you had a class with at least three different language and cultural groups, which of the strategies in the clip and in the list on page 306 would you utilize?

Being able to adapt your instruction is a valuable skill when English Language Learners are in your classroom. One middle school teacher calls herself the "Overhead Queen." She uses an overhead projector for each paper she gives to her students. They can see exactly what she wants. The visual learners benefit, as do the English learners. She maintains a notebook for each period, organizing the overheads in plastic sleeves and using them from year to year.

Experienced teachers and leaders in the field of ESL (English as a Second Language) such as Peregoy and Boyle (2005), Lessow and Hurley (2005), and Diaz-Rico and Weed (2006), among others, suggest the tips in the box on the following page to promote English language development in a natural and meaning-centered approach.

Help is available if you are new to these ELL strategies. Confer with teachers and resource personnel at your site or at the district level. Share ideas with teachers who are more experienced than you. Read factual and fictional accounts about the cultures represented in your classroom. Ask your principal for advice as needed. Avail yourself of the references at the end of this unit.

Apply It!

Most of the strategies for English learners involve excellent teaching practices: hands-on, active learning in a student-centered environment. Think about a lesson you will be teaching at your grade level or in your subject area. How will you differentiate instruction using some of the techniques suggested in the video and in the chapter?

Establish and maintain connections with the parents of your English learners. Check to see if your school district provides informational materials in translation and/or an interpreter during parent conferences. Increasingly, many school districts with diverse populations provide such services. Ask the bilingual coordinator and other bilingual teachers to help you out. Parents often bring a relative or older sibling to translate for them during parent conferences. Use the translation website http://babelfish.altavista.com for translating simple messages to parents. You can invite parents to share native costumes, foods, music, dance, photos, traditional stories, and family history.

Teacher Talks . . .

Language and culture are inseparable. Learning a foreign language makes a language learner appreciate his or her own language more, as well as cultures from other countries. In this global world, the distance between people is shortening because of the international language—English. Nowadays, people around the world need to be able to use English fluently to get others to understand or appreciate their culture. Therefore, learning to use English to present or describe one's own culture is a very important skill. A good way to develop this ability/skill is to have students explore specific aspects of Chinese culture in depth and to ask them to design and produce a video to introduce it to people from different countries.

*Huifen Lin
Ninth Grade, ESL/EFL
Tainan Hsieh, Taiwan
Doctoral student, Penn State University
State College, Pennsylvania*

(As seen on http://www.LessonPlansPage.com)

Teacher Talks . . .

I am an ESL teacher in São Paulo, Brazil. I thought I could motivate my students to use English to show their feelings or impressions about pictures. I chose pictures that might elicit students' thoughts and feelings, and posted them in my fifth–ninth grade ESL classroom. The students examined the photos and after a week, wrote original captions, in English.

Next, my students took their own photos and wrote about something they considered important, interesting, or funny. The first thing the students did when they entered the class was to look for new captions written by other students. This was created to be a writing project, and it turned out to be a reading project as well. It was amazing to see students reading and talking about what other students had written.

Katia Martins Pereira
Grades 5–9 ESL, Colégio Pueri Domus
São Paulo, Brazil

(Quoted on www.EducationWorld.com)

Thirty Ways to Promote English Language Development

1. Provide direct experiences such as field trips.
2. Include instructional simulations of real-life experiences and role playing.
3. Preview and review material graphically (concept maps, graphic organizers, Venn diagrams).
4. Incorporate substantial oral language opportunities in each lesson.
5. Schedule time for uninterrupted, silent, sustained reading.
6. Encourage the use of student journals and learning logs.
7. Support instruction with technology and audiovisual materials such as films, posters, and videos.
8. Design cooperative learning and collaborative projects.
9. Develop thematic units that integrate curriculum areas.
10. Use maps, graphs, props, concrete materials, visuals, and posters.
11. Dramatize content with gestures and facial expressions.
12. Model clear and understandable written and oral language.
13. Encourage your students to maintain their primary language.
14. Subject your English learners and native English-speaking students to a language unknown to both groups to build empathy.
15. Encourage all students to make personal history and culture books.
16. Recruit native-speaking volunteers or peer mentors.
17. Label objects in the room in all languages represented.
18. Encourage English language learners to keep picture journals.
19. Provide notes (perhaps an outline of the lesson) to students for later review.
20. Allow sufficient time for responses and discussion.
21. Invite your students to share their traditions, stories, and culture with the class.
22. Use research-based active learning strategies described in previous chapters.
23. Use interactive dialogue journals in which students and teachers write to one another in journal format.
24. Encourage choral readings and partner reading.
25. Use reciprocal teaching techniques.
26. Keep routines consistent.
27. Maintain a library of multicultural books.
28. Give clear directions, and review and summarize frequently.
29. Define new words and avoid using idioms and slang.
30. High Expectations, High Expectations, High Expectations.

Classroom Artifacts

(As seen on http://www.LessonPlansPage.com)

Gaynor Morgan, an 8–12 Language Arts and EFL teacher in Oostende, Belgium, offers the following lesson designed for English language learners. It can be adapted for English-speaking classes as well.

Title—The Buzz Poem
Language Arts, Grades 8–12

1. Open discussion about any topic (five min. max).
2. Get feedback on feelings (fluency language).
3. Split class into groups of four or five.
4. Brainstorm a title and write all titles on the board; agree on a title and the style (rhyming or non-rhyming poem), using the majority.
5. Explain that the class will make a joint poem, and each group has two lines each to write. The poem could either be split into verses or kept as a continuing poem.
6. Get each student to write two lines of a poem. The group must then decide in which order the lines are going to be, e.g., Johnny's two lines first, then Sarah's two lines, etc. (good team work spirit).
7. The group members must then check each other's spelling using dictionaries (good practice for team work and precision work).
8. One person in the group will then write out the groups' lines on one piece of paper to be handed to the teacher.
9. The teacher, a chosen student, or a chosen person from each group reads out each verse.
10. If facilities allow, photocopy the poem onto a transparency and show the end result on an overhead projector or photocopy the final poem and give each student a copy of their work.

This lesson plan encourages fluency, teamwork, and accuracy, but above all allows students to show their innermost feelings without feeling self-conscious.

A Proud Parent Sharing

Multicultural Studies

Multiculturalism should be an integral part of every day in your classroom. Multiculturalism should not be an add-on; everyone benefits from learning about other cultures. The importance of valuing the cultures represented in your classroom

Around the World in
One Day at School

cannot be overemphasized. You can learn about your students' traditions, clothing, foods, music, and countries of origin directly from them and they can learn about yours. Think about how valued a student feels when he or she is asked to share. Consider how enriched everyone in the class will be by the experience.

Where my son teaches—a school designated for global studies—each year, teachers and students create a global fair. Each classroom becomes a different country and the room is decorated to reflect that place. Activities are set up in each room—crafts, food, art, dance, music, stories, etc. Each student gets a passport at the beginning of the day and travels to four or five countries during the day.

Avoid It!

Some people speak louder when they meet someone who is learning English. Use the suggestions in this chapter to make your message clearer, not louder. Remember that some English language learners are learning cultural norms as well as a new language. Be sensitive to gestures and body language from them that signal discomfort. Don't expect that they know that in our culture, for example, looking directly at the teacher is a sign of respect. In many cultures, it is just the opposite.

Classroom Artifacts   (As seen on http://www.LessonPlansPage.com)

Fourth-grade teachers Brandi Stephens and Cindy Brewer of Mebane, North Carolina share the following multicultural lesson plan that illustrates how well-chosen literature can be the hook to teach students about their own cultures. Multiple curriculum standards are incorporated, the lesson is differentiated, and the lesson culminates in a collaborative product.

Title—"What's on Your Quilt?"
Primary Subject—Language Arts, Grade 3

Essential Questions:

1. What can we learn from studying an author's craft concerning cultures around the world?
2. How can we apply what we learn about Patricia Polacco's works to our own writing styles?
3. How can we apply what we read to our own lives?

Standards & Content Areas:

Language Arts:

Goal 1.04—Increase sight vocabulary, reading vocabulary, and writing vocabulary through wide reading, listening, discussion, book talks, viewing and studying author's craft.

Goal 2.08—Listen actively by facing the speaker, making eye contact, asking questions to clarify the message, and asking questions to gain additional information and ideas.

Art:

Goal 4.05—Know, discuss, and/or write about how an artist's background and experiences are important in shaping the artist's work.

Math:

Goal 2.02—Identify symmetry and congruence with concrete materials and drawings.

Goal 2.06—Estimate and measure length (inches).

Social Studies:

Goal 2.02—Analyze similarities and differences among communities in different times and in different places.

OUR CLASSROOM QUILT

Description: After reading the story *The Keeping Quilt* by Patricia Polacco, the class will take part in a discussion about the story. For instance, the class will discuss the new words they learned, such as *babushka* (grandmother), and discuss the Russian customs and traditions presented in this book. Next, the class will talk about the significance of the quilt in the story and the teacher will show the class a quilt that he/she personally designed, while explaining the meaning. This is a great opportunity for the teacher to share his/her background with students. The students will be able to design their own quilts with construction paper. The quilt must represent each individual person, such as where they were born, birth date, hobbies, favorite foods and so forth. The students will be given squares of construction paper to represent the patches of the quilt, that they will glue to the background of the quilt. In addition, students will be encouraged to use markers and crayons to draw and decorate their quilts. The teacher will call attention to the sides of the squares and ask students to measure them in inches. They will notice that each side is the same length (3 inches). Students can share their quilts with the class and a class quilt can be made by linking them all together and attaching them to a bulletin board to showcase artwork. This is a great activity for encouraging community within the classroom.

Differentiation: Reading the story aloud to the class while showing them pictures from the story will help both auditory and visual learners. Providing an example of the quilt will aid the visual and global learners, while designing the quilts will help kinesthetic learners. Because students produce a visual representation, this project appeals to spatial intelligence. It is also good for logical learners because of the math involved. This project is also appropriate for intrapersonal learners because they are creating quilts about themselves.

Assessment: The teacher will assess students through informal observation throughout class discussions and by viewing the quilts.

Resources:

- *The Keeping Quilt* by Patricia Polacco
- Black or white construction paper for background of quilt
- Multi-colored squares (3-inch sides) for quilt patches
- Glue
- Crayons, markers or colored pencils

Unit 6 Checklist

Engaging All Learners Checklist	For more information go to:
☐ Am I communicating positive expectations to my students?	Chapter 25
☐ Do I treat all my students equally?	Chapter 25
☐ Am I making an attempt to get to know all my students on a personal level?	Chapter 25
☐ Am I using a variety of research-based strategies, including cooperative learning?	Chapters 26, 27
☐ Do I incorporate multiple intelligences into my lesson plans?	Chapters 22, 28
☐ Have I determined the policies for referring a student with special needs?	Chapter 28
☐ Do I differentiate learning as needed?	Chapter 28
☐ Have I determined the proficiency level of the English learners in my classroom?	Chapter 29
☐ Have I prepared materials for parents in their native language or found someone to translate for me?	Chapter 29

Further Reading: Engaging All Learners

Diaz-Rico, L., & Weed, K. (2006). *The cross-cultural language and academic development handbook: A complete K–12 reference guide,* 3rd ed. Boston: Allyn & Bacon. This handbook will be a key resource for mainstream teachers, K–12, with English language learners in their classroom. The relationship between language and culture is clearly explained and many strategies with a solid theoretical base are included to help teachers ensure success of diverse populations.

Friend, M., & Bursuck, W. (2006). *Including students with special needs: A practical guide for classroom teachers,* 4th ed. Boston: Allyn & Bacon. This is a guide to teaching students with special needs in an inclusive setting. It contains many practical suggestions, vignettes, and methods. The text examines the needs of students with high- and low-incidence disabilities in K–12 inclusive settings.

Johnson, D., & Johnson, R. (1999). *Learning together and alone: Cooperative, competitive, and individualistic learning* (5th ed.). Boston: Allyn & Bacon. This is a comprehensive cooperative learning manual with guidelines for when and how to use cooperative learning approaches. Issues such as resolving conflict among group members and assessing competencies and individual participation make this a unique resource.

Marzano, R., Pickering, D., & Pollack, J. (2001). *Classroom instruction that works: Research-based strategies for increasing student achievement.* Alexandria, VA: Association for Supervision and Curriculum Development. This is a synthesis of what works, and it is easy to read and apply. The most effective teaching strategies are clearly explained in ways that make them applicable in any grade or subject matter classroom.

Tomlinson, C. (2001). *How to differentiate instruction in mixed-ability classrooms* (2nd ed.). Alexandria, VA: Association for Supervision & Curriculum Development. The second edition provides many field-tested examples of how to differentiate instruction in diverse classrooms by assessing readiness levels, interests, and learning profiles. Many examples of differentiating content, processes, and products of lessons are included.

Informative Websites

Teaching Special Kids: Online Resources for Teachers

http://www.education-world.com/a_curr/curr139.shtml

This online article on the *Education World* website provides one stop shopping for information about facilitating the success of students with special needs. There are links to outstanding resources and articles chock full of information, ideas, and strategies.

One Stop English

http://www.onestopenglish.com/lessonshare/archive/young

This website offers lesson plans, free resources, and articles for teachers with English language learners.

Ed Helper

http://www.edhelper.com/

This is a very teacher-friendly website with lesson plans, worksheets, ideas, and much more. The page is organized by subject matter and has skills for middle and high school in addition to monthly unit plans.

The Lesson Plans Page

http://www.LessonPlansPage.com/

This website offers ideas and lessons organized by subject and grade level, K–12. If you need an idea, lesson, or complete unit, this is the place to go. You will find educational links, discussion forums, inspirational stories, and much, much more.

Unit 7

Assessing and Communicating Student Progress

Chapter **30**

How Can I Assess Student Performance?

Effectiveness Essentials

- You can design your own easy-to-score diagnostic tests for basic skills and concepts to determine the appropriate starting level for instruction or to assess progress.
- Norm-referenced tests measure student scores in relation to those of other students.
- Authentic assessments focus on the process and continuum of learning, not just on the outcomes.
- Performance or authentic assessment helps you focus on assessment as an integral part of the teaching-learning cycle.
- Performance-based assessments help you determine how much of what you are teaching is getting through to your students.
- Portfolio assessment is an organizational and management system for collecting evidence to monitor student progress.
- Parents and former teachers can provide you with a great deal of information that will be helpful in assessing students' strengths and pinpointing their weaknesses.

Teachers approach student evaluation with trepidation. They often find this particular aspect of teaching difficult because they don't want to hurt students' feelings; they don't feel they know enough about assessment techniques; and they don't know how to factor student effort, as opposed to actual performance, into the grading equation.

Assessment has always been a part of the teaching-learning cycle, and, therefore, it is a key component of effective practice. Today's standards-based education climate and concomitant high stakes testing have focused educators' attention on assessment more than ever. Teachers do not teach in a vacuum. At strategic points, they have to determine the effectiveness of their instruction. The feedback teachers receive, based on their assessments, is used to guide further curriculum and instruction decisions. Students also benefit because the assessment data let them know where they stand in relation to the standards they are expected to reach.

Assessing Your Students

Assessment involves ongoing evaluations of your students' progress on a number of fronts. The process begins with the first day of school. The diagnosis you plan for the beginning of school should be "underwhelming" for you. You will be very preoccupied by a multitude of tasks, but diagnosis is very important at the outset and needs your attention. Why? Because you do not want to overestimate or underestimate your students' readiness. You may turn them off if the work is too hard, or you may bore them if they have already mastered the material in another class. You will want to use existing records and some diagnostic measures that are easy to administer and score; short and relevant to your standards-based educational objectives; non-threatening to the students; and administered in a group rather than individually, to save time.

As the year goes on, you can monitor student progress in a number of ways. Assessment generally falls within three general categories or types: norm-referenced, criterion-referenced, and performance-based or authentic. The first two are considered standardized tests because they are administered and scored in a standardized manner. The third type uses rubrics to assess performance and it is not as easy to control all the variables of administration

statistics

Tienken & Wilson (2001) report that thirty-five out of fifty states have no requirements that teachers demonstrate competency or pass a course in assessment.

Informal Reading Inventory
A sixth-grade teacher administers an Informal Reading Inventory and observation survey. What is the purpose of an Informal Reading Inventory? What procedures are demonstrated in the clip?

Teacher Talks . . .

I would advise teachers in our district to use an Independent Reading Inventory to assess all new students. Scores for students who were in our district the year before should have been recorded and passed on to the next teacher. Use the IRI to establish a reading and comprehension level for each student. If more information were needed I would administer an Observation Survey. While giving this test, I am able to grasp the student's grasp of letter names, sight word reading vocabulary, a written word knowledge, understanding of hearing and recording sounds during dictation, and the student's understanding of how print works.

I would collect writing samples from each student and assess them using a Six Trait Writing Rubric. If I needed information on the student's phonics knowledge, I would give the 20 word spelling test from Words Their Way (Bear et al., 2003).

Joan Marie Smith
District Curriculum Program Specialist
Colton, California

and scoring. The three types of assessment are all equally important and they all give you essential, albeit different, information.

Norm-Referenced Assessment

Norm-referenced tests measure student scores in relation to those of other students. Half of your students will always fall below the 50th percentile by virtue of the bell-shaped curve. Some standardized tests such as the GRE, the SAT, and the Wechsler Intelligence Scale for Children (WISC) are norm-referenced. Many state achievement tests are norm-referenced if they measure students against the group taking the test. The feedback from norm-referenced tests is helpful for comparing classes, schools, and districts in relation to one another. The information you receive as the actual teacher, however, does not tell you precisely where individual students have fallen short or excelled.

Criterion-Referenced Assessment

Like norm-referenced tests, criterion-referenced tests are standardized in that they are administered and scored in a standardized manner. However, instead of measuring students against one

Myth Buster!

Standardized tests are the best way to measure progress.

Standardized tests are only ONE way of measuring student progress. It is important to look at the "whole child." Testing is only one piece of the total picture. It is a fact that many children (and adults) do not perform well in testing situations. However, if given the opportunity to demonstrate the same knowledge in an alternative manner, the child is successful. The true picture of a child's ability contains teacher observations, and classroom performance, as well as testing achievement.

Joan Prehoda
Coordinator Early Education
Fontana USD
Fontana, California

another, criterion-referenced tests measure the students against set criteria. These tests defy the bell curve and assume that every student can achieve a "passing" score or meet the standard. If this sounds familiar, it is because standards-based tests are a form of criterion-referenced tests. There is a great deal of controversy surrounding "high stakes" testing that has been mandated by the *No Child Left Behind* Act. No child is to be left behind and every child, therefore, should meet the criteria established for passing the standards-based tests. Exit exams are also criterion-referenced tests with a passing score established that all students are expected to meet or exceed.

Ready for the Test

Bubbles, Bubbles, Bubbles

Authentic Assessment

Authentic assessments, also called performance-based assessments, are not easily standardized and focus on the process and continuum of learning, not just on the outcomes. They take into consideration many more facets or dimensions of a student's progress than norm-referenced or criterion-referenced standardized tests. Authentic assessments require that students perform real world tasks that show what they have learned vis-à-vis the standards or objectives that have been set. They are evaluated using a rubric with several

proficiency levels that are made known to students in advance. All students can succeed at the highest proficiency levels since they know up front what the objective is, what the task is, and how it will be evaluated.

Performance, or authentic, assessment can go a long way toward helping you focus on assessment as an integral part of the teaching-learning cycle. The feedback from authentic assessments will help you determine how much of what you are teaching is getting through to your students. Then you can modify or adapt the instructional process to better meet the needs of your students along the way instead of waiting for a one-time-only standardized test. These assessments can

The Big Day!

Watch It! *video*

Standardized Tests
Gerald Bracey discusses the difference between norm-referenced and criterion-referenced tests. After viewing the clip, define both types of tests, including the strengths and weaknesses of each type. What do you think is the best way to effectively measure student progress?

also be fun for your students. For example, students may have to make a model, demonstrate a procedure, or conduct an experiment to show what they have learned. These activities are intrinsically enjoyable in and of themselves.

***Five Steps to Authentic Assessmen*t** At first blush you may be a bit intimidated by designing authentic assessments. However, you use authentic assessments all the time, for example, when you observe your students conducting an experiment in a science lab or creating a still life watercolor based on your criteria. You observe their behavior, check on their handwriting, and listen to them read. This is ongoing and you may not even be aware you are doing it. Authentic assessments could be called "What you have students do every day" assessments. The real challenge is tying the tasks to the standards and scoring the students' work. Here are some steps to help you design an authentic assessment.

1. **Identify what you are assessing.** Look closely at your standards. They will identify *what* students should know or be able to do and at what level. Some specific ideas for assessing the attainment of the standard or objective may jump out at you. For example, if your standard reads "Students will deepen their understanding of the measurement of solid shapes," you may contemplate a task of actually constructing a pyramid to scale. This becomes your performance objective.

2. **Decide what activity will provide context for assessment.** You may decide that you will indeed have students work in cooperative groups to construct a pyramid, with each member of the group assigned one of three equal tasks that include measuring the pyramid faces and base. Make sure that whatever task you delineate, you have enough materials, supplies, and space. Organize the responsibilities of each task and give very clear directions to avoid confusion.

3. **Define the criteria and let the students in on them.** You can often locate the criteria for attainment of the standard by looking at the benchmarks that your district has set up. They won't come out of thin air. Focus on the skills and concepts your district or your state has designated as essential. When you are assessing formally, always let the students in on the task and the established criteria and performance levels. The task may be any hands-on activity that

Figure 30.1

Paragraph Writing Rubric

Criteria	4 Points	3 Points	2 Points	1 Point
Topic Sentence	Clear, properly placed and restated	Either unclear or not placed properly, but restated at end	Unclear, not properly placed, but is restated	Unclear and neither properly placed nor restated
Supporting Details	3 supporting detail sentences	2 supporting detail sentences	1 supporting detail sentence	0 supporting sentences
Mechanics Spelling Punctuation Grammar	No errors	1–2 errors	3–5 errors	6 or more errors
Legibility	Legible in all places	Marginally legible	Illegible in some places	Illegible in all places
Teacher Comments				

you observe or products that the students complete. Let the students tell you what they think a successful project would look like, based on the standard.

4. **Create a rubric.** Your rating system should be based on the criteria you set up along with performance indicators for each of the criteria. You can create your own rubric or use ones designed at your site or district level. I utilized a free rubric-generating website, www.teachnology.com, to generate Figure 30.1. Design fair and simple rubrics since you will be sharing them with your students. Other rubric-generating sites are listed in the references at the end of this unit.

5. **Provide feedback.** Translate the results into feedback through anecdotal reports or grades. Decide how the point range on the rubric corresponds to each of the letter grades, or have your rubric total points add up to a score easily multiplied to give a traditional top score of 100.

> ## Teacher Talks . . .
>
> *We have developed rubrics covering areas from student behavior to academic projects. But before using a rubric at all, I've recommended developing one for something simple and using it as a shared reading and discussion point. After the rubric has been thoroughly "worked," then each group writes their own for a group project or group participation. In this way, the students come to "own" the idea and understanding of a rubric. Anything put into use for greater understanding eliminates the need to go back and reteach. The students also designed a rubric for family participation at a school family night. The parents really enjoyed it because it also gave them a focus for their participation—enabling them to take part in some activities that they might have skipped.*
>
> *Brenda Downs*
> *Reading Specialist/Literacy Coordinator*
> *Pinon Hills Elementary School*
> *Minden, Nevada*

Apply It!

Access the website www.teachnology.com and create a rubric for one of the performance standards you are required to assess. Then try it out on an assignment in your classroom. If you are already familiar with rubrics and the process for generating them, take it a step further and involve your students in creating a rubric. Even first graders have created their own writing rubrics!

You can challenge your students to create rubrics. For example, before sharing the rubric in Figure 30.1, I might have shown my students copies of paragraphs I identified as having a wide range of proficiency. I would ask the students to identify the elements of a good paragraph and then ask them (in groups, possibly) to develop four levels of proficiency for each criterion. I would then show them the one I generated by comparison and they could alter theirs if need be. Students can often assess their own work using rubrics.

Creating Rubrics in a Nutshell Rubrics for common standards are often shared among teachers, so don't reinvent the wheel if you don't have to. Many districts have teams of teachers creating rubrics for the essential standards. Don't be shy! If there are no rubrics for selected standards, either adapt a similar one or create one yourself. Here's how:

1. Share sample assignments with gradations from good to poor with your students.
2. Make a list of criteria for assessing the assignment with the class.
3. Reduce the list of criteria to a manageable few elements.
4. Sketch out approximately four levels of performance for each criterion. These levels can have values attached for easier grading: 3, 2, 1, 0 or 4, 3, 2, 1.
5. Create a draft of the rubric.
6. Apply it to the assignment.
7. Revise and perfect it.

Assessment Using Portfolios

Portfolio assessment is the term that describes an organizational and management system for collecting evidence to monitor student progress. Portfolios include samples selected by the student and teacher as well as reflections about and comments on the work. They may include audio tapes of a student's oral reading at various times during the year, CDs of their writing, homework, tests, artwork, and photos of projects, among other things. Periodically, the students and teacher review portfolio contents and assess progress. This reflective aspect empowers students to make decisions and to evaluate their own progress based on established criteria.

Portfolios are shared with parents at conference time and serve as your data, along with the more objective measures, when you complete report cards. Portfolios can be passed on to the next teacher along with other records or given to the student to take home at the end of the year. It is tangible evidence of how far the student has progressed.

Read all you can about managing portfolios, talk to colleagues, and attend all inservices or seminars on this topic. Some practical resources on authentic assessment are listed at the end of the unit. In these references, you will find very practical advice about portfolio management. Here are a few key timesaving ideas:

1. Take some time each day to examine a few portfolios with the students so the work doesn't get overwhelming. In this way, you can be on a two-week cycle of review.

2. Use Post-it™ notes for comments and add them to the folder, attached to a larger reflection sheet for your expanded commentary.

3. Videotape your class doing oral reports, plays, debates, and other activities. Copies of the tapes can be edited for the students to keep as part of their individual portfolios.

4. Collect reading samples from individual students on their own audiotapes every few weeks.

5. Organize writing portfolios on a computer if each student is able to have his or her own disk. The drafts, edited versions, and final products, along with reviews by peers, the teacher, and even parents can all be included on the same disk.

Portfolios and Self-Assessment
A teacher discusses the advantages and management of portfolio assessment in the primary grades.

Portfolios
A seventh grade teacher and a fifth grade teacher discuss how they assess students using portfolios.

Portfolio Exhibition
A teacher describes a school-wide exhibition of writing portfolios.

After viewing the three video clips, discuss the commonalities in approach that you saw. How do the middle school teachers differ in their portfolio management from the primary teacher? What are the advantages of a school-wide exhibit of the portfolios as opposed to a class exhibit?

Apply It!

Gather information about diagnostic testing resources and procedures at your site and district as soon as possible so you don't reinvent the wheel. Teacher's manuals often include relevant diagnostic tests and directions for their administration and interpretation.

Other Diagnostic Tools

Although you may not use all the following data-gathering methods for each student, this listing, suggested by experienced teachers, gives you a variety of choices. Completed diagnostic assessments can be added to the student portfolios as well.

Teacher-Made Tests

You can design your own easy-to-score diagnostic tests for basic skills and concepts to determine the appropriate starting level for instruction or to assess progress. Speak to other same-subject or same-grade level teachers. They may have diagnostic and review tests on file that are appropriate for your class as well.

Conferences with Other Teachers

To find out more about a student's academic history, seek out a previous year's teacher and present your concerns and questions. You may find that (1) your perceptions are confirmed and/or (2) the teacher saves you from reinventing the wheel by sharing how he or she was able to reach the student last year. Enlist the help of other resource persons at school: the special education resource teacher, the principal, the school psychologist, or the student study team.

Conferences with Parents

Parents can provide you with a great deal of information that will be helpful in assessing a student's strengths and weaknesses. You don't have to wait until formal parent conference times. If you need data that parents can provide, call them and let them know that you need their help in providing the best possible learning situation for their son or daughter. Chapter 34 provides more detail about how you can work with parents to maximize the learning experience for each of your students.

One kindergarten teacher I know interviews each child's parent(s) or guardians during the first few weeks of school, using a non-threatening set of questions that elicit information about the child's strengths and weaknesses, interests, fears, food preferences, traumas, developmental milestones, health problems, and other concerns. Arrange for an interpreter in these interviews if you need one. These extra efforts result in greater parental cooperation and support and provide a wealth of insightful information not otherwise available.

The Cumulative Record

The cumulative record provides continuous and succinct documentation of a student's educational experiences from elementary school through high school. They are used extensively by teachers and other school personnel, since they follow students from grade to grade and provide an easy reference for many aspects of growth and development, academic performance, and behavior in school.

Apply It!

Teachers disagree about whether or not to look at cumulative records before they have made their own judgments about a student. What are the pros and cons? What is your position in the debate?

teaching, learning, test taking, career choices, etc. My students have told me that they "always think of the teacher being tested" when they are taking tests because of our conversation back in September. I think it helps students to know that testing and feedback is not just a process that applies to schoolwork, but it applies throughout life in every profession—and especially in the teaching profession.

Sharon Vanderford
Fifth Grade
West Memphis, Arkansas

As seen on
http://www.LessonPlansPage.com

Avoid It!

Do not make definitive judgments about student achievement just from standardized tests. Gather as much information about a student as you can from all the sources mentioned in this chapter.

*Attitude is a little
thing that makes
a big difference.*

Chapter **31**

How Can I Assess Student Interests and Attitudes?

Effectiveness Essentials

■ Your students can provide you with a wealth of information not obtainable elsewhere and can give you a baseline for building on the diversity in your classroom.

■ A number of strategies exist for collecting information about your students that can help you identify their individual needs.

Although much of the focus in education today is on testing and academic progress, your role as assessor doesn't stop there. Gathering feedback from your students and collecting information about your students expands your role. Your students are more than numbers or names on a seating chart, and finding out what they are thinking, feeling, and believing is key to your success as a teacher. You are not just teaching in the abstract. You are teaching important content and skills to *students,* and you want to dig deeper to find out who they really are. An inquisitive and sensitive teacher knows that students can provide you with a wealth of information not obtainable elsewhere and can give you a baseline for building on the diversity in your classroom. There are a variety of techniques you can use to collect information about your students' attitudes, especially toward instruction, as well as their interests.

Feedback on Instruction

To improve your instruction, take some time at the end of each class period to gather student feedback. I have found this to be very helpful at all levels of instruction—from elementary to university. Adapt any of these formats or make up your own.

Quick Write

Have students write a paragraph in response to a probe to evaluate their understanding of a topic. For example, *what was the most important* (confusing, troubling, interesting) *thing you learned about the Civil War? What was hard to understand? Next time....*

Pass the Envelope, Please

Write a question about the lesson on the front of an envelope and pass it around the class. Every student submits a response to the question and places it in the envelope. You can decide whether or not to make this anonymous.

Summary or Explanation

Have students write a paragraph about what they learned during the period. They can be asked to explain the concept in simplest terms or to give an example. They can write these paragraphs on index cards or in their notebooks, but you should collect them and read them to see how well they understood the lesson.

Rating Scales

Have the students rate the session in terms of comprehensibility, interest, etc. They can use a scale of 1–5 or a yes/no format.

(1 is low, 5 is high)

I learned a great deal	1 2 3 4 5
Material was understandable	1 2 3 4 5
Material was interesting	1 2 3 4 5

Comments:

Interviews

Anonymity is the state of not being known, and every student wants literal and figurative recognition. It is understandable when you forget the name or face of a student you had two years ago. It is embarrassing if that student is currently in your class. Some teachers take time during the first weeks to interview each student for a few minutes. Although this is very time-consuming, the face-to-face exchange allows you to ask follow-up questions and individualize the questions to suit each student. Students have a chance to have special time with you, and the interest you show will pay off in instructional matters. You might prepare ahead of time a list of questions from which you draw as appropriate. Make sure that the questions can all be justified as school-related and do not infringe on family privacy. Some sample questions follow:

- What is your favorite family tradition?
- What do you like to do after school?
- What kinds of books do you like to read?
- What would be the best birthday present?
- What are your favorite television programs?
- How much time do you spend watching television each day?
- What are your favorite possessions?
- What subjects do you like best in school?
- What are your least favorite subjects?
- What sports interest you? Do you play on any teams?
- Who is your favorite sports star?
- What faraway place would you like to visit?
- Do you have a pet? Tell me about it (them).
- What question would you like to ask me about the coming year?
- Describe yourself in three words.
- Tell me one thing you are very good at.
- What new thing would you like to learn to do?
- What do you want to be when you grow up?

Apply It!

Design an interest inventory, using either interview questions or a self-assessment for the appropriate grade level or subject matter. You can use pictures for younger students.

Interest Inventories

Students can fill in the inventories themselves or interview a classmate and then fill in the answers. Although this saves a great deal of teacher time, it does not allow the teacher to follow up and give each student individual attention.

Your students' favorite activities can be determined by compiling a long list of choices. Have them use appropriate symbols to mark the ones they are good at and the ones they want to get better at, or the ones they like versus those they don't like at all. See Figure 31.1 for a pictorial interest inventory for young children.

Figure 31.1
Pictorial Interest Inventory for Young Students

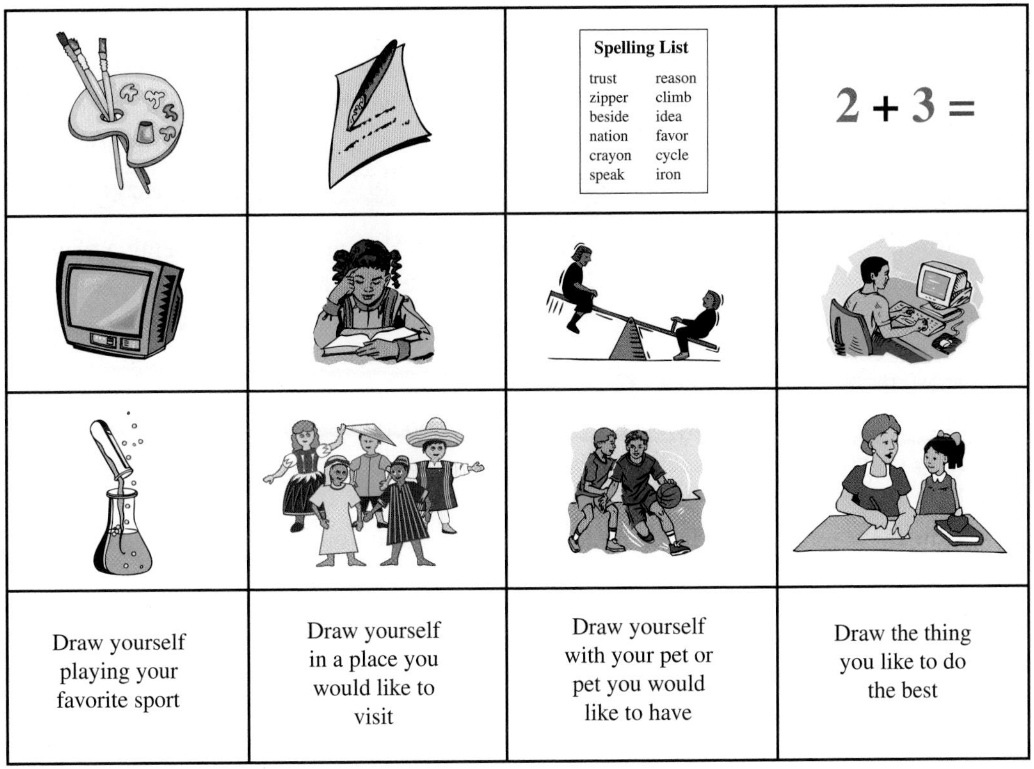
Spelling List
trust reason
zipper climb
beside idea
nation favor
crayon cycle
speak iron
2 + 3 =
Draw yourself playing your favorite sport
Draw yourself in a place you would like to visit
Draw yourself with your pet or pet you would like to have
Draw the thing you like to do the best

statistics

Twelfth graders' interest in school declined from 1983–2000. Whereas 40% of seniors in 1983 said their schoolwork was "often or always meaningful," only 28% of seniors responded this way in 2000 (NCES, 2002).

Good at	✓	speaking in front of	puzzles
Want to get better at	➡	the class	skateboarding
Like	♥	video games	skiing
Don't like	✗	math	snowboarding
		science	basketball
reading aloud		social studies	baseball
reading silently		art projects	swimming
singing		science experiments	tennis
writing stories, poems		drawing	
dancing		board games	
		computer work	

(add your own)

Getting to Know Your Students

Apply It!

Design an attitude inventory appropriate for your grade level or subject area.

Attitude Inventories

Attitude inventories are self-assessment measures that involve a scaled response from high to low. You might use numbers for your scale or even a progression of faces from happy to sad. Some sample questions follow:

- How do you feel about reading (in a group)?
- How do you feel about coming to school each day?
- How do you feel about math?
- How do you feel about science?
- How do you feel about social studies?
- How do you feel about art?
- How do you feel about listening to music?
- How do you feel about watching television?
- How do you feel about speaking in front of the class?
- How do you feel about being a class monitor or assistant?
- How do you feel about writing assignments?
- How do you feel about working in cooperative groups?
- How do you feel about working on computers?
- How do you feel about taking important tests?
- How do you feel about doing homework?
- How do you feel when you receive your report card?

Autobiographies

Students can write autobiographies as an early assignment. You can structure the task with key questions if students need more direction. These essays will be quite revealing and may answer questions you never even thought to ask.

Sentence Stems

In our local newspaper each week, a teen is highlighted and responds to the following prompts in addition to all the "favorites" such as CD, pro team, junk food, web site, etc. You can adapt these ideas to your grade level.

- I go online to . . .
- Few people know that . . .
- What I will drive one day
- Where I will go to college
- What I will do for work
- Where I will live someday
- Where I will vacation one day
- If I could meet one famous person
- With a $____ gift I would buy . . .
- The person who has influenced me most so far
- Favorite quote
- How you want your classmates to remember you?
- Describe yourself in 20 words or less

Avoid It!

Do not ask students questions that would invade their privacy or prove embarrassing. Any questions you ask must have the sole intention of providing information to better adapt the curriculum to meet the student's needs. Here are some no-no's. Use your judgment. If you have doubts as to the propriety of a question, seek advice from your principal.

What does your mom (dad) do for a living? ▪ Why doesn't your dad live with you? Are your parents divorced? ▪ How many relatives live in your house?

statistics

What American middle and high school students do after school and on weekends (Public Agenda, 2004).

- 66% say they participate in sports activities
- 62% are in school clubs or extracurricular activities
- 60% do volunteer work
- 54% attend religious instruction or a church youth group
- 52% take lessons in things like music, dance, or art
- 52% are in an after-school program at school or another locale
- 37% of high-school students have a part-time job
- 30% get regular tutoring or extra academic or test preparation
- 19% belong to an organization like the Scouts

*Not everything
that counts can
be counted, and
not everything
that can be
counted counts.*

Sign hanging in Albert
Einstein's office at Princeton

Chapter **32**

What Are Some Paperwork and Grading Shortcuts?

Effectiveness Essentials

- Record keeping by teachers is needed on a daily basis to address both the requirements of the district and the needs of students. Therefore, it's important to establish an efficient system for dealing with paperwork at the very beginning.

- Learn right away what your school district's policies and requirements are for the paperwork that needs to be completed.

- Keep records of all contacts with parents.

- Make accurate and up-to-date entries on student achievement in relation to standards.

- Find creative ways to save time when grading student work.

Many teachers report that a major challenge in their school day is dealing with the seemingly endless parade of papers across their desks. The records teachers keep fall into two categories: the official district records and the day-to-day student paperwork that needs to be graded in order to assess student progress. The more carefully you organize your own assessment and record-keeping procedures at the outset, the less overwhelmed you will be by the additional record keeping dictated by your district.

Apply It!

Buy a big loose-leaf binder with divider tabs. Begin to collect copies of all the forms you will be required to complete. The tabs will enable you to find what you need at a glance. Some districts even provide new teachers with a guide to the required forms. Keep your binder in a location that is accessible.

Official School and District Paperwork

Your school and district requirements for record keeping are demanding, yet necessary. The *No Child Left Behind* Act has mandated very accurate reporting by districts, and your records of student progress are part of the big picture. There are times when you'll want to hire a part-time secretary when you look at the papers that have covered your desk. School districts generate copious forms. The paperwork goes with the job! You'll learn all about these forms at staff meetings. Some schools provide new teachers with buddies or mentor teachers to help lead you through the maze of forms. Veterans will be happy to explain the forms and offer helpful suggestions.

Set aside a time each day, preferably in the morning before school, to fill in any forms, compose any reports or letters, write your report cards, and do similar chores. Keep a large calendar on which you mark due dates and special events so you can plan ahead, and keep on top of any deadlines. The following sections discuss some of the official records you may be asked to keep.

Grade Book and Attendance Book

Many of your records will be kept in a grade book, marking book, or in a computer program as soon as the final class roster is set. Remember to keep careful

The Class Roster

Plans Ready for the Day

attendance records, as these are legal documents. Daily average attendance determines how much money districts receive from the state, and since school attendance is compulsory, your attendance records alert authorities to truancy or more serious problems at home. Each page in a grade book has room for a roster of student names and columns for recording attendance, test grades, and work completed. It's probably best to use a separate page for attendance and for grading each of the major curriculum areas.

You can save yourself some time by simply duplicating class rosters with columns and with the names already typed in. These sheets can be used for innumerable purposes besides grading and attendance, such as checking receipt of field trip permission slips, recording monies collected, and checking off homework. There are many computer grading programs that you can access, but computers crash and you always want to have a hard copy of all your data.

Plan Book/Lesson Plans

Practically all schools have a policy regarding the format and length of lesson plans. Some districts require plans to be turned in weekly, some semi-

monthly, others not at all. In almost all districts, teachers are required to leave their plan books in school so that substitutes have access to them in case of emergency.

Find out about the policy in your school or district regarding lesson plans and when and if they need to be turned in, if you haven't already done so. This is one of the first questions you should ask as a beginning teacher. Complete your plans in appropriate detail and format and then hand them in on time!

Parent Conference Records

It is wise to keep records of all contacts with parents. Keep all correspondence from home, no matter how trivial. If you want to be safe rather than sorry,

Apply It!

Buy a card file box and index cards. Use one card for each student to keep records of conferences and telephone calls, or use individual sheets in your loose-leaf notebook. Use different color index cards for each class you teach so you can access parent information easily.

save copies when you communicate with parents. You can clear up many a misunderstanding if you can produce the evidence by simply opening up your loose-leaf binder or index card file. It is also wise to make a record of all telephone calls to parents, including the date, time, and nature of the call.

Standards-based Records

Teachers stress how important it is to make accurate and up-to-date entries on student achievement in relation to standards. Use district standards-based forms to focus instruction on those concepts and skills required at your grade level. These lists enable you to focus on specific remedial efforts for individuals who have not met the standard(s). Finally, reporting to parents and enlisting their aid at home becomes easier if you can be quite specific about which standards have been mastered by any particular student and which have not.

Student Paperwork

To be perfectly honest, I love everything about teaching except grading and paperwork. Night after night, we teachers lug home bags full of student papers. The good news is that I became

motivated to compile a list of labor-saving suggestions from experienced teachers so I could lighten my load . . . and maybe yours as well. Some are appropriate for all levels and some are more grade-level-specific. Choosing the type of strategy to deal with the paperwork depends to some degree on the level of thinking the assignment requires. In middle and high school, for example, assignments are geared to the higher levels of Bloom's taxonomy, so the written work is extensive, more complex, and more time-consuming to grade.

Grade on the Spot

As students finish their work, check papers on the spot when it is feasible. Primary youngsters have worksheets that have a reasonable number of items that can be graded right away. Use a "good job"-type stamp to make the grading fun for elementary students, or apply a sticker to the paper. Secondary grading can be more time consuming, so use your preparation time or free period to evaluate student work as soon as possible.

Student Exchange

Have your students exchange papers or correct their own. One teacher I know

Good Work Stamp

Figure 32.1

Grade Book Set Up Numerically

Number	Name			
1	Cho, Steve			
2	Smith, Jane			
3	Lee, Theresa			
4	Singh, Paul			
5	Stein, Jason			
6	Bloom, Emily			
7	Martinez, Javier			
8	West, Talitha			
9	Lopez, Kathy			

assigns students a number in random order that is to be placed on every assignment instead of their name. The students do not know who is who and the papers can be distributed and then collected in numerical order. If you set up your grade book in numerical instead of alphabetical order, your work is lessened in the marking and the entering grades phases.

Every Pupil Responses

Use hand signals, choral responses, and individual sets of flash cards to check understanding without having every response written down. Use thumbs (or pencils) up, thumbs down, thumbs across for agree, disagree, or not sure.

Use fingers to denote numbers for any mathematical responses. For example, 24 x 8 = ___. Students are asked to hold up the number of fingers representing the number in the ones

Figure 32.2

Thumbs Up and Down

Figure 32.3

Flash Cards

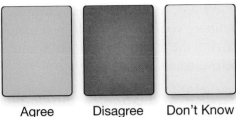

Agree   Disagree   Don't Know

Figure 32.4

Numerical Response
with Fingers

column, then the tens column and then the hundreds column. You can tell at a glance who needs extra attention.

Individual Response Boards

Use individual chalkboards or dry erase white boards if you have them. Floor tiles with grease pencils work well too. Or, laminate response cards made of file folder cardboard and give each student a card, a grease pencil, and a wiper. In each case, the students respond by holding up their plastic cards, tiles, chalkboards, or white boards.

Students respond on individual boards.

Students Self-Marking

Make a transparency of the worksheet and illuminate it on the overhead projector with the answers filled in all at once or one at a time. You will save a great deal of time by following these steps:

1. Make a copy of the worksheet.
2. Fill in answers.
3. Make a transparency.
4. Uncover the correct answers as the students respond.
5. Have them mark their own work or exchange papers with someone.

Answer Keys

Provide answers on a key or overhead projector to all but the last 5 items. These you check yourself, thus determining if the student simply filled in the answers or has really mastered the material.

Teacher Talks . . .

Teaching middle school can be a challenge for some and a great pleasure for others. I love it because my students can begin to make their own choices about which way their lives are headed.

I had a student who came into my office last week. She was very concerned about her grade in my class. As an 8th grader preparing for the trials of high school, she knows that she needs to do well. Her grade was slowly slipping below average. This student decided it was time to get to work and find out what she needed to do to pass. So Friday afternoon she came to speak with me.

I told her that all she needed to do was to complete the assignments that I had given her. I reminded her that at the beginning of the year I told the class:

"It's your choice! You choose your attitude. You choose how

(continued on facing page)

Less Is More

Recognize that you don't have to test each skill or concept with multiple examples when fewer will suffice. If a preprinted worksheet has 25 examples, cut the sheet in half, or tell your students to complete only the odd-numbered ones or the last 10. Or, have them do all the examples, but you'll have a fair idea of how they have done if you only do spot checking.

Volunteers

Engage parent volunteers to help in the marking. This will only work if you have students use numbers instead of names on their papers.

Eyeball Some Assignments

Recognize that not every assignment needs careful attention and, additionally, that not every assignment needs to be returned to your students. You can eyeball the work to check for major error patterns, and honestly tell students that some papers won't be returned, but all are examined.

Oral Review

Review orally as a sponge activity instead of requiring so much written work. This is especially effective at secondary levels when the work is often more conceptual. Tasks such as summarizing the plots of literary selections, reviewing spelling words, defining vocabulary words, and memorizing the multiplication tables can be evaluated orally.

Review in 8 Boxes

Cochran (1989) suggests that kids make up their own worksheets on papers folded into eighths. In each box, students demonstrate mastery of what they have learned during the day. They can, for example, draw a mammal in box 1, write three nouns in box 2, and solve an addition problem in box 3. In just three spaces you have reviewed three subject areas with a primary class and have very little grading to do at home. (See Figure 32.5.)

Answer Columns

Ask students to use answer columns on their papers to record their final solutions to math problems, for example. Instruct them to fold a 2-inch-wide column or draw a 2-inch line down the right- or left-hand side of their papers to record just their answers. Teachers can quickly scan the answer column for instant feedback and either grade on the spot or take the papers home to review in their entirety.

Figure 32.5

Homework in 8 Boxes

4 + 3 = 2 + 3 = 1 + 3 = 3 + 5 = (Math)	Draw and color 3 yellow balloons and 3 green balloons. How many all together? (Number and color concepts)	Write the letter Aa 3 times. (Handwriting)	Color this stop sign. 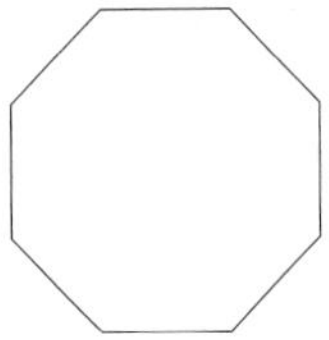 ⬡ (Social studies safety unit)
Complete this pattern. △●■♥△ — — — — — — — (Math)	Write your spelling words here. (Spelling)	Draw a picture of the main character in our story. (Reading)	Draw a nest with 4 eggs. (Science—animal homes unit and math)

successful you will be in life. It's not we teachers, or your parents, or any other adult. We are here to guide you. Ultimately it is your choice!"

The student remembered that topic from the beginning of the year. I reminded her that it was possible to meet her goals. She spoke about how she wanted to make her mother proud. I kindly reminded her that it was her choice to make those who mattered most in her life proud of her.

Now when she walks past me, she reminds me that she is going to raise her grade because it is her choice.

Jennifer Ponsart, Music Director
Four Corners Charter School
Davenport, Florida

As seen on
http://www.LessonPlansPage.com

Rubrics

Use rubrics and have students grade their own work before they turn it into you. The website, TeAchnology.com (www.teachnology.com) can help you generate rubrics. You also can return to Chapter 30 to read more about rubrics. See Figure 30.1 in Chapter 30.

Cooperative Group Grading

Use cooperative groups to peer edit writing assignments so that you do not have to correct every spelling error, punctuation mark, and capitalization error. In groups of four, assign these tasks: Capitalization Editor, Punctuation Editor, Spelling Editor, and Grammar Editor. There are four papers to edit and each student has a job and a different color pencil for editing. Students pass the paper to the next editor when they have finished their job. Then you are free to focus on the content and organization of the assignments.

Emmer and colleagues (2003) offer some useful suggestions that are applicable to all teachers: Become familiar with grading practices in your district, at your school, and in your department and/or team. Most likely, each already has a set of norms. Next, identify how your own ideas about assessment fit in with theirs. Consider the percentages that will be awarded for neatness, organization, mechanics, participation, test grades, homework assignments, and other assignments. What will you do about late assignments? Will there be due dates on a master syllabus? Will big projects be broken down into smaller assignments?

Ask yourself these questions. I do each and every quarter before I type up a final syllabus.

- What are the grading practices in your school?
- What is the weight of each assignment?
- Will you use points, averages, or percentages?
- Are the requirements clear, and are due dates established?
- Will you have a syllabus?
- How will you factor in effort?
- Do you have a grading rubric for each assignment?
- Are the assignments varied so all learners can succeed?
- How will you give feedback to the students and how soon?
- Will big assignments have incremental deadlines?
- What will you do about late assignments?

Avoid It!

- Avoid arguments about points and criteria by making your grading system clear, fair, and justifiable. I can't emphasize this enough because even very experienced university professors get caught in the grade grievance trap because something wasn't spelled out clearly enough. Students can be great detectives when they set about challenging a grade!

- Avoid holistic grading that you can't justify. Use specific criteria or rubrics, instead of "I just think you deserved a C."

Chapter **33**

How Can I Prepare My Students for Taking Standardized Tests?

Effectiveness Essentials

- Prepare your students for "high stakes" tests all year long by covering the standards in your instruction.
- Integrate test prep and test-taking skills with your instruction.
- Build up test endurance incrementally by increasing time on-task.
- Alert parents to the need to be well rested and to eat breakfast on test day.

I didn't fail the test, I just found 100 ways to do it wrong.

Benjamin Franklin

But there are advantages to being elected President. The day after I was elected, I had my high school grades classified "Top Secret."

Ronald Reagan

As surely as the daffodils bloom each spring, your school testing coordinator will arrive with packages of standardized tests and test directions. With so much attention on school progress due to NCLB, this can be a stressful time for many communities. Schools and districts that do not score well or miss their targets for adequate yearly progress (AYP) on state tests may be sanctioned and lose funding. In extreme cases, principals may be removed. School scores are reported to parents and are published in many newspapers for all to see.

In addition, some districts give other achievement tests such as the Iowa Test of Basic Skills or state achievement tests. Many states, also, now have high school exit exams, and students who do not pass them may not graduate with a diploma. Students will be attuned to your anxiety levels, so make this a positive and upbeat time, not a nail biter for you or for them! You can help alleviate their anxiety as well as your own by careful attention to standards and sustained test preparation all year long.

You have been preparing your students for these tests all year long by doing your best teaching and adhering to the subject standards. Keep in mind that your students have been engaged in meaningful learning throughout the year and will do their best to make you proud. Excessive worrying won't help.

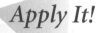

Apply It!

Find out what tests your students will be taking since not all grade levels take every test. Then get a calendar and mark in the dates of the tests in big red letters. Ask the testing coordinator or principal if there are sample tests or materials and teacher booklets that would be useful to you in preparing your students for the format of the test and types of questions asked. Some testing corporations even provide short, sample practice tests for students to take. You should inquire about what test prep materials are available sooner rather than later. The more information that your students have about the types of questions and the formats, the less anxious they will feel. Think of this preparation as teaching to the format, not teaching to the test.

Standardized Test Preparation Throughout the Year

Standardized tests, as defined in Chapter 30, are administered and scored in a standardized manner. They can be norm-referenced (comparisons of a student's scores to the group that took the test, resulting in a bell-shaped curve), such as the SAT or ACT, or criterion-referenced (students can all meet the passing scores), such as many state standards-based assessments. For example, in my state, students take the California Standards Test, a criterion-referenced test with five levels of performance for each subject tested: advanced, proficient, basic, below basic, and far below basic. They also take the California Achievement Test, which is a norm-referenced test with scores reported in percentiles for each school and district, and the High School Exit Exam, which is a criterion-referenced test with a set passing score. There are other tests as well for particular subgroups.

Throughout the year, when discussing assignments or administering any kind of test, emphasize that your students need to follow directions closely, budget their time carefully, and check their work continually. For vocabulary work, encourage your students to use flash cards and pictographs, and to play games such as Jeopardy, Pictionary, and Word-Definition

		trustworthiness	fluid
affable	integrity	wily	sticking together
easy flowing			
cunning	cohesive	friendly	

Test Preparation

Teacher Talks . . .

In California, in elementary school, the standardized tests are based on the language arts standards and math standards. I advise teachers to have a thorough knowledge of the standards for their grade level. If the teacher teaches a good curriculum and accounts for the standards being covered, students should have no trouble with standardized tests. It helps to familiarize students with test formatting so that the format does not cause any confusion. Test formatting practice can be done throughout the year or a few weeks before the test.

Besides that, I always emphasize that students should READ, READ, READ, and WRITE, WRITE, WRITE.

Joan Marie Smith
District Curriculum Program Specialist
Colton, California

Apply It!

Build a vocabulary word wall all around the baseboards in your room, encouraging your students to add synonyms, antonyms, and definitions.

Vocabulary
Word Wall

Word	Definition	Synonyms	Antonyms
affable	friendly	genial, pleasant, gracious, amiable	unfriendly, aloof, distant, surly
aggravate	make worse, annoy someone	worsen, inflame	alleviate, soothe, mollify
austere	strict, without decoration	simple, basic, stark	fancy, elaborate, ornate

Concentration. Incorporate key skills into your instruction. For example, teach your students to recognize prefixes, suffixes, and root words.

Many teens will be taking the SAT or ACT. The SAT was revised in March 2005 and is 3 hours and 45 minutes long. New to the SAT are a 25-minute essay exam and multiple critical reading sections, replacing the older verbal sections. The maximum score is now 2400 instead of 1600. An alternative college entrance exam is the ACT. It assesses high school students' ability to complete college-level work and is composed of multiple-choice tests in English, mathematics, reading, and science, as well as an optional essay test. The writing portion on these exams has caused consternation among students, so you can alleviate anxiety by helping them respond to sample writing prompts.

⊘ Myth Buster!

Good teaching can be measured by how well your students do on standardized tests.

I believe good teaching is the ability to provide students with experiences which engage them in the subject matter, help them develop a deep understanding of concepts and processes in the chosen subject, and encourage a love of learning. . . .

The main thing that these sorts of tests show is a student's ability to do well, or poorly, in these sorts of tests!

Shirley Casper,
Science & Biology teacher
Years 7–12 (High School)
Sydney, New South Wales
Australia

Avoid It!

Do not get caught up in the high stakes testing frenzy. You will be communicating your anxiety to your students. What they need is a cheerleader, a teacher who encourages and builds their confidence—not a worrywart.

Do not assume that students are familiar with the format of standardized tests. Do not assume that students have come to school with a good night's sleep and a full stomach. Make sure you have high protein stacks available for students prior to the test session.

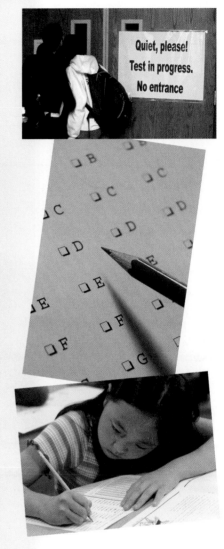

Standardized Testing

Some students will take review courses and buy numerous review books. You can help all of your students by buying the books yourself and focusing on the format and samples. Even though not all of your students are college bound, it is important to focus on essential writing skills at all levels.

Ten Suggestions for Standardized Test Preparation

The following ten suggestions come from experienced teachers and will help you through this stressful time of year. Remember that you have maintained a standards-based focus all year and that your students will rise to the challenge.

1. Do some test preparation each day to avoid the before-test crunch

2. Integrate test prep with your instruction and make it just another exercise.

3. Teach test-taking skills such as:
   - Bubble filling
   - Using scratch paper if allowed
   - Completely erasing any changes in responses
   - Estimating answers in math and checking work
   - Using the process of elimination
   - Making reasonable guesses when all else fails
   - Webbing an essay response
   - Using memory aids such as acronyms
   - Reading the questions prior to reading the passage

- Looking for key words in math problems that give clues to the operation
- Using the "does the answer make sense?" test
- Working all the easy ones first
- Pacing
- Reviewing for careless errors

4. Review different types of questions and question formats:
   - Factual
   - Inferential
   - Application
   - Evaluation
   - Opinion

5. Discuss why the right answer is right and how to arrive at the correct response.

6. Discuss why the wrong answers are wrong.

7. Build up test endurance incrementally by increasing time on task.

8. Stress to parents and students the need to be well rested, to eat breakfast, and to wear comfortable clothes on test day.

9. Bring healthy snack to class on the day of the test.

10. On the day of the test, some teachers give out "magic" cookies, special pencil toppers, or good luck charms.

Apply It!

Ask at least three experienced teachers how they prepare their students to do their best on standardized tests. Create a pre-testing period timeline for implementing these and other suggestions.

Chapter 34

How Can I Enlist Support from and Communicate with Parents and Guardians?

If you want your children to improve, let them overhear the nice things you say about them to others.

Haim Ginott,
psychologist and author

By the year 2000, every school will promote partnerships that will increase parental involvement and participation in promoting the social, emotional, and academic growth of children.

Goals 2000: Educate America Act

Effectiveness Essentials

- Your students' parents/guardians play a fundamental role in the educational process.

- Convey in word and deed to parents/guardians that you will treat their child with the same concern and respect as you would your very own.

- A two-way positive communication channel opened early and used regularly throughout the year is the key to success.

- Your communication with parents/guardians should probably begin on the very first day, if you haven't started sooner.

- Parent-teacher conferences coincide with report cards, but additional conferences with parents/guardians should be scheduled as needed.

statistics

According to the latest U.S. Census Bureau report (2001), these are the percentages of children ages 0–17 living in various family arrangements:

No Parents

Grandparent	48.2
Other Relatives	27.4
Nonrelatives	8.5
Foster Parent(s)	8.9
Other Relatives and Nonrelatives	5.3
Own Household or Partner of Householder	1.7

One-Parent Families

Single mother	78.2
Single mother with partner	9.4
Single father	9.4
Single father with partner	2.0

Two-Parent Families

Two biological/adoptive married parents	86.8
Two biological/adoptive cohabiting parents	3.6
One bio/adoptive parent and stepparent	9.6

Parent, teacher, and student

It was my fourth year of teaching and my first year in a university demonstration school. The parents were connected to the university as either students or professors. One non-reader in my sixth grade class had a father who taught in my doctoral program. "Well, your sixth grader still can't read," I told this parent with trepidation. I was ready to accept all the blame for the previous six years. After all, this father could be my professor next semester! "We don't want to push him, don't worry. He'll either "learn to read or he won't." The child learned to read and is now a dad with two readers of his own.

Although you may have entered the teaching profession to work with kids, your students' caretakers play a fundamental role in the educational process. It is important to recognize that family configurations are as diverse as the students themselves. Some of your students may have two parents. Some may live with one parent. Some may be raised by a grandparent or other relative. Others may be raised by an unrelated guardian. In all cases, your students' parents or guardians are entrusting their precious offspring to you, and it is the best situation for you and for your students when parents/guardians are on your side, working along with you and not at cross-purposes.

Establishing a Partnership

To engender confidence and gain respect from parents and guardians, convey in word and deed that you will treat their child with the same concern and respect as you would your very own. This attitude will bring out the best that parents/guardians have to give. Engaging their cooperation in the school setting can provide you with a critical mass of support during the rough times and enable you to impart the greatest possible benefit to your students.

Having a majority of the parents/guardians in your corner cheering you on is well worth the time and effort you take cultivating their support. Parents and guardians, when informed about your goals, program, and procedures, can serve as a valuable backup system. Moreover, they have a right to be informed about a student's progress—both strengths and weaknesses. There are numerous opportunities and processes for encouraging the partnership. Consider the following ways you can strengthen this partnership.

1. Attend parent organization (PO) or PTA meetings.

2. Invite parents to volunteer in your classroom.

3. Provide parents with a list of grade-level or subject standards.

4. Accommodate caretakers' work schedules and schedule conferences for siblings on the same day.

5. Read up on cultural norms and learn some welcoming words in languages represented in your class.

6. Encourage parents/guardians to share their life experiences and culture with students in your classroom.

7. Start a lending library of education and parenting books of interest to parents/guardians.

8. Invite parents to shadow their kids during class time and participate in all activities.

9. Send home commendations and awards.

10. Take photos of your students and send copies to parents/guardians.

11. Let parents or guardians know when tests begin and send home suggestions such as: get a good night's rest, eat breakfast, and dress comfortably.

12. Invite parents/guardians to performances, fiestas, debates, award assemblies, etc.

Fostering Communication

Parents/guardians and teachers have a lot to offer and teach one another. Parents or guardians and teachers usually share equally the amount of time kids spend awake each day. Parental insight and experience will bring to light additional information that may help you better serve the needs of the student. A two-way positive communication channel opened early and used regularly throughout the year is the key to success. If the right hand at home knows what the left hand is doing at school and vice versa, how much better both will be at understanding and doing what is best for the student. Anticipate that every communication with parents, whether oral or written, may need interpretation or translation for those parents whose primary language is not English.

statistics

For the parents polled, 83% say their most important role is that of homework checker and cheerleader for learning. Of teachers polled, 57% want parents to supervise homework for accuracy or at least completion, but only 16% of teachers feel that parents are doing that conscientiously. Half of the parents report having serious arguments about homework and a strong 22% report doing their son's (or daughter's) homework themselves! (Farkas et al., 1998).

Award Certificate

Teacher Talks . . .

I establish open communication with parents early on in the school year. I ask students to have their parents sign the opening letter I write for students. It's a chatty letter that I love writing each summer in the days before school begins. I always introduce my cats (and describe what they've been doing that summer), and I share my philosophy of education and the English classroom.

At open house, I provide my home e-mail and phone number, and I invite parents to complete a writing assignment: "In one million words or less, tell me about your child." I've had hilarious and touching, informative, and crucial information shared.

I also call parents for good reasons—just to tell them their kids did something well, that they have a polite and considerate child, that their kid is improving. . . . Some

(continued on facing page)

Five Ways to Open Communication Before School Starts

You can start establishing a solid foundation by contacting parents or guardians at the beginning. You don't need to spend a lot of time on these introductory communications, but they will set the right tone when and if you later have to call and deliver unpleasant news.

1. **Phone.** Telephone each parent/guardian during the week preceding the start of the school year. Be brief in making the point—"I care; I want to work with you for your student's sake; let's get together." Few parents/guardians can resist this sincere expression of welcome.

"Just called to say, all is well."

2. **Letter.** Type a duplicated letter to each parent/guardian before the school year starts. Make sure to have letters translated into the languages represented in your classroom population and send them appropriately to non-English speaking parents. Below is an example of such a letter.

Dear Parent or Guardian,

My name is _____ and I will be your son's/daughter's _____ teacher this year. I'm writing to let you know that I look forward to working with you so that your son/daughter can develop new talents, skills, and abilities this year. I really love teaching and will do everything I can to make this year a very successful and happy one.

Our Open House is scheduled for the first week in October. If you have any questions or would like to talk with me before then about any of your concerns, please call the school (phone no.). I will return your call as soon as possible. I look forward to meeting you in person.

_____ (name)

_____ (school)

---

3. **Interview.** Interview each parent/ guardian during the first weeks of school. The interviews will enable you to gather firsthand information about strengths, abilities, health status, developmental milestones, and other factors. Above all, the very act of scheduling the interview conveys that you really care about your students and respect their parents and guardians.

4. **Autobiography.** Have parents/ guardians send an autobiographical poem or their son's or daughter's autobiography to you before school starts. Encourage parents/guardians to sit down and compose it jointly. The autobiographical poem format is found in Chapter 7.

5. **Home Visits.** Consider making home visits to each of your students. Although this takes a great deal of time, you can gain a lot of information about behavior and home environment. Many parents and guardians will be delighted that you took the time to actually visit their homes.

First-Day Communications

Your communication with parents/ guardians should probably begin on the very first day if you haven't started sooner. Those who are included from the first day may have fewer questions, comply more readily with requests for assistance, and generally feel better

about you and the school.

The content of first-day notes varies according to how much information is provided by the school itself. Your letters can be prepared ahead of time and filed from year to year with only updates added. First-day letters are explained in Chapter 9. Keep your letters, notes, and handbooks short and to the point and avoid using any jargon.

Open House

Open House may be your first opportunity to meet a majority of the parents and guardians and make a pitch for cooperation. You can increase attendance by having your students write the invitations. Teachers feel it is vital to establish a time during the Open House when parents and guardians stop milling and wandering around the room and come together for a brief program. The schedule might look like this:

8:00–8:20 P.M.	Sign the guest book
	Walk around the room
	Look at texts, materials, and students' portfolios
	Play with the computers, etc.
8:20–8:30 P.M.	Program begins
8:30–8:45 P.M.	Questions and answers

parents have returned my calls in fear, and then cried when I said, "I'm just calling to say how great she is."

Camille Napier
Eleventh Grade English
Natick High School
Natick, Massachusetts

Quoted on
www.EducationWorld.com

Ten Ideas for a Successful Open House

1. **Refreshments.** Set up a table with some snacks. Food helps create a warm social atmosphere. Note that in some cultures it is traditional to bring food to functions. Some parents and guardians may feel better about attending if they can contribute something, no matter how small. You might extend an invitation, for example, to bring a piece of fruit to cut up and add to a big fruit salad.

2. **Student Work.** Have representative samples of each student's work displayed around the room and have each student's portfolio along with a name card on his or her desk.

3. **Nametags.** Provide nametags for parents and guardians instead of making well-reasoned assumptions about who belongs to whom, which may turn out to be mistaken. Have a space for the names of both caretaker and student.

4. **Schedule.** Write the daily schedule on the board so parents and guardians can actually see what the students do all day or all period long.

5. **Body Tracings.** Some teachers have students trace their bodies on butcher paper, color them with tempera paint, cut them out double, stuff and staple them, dress them in clothing brought from home, and prop them up on their chairs.

6. **Sample Texts and Materials.** Have sample texts and materials out for display. Students enjoy having their parents or guardians look at their books and showing off a special science kit, math lab, computer program or DVD.

7. **Questions on Cards.** At the door when parents and guardians sign in, provide index cards and encourage them to print their questions on the cards and leave them in a specified box. This will spare parents/guardians the embarrassment of asking what they may consider to be a "dumb" question. Collect the cards before your program starts, and answer the most frequently asked questions on the spot. Announce your intention to deal with the others in newsletters.

8. **Student Guides.** You can make Open House into a learning experience for your students when you prepare them as tour guides, pointing out the classroom landmarks and high points. One teacher has a guide of the day, every day, whose responsibility it is to greet and show visitors around the room.

9. **E-mail and Websites.** Promote the use of e-mail and websites to encourage ongoing communication. Let parents and guardians know that if they have and are willing to write their e-mail addresses on the sign-in sheet, you will be able to make a listserv and advise them of general happenings and specific reports on grades, behavior, and other matters. If you have a website, give the address to parents/guardians and ask those with Internet access to communicate with you that way. Otherwise, let them know you will communicate by phone or note.

10. **Handouts.** Provide handouts with all relevant information and in translation if necessary. You can send the information home to parents/guardians who are unable to attend, and those who do attend will be able to have easy reference as needed. Otherwise, let them know you will communicate by telephone, notes, and monthly newsletters. Avoid speaking in jargon or acronyms.

Open House

When your program begins, you might want to consider covering the following topics and issues:

- Class rules and discipline policies
- Homework policy
- Curriculum overview
- Reporting, grading, conferencing
- Invitation to serve as a room liaison or volunteer
- PowerPoint presentation with student photos
- Students acting out their day

In middle school and high school, the parents/guardians generally follow

Open House Sign

their son or daughter's schedule in an abbreviated way. So, if you have a program to present, make it very short because the parents/guardians will need to move on to the next room that may be way across campus.

The Parent- or Guardian-Teacher Conference

Parent- or guardian-teacher conferences coincide with report cards, but additional conferences should be scheduled as needed. The dual goals of such a conference are the exchange of information about an individual student and the formulation of cooperative strategies to solve any problems. This is a time of high anxiety for both you and the parents or guardians. The parents/ guardians are worried about what you have to say, and that's why, no matter what, you should start out on a positive note. You will be worried that you are not qualified to give advice about someone else's child or that parents will attribute any difficulties to your inexperience. You both can relax! This is a partnership in the best interests of the child. On pages 357 and 358 is a checklist to help you have a successful conference.

statistics

Public Agenda (2000) reports that:

- 9% of parents say that teachers are putting too much academic pressure on students.
- 10% say their youngster is getting too much homework.
- 10% say their youngster's school fails to provide extra help to students who are struggling.
- 11% say their youngster's school requires them to take too many standardized tests.
- 12% say the standardized tests that their son (or daughter) takes ask "questions so difficult or unfair that students cannot be expected to answer them."
- 18% say the teachers in their youngster's school "focus so much on preparing for standardized tests that real learning is neglected."

A Report Card

Myth Buster!

Parents and guardians don't want to be involved in school.

Almost all parents want to be involved in their child's education in some way. It just varies how much they would like to participate. I have found that there are three groups of parents or guardians in schools. The first are the "Super Room Parents." These are the parents that want to be in your classroom everyday all day if you would let them. Next, you have your "Working Parents." These are the parents that want to be involved, but don't know how to do this as a full-time working parent. Lastly, you have the "You do it" parents. These are the parents that are content to let others get involved and want everything to run "on automatic."

The "Super Room Parent": New teachers take advantage of the help. Have a "volunteer sign-up" list posted at the "Back to School Night" and get the helping hands started. Plan for a volunteers meeting soon after to set up a schedule. For new teachers it would be advantageous to have an assistant almost every day. These parents can organize your celebrations, find your donations, and will work for you as much as you want (or let them in some cases). On average they are very supportive and work well with small groups, allowing you more time for one on one with your students.

The "Working Parent": Have a separate sign-up at "Back to School Night" entitled "Can Work From Home." You will find that many of your "working parents" love to help this way. At home, many of them can trace, cut, staple, sort and do many other tedious things that take time from your day. An easy way to do this is by laminating a large manila envelope and creating a cute and fun cover entitled "Home Helper." In this envelope you can slip in whatever you need done with a quick post-it giving the parent instructions, and send it home with their child. This makes the parent feel involved and allows you to get more things done.

The "'You Do It' Parent": It may appear that this set of parents wants nothing to do with your classroom, but once motivated, they can be a great resource. They usually are a great help in donating supplies or money for necessities in your classroom. They like to feel involved without having to do too much "hands on." Some parents may need some direct prompting with a phone call rather than just a send-home sign-up sheet. A highly motivated "super room parent" can often make the calls to get you the supplies you need.

One final note: All parents and guardians want what is best for their child. As a parent it can be difficult to have your child away from you for a large part of their day. Having parents involved in the classroom brings peace of mind and fulfillment to the parent, teacher, and student. Create a community where everyone is welcome and you will find the most successful classroom.

Ivania Martin
Parent and teacher on parental leave
Benicia, California

A Conference Checklist

Prior to the Conference:

☐ Confirm the date, time, and place with the parent/guardian.

☐ Coordinate parent conference schedules with team members in middle school and/or with homeroom/advisory teachers at the high school level and with same school teachers of multiple siblings.

☐ Inform parents/guardians ahead of time about the purposes of the conference.

☐ Have them bring to the conference a list of questions or concerns.

☐ Arrange for an interpreter if needed.

☐ Examine the student's portfolio and have your marking book and any anecdotal records accessible.

☐ Make a list of three or four points to cover, beginning with strengths.

☐ Think about three adjectives to describe the student.

☐ Establish a waiting area for early arrivals to maintain confidentiality during the conference in progress.

☐ Dress professionally in an outfit that will not intimidate.

☐ Make sure the chairs are adult-sized—even if you have to raid an upper-grade classroom or the teacher's lounge.

☐ Sit side by side at a table with all of the documentation in front of you.

The Conference Itself

☐ Start the conference by meeting the parent/guardian at the door.

☐ Have a space available for coats and umbrellas.

☐ Be as gracious a host/hostess as you would in your own home.

☐ Thank the parent(s)/guardians(s) for coming and lead them to the conferencing area.

☐ Start out on a positive note and find something good to say about the student.

☐ Begin the six-step process:
- Provide data.
- Seek information.
- Listen actively to parents/guardians.
- Synthesize their suggestions with your own.
- Devise a plan of action.
- Arrange for follow-up.

Teacher Talks . . .

Each parent comes in not knowing what will be said. All have hope that things are going well. What you have to say should not be the first time you are saying it. In other words, there should be no surprises on conference day. My first question is: What do you think? Usually their response is just on target and it's a great opener to what you have to say.

Kris Ungerer
Kindergarten
Riverside, California

A Parent–Teacher Conference

Teacher Talks . . .

One of the most important secrets to achieving students' success is to get the families involved in the academic process. Parents are important participants who can channel a student's success or failure. To illustrate my point I would like to share the story of one of my students: After two months of class, she still didn't know any letters or sounds. I tried my best to make her mom understand that it was important for her to get involved in her daughter's education. She listened to me and followed up with my recommendation. After eight months of school, this girl reads at level 14 with great ability to retell stories. To reach high expectations, three components are necessary: student, teacher and family.

Maria Cleppe
School Counselor
San Bernardino, California

Teacher Data	*Guardian Data*
■ test scores	■ talents and abilities
■ academic performance	■ overall health and concerns
■ behavior in the classroom	■ interests, hobbies, sports
■ social interaction with other students	■ attitude toward school subject(s)
■ effort	■ responsibilities at home
■ cooperation	■ homework habits
■ peer relationships	■ responses to rules at home

Conference Closure

☐ Summarize the major points.

☐ Clarify what action will be taken, if any.

☐ Set a date for a follow-up note or conference.

☐ See the parents/guardians to the door.

☐ Express your sincere thanks for their attendance.

☐ Make notes about the conference as soon as the parents/guardians leave.

☐ Take a breather before you start talking to the next set of parents/guardians.

☐ Send a brief note to each parent/guardian, thanking them for attending and listing the major points covered. This can be a fill-in-the-blanks type note in the interest of time.

Avoid It!

Do not be intimidated by parents or guardians. They, like all of us, need to feel significant, and when invited to participate with you as a partner in education, they will jump at the chance. They simply need encouragement to do so. They can participate in big ways, in small ways, in any way at all. They are more intimidated by you than you are frightened of them. Extend a hand to them. It will make a difference to you, to them, and to their kids.

Unit 7 Checklist

Assessing and Communicating Progress Checklist

For more information go to:

☐ Have you found out which tests your students will be required to take and when? — Chapters 30, 33

☐ What authentic assessments and diagnostic tools are used at your site? — Chapter 30

☐ Have you checked out what grading practices are the norm at your site? — Chapter 30

☐ Have you gotten a copy of the reporting forms and rubrics? — Chapter 30

☐ Have you made a list of questions for an interest interview or inventory? — Chapter 31

☐ What grading shortcuts seem most feasible to use? — Chapter 32

☐ Have you decided on a pre-testing period timeline for test preparation? — Chapter 33

☐ Are you prepared for parent conferences or do you need more information? — Chapter 34

☐ Have you familiarized yourself with the cultures represented in your room? — Chapters 34, 39

☐ Have you provided parents with the information they need to help at home? — Chapters 34, 39

Further Reading: Assessing and Communicating Student Progress

Clark, L. (2000). Get ready for testing: Sensible ways to help your students prepare. [Online] Available online at http://www.microsoft.com/ Education??ID+GetReadyTesting March 2, 2005. This is an excellent resource as you prepare your students for high stakes testing.

Popham, W. J. (2004). *Classroom assessment: What teachers need to know* (4th ed.). Boston: Allyn & Bacon. This text offers a range of assessment techniques that teachers most often use in classrooms. It address the mandates of NCLB, but focuses as well on alternative assessment tools.

Silvaroli, N., & Wheelock, W. (2003). *Classroom reading inventory* (10th ed.). New York: McGraw-Hill. This is an easy-to-use classroom reading inventory that is useful for novice teachers. It can be administered in about fifteen minutes and will enable teachers to assess comprehension and word recognition skills with pretests and posttests.

Stiggens, R. J. (2004). *Student-involved assessment for learning* (4th ed.). Upper Saddle River, NJ: Prentice Hall. This is a comprehensive book about developing assessments that reflect learning. There are clear step-by-step instructions on how to construct all types of classroom assessments and a discussion of what they can and cannot assess.

Assessment Websites

National Education Association

www.nea.org/index.html

Find resources about assessment techniques and issues by searching this comprehensive and easy to navigate website.

Rubric Generator

www.teachnology.com

At this website you can personalize already created rubrics or design your own from scratch.

Rubric Construction Set

www.landmark-project.com/classweb/rubrics/index.html

You can create rubrics online at this useful website.

Checklists Online

www.4teachers.org/projectbased/checklist.shtml

Create your own checklists online.

7–12 Educators' Website: Assessments

http://712educators.about.com/od/assessments/

There are inventories and rubrics and very up-to-date information about assessment and testing for secondary educators, including SAT information.

Unit 8

A Professional Life in Balance

The real man

smiles in trouble,

gathers strength

from distress, and

grows brave by

reflection.

Thomas Paine,
patriot and philosopher

Chapter **35**

What Is Reflective Practice and How Do I Engage in It?

Effectiveness Essentials

- New teachers go through five phases in the induction year (Moir, 1990).

- The reflective teacher is open to change, takes responsibility for outcomes, and teaches with enthusiasm and openness to diversity.

- There are a number of ways a teacher can gain feedback about his or her own teaching that can encourage reflection.

All of the preceding chapters have focused on what you do for your students to make their year rewarding. This unit explores how you can use your insight to make this and future years gratifying for you.

Moir (1990) and colleagues identified five phases in the induction year. You may remember these were described and diagramed in Chapter 3. The *Anticipation Phase* is characterized by excitement when you land a position. Then comes the *Survival Phase,* in which you are just happy to keep your head above water. The *Disillusionment Phase* and the *Rejuvenation Phase* follow this. A *Reflection Phase* follows and leads to another *Anticipation Phase* for the next school year. This chapter spotlights the *Reflection Phase* and focuses on how you can become a reflective teacher.

Toward Reflective Practice

One of the most important decisions you will make is whether or not you will become a reflective teacher. What is a reflective teacher? Grant and Zeichner (1984) suggest three requisite attitudes for the reflective teacher. They are *open-mindedness,* a willingness to consider and even to admit that you are wrong; *responsibility,* a willingness to look at the consequences of your actions; and *wholeheartedness,* a willingness to accept all students and to practice what you preach.

(⊘ *Myth Buster!*

Teachers are born, not made.

New teachers should allow themselves five years. The first year you are totally overwhelmed and a bit confused with all the record keeping, curriculum requirements and testing schedules and wondering why you entered the teaching profession! The second year you recognize the materials and manage the schedule. The third year you not only recognize the materials and manage the schedule but are now able to add one or two creative ideas of your own to energize your program. The fourth and fifth years you realize how much fun teaching is and find yourself searching for materials. methods, and opportunities to provide enrichment and enhance the learning experience of your students.

Lynn Sleeth
Former elementary and middle
school teacher and principal
Special Education Mild/Moderate
Fontana, California

I applied for National Board status because I felt I had reached a plateau in my delivery of instruction. I knew I could be a better teacher, but I needed the impetus to find out how. Going through the National Board process forced me to take a comprehensive look at my teaching practices and analyze them in detail as they related to national standards and best practices. I truly believe that this year of intense reflection was by far the best professional development I have ever done. That being said, the process is not for everyone. It requires ongoing self-motivation and the ability to recognize one's own strengths and weaknesses. Many people, also, do not achieve [certification] the first time around. With this in mind, I would definitely encourage a teacher to apply. There is no better way to improve one's teaching.

Virginia Strong Newlin, NBCT, Principal
Rock Hall Middle School
Rock Hall, Maryland

Quoted on www.EducationWorld.com

"We have always done it that way," is a saying that is all too common in many fields. You may even hear this at your school site. There is a widely held belief that teachers teach the way that they were taught, and some do so without considering whether those methods were effective. The reflective teacher, on the other hand, discounts the notion that because something has always been done a certain way, it must be good. It may be true that many teaching strategies are as effective today as they were twenty years ago, but the reflective teacher does not take this for granted. Reflective teachers are analytical. They examine what they are doing in light of research and experience, and they seek out feedback in order to grow professionally. Reflective teachers constantly examine their practice and decide what is best for the current group of students. They can admit they have been mistaken and they take full responsibility for their decisions. I tell student teachers to realize "It seemed like the best solution at the time," so they can forgive themselves and learn from their mistakes.

A Five-Point Plan to Get You Started

The reflective teacher is open to change, takes responsibility for outcomes, and teaches with enthusiasm and openness to diversity. Once you decide to be a reflective teacher instead of one who relies on the way things have always been done, how do you take the first steps?

Apply It!

Buy a blank journal to write down all your reflections. The first section should be reserved for your teaching credo, no more than 1–2 paragraphs per question. What do you believe makes a good teacher? What do you believe about the way kids learn best? What is your discipline plan? What are your beliefs about parental involvement? Look at what you have written from time to time throughout your first year of teaching and revise it as your belief system grows with your experience. There may be additions, deletions, and revisions. Keep all your versions in your reflection journal.

Apply It!

In your reflective journal, list at least ten qualities, skills, or attitudes that make you an effective teacher. Don't be shy! Then write down five areas that you would like to strengthen. Don't be shy here either. What alternatives have you considered? Write these down as well.

1. Recognize your own implicit theories and beliefs about teaching, learning, and kids. You have gone through your own childhood, schooling, university education, and student teaching. You have read a great deal and heard many diverse theories in classes. Now it's your turn to put it all together.

2. Acknowledge your own strengths and relinquish the notion that you have to excel at everything. Question the way you do things and seek alternatives.

3. Design a five-year plan of goals you would like to achieve, and seek help from all sources (parents, colleagues, local businesses, professional organizations) to reach them.

4. Find ways to love, respect, and treat yourself well. Do not become your own worst naysayer. Teachers are all too quick to dwell on their mistakes and forget all the good. Students have a knack for draining confidence from their teachers with raised eyebrows, whispers to friends, notes passed, yawns, makeup touch-ups, doodling, bored expressions, wise remarks, clowning around, jokes, etc. You will need to learn to ignore these seemingly hostile manifestations of disinterest. Students may simply be posturing and trying to impress their peers. Do not become discouraged. Seek feedback from the students through a suggestion box in your classroom and ignore the outward expressions that may not be a reflection on you but rather on their need to impress their classmates with their cool "world-weariness."

5. Blow your own horn and take every opportunity (conferences, videos, presentations) to demonstrate your expertise. Viewing your successes through

Apply It!

Sketch out a tentative five-year plan and keep it in your reflective journal. You can make changes, but keep all the versions.

statistics

Findings from the 2000 survey by the National Center for Educational Statistics (NCES) found that practically all public school teachers had a bachelor's degree, and 45% had earned a master's degree and 1% obtained a doctorate or some other degree, and 18% reported having other certifications.

Newer teachers were less likely than more experienced teachers to report holding a master's degree, ranging from 20% of teachers with 3 or fewer years of teaching experience to 54% of teachers with 10 or more years of teaching experience (NCES, 2000).

Ed Watson

4th Grade Teacher
Franklin Elementary School

Teacher Business Card

Apply It!

Write a *Dear Me* letter to yourself. Write what you value most about yourself and why you have earned respect from colleagues, family, and friends. Don't be shy. This letter is for your eyes only, and you should keep it in your reflective journal.

the eyes of the public will help you validate your practice. You will have to acknowledge your own strengths when they are so visible to others. Notify the local media that a special, newsworthy activity is coming up. For example, a third-grade teacher friend of mine also directs the *Nutcracker* ballet each year, and she brought several performers to her school for a special assembly. The local paper carried the story. Make up business cards with your name. Wear a nametag at school. Take and share photos of your classroom activities. Submit a conference proposal.

Engaging in Reflective Practice

Use objective techniques of videotaping or audiotaping lessons to help you reflect on your practice. Also, your students can give you some honest and useful feedback if you ask them. At the end of the school year, one teacher I know has her students write down the three best things about the year, and she rereads them for confidence on the very first day of the following school year. Another has the current class write letters to the next year's class about their experiences. One teacher has her students make report cards for her at the

end of the year. The design and categories are of their choosing, and it is a creative way to gather material for reflection.

You may want to design a questionnaire for your students to fill out anonymously at the end of the year. Answers to open-ended questions such as those in the Apply It! feature will provide you with data to ponder before the beginning of the next school year.

Peer coaching or just talking informally with colleagues will help you think about your practice. School-based collaborative teacher reflection should be ongoing and teachers can become the initiators of their own professional development. When teachers come together with school colleagues to

Report Card for Teacher

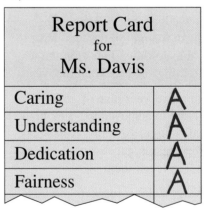

Report Card for Ms. Davis	
Caring	A
Understanding	A
Dedication	A
Fairness	A

Myth Buster!

If I try hard enough I can reach every student.

I think many teachers enter the classroom thinking that they will be able to "rescue" all of their students. Then when they fail, they feel like they aren't good at teaching and might as well quit the profession. Teaching students is not about "rescuing" them, but rather about giving them the tools to rescue themselves when they need it. It is important that the students know they have choices and that the outcome of their life is based on the choices they make.

Jennifer A. Ponsart
M.S. Music Director
Four Corners Charter School
Davenport, Florida

openly discuss discrepancies between theory and practice and give voice to their opinions, they become intellectually stimulated, less isolated, and more empowered.

Jot down your feelings, your successes, your questions, and ruminations about the day, every day in your journal. Keep your reflective journal in your desk drawer and write down at least three successes every day. When all seems futile, take out your journal and read it from start to finish. That should cheer you up and restore a "can-do" attitude.

Date: 9/28   Success #1
Instead of calling out, Mary raised her hand for the first time

9/28   Success #2
Sean sat in his place on the rug during story time, and didn't bother anyone

9/28   Success #3
Principal complimented class during math

Success-of-the-Day Page from Journal

Avoid It!

Never put yourself down. Even if you have had a very bad day, you need to focus on what went right and how you can ameliorate any problems the next day. There are really no perfect decisions. Recite this to yourself, "It seemed like a good idea at the time." Think back on or rent the movie, *Groundhog Day*. Bill Murray was able to relive each day until he got it right. Teachers have this opportunity to start fresh each and every day all year long!

Respect your fellow human beings, treat them fairly, disagree with them honestly, enjoy their friendship, explore your thoughts about one another candidly, work together for a common goal and help one another achieve it.

Bill Bradley,
NBA player and presidential candidate

Adding "just kidding" doesn't make it okay to insult the Principal.

Bart Simpson,
cartoon character

Chapter **36**

How Do I Establish Relationships with Administrators and Colleagues?

Effectiveness Essentials

■ A school is a community within a community.

■ Seek out other teachers and take the initiative to introduce yourself. The veteran teachers will most likely be delighted if you ask for ideas or help.

■ Get to know the key personnel at the district office, in the audiovisual center, and in the resource center.

■ Familiarize yourself with the school norms and operating procedures.

■ A successful year depends on an open, honest, and professional relationship with your principal.

■ Present yourself as a prepared professional who is positive and enthusiastic about the challenges of the first year.

■ Perhaps your greatest allies in your school setting are your colleagues and school staff. Contact with your colleagues will help you discover their special talents and skills.

A school is a community within a community. We all have a primary need to belong and gain acceptance, so you will want to quickly adapt to your adopted community. As the new kid on the block, you will need to orient yourself to the physical environment, get to know the key players, and learn the ropes. You will want to establish productive, positive, and professional relationships with your administrator, colleagues, other staff, and support providers. Good working relationships can make or break the school year.

Getting Oriented

When you arrive at your school, the first thing you need to do is acclimate yourself to the building so you can find your way around. Depending on the size of your school, this could be a daunting task. The second most important thing is to identify the key people in the school. Who will be able to answer questions? Whom do you go to for supplies? Who REALLY runs the school?

Key Locations

Most schools have campus maps, and you need to ask for one even before school starts. If none is available, take out a piece of paper and start drawing. Annotate it with the following important campus locations:

- restrooms for your students
- restrooms for you
- water fountains
- the teacher's lounge/refrigerator
- the custodian's space
- the cafeteria
- the resource room
- the computer lab
- the gym
- the library
- the nurse's office
- the audiovisual equipment room
- textbook storage closets
- the assembly room
- the supply room
- the school office
- telephones
- the principal's office
- the school counselor's office
- the mailboxes
- the workroom: copier, laminator, etc.
- the school bus depot
- your spot for class lineup
- your spot for emergency lineup
- a place to park your car
- mass transit stop
- and, of course, your classroom!

Teacher Talks . . .

When I started teaching in my high school, it didn't take me long to figure out that the most important people in the school to know were the secretary in the main office and the custodian. They knew all the behind-the-scenes workings of the school, and those are important things to know. It also became very clear which teachers had the most clout, and you didn't want to get on their bad side. But the real power was with the support staff.

Mary K.
High School, Social Science
Wellman, Iowa

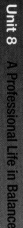
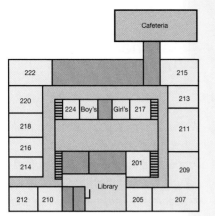

Map of a School

The Tech Place

A Teacher's Work Is Never Done

Apply It!

Secure a faculty and staff roster. Annotate the list as you sit in faculty meetings so you can quickly learn the names and roles each person plays at your school. Make notes to connect names and faces, and write down any particular skills or talents that come to light.

For the first few weeks, you will probably refer to the map fairly often, but in time, it will become less necessary.

Key People at School

Obtain a staff roster as soon as possible to find out who's who at your site. From time to time, you will be seeking the advice of other professionals and support providers in the school. Knowing them by name will help you develop rapport more easily.

Introduce yourself to the key players at school and make notes about the hours and days they are available for consultation and what information they need from you.

- school nurse or health aide
- community worker
- special education resource teacher
- psychologist or school counselor
- bilingual resource teacher
- reading specialist
- language and speech specialist
- library aide
- technology resource person
- school secretary
- custodian
- other _____

Seek out other teachers and take the initiative to introduce yourself. You will need the support they have to offer later, and they will appreciate your support as well.

Get to know the key personnel at the district office, in the audiovisual center, and in the resource center. Don't be shy. You will reap great benefits from just walking in and introducing yourself. Attend school board meetings from time to time, and become familiar with the community leaders and the issues they wrestle with each month.

It won't take long before you identify the "movers and shakers" at your site. Key "players" are not always the people with titles. Find out who has influence and who is a leader. Identify those people who seem to make things happen and those whose comments are held in high regard. As with any community, schools have the same political dynamics that play out both in front of and behind the scenes. It may take time to gain an understanding of these dynamics, but this information will prove to be very valuable over time.

The School Secretary

Key Procedures

You need to familiarize yourself with the school norms and operating procedures without delay. Some districts provide new teachers with a general policy manual that will answer many of your questions. Questions beget questions, and the answers to these and to all other questions should be made a permanent part of your own policy manual. Some of these procedural questions might include the following:

- How do I refer a student for special testing?
- What do I do first if I suspect child abuse?
- How do I get into the school on weekends?
- How does the laminating (copy, die press, bookbinding) machine work?
- How do I sign up to use the multiuse or assembly room?

- How do I order media and technology?
- How many times will the principal visit me, and will I have notice?
- How do I get more desks (books, materials, pencils, etc.)?
- How do I get repairs done in the room?
- What do I do when a student gets sick?

The one quality I try to find is a teacher who will be a "kid magnet." Once a student really connects emotionally to the teacher, then the rest will follow! Many things might lead me to believe that the candidate is a "kid magnet." Some are based on instinct—a feeling that I get from a young, enthusiastic person who has that "je ne sais quoi," that intangible spark that would attract kids. I also look for people who are involved with kids outside of the school setting, especially music groups, theater, and sports. If I ask the right kinds of questions to let the personality of the candidate emerge, I can usually find this quality if it's there.

Our committee just finished interviewing 26 candidates, and we found 3 or 4 with those qualities. All agreed that the candidates have that special something to become superstars—and we will settle for nothing less!

Steven Podd, Principal
Nesaquake Middle School
St James, New York
Quoted on www.EducationWorld.com

Apply It!

Use a loose-leaf notebook and begin to collect all of the policy and procedures documents that cross your desk. Classify them under larger headings and use dividers. Have blank sheets in each section for your own annotations. Prepare a list of questions and get answers to them as soon as possible.

Working with Your Principal and Other Administrators

A successful first year depends on an open, honest, and professional relationship with your principal. You are at least 50% responsible for establishing a productive relationship with your principal and 100% responsible for meeting the expectations that your principal has of you.

Present yourself as a prepared professional who is positive and enthusiastic about the challenges of the first year. You can demonstrate this overtly through your dress and demeanor. Any

The Principal's Space

first-week difficulties such as overcrowding can be viewed as problems to be solved rather than as tragedies to lament. When requesting changes of any sort, provide an instructional rationale. For example, if you want the unused piano moved into your room, explain that you play piano and use songs to teach concepts.

Working with Other Teachers

Perhaps your greatest allies in your school setting are your colleagues. You may have a formal mentor or you may be assigned buddies, but you definitely will have your peers who are ready and willing to help you. They were in your shoes once, and, like most of us, they remember vividly those first years of teaching.

It is important to be friendly to everyone and resist getting pulled into cliques. Try to steer clear of any

Ten Ways to Convey a Positive Impression to Your Principal

1. Use great discretion before you send a student to the office for discipline. As a beginning teacher, you want to convey the impression of competence, even though you won't be feeling it all the time.

2. Keep your principal informed at all times so that surprises are kept to a minimum. Discuss problem students with your principal well before the parents storm his or her office. Principals don't like to be left in the dark, and they especially don't want to utter or even think the words, "I don't know anything about this."

3. Share with the principal any letters or communications before you send them home to parents. The principal may notice any policy discrepancies and spare you the embarrassment of having to retract what you have written.

4. Inform your principal about any impending outside activities. Field trips, conferences, in-services, or absences will require that you obtain substitute coverage sooner than later.

5. Inform the principal about guest speakers and special presentations. Share with your principal all the wonderful activities you are engaging in with students.

6. Send samples of students' work to the office from time to time. Class newspapers, art projects, stories, and cooked or baked goods will be favorably received.

7. Invite your principal to special events such as plays or debates in your classroom. Your students can design the invitations and escort the principal to a good vantage point upon arrival.

8. Be on time to school and to meetings, and turn in any reports or rosters on or before your deadline. Punctuality rates very high with administrators.

9. Maintain an attractive, orderly, and clean room environment at all times. Your room speaks for your program, especially during a quick walk-through by the principal.

10. Present a positive demeanor. Smiling beats whining and even if you have had a very hard day, remember that although "this too will pass," an administrator may not forget your downbeat reaction.

Principal Talks . . .

- *Surviving your first year is simple if you are not afraid to ask for help. There is no reason to reinvent the wheel. Ask, ask, ask and share, share, share.*

- *To stay organized you MUST stay after school and get ready for the next day. This will make your mornings and days run smoother. It will also lower your anxiety because you'll be prepared.*

- *Remember students only have one year to experience this grade with you. Make it the BEST you can and don't be afraid to ask them how to make it even better. Your students can be one of your best teaching assets.*

- *Don't be a perfectionist when it comes to room environment. Get their work up on the board and if they are old enough maybe (third to twelfth grade), let them put it up for you. They will have a sense of ownership.*

(continued on following page)

- *Be firm, fair and ALWAYS follow through with what you say. You will gain their respect this way. Remember they don't have to like you but they should respect you. The easiest way is to show them respect ALWAYS.*
- *Praise in public and correct in private.*
- *Remember to make time for your home life. Teaching is just a job—not your life. You will be better for the students if you have balance with life and work.*
- *Your principal is your FRIEND! He or she is there to help you succeed. Don't be afraid to ask for help. A reflective first-year teacher is high on a principal's list of desirable traits.*

Nina Conine
Teacher K–12 (13 yr)
Junior High and Middle School Vice
    Principal (2 yr)
First Year Principal
Olivehurst, California

Working with Other Teachers

Avoid It!

Don't stay in your room during lunch or recess breaks. It is much more important to socialize and break out of the isolation of the classroom. You need that cup of coffee or glass of juice, not only to refresh yourself but also to feel a sense of belonging with your colleagues.

Do your fair share of committee work, but guard your precious time. Your first year's focus is on your classroom and teaching. Practice tactful ways to decline invitations for extracurricular involvement. Rather than complaining, seek solutions and support from your colleagues.

colleagues you identify as whiners, complainers, or gossips, but remain friendly just the same. There are wonderful opportunities on a staff for collegiality and even deep and lasting friendships.

Contact with your colleagues will help you discover their special talents and skills. Find out who the experts are in various curriculum areas. Who is adept at computer-based instruction? Who knows every art project ever invented? Who plays guitar and may be willing to swap music for art? Who runs a well-managed classroom? Whom can you go to for science or social studies ideas? You'll discover this information informally. Don't be shy. Ask for help.

The veteran teachers will most likely be delighted if

you ask for ideas or help. One or two colleagues may take you under their wing. Swallow your pride and seek them out. This book could not have been written except for the willingness of experienced teachers to share what they have learned either by trial and error or from other teachers.

In middle school, you will probably have an interdisciplinary team to look to for advice. If your school has block scheduling, you will hopefully be teaming with teachers who are a bit more experienced than you are. In high school, you will probably depend on your department head to guide you through the ins and outs of your first year of teaching. Grade-level colleagues in elementary school will see you through the first year.

Chapter **37**

How Can I Manage My Time and Balance My Life?

Effectiveness Essentials

- Learning to manage your time efficiently both at home and at school is important for maintaining a healthy and balanced life.

- A number of planning aids and strategies can help you prioritize your day.

- Overcome obstacles: Perfectionism, Procrastination, Indecisiveness, and Interruptions.

- Stress can manifest itself in both positive and negative ways.

- Stress can derive from the very nature of the teaching profession, the reality of high stakes testing, and accountability demands.

- There are a number of effective ways to keep stress at bay.

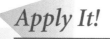

YOU'RE INVITED
TO
LYDIA JOHNSON'S
RETIREMENT PARTY!

In the first few years of teaching, it's not at all unusual to feel sleep deprived and to wonder how you will juggle every personal and professional demand. Balancing all your responsibilities while establishing yourself in the classroom and in your school takes time and can be stressful. But you need to feel assured that with time, the demand on your time does get better. In the meantime, there are a number of things you can do to reach a healthy balance.

Apply It!

Reflect on why you chose the profession of teaching. Did you want to drive yourself into being a workaholic? Did you want to make sure that each and every lesson has a motivation to knock your socks off? Write a speech for your future retirement party. What do you want your legacy to be? Only when you decide on a realistic legacy by writing a retirement speech will you be more open to the stress-busting and time saving suggestions that follow.

Myth Buster!

Teaching is a cushy, part-time job.

It is Sunday, my day off, and I just spent three hours doing lesson plans, grading papers, and completing a project for my classroom. I always feel like there is never enough time to do all the things I need to get done as a teacher. I could stay at school for hours after my contract time. I have learned to manage my time better and to just cut myself off at a certain time each day whether I am done or not. I say to myself, "Tomorrow is another day!" I always bring home work to grade and lesson plans and projects to complete. There is always something to do that you just can't seem to get done. I put in a lot more time than my contract hours; I think that most teachers do. During time off, I find myself taking extra classes, going to conferences and constantly thinking about how I can become a better teacher. A teacher's work is never done!

Diane Amendt
Third Grade
Colton, California

Time Management

Time management is a skill you will need to learn. When my student teachers tell me they are "burned out," I reply, "How can that be? You haven't even been lit yet!" Beginning teachers often bemoan the lack of time in a day. They spend long hours writing lesson plans, grading papers, and dealing with the day-to-day needs of the job. These tasks can leave you feeling harried as you try to do it all and have it all. Instead, you should take out a crystal ball and look ahead. There will come a time, sooner than later, when you are managing your time more efficiently and have more to spend on other aspects of your life.

Time Management at School

It is important to protect teaching and learning time at school. Maximizing teaching and learning time in the classroom will lessen some of the pressure you feel to accomplish your objectives and will ensure that students will succeed. The routines suggested in Unit 3 and the additional ones that follow will give you more time on task and fewer repetitions of the new teacher mantra, "I never have time to finish anything."

Apply It!

The first task you must do when trying to regain some time at school and at home is to honestly record your activities. Choose a typical weekday, and in shorthand record what you did in half-hour intervals. Did you chat with a friend on the phone for a half hour? Did you dawdle over the post-school snack? Did you watch a half-hour "Jeopardy" rerun? Did you pet the cat mindlessly, avoiding the stack of papers on your desk? Could you make more time by adding just one half hour at the end of the school day for marking papers and tidying your desk? Can you find one half hour to exercise during your day?

Teacher Talks . . .

Mrs. W. was my fifth grade teacher, and if ever there was a teacher that deserved a gold star, it was she. She did not make me feel defeated. On the contrary, she went out of her way to let me know that I could be whatever I wanted to be. She helped me in so many ways and built my self-concept to the point where I actually did believe that I could do something special. And that is just what I did.

For the past 22 years, I have been a fifth grade teacher. Because of Mrs. W's influence in my life, I am now encouraging students who have had difficulties in their lives to believe that they can overcome and become someone. I have won numerous awards such as Teacher of the Year and have been nominated to Who's Who Among America's Teachers *four times by former students, but I owe it all to one fifth grade teacher who believed in me and challenged me to be all that I could be.*

Charles Skinner, Science Coach
South Carolina State Dept. of Education
Cottageville, South Carolina
As seen on
http://www.LessonPlansPage.com

1. Keep your students on task and away from socializing in order to maximize learning.
2. Sit down and work while your students are working, once they understand the assignment.
3. Routinize your transitions to increase teaching time.
4. Maximize your instructional time by relegating rote practice to homework.
5. Post an agenda on the board and stick to it.
6. Use an alarm clock or a timer to keep yourself focused and away from detours and diversions.

Teachers are "meeters." Middle school teachers will meet with their teams, and high school teachers may have curriculum or department meetings. Elementary teachers have grade level meetings. Since you know one another and work so closely together, there is a risk that you will waste time talking about personal issues, complaints, or side issues. Usually meetings have set times dictated by the union and school district, and every minute counts. Try to redirect the conversation diplomatically when it gets off track.

Time Management at Home

Saving time at home is key to your mental and emotional health. At home, try to implement the following ten steps to conserve time for such important activities as sleeping, exercising, preparing a healthy meal, spending time with your family and friends, or just taking some time for yourself.

1. Commit to balance in your life.
2. Decide what's important to you.
3. Prioritize and plan. (Prefer not to do the extra things like the family reunion or Thanksgiving dinner for forty.)
4. Make "to-do" lists and use planning aids, especially technology.
5. Overcome obstacles:
   Perfectionism
   Procrastination
   Indecisiveness
   Interruptions
6. Get rid of clutter and organize your workspace.

Family Time

7. Socialize with some non-teachers after school hours.

8. Go to sleep and awaken at the same time each and every day.

9. Take up a new hobby like biking, golf, or photography.

10. Travel and share your experiences in the classroom. Keep yourself energized by seeking out new interests.

Managing Stress

Sometimes the pressure and imbalance of those first years of teaching can be stressful. Stress is like a chameleon, changing its manifestations just as effectively as the lizard changes color. Have you ever felt tired, unable to concentrate, overwhelmed, anxious about going to school, withdrawn, sick to your stomach, unable to sleep, depressed, irritable, insignificant, discouraged? These can all be symptoms of a debilitating state of stress.

Moderate stress is not always bad, but super-sized stress or distress serves no purpose. Moderate stress can energize us to get things done. Super stress immobilizes us.

Stress can derive from the very nature of the teaching profession. You

Avoid It!

Avoid comparing yourself to experienced teachers. Do not over-commit your time to anyone, including friends, family, and community organizations, to name a few groups who would like you to clone yourself so you can give more and more. You have a valid justification for guarding your free time, and you can develop nice ways of extricating yourself from situations that place excessive demands on your time. "I would like to help you out, but during this first year of teaching, I need to focus on my professional responsibilities. Please, contact me to serve on that board next year."

may feel discouraged by low pay, high expectations, and the low respect associated with teaching. You can pick up the morning paper most days and read teacher-bashing editorials. Those editorials always get my stress level elevated.

Stress can derive from the reality of high-stakes testing and accountability. Other stress-inducing factors include a sense of isolation, a lack of autonomy, cascades of paperwork, and a dilapidated physical plant.

Stress can also be caused by poor health choices you make. You know what they are: smoking, drinking, neglecting exercise, and poor eating habits.

Conquering Stress at School

One of the most important things you can do to keep stress at bay is to maintain a positive perspective about your work. When you read negative reports about schools or schooling, you can become stressed out. Do your part to promote respect for teachers. Network with other teachers to brainstorm ways of polishing your profession's image in the community. Parents are your best partners, and they can promote you in the community.

What Is Your R&R Ritual?

Maintaining Perspective

There are a number of ways to maintain a healthy and positive perspective about your professional life and avoid becoming immobilized by stress or negative thinking. Here are some to consider:

1. Set realistic expectations for yourself and your students. Keep careful and up-to-date records, and communicate often with parents and your administrator about your progress with the class as a whole and with individual students.

2. View your students holistically, and recognize that test scores are only one facet of a student's development. Ask yourself, when you are feeling low, "Where was she at the beginning of school? Where is she now?" Justify your program with confidence.

3. Counter any sense of isolation by establishing collegial relationships at school. Make a promise to yourself to socialize during lunch and recess no matter how much work you have. Team with other teachers, plan with other teachers, jog with other teachers. Organize a support group of new teachers that meets

once a week during lunch or at someone's house.

4. Students appreciate teachers who have a sense of humor. Use your sense of humor to relieve any tension in your classroom and your own stress level. There are plenty of sources for jokes and humorous stories on the Web. Use cartoons or funny photos in your PowerPoint or overhead transparency presentations.

5. Make frequent contact with a mentor or a buddy who has been officially designated, or simply find a friend at school with whom you can talk.

6. Design a learning environment you want to live in for six hours each day. Clean up, organize, and redecorate your room from time to time. Throw things out that are dog-eared or are no longer useful. Play soft music during work time. The room environment is a key factor in how teachers feel about coming to school each day.

7. Devise ways to break the routine for yourself and your students. For example, an elementary teacher might have a backward day when the schedule goes in reverse and so do students' shirts. Other themed days teachers have tried and thor-

oughly enjoyed include an all-day read-a-thon, crazy-hat day, wearing-slippers day, students-teach-the-class day, bring-your-stuffed-animal-to-school day, and wearing-a-certain-color day.

8. Do some silly things like jumping rope with the kids or playing basketball with them at recess. Bring in a Frisbee and toss it around with them. Take them out for an unexpected walking field trip on the first day of spring. Create new projects like a classroom window garden or a class newspaper. Cook with them.

9. Take a few minutes out of the day for your own R and R ritual, which may include deep breathing, easy stretching, and muscle-flexing exercises. Or, take a few minutes during recess to engage in visual imagery techniques. Regulate your breathing and take a mental trip to a quiet, secluded, peaceful place you have been to or hope to visit. A few minutes in Tahiti or on a hike in the woods during a break will put you in a better frame of mind.

10. Know your limits and be assertively polite about saying no to extracurricular assignments that are not part of your responsibilities.

Crazy Hat, Anyone?

Teacher vs. Students

Teacher Talks . . .

New teachers spend every waking moment on school-related tasks: lesson plans, grading, preparing materials for lessons, etc. You need to take one day each weekend for yourself and your family instead of devoting both days to work. On Friday evenings, I enjoy lighting a candle and sipping a glass of sparkling cider as I soak in a bubble bath. Even just 20 minutes for myself makes me feel refreshed and renewed.

Becky Monroe
Middle School Language Arts
San Bernardino, California

Conquering Stress at Home

You might have to negotiate responsibilities at home to allow yourself more free time. School has a way of consuming teachers, especially new ones, so learn to make yourself top priority. Give yourself time between school and arrival home to unwind, or take a few minutes upon arrival to make the transition. Try to complete most paperwork at school, even if it means staying there to do it. Establish a schedule that gives you some free nights, even your first year, and use grading shortcuts.

Your personal stress busters are unique to you. They might include attending a sporting event, taking a trip to the day spa, going on a mini-vacation on Saturday, or going out to dinner with a friend. Here are some other low-cost suggestions from teachers to get you started on your own personal rejuvenation plan.

1. Plan a weekend away (or stay home and hibernate).
2. Take up a new hobby.
3. Read a book you "don't have time for."
4. Call a friend and talk out issues that are bothering you.
5. Practice relaxation techniques like meditation or yoga.
6. Spend some time alone.
7. Shop (my personal favorite).
8. Cook a healthy meal and freeze individual portions for lunch.
9. Listen to music or watch a DVD you "don't have time for."
10. Go to the gym, ride a bike, or take a hike.
11. Have your house or apartment cleaned by someone else.
12. Get a babysitter.

Apply It!

Make a list of at least ten ways you relax or would like to relax after a day at school. Tape the list on your mirror so you can look at it every day.

Apply It!

Buy a calendar and record all the rejuvenating activities you engage in each month. Make sure that each month your calendar is filled with restorative activities so you can be of sound mind and body for the students in your class. They rely on your well-being more than you know.

Rejuvenation Calendar

Month: _____

Record All Rejuvenation Activities

Sunday	Monday	Tuesday	Wednesday	Thursday	Friday	Saturday

Principal Talks . . .

I love books of every kind, but my favorite stress reliever is to read a murder mystery. I take time to read every night, even if only for a few minutes. It gets my mind off the hamster wheel of worry for at least a little while and lets me relax enough to fall asleep quickly.

Virginia Strong Newlin, NBCT, Principal, Rock Hall Middle School (Grades 5–8) Rock Hall, Maryland Quoted on www.EducationWorld.com

Sundays can be especially stressful if you wait until the last minute to plan for the week. Try to parcel out your planning so you can get it out of the way and have some free, unstructured time to pursue your own interests and hobbies or to catch up on family time or sleep!

Avoid It!

Do not allow anyone in your life to undermine your career choice. Remember always, whatever the public perception, that you are engaged in significant work that makes a difference in the lives of children and adolescents.

*Your work is to
discover your
work and then
with all your
heart give your-
self to it.*

Buddha

Chapter **38**

What Professional Opportunities Are Open to Me?

Effectiveness Essentials

- A profession by its very definition requires continuing education. Explore every possible way you can continue to grow in your field.

- Keep reading all you can about teaching and learning, classroom discipline, and management.

- Extended education courses can help you stay up to date on the latest trends in teaching.

- Create your own teaching portfolio.

- Get involved with local or regional councils of national professional organizations, and attend conferences.

- Seek out grants that can help you professionally and in the classroom.

- Work with an eye toward applying for National Board Certification granted by the National Board for Professional Teaching Standards.

A profession by its very definition requires continuing education. Even after retirement, you will find yourself keeping up with innovations.

Professional Development Opportunities

There are many ways to broaden your knowledge about teaching and learning.

1. Keep reading all you can about teaching and learning, classroom discipline, and management. Some teachers suggest getting subscriptions to magazines that are filled with numerous specific teaching ideas and units. Many can be accessed online as well. At the end of this chapter, you will find a list of periodicals you may want to look for in the resource center or university library and then order for your own professional library.

2. Collaborate with your colleagues and absorb all the information you can. Experienced teachers have made their share of mistakes and can help you avoid some of the common pitfalls. You need only to seek advice and they will be more than happy to share their experiences with you.

3. You may be required by your state credential laws to continue your education right away. Veterans advise

that you take the least demanding courses first and none during the first semester of teaching. Your district will likely require you to attend new teacher in-services and meetings that will consume your time during those first few months, in addition to the adjustments you will be going through. You don't want to over-commit yourself.

4. Periodically, take some extended education courses to bone up on some practical aspect of teaching. Take these courses on a need-to-know basis so they are useful to you in your everyday life in the classroom. Consider extension courses with titles such as "100 Ways to Enhance Literature" (or Creative Writing or Science, etc.), or that focus on bulletin boards or using new technologies. Or you might just take a course for fun that has absolutely nothing to do with teaching! "The Care and Feeding of Your Reptile" was one I came across recently.

5. Learn or brush up on second language skills by studying any of the languages your students speak. Conversation tapes and CDs are available in libraries and bookstores, and it would be well worth your effort to speak some simple phrases to your English learners and their parents.

statistics

During 2000, 92% of public school teachers participated in a collaborative professional development activity, the most common of which was regularly scheduled collaboration with other teachers (69%). Networking with teachers outside their school was mentioned by 62%, a common planning period for team teachers was mentioned by 53%, and individual or collaborative research on a topic of professional interest was mentioned by 52% (NCES 2000a).

Teacher Talks . . .

The best teaching ideas are the ones I got from my colleagues. I am always looking for new and innovative teaching strategies and I continually ask my colleagues for advice or ideas on how to teach a certain topic.

> Kelly Rubio
> Fourth Grade
> Manhattan Beach, California

statistics

The number of hours teachers spent in professional development activities was related to the extent to which teachers believed that participation improved their teaching. Teachers who participated for more than 8 hours were more likely than those who spent 1 to 8 hours to report that participation improved their teaching a lot (NCES, 2000).

I am a teacher. I have an inner need to make a difference, to matter. My way of making a difference is to strive to inspire people within my circle of influence—primarily my students. I went through the process of becoming a National Board Certified Teacher to explore current strategies and best practices available to improve my teaching practice. In this time of our teachers' skills constantly being called into question, I wanted to ensure that I was doing everything I could to prove myself worthy and ensure that I was doing the best for my students and community.

After seven years of teaching I applied to be a candidate. I joined a local support group, collaborated with other teachers and administrators and read everything I could about best practices and strategies, and then began the reflective process. The most rewarding

(continued on facing page)

Professional Development Opportunity

6. Create your own teaching portfolio. You will be able to see your evolution as a professional and have direct evidence, on those "bad" days, that you really are doing wonderful things. From time to time, you can reflect on your progress, and share your portfolio with colleagues, mentors, administrators, and parents. Include in your portfolio:

- videos of lessons you have taught
- samples of pupil products
- videos of performances
- photos of special bulletin boards or displays
- observations and evaluations by your administrator
- letters from parents
- notes from your students
- units you have developed
- special lesson plans
- lists of professional books and articles you have read

- notes and agendas from committee meetings
- annotated agendas and handouts from conferences and in-services

7. Join local or regional councils of national professional organizations. Read the very informative professional journals they publish. The websites are listed at the end of the chapter. These local councils provide meeting and in-service opportunities.

8. Present at local and national conferences. You can start out by co-presenting with someone who has done this before. Many of the grant and conference presentation opportunities are more available to secondary teachers since there are only a few national organizations solely devoted to elementary concerns. Elementary teachers are usually subsumed within the major subject area organizations. Choose a curriculum area that you feel is one of

your strengths, join the organization that represents that area, and start to attend meetings. In time, you can start to submit presentation proposals.

9. Apply for grants of all sorts. Grant monies exist to help you expand your own knowledge and skills, as well as to help finance projects in your classroom. The challenge is identifying the sources of the grants. Grant forms are pretty simple, and many professional organizations list grant opportunities on their websites. You will also find out about grant opportunities in professional journals. Take advantage of grants to attend seminars and workshops in foreign countries. Combine travel with international conference opportunities. All of my most exciting travel experiences resulted from grants such as Fulbright summer seminars for teachers. Travel grants have taken me to Indonesia, Israel, Vietnam, and Japan.

10. After a few years of teaching, consider applying for National Board Certification granted by the National Board for Professional Teaching Standards. National Board certification will give you nationwide access to certification and will carry with it a stipend and, more importantly, a sense of accomplishment. You will need to take certain tests and submit a portfolio, so it's never too early to gather evidence of your accomplishments.

Avoid It!

During your first year of teaching, it will be sufficient to limit your professional development options to the essential, required in-services and new teacher workshops. Ease into the other professional development opportunities, and engage in those activities that will provide practical and sensible solutions to your immediate needs.

Professional Development Resources

Here is a listing of professional development resources, including generic teacher websites and magazines, websites and journals for discipline-specific professional organizations, websites for general issues, programs and technology, and union websites. Many schools subscribe to some of the journals listed and make them available in the library, staff, or resource room. You may find some you want to subscribe to for your own professional library.

thing about creating a portfolio and taking the National Board test was seeing the growth in student performance from my application of learning. The more I would reflect, plan, and apply what I learned from my students, the more connected they became to the material. The process was a very rewarding professional growth experience. It has long lasting effects on the teacher experiencing it, as well as all those within their circle of influence.

Eileen Mino
Fifth Grade
National Board Certified Teacher
Colton, California

Eileen Mino asks, "Is National Board Certification in Your Future?"

Teacher Talks . . .

Many new teachers getting ready for their first year have the idea that teaching is going to be easy, but it isn't. The first year is perhaps the hardest year because there are so many things you have to go through such as state certification require-ments, administration expectations, not letting your students down, and not giving up after the first day. If you need to, go back to your men-tors, college professors, and other experienced teachers to help you through that first year. Observing teaching techniques and going to educator conventions can help you come up with creative ideas on making your classroom an awe-some learning experience for your students. It's also important to find an outlet for yourself after school that helps relieve your stress from the day. Remember, every teacher has had their first year and made it through, and so will you!

Jennifer A. Ponsart
M.S. Music Director
Four Corners Charter School
Davenport, Florida

Generic Magazines and Websites

Instructor
http://teacher.scholastic.com/products/instructor/

Teaching Pre K–8
http://www.teachingK-8.com

Education World
www.education-world.com/

Middle and High School Teachers Website
http://712educators.about.com

Discipline-Specific Professional Organizations and Journals

Social Studies

National Council for the Social Studies
http://www.ncss.org/
  Social Studies and the Young Learner
    (elementary)
  Middle Level Education (middle school)
  Social Education (high school)

Mathematics

National Council of Teachers of Mathematics
http://www.nctm.org/
  Teaching Children Mathematics (elementary)
  Mathematics Teaching in the Middle School
    (middle school)
  Mathematics Teacher (high school)

Science

National Science Teachers Association
http: //www.nsta.org
  *Science and Children (*elementary)
  *Science Scope (*middle and junior high)
  *The Science Teacher (*secondary)

Reading/Language Arts

National Council of Teachers of English
http://www.ncte.org/*Language Arts*

The International Reading Association
http://www.reading.org/
  The Reading Teacher
  Journal of Adolescent & Adult Literacy

Technology

Computer-Using Educators, Inc.
http://www.cue.org/
  On Cue

Special Education

Council for Exceptional Children
http://www.cec.sped.org/
  Exceptional Children
  Teaching Exceptional Children

Bilingual Education and English Language Development

National Association for Bilingual Education
http://www.nabe.org/
  Language Learner

Issues, Practices, and Programs

Association for Supervision and Curriculum Development
http://www.ascd.org
  Educational Leadership

National Middle School Association
http://www.nmsa.org/
  Middle School Journal

National Board for Professional Teaching Standards
http://www.nbpts.org

Association for Childhood Education International
lhttp://www.acei.org/jour.htm
  Childhood Education

Teacher Organizations/Unions

American Federation of Teachers
http://www.aft.org/
  American Educator
  American Teacher

National Education Association
http://www.NEA.org
  NEA Today

Unit 8 Checklist

A Professional Life in Balance Checklist	For more information go to:
☐ Have I decided to become a reflective teacher?	Chapter 35
☐ Will I make a list of my strengths and weaknesses?	Chapter 35
☐ Have I located key places and people at school and in the community?	Chapter 36
☐ Have I begun to establish professional relationships with my principal, the support staff, and my colleagues?	Chapter 36
☐ Have I committed to leading a balanced life?	Chapter 37
☐ Will I accept that I am a work in progress?	Chapter 37
☐ Have I identified my stressors at home and at school?	Chapter 37
☐ Have I explored my state requirements for continuing professional development?	Chapter 38
☐ Will I create my own teaching portfolio?	Chapter 38

Further Reading: A Professional Life in the Balance

Costantino, P., De Lorenzo, M., & Kobrinski, E. (2006). *Developing a professional teaching portfolio: A guide for success* (2nd ed.). Boston: Allyn & Bacon. This book provides information on how to create and maintain a teaching portfolio, paper or electronic, including what should be included, how to reflect on your work, and how to design your portfolio in a creative and engaging manner.

Losyk, B. (2005). *Get a grip: Overcoming stress and thriving in the workplace.* Hoboken, NJ: John Wiley and Sons. This book provides tips and strategies for reducing stress through visualization, diet, exercise, etc., to revitalize the mind and body at home or in the workplace.

Morgenstern, J. (2004). *Organizing from the inside out: The foolproof system for organizing your home, your office and your life* (2nd ed.). New York: Henry Holt and Company. This book first discusses the reasons people are disorganized and then goes on to list specific instructions for organizing work and home spaces for maximum efficiency.

Morgenstern, J. (2004). *Time management from the inside out: The foolproof system for taking control of your schedule and your life* (2nd ed.). New York: Henry Holt and Company. In this easy-to-read book, the author discusses the reasons people run out of time, and discusses how to set realistic goals and use a device called the personal time map to conquer procrastination and lateness.

Epilogue
Final Tips

No more pencils,
no more books,
no more teachers'
dirty looks.

Nursery Rhyme

There will come
a time when you
believe everything
is finished. That
will be the
beginning.

Louis L'Amour

Chapter **39**

The Last Days of School

Effectiveness Essentials

■ Maintaining order and interest up until the last day can be challenging.

■ Use the time to have some fun with students, but never lose the focus on learning. Even fun projects can be used to assess student progress.

■ Engage your students' help in reflecting back on the year and assessing what worked and what didn't.

Before closing, I have a few more tips for ending the school year. Books such as this one often provide numerous suggestions on how to get through a school year, but they rarely ever talk about how to wind down a school year. In fact, the final days of school are as important as the first days. They are a time for you and your students to reflect on the entire year or semester, and to solidify memories of your time together. It's a time to engage students in projects you didn't have time for all semester or year and to have fun with your class after all the test taking is over. It is time to deconstruct your room and to plan for your own free time.

Maintaining Routines and Sustaining Interest

It's really not over until the report cards have been distributed, the tears have been shed, the hugs have been given, and the final goodbyes have been spoken. Your year-end activities will be influenced by the ages of your students, and the way you approach the final day or days will vary accordingly.

Kindergarteners will have no idea that their school year is coming to an end because this is their first year of

school. Since very young children don't handle change well and have a great need for structure and security, seasoned kindergarten teachers suggest that you maintain routines, schedule, activities, and the room environment up to the very last day. Your job will be to reassure the little ones and provide a very smooth transition to vacation on that last day. You can read their favorite books; sing their favorite songs; and revisit their favorite field trips, experiences, and memories. Only after they are gone should you deconstruct your room. Otherwise, they may be as upset as they were on the first day of school.

On the other hand, your older students will be chomping at the bit for vacation to begin. They know what the last day of school means and they will be counting down the days. Maintaining order and your students' interest can be a serious challenge. However,

Teacher Talks . . .

At our school we have what is called an "Exam Jam" (after End of Grade Tests). We have a theme among our four fourth grade classes. We rotate the kids throughout the day to different classrooms. For example, we had a Fiesta one year with making Mexican style hats, learning Mexican dances, making fried ice cream, and breaking piñatas.

Teachers can divide up topics and kids will switch classes. For example, in one class a teacher will do a thematic unit on tornadoes, while another class studies geography. There are so many things that teachers can do to keep students interested and it's fun for all :-) I think most everyone is burned out by the end and need a nice break! Take care!

Brandi Stephens
Fourth Grade
Mebane, North Carolina

I was able to add an extra curriculum that enhanced my students' higher thinking skills through interdisciplinary projects within my classroom. Some of our projects included constructing a 23 ft. Great White mechanical shark, a 17 ft. Brooklyn Bridge, a full scale 1903 Wright Brother's Flyer hanging from the classroom ceiling, and seven 1903 Wright Flyer 1/8 scale models.

Perry Lopez
Fifth Grade
Bronx, New York

The Great White Mechanical Shark

attendance is mandatory and you will need to sustain their interest with engaging and motivating activities—for both your sake and theirs. This is the time to introduce some exciting projects since the standardized testing no longer dictates your curriculum. The last days of school may provide opportunities to go beyond the standards and design unique projects that will capture the students' interests and make them anxious to come to school each day.

One such teacher, Perry Lopez, creates these projects all year long, but as a novice you probably will feel more comfortable doing large-scale projects such as these at the end of the year when interest tends to flag.

Having Fun with Your Students

At the end of the year you can have some guilt-free fun with your students and change both the content and the structure of the day or period. This is the time to try out some different structures, activities, materials, and media. Even though the curriculum has been covered and the standards are all checked off in your planning materials, you still have to make sure that the activities you plan, although fun, are substantive and justifiable to parents and administrators.

One way to ensure that students do not equate fun with goofing off is to assure them that projects are graded up until the very end when the report cards are distributed and/or are sent home. Older students, who are already familiar with your rubrics, can even design their own rubrics to assess the "fun" projects. Here are some ideas for elementary and secondary students.

Ideas for Elementary School

The list of possible exciting end-of-year ideas is as long as your imagination can extend, but here are some to get you started. Many will relate to the curriculum, others are add-on fun activities that extend the curriculum or create new interests. Students can:

- Build a diorama reflecting a literature selection
- Construct story character puppets and recreate stories they enjoyed
- Study a new topic like bubbles or anime drawing or any other mini unit
- Take guided walks to collect materials for collages or pressing flowers
- Design, construct, and fly kites
- Spend one whole day on each subject
- Rotate to centers set up in each classroom (crafts, stories, projects)
- Present unique book talks
- Participate in scavenger hunts online

- Create mini skits or plays about subjects they have studied
- Cook simple recipes or make ice cream
- Read books about the last days of school such as:

  Last Day Blues (2006) by Julie Danneberg and Judith Dufour Love. Watertown, MA: Charlesbridge Publishing.

  The Last Day of School (2006) by Louise Borden and Adam Gustavson. New York: Margaret K. McElderry, imprint of Simon and Schuster.

Ideas for Middle and High School

Your older students might enjoy some of the aforementioned activities, but here are some other ideas that might appeal to preteens and teens. These students can:

- Compare and contrast the movie version with a book they have read
- Create mini science, math, or art projects
- Present in any format what they learned
- Evaluate the class, i.e., what did you like most, least about this class?
- Write a letter to next year's students about the class
- Play games such as basketball against the staff

- Play year-end "Jeopardy"
- Become "Student teachers" and teach the class in pairs or triads based on their interests
- Develop and implement a community service project
- Create a commercial, poster, or brochure for the class or course
- Make a year-end video or PowerPoint with photos of every student

Teacher Talks . . .

In my first year of teaching, on the very last day, I was so emotional saying goodbyes to my first graders that I forgot to distribute their report cards. Freud might say I had a hard time letting go. That aside, I had to hand-deliver each and every report card individually that afternoon. That gave me a chance to say goodbye to parents as well.

Jason Paytas
Fourth Grade, formerly first grade
Arcata, California

Apply It!

Make a list of at least ten post-school activities you have planned. They can be simple ones such as "read three mystery books" or as complex as "take a long awaited trip to a vacation destination."

Reflecting on the Year

The end of school is also a time for creating lasting memories of the year and reflecting back, especially for those students who will be moving on to another school. There are many activities that fall into this category and here are some to choose from:

- Have the students put together autograph books or anthologies of their writing.
- Create slide shows on PowerPoint with photos and artifacts of the year.
- Have each student create a PowerPoint slide of his or her fondest memory.
- Create calendars for next year with photos of main events or activities.
- Have students write autobiographies for a mini "yearbook."
- Take class photos and make a collage for everyone to take home, or take a class photo.
- Make a book of class records—something unique to each student or awards for each student.

This is also a time for you to reflect back on your year. Look over your class list, and think about your successes and what you might have done differently to better engage each of your students. During your vacation, you can think about what you have learned from the Apply It! activity on the following page.

Dismantling Your Room

To make your life easier next year, use the same care in dismantling your classroom as you did in assembling it. If you do this slowly and enlist the help of your students, the job will be done in a week or less. Remember to wait until school really ends before dismantling the room while your kindergarteners are still there. Carefully pack away your materials, bulletin board items, supplies, etc., in see-through plastic tubs. To be extra meticulous, paste a list of contents on each tub.

Apply It!

Complete these sentence stems and have each student do the same. Compile them into a list to reflect on during your free time. This feedback will make you a better teacher.

The best three things about this year were . . .

The three projects I liked best were . . .

Five words to describe your students . . .

This year could have been better if . . .

If I could change the class rules . . .

If I could change the class schedule . . .

We could have used more . . .

We could have used less . . .

The most interesting subjects/ topics were . . .

The most boring subjects/ topics were . . .

Saying Your Goodbyes and Planning Ahead

The last day of school is a celebratory time. You want to celebrate with your students and say your goodbyes to them and to the staff. This might be a time to thank those staff members who have helped you out with a small token of appreciation or a note. If the staff is having an after school get-together, make sure you attend. Those events bring closure to the year and create a sense of community. Some staffs have one every Friday, but the last one is special. The staff members will probably share their vacation plans and you should already have some plans, too.

Student Says . . .

At the end of the year my teacher had "Awards Day." This was good because we got to give awards to each other and it showed how well we did in things through the year.

Erik
Grade 4
Brookline, Massachusetts

Anyone who has never made a mistake has never tried anything new.

Albert Einstein

There are no secrets to success. It is a result of preparation, hard work, and learning from failure.

Colin Powell

Chapter 40

Now It's Time to Teach!

Effectiveness Essentials

■ Recognize that there will be good days and bad days and you need to be self-forgiving of mistakes.

■ Teaching is a dynamic interaction between you and your students.

■ Learn to trust yourself and internalize your own unique teaching style from all the well-intentioned advice you receive.

■ Your professional development is a process that can't be short-circuited and will continue as long as you call yourself teacher.

Some Final Tips

There will be good days and bad days, so you need to be self-forgiving of mistakes. Don't try to implement every teaching strategy and idea learned in your credential program during the first week. Ease up on yourself, and all will fall into place. At all costs, don't overextend yourself at the outset. You'll tire yourself out and be ready for a vacation two weeks into the school year. There are way too many good, qualified teachers in this country who gave up on the profession after only a year because they pushed themselves too hard in the beginning. Be patient! Pace yourself!

This guide will help you take the first tentative steps across the threshold of your teaching career. When all is said and done, there is so much else that could have been said, but not nearly the space. Your experience will mold and shape you, and you will continue to grow and learn with each successive year.

Teaching is a dynamic interaction between you and your students. The experience will mutually change your lives in both big and small ways. Let your students guide your development as you guide theirs.

You have to trust yourself and internalize your own unique teaching style from all the well-intentioned advice you receive. That said, take the advice contained in this book and in other books, and the advice offered by colleagues and in courses, and incorporate what works for you.

Your professional development is a process that can't be short-circuited and will continue as long as you call yourself teacher. Listen, learn, ask questions, but ultimately, during your first year of teaching and beyond, your personal teaching style will emerge and you'll find your own way.

I end with an expression of gratitude to all the teachers, administrators, teacher educators, and students who contributed the practical advice and realistic depiction of this admirable profession. This book could not have been written without your participation. If you would like to be included in the Teacher Talks ... or Myth Buster! features in the next edition, please contact me at professorellen@roadrunner.com. If your children or students would like to contribute to the Student Says ... feature, I will send permission slips to them as well.

Now as my mother used to say when I was starting any new endeavor, *"Put your right foot forward and do it!"*

Student Says . . .

I want to be a teacher. It seems like fun and I like to do all of the things teachers do—like teaching, grading, making decorations for the classroom, making charts and giving stars. I'd like to teach first grade because I like little kids. I have two younger brothers and one younger sister and I like to play school with them, and teach them things I know how to do. My sister Megan thinks I would be a good teacher because she says I'm a great sister, very nice, good with little kids, smart, patient, and treat everyone the same.

My older sister gave me a teacher's kit for Christmas and I use all of the things in the kit when we play school—an outfit, pointer, letters, numbers and arithmetic signs. My teacher talks about current events and I would like to do that with my students. I like talking about real things that are going on in the world and I would have my students bring in newspaper articles and I'd put them on the bulletin board.

*Erin
Age 9, Fourth Grade
Glenview, Illinois*

395

Teacher Talks . . .

I will always remember what one of my professors told me, "You've got to be gentle as a dove and yet sly as a fox when dealing with students." He was right! Regardless of what we hope for, our students are thinking up great ways to raise our blood pressure. New teachers are a great target because of a lack of experience in the classroom. Whatever age you teach in any subject, stay one step ahead of the kids by thinking like them. I've noticed that they try the same things I did when I was a kid, just with new toys. They always ask me, "How did you know?" I simply reply, "Because once, a long time ago, I tried the exact same things."

Jennifer A. Ponsart, M.S.
Music Director
Four Corners Charter School
Davenport, Florida

Apply It!

- Review the Effectiveness Essentials for each chapter or go back over the entire book. For each chapter, highlight or note those ideas that you will implement. Use your reflection journal to note these ideas, strategies, and activities.

- In your reflective journal, make a list of unanswered questions or concerns and find resources to address them.

- Recite ten times per day the following wise sayings teachers have suggested: I will be as forgiving of myself as I am of students. • I will be realistic and won't dwell on mistakes. • This too shall pass. • Everything is a learning experience. • It seemed like the best thing to do at the time. • Mistakes are learning opportunities. • I'll do my best every day; then I won't worry.

Student Says . . .

In response to the question "Would you like to be a teacher when you grow up?"

No, because I don't want to be a teacher that stays indoors all the time. But I wouldn't mind being a sports, art, or any other teacher that is outside for at least some of the day. I also don't want to be staying indoors while I could be doing something fun like art, dance, helping people, or even playing a team sport.

Annie Casper
Age Eleven, Grade Six
Cremorne, Australia

Avoid It!

The "super-teacher syndrome" is characterized by a debilitating perfectionism. You will make mistakes. We all make mistakes. You can either learn from your mistakes or be paralyzed by them. The quest to be perfect, to be a super-teacher, can be replaced with "can-do" attitudes.

Teachers Talk . . .

If I had it to do all over again, I'd most definitely still become a teacher. Being a teacher has helped me personally to be more patient, kind, considerate, and understanding. Being a teacher has fostered my ability to learn and grow, to embrace lifelong learning, and to keep current with the many changes taking place in curriculum, education, and technology.

It is important to enter teaching for the right reasons. If you are becoming a teacher to have June, July, and August off, think again. Most summers are filled with courses, in-service training, writing curriculum, and more. If you are becoming a teacher because you love learning and helping others learn, because you want to make a difference in the lives of youth, because you're willing to work hard and against many odds to help students learn; then teaching probably is for you.

Robin Smith
Educational Technology Specialist
Hollidaysburg District, Hollidaysburg, PA
Quoted on www.EducationWorld.com

In September 2002, I walked away from a secure, high-paying job in the corporate world to fulfill my lifelong desire to teach. Today, I have the job of my dreams, teaching K–4 students at my local elementary school about technology. Although the financial sacrifice (a cut in pay of almost two-thirds) was enormous, I would do it all again in an instant. Why? I am surrounded every day by the two things I love most in the world: children and technology. And "extra-curricular" work outside of school has substantially reduced the financial impact of my career move. I have never been happier.

Kevin Jarrett
Technology Facilitator, K–4
Northfield Community School, Northfield, New Jersey
Quoted on www.EducationWorld.com

Several years ago, I received a Christa McAuliffe Fellowship, which led to me leaving the classroom for a few years to take a position at our State Department of Education. Although my experiences there were invaluable, because I got to work with teachers from all around the state, I missed the classroom. After nearly five years away, I returned to teaching fourth grade. I can honestly say that the only thing I miss is the longer lunch period. I love being in a school again!

It's true that I don't make a lot of money and the hours are long, but if you like working with children, there is nothing better to do with your life.

Kathleen Cave
Fifth Grade
Sparks Elementary School, Sparks, Maryland
Quoted on www.EducationWorld.com

References

Unit 1

Brock, B., & Grady, M. (1996). *Beginning teacher induction programs.* Paper presented at the annual meeting of the National Council of Professors of Educational Administration, Corpus Christi, TX. (ERIC Document Reproduction Service No. ED 399361).

Dewey, J. (1993). *How we think: A restatement of the relation of reflective thinking to the educative process.* Boston: Houghton Mifflin Company.

Hall, J. L. (2005). Promoting quality programs through state-school relationships. In H. Portner (Ed.), *Teacher mentoring and induction* (pp. 213–223). Thousand Oaks, CA: Corwin Press.

Hayasaki, E. (2004, August 15). *Teachers lose tax breaks for class supplies.* Los Angeles Times, pp. B1, B9.

Interstate New Teacher Assessment and Support Consortium (INTASC). (1992). *Model standards for beginning teacher licensing, assessment: A resource for state dialogue.* [Online] Available ww.ccsso.org/contents/pdfs/corestrd.pdf, October 2, 2006.

Lidstone, M., & Hollingsworth, S. (1992). A longitudinal study of cognitive change in beginning teachers: Two patterns of learning to teach. *Teacher Education Quarterly 19*(4), 39–57.

Moir, E. (1990). Phases of first-year teaching. *California New Teacher Center Newsletter.* Sacramento: California Department of Education.

National Board for Professional Teaching Standards (NBPTS). (1989). *What teachers should know and be able to do: The five core propositions of the National Board for Professional Standards.* [Online] Available http://www.nbpts.org/standards, November 30, 2004.

NCTAF. (2005). *The cost of teacher turnover study.* [Online] Available http://www.nctaf.org/article/?c=7&sc=48&ssc=0&a=367, August 15, 2005.

NEA. (2005). *Rankings and estimates: Ranking of the states 2004 and estimates of school statistics 2005.* Atlanta: National Education Association.

NEA. (2004a). *Assessment of diversity in America's teaching force.* Atlanta: National Education Association.

NEA. (2004b). *Staying power: What we must do to end the teacher retention shortage.* [Online] Available http://www.nea.org/teachershortage/04threshold.html, August 10, 2005.

NEA. (2003). *Status of the American public school teacher 2000–2001: Highlights.* [Online] Available http://www.nea.org/edstats/images/status.pdf, August 10, 2005.

Payne, R. (2001). *A framework for understanding poverty,* revised ed. Highlands, TX: Aha Press.

U.S. Department of Education. (2002). *No Child Left Behind.* [Online] Available http:// www.nochildleftbehind.gov/start/facts/teachers.html, August 10, 2005.

Unit 2

Johns, K., & Espinoza, C. (1996). *Management strategies for culturally diverse classrooms.* Bloomington, IN: Phi Delta Kappa.

Fisher, A., and Sandin, J., Ill. (1991) *Always wondering: Some favorite poems of Aileen Fisher (*10th ed.) New York: HarperCollins Children's Book Group.

Unit 3

Emmer. E. T., Evertson, C., & Worsham, M. (2003). *Classroom management for secondary teachers* (6th ed.). Boston: Allyn & Bacon.

Hannah, G. (1984). Jazzing up your classroom. *Learning, 13*(1), 68–71.

Kottler, J. (1998). *Secrets for secondary school teachers: How to succeed in your first year.* Thousand Oaks, CA: Corwin Press.

Kounin, J. (1977). *Discipline and group management in the classroom.* New York: Krieger Publications.

National Education Association. (2003). *Status of the American public school teacher 2000–2001: Highlights.* [Online] Available http:// www.nea.org/ edstats/ images/ status.pdf, November 30, 2004.

Unit 4

Canter, L., & Canter, M. (2001). *Assertive discipline: Positive behavior management for today's classroom* (3rd ed.). Santa Monica, CA: Canter & Associates.

Dreikurs, R., Grunwald, B., & Pepper, F. (1998). *Maintaining sanity in the classroom* (2nd ed.). Philadelphia: Taylor and Francis.

Jones, F. (2000). *Tools for teaching.* Santa Cruz: Fred Jones & Associates.

Jones, F. (1992). *Positive classroom discipline.* New York: McGraw-Hill.

Kounin, J. (1971; 1977). *Discipline and group management in classrooms.* New York: Holt, Rinehart and Winston.

Marzano, R., Marzano, J., & Pickering, D. (2003). *Classroom management that works.* Alexandria, VA: Association for Supervision and Curriculum Development.

Maslow. A. (1987). *Motivation and personality* (3rd ed.). New York: HarperCollins.

National Center for Educational Statistics. (2004). Indicators of school crime and safety. [Online] Available http://nces.ed.gov/ pubs2005/crime_safe04/index.asp, December 28, 2004.

Nelsen, J., et al. (2000). *Positive discipline in the classroom* (3rd rev. ed.). Roseville, CA: Prima Publishing.

Payne, R. (2003). *A framework for understanding poverty* (3rd rev. ed.) Highlands, TX: Aha! Process.

Pfister, M., & James, J. A. (1992). *The rainbow fish.* New York: North-South Books.

Starr, L. (2002). *Corporal punishment: Teaching violence through violence.* [Online] Available http:// www.educationworld.com/a_issues/starr/starr051.shtml, December 28, 2004.

Unit 5

Bloom, B., Mesia, B., & Krathwohl, D. (1964). *Taxonomy of educational objectives: The affective domain & the cognitive domain.* New York: David McKay.

BSCS. (1997). *Science for life and living* (3rd ed.) Dubuque, IA: Kendall-Hunt Publishing.

Bureau of Labor Statistics, U.S. Department of Labor, *Occupational Outlook Handbook, 2004–05 Edition, Teachers—Preschool, Kindergarten, Elementary, Middle, and Secondary.* [Online] Available http://www.bls.gov/oco/ocos069.htm, January 27, 2005.

Charles, C. M., & Senter, G. (2005). *Elementary classroom management* (4th ed.). Boston: Allyn & Bacon.

Davidman, L., & Davidman, P. (2001). *Teaching with a multicultural perspective* (3rd ed.). Boston: Allyn & Bacon.

Editors, (2001). *Free stuff for kids.* Deephaven, MN: Meadowbrook Press.

Florian, J. (1999). *Teacher survey of standards-based instruction: Addressing time.* [Online] Available http://www.mcrel.org/topics/, January 27,2005.

Gardner, H. (1999). *Intelligence reframed: Multiple intelligences for the 21st century.* New York: Basic Books.

Gardner, H. (1993). *Multiple intelligences: The theory in practice.* New York: Basic Books.

House of Representatives. (1994). Goals 2000 Educate America Act. [Online] Available http://www.ed.gov/legislation/GOALS2000/TheAct/sec102.html, October 12, 2006.

Marzano, R. J., & Kendall, J. S. (1998). *Awash in a sea of standards.* [Online]. Aurora, CO: Mid-continent Regional Educational Laboratory, Inc. [Online] Available http://www.mcrel.org/standards/articles/awash-printer.asp, January 27, 2005.

U.S. Congress. (2001). No Child Left Behind Act. [Online] Available http://www.ed.gov/policy/elsec/leg/esea02/index.html, October 12, 2006.

Williams, J. D., & Snipper, G. C. (1990). *Literacy and bilingualism.* White Plains, NY: Longman.

Unit 6

Ausubel, D. (1968). *Educational psychology: A cognitive view.* New York: Holt, Rinehart & Winston.

Coelho, E. (1996). *Learning together in a multicultural classroom.* Markham, Ontario: Pippin Publishing.

Coles, A. D. (2000). Immigrant health. *Education Week, (19)*29, 12.

Cotton, K. (1990). Expectations and student outcomes, Close up #7 in *School Improvement Research Theory Series.* Portland OR: Northwest Regional Laboratory. [Online] Available http://www.nwrel.org/scpd/sirs/4/cu7.html, February 20, 2005.

Diaz-Rico, L., & Weed, K. (2006). *The cross-cultural language and academic development handbook: A complete K–12 reference guide* (3rd ed.). Boston: Allyn & Bacon.

Gardner, H. (2000). *Intelligence reframed: Multiple intelligences for the 21st century.* New York: Basic Books.

Gardner, H. (1993). *Frames of mind: The theory of multiple intelligences* (10th ed.). New York: Basic Books.

Good, T. L. (1987) Two decades of research on teacher expectations: Findings and future directions. *Journal of Teacher Education, (38),* 32–47.

Johns, K., & Espinoza, C. (1992). *Mainstreaming language minority children in reading and writing.* Bloomington, IN: Phi Delta Kappa Educational Foundation

Joyce, B., & Weil, M. (2003). *Models of teaching* (7th ed.). Boston: Allyn & Bacon.

Lessow-Hurley, J. (2005). *The foundations of dual language instruction* (4th ed.). Boston:Allyn & Bacon.

Marzano, R., Pickering, D. & Pollack, J. (2001). *Classroom instruction that works: Research-based strategies for increasing student achievement.* Alexandria, VA: Association for Supervision and Curriculum Development.

National Center for Educational Statistics. (2001). [Online] Available http://nces,ed,gov/pubs2001/dropout/, February 2, 2005.

Ogle, D. S. (1986). K-W-L group instructional strategy. In A. S. Palincsar, D. S. Ogle, B. F. Jones, & E. G. Carr (Eds.), *Teaching reading as thinking* (Teleconference Resource Guide, pp. 11–17). Alexandria, VA: Association for Supervision and Curriculum Development.

Paige, R. (2004). Remarks of U.S. Secretary of Education Rod Paige at the press conference announcing new policies for English language learners. [Online] Available http://www.ed.gov/print/news/speeches/2004/02/02192004.html, February 2, 2005.

Palincsar, A. (1984). *Teaching reading as thinking.* Alexandria, VA: Association for Supervision and Curriculum Development.

Peregoy, S., & Boyle, O. (2005). *Reading, writing and learning in ESL: A resource book for K-12 teachers* (4th ed.). Boston: Allyn & Bacon.

Public Agenda. (1997). Public school teenagers call for higher standards, more order and discipline in classrooms. [Online] Available www.publicagenda.org/press/press_release2.cfm, February 25, 2005.

Riley, R. (2000). *Excelencia para todos —Excellence for all: The progress of Hispanic education and the challenges of a new century.* Speech given by U.S. Secretary of Education Richard W. Riley. Washington, DC: [Online] Available: http://www.ed.gov/Speeches/03-2000/000315.html, February 2, 2005.

Rosenthal, R., & Jacobson, L. (1996). *Pygmalion in the classroom: Teacher expectation and pupils' intellectual development* (New and Expanded Edition). New York: Irvington Publishers.

Rowe, M. (1972). *Wait-time and rewards as instructional variable, their influence in language, logic, and fate control.* Paper presented at the National Association for Research in Science Teaching, Chicago, IL, Edo61 103.

Snyder, T., & Hoffman, C. (2002). Digest of education statistics 2001 (NCES 2002-130). [Online] Available http://nces.ed.gov/pubs2003/overview03/#4, February 20, 2005.

Stahl, R. (1990). *Using "think-time" behaviors to promote students' information processing, learning, and on-task participation: An instructional module.* Tempe, AZ: Arizona State University.

Tomlinson, C. (1999). *The differentiated classroom: Responding to the needs of all learners.* Alexandria, VA: Association for Supervision and Curriculum Development.

Unit 7

Bear, D., et al. (2003). *Words their way (*3rd ed.). Upper Saddle River, NJ: Prentice Hall.

Cochran, J. (1989). Escape from paperwork. *Instructor, 99*(3),76–77.

Emmer, E., Evertson, C. M., &Worsham, M. (2003). *Classroom management for secondary teachers (*6th ed.). Boston: Allyn & Bacon.

Farkas, S., et al. (1998). *Playing their parts: Parents and teachers talk about parental involvement in public schools.* New York: Public Agenda.

National Center for Educational Statistics. (2002). *Student effort and educational progress.* [Online] Available http://nces.ed.gov/programs/coe/2002/section3/indicator18.asp, March 2, 2005.

Public Agenda, 2000. *Survey finds little sign of backlash against academic standards or standardized tests.* [Online] Available http://www.publicagenda.org/press/press_release_detail.cfm?list=29 March 2, 2005.

Public Agenda, 2004. *Survey: Sports, arts, clubs, volunteering: Out-of-school activities play crucial, positive role for kids.* [Online] Available http://www.publicagenda.org/press/press_release_detail.cfm?list=59 March 2, 2005.

Tienken, C., & Wilson, M. (2001). Using state standards and tests to improve instruction. *Practical Assessment, Research & Evaluation, 7*(13). [Online] Available http://ericae.net/pare/getvn.asp?v=7&n=13., March 2, 2005.

U.S. Census Bureau. (2001). *Survey of income and program participation (SIPP): Living arrangments of children.* [Online] Available http://www.census.gov/population/www/socdemo/children.html, November 8, 2006.

Unit 8

Grant, C., & and Zeichner, K. (1984). On becoming a reflective teacher. In C. Grant (Ed.), *Preparing for reflective teaching* (pp. 1–8). Boston: Allyn & Bacon.

Moir, E. (1990). Phases of first year teaching. Originally published in *California New Teacher Center Newsletter.* Sacramento, CA: California Department of Education. [Online] Available http://www.newteachercenter.org/ti_article2.php.

National Center for Educational Statistics. (2000a). *Teacher preparation and professional development: 2000.* [Online] Available http://nces.ed.gov/programs/quarterly/Vol_3/3_3/q3-3.asp

Index